I0821774

The Battle for Peace

The Battle for PEACE

The Long Road to Ending a War with the World's Oldest Guerrilla Army

JUAN MANUEL SANTOS
Winner of the Nobel Peace Prize 2016

Translated by Joe Broderick
Foreword by John Kerry
Prologue by Felipe González

Published by the University Press of Kansas (Lawrence, Kansas 66045), which was organized by the Kansas Board of Regents and is operated and funded by Emporia State University, Fort Hays State University, Kansas State University, Pittsburg State University, the University of Kansas, and Wichita State University.

Originally published in Spanish as *La Batalla por la paz: El largo camino para acabar el conflicto con la guerrilla más antigua del mundo*
Juan Manuel Santos, 2019
Editorial Planeta Colombiana S. A. 2019

Library of Congress Cataloging-in-Publication Data
Names: Santos, Juan Manuel, author.
Title: The battle for peace : the long road to ending a war with the world's oldest guerrilla army / Juan Manuel Santos ; translated by Joe Broderick ; foreword by John Kerry ; prologue by Felipe González.
Other titles: Batalla por la paz. English
Description: Lawrence : University Press of Kansas, 2021. | Includes index.
Identifiers: LCCN 2020036205
ISBN 9780700630660 (cloth)
ISBN 9780700630677 (ebook)
Subjects: LCSH: Colombia—Politics and government—1974– | Fuerzas Armadas Revolucionarias de Colombia—History. | Insurgency—Colombia. | Peace-building—Colombia. | Santos, Juan Manuel.
Classification: LCC F2279 .S256913 2019 | DDC 986.106/34—dc23
LC record available at https://lccn.loc.gov/2020036205.

British Library Cataloguing-in-Publication Data is available.
Printed in the United States of America
10 9 8 7 6 5 4 3 2 1
The paper used in this publication is acid free and meets the minimum requirements of the American National Standard for Permanence of Paper for Printed Library Materials Z39.48-1992.

To the more than eight million victims of Colombia's armed conflict, the center and raison d'être of the peace process.

To those who were victims and for those who now will never be so.

To Celeste and Mariano, my first grandchildren, who will only learn about this war from the history books.

Santos was able to see—to have the imagination and the vision to see—that this was the moment when you could pivot to peace. . . . This was someone who was completely sincere in his genuine desire to change the lives of the people and to bring peace where before conflict had been the norm of thousands and thousands of people suffering. . . . This was a really tough thing to do. This was frankly tougher than Northern Ireland, tougher I think than any conflict I have been involved in, and I would put the Israeli-Palestinian conflict in the same bracket. To have taken it this far is an extraordinary achievement. . . . I'd say to the people of Colombia: just remember the darkest days of this conflict and what that was like. Debate, by all means, the right way to go forward but don't let this slip back. That would be a big mistake.

—*Tony Blair*

Making peace after a long and bloody conflict is not a work for the fainthearted and you can't expect to be appreciated in the short run. You should do it if you believe it is the best way to give your kids and grandkids a better future. . . . I think Santos wanted to give all the Colombians a different sort of choices, and I think he was willing at the end to risk his standing in the short run to enhance Colombians' standing and quality of life in the long term. . . . Slowly but surely, a more peaceful and more normal life has returned, making it possible for people to develop the natural resources of the country.

—*Bill Clinton*

With the finalizing of a peace agreement between Colombia and the Revolutionary Armed Forces of Colombia, the longest-running war in the Western Hemisphere is coming to an end. We have witnessed, once again, that a sustained commitment to diplomacy and reconciliation can overcome even the most entrenched conflicts. This accord is a tribute to the hard work and cooperation of countless Colombian leaders and citizens—across parties and administrations—who painstakingly laid the groundwork for this milestone. I especially want to commend President Juan Manuel Santos for his courageous leadership during four years of difficult negotiations. . . . I think this is an achievement of historic proportions. It ultimately will be good for the region, as well as the people of Colombia. It took a lot of courage and a lot of hard work by a lot of people. And we are very proud to have played a modest part in helping the dialogue go forward.

—*Barack Obama*

No matter what sacrifice awaits me along the path on which I begin my
journey today, I will receive it happily if, in exchange,
I can bring to Colombian families a little more well-being,
a little more justice and the divine gift of peace.

—Eduardo Santos, inaugural address on assuming the presidency of Colombia, August 7, 1938

For peace I am prepared to take all the necessary risks . . . .
Peace in Colombia is more important, very much more important,
than any personal aspiration, any dignity or any individual person.

—Juan Manuel Santos, letter to President Ernesto Samper, October 11, 1997

Contents

Photographs follow page 162.

Acknowledgments

Governing is a lonely job. In my case, however, I was fortunate to have been accompanied by many men and women who committed themselves to Colombia's future and, as a result, to the search for peace. The process we carried out over more than six years enjoyed the support of a great many people, to whom all Colombians owe a debt of gratitude.

I especially want to thank the high commissioner for peace, Sergio Jaramillo; the head of the negotiating team, Humberto de la Calle; the plenipotentiary negotiators: generals Óscar Naranjo and Jorge Enrique Mora, Frank Pearl, Luis Carlos Villegas, Gonzalo Restrepo, María Paulina Riveros, Nigeria Rentería, María Ángela Holguín, and Roy Barreras; the alternate negotiators: Jaime Avendaño, Alejandro Éder, Elena Ambrosi, and Lucía Jaramillo, and the dedicated team at the Office of the High Commissioner for Peace, including Gerson Arias, Mónica Cifuentes, Juanita Goebertus, and Marcela Durán. I also wish to thank the high-level government officials who intervened in the process, including Juan Fernando Cristo, Rafael Pardo, and our ambassador in Havana, Gustavo Bell. And my brother Enrique Santos Calderón, who accompanied us at crucial moments in the negotiations.

Thanks, also, to those who served as facilitators: Henry Acosta, Álvaro Leyva, and Iván Cepeda; and to the legal consultants: Manuel José Cepeda, Juan Carlos Henao, Douglass Cassel, and Yesid Reyes, as well as those high-ranking military officers in active service who made up the subcommission for the ending of the conflict, the generals Javier Flórez, Martín Fernando Nieto, Alfonso Rojas, Oswaldo Rivera, and Álvaro Pico, and vice-admiral Orlando Romero.

It takes two to make peace. Which is why I want to acknowledge the commitment, seriousness, and goodwill shown by the Farc negotiators and their leader Rodrigo Londoño—formerly Timoleón Jiménez or Timochenko—who made it possible for us to reach an agreement. Ours was a debate between adversaries, arduous and difficult because of the deep differences that separated us, and if we achieved our goal it was due to the work and the persistence of everyone.

I want to emphasize and express my thanks for the invaluable support I received from my international advisers: Shlomo Ben-Ami, Jonathan Powell, Dudley Ankerson, Joaquín Villalobos, and William Ury, who shed light on, and provided a context for, our search for peace. I also thank the special envoys: Bernie Aronson from the United States; Eamon Gilmore from the European Union; Tom Koenigs from Germany; and the International Red Cross and the presidents of its delegation in Colombia, Jordi Raich and Christopher Harnisch. I thank, too, the former prime minister of Spain—a great friend and ally for peace—Felipe González, and the former president of Uruguay, José "Pepe" Mujica.

Thanks to the international community in general, which, without exception, supported our peace process, and very especially to Cuba—our host country—and its president Raúl Castro, along with Norway, Chile, and Venezuela, who served as guarantors and accompanied us in the process. Naming all the countries, heads of state, ministers, and heads of international organizations would be an interminable task. But I must pay a special tribute to the fundamental role played by the United Nations through the Security Council and the UN secretaries-general Ban Ki-moon and António Guterres, and the latter's delegate Jean Arnault; I also thank the United States and President Barack Obama, Vice-President Joe Biden, and Secretary of State John Kerry, and the European Union through its high representative for foreign affairs and security policy, Federica Mogherini.

My gratitude and deep respect go to Pope Francis, one of the great spiritual leaders of our times, who at every moment supported and promoted peace in Colombia and insisted on the need for reconciliation.

Peace with the Farc was not achieved in eight years. It was a long, drawn-out process with many ups and downs, advances and regressions, suspensions and new beginnings—as if we were applying the method of trial and error. It began in 1982 with the efforts of the government of Belisario Betancur (RIP), and bore fruit three decades later, during my administration. So I value and am grateful for the contributions made, at various moments and with different degrees of intensity, by my predecessors in the presidency of the republic.

I acknowledge most especially the victims of the conflict, since it was for them, because of them, and *with* them that we undertook the peace process. Their stimulus and generosity helped me not to fall by the wayside. And I want to acknowledge the members of our armed forces and police, because it was thanks to their self-sacrifice and courage that the guerrillas came to understand they would never achieve their goals by force of arms, and that the only way forward was through dialogue.

Thanks, many thanks, to every single Colombian. For the peace we are building, and will continue to build, is something we, all of us, do together: the congressmen and women who sealed the accord and passed the laws and reforms required to implement it; the magistrates who gave it legal status; the young people who filled the streets and the public squares to make sure the agreement would not be thwarted; the millions who voted yes in the plebiscite, and even those who voted no, since they obliged us to obtain an even better accord. Our peace is Colombian, and we Colombians are the ones who achieved it.

Finally, my heart goes out to my family: my wife, María Clemencia; our sons, Martín and Esteban; our daughter, María Antonia, and her husband, Sebastián; and little Celeste and Mariano, who have arrived to gladden our lives and who will enjoy, along with all the children of our beloved country, the peace which together we have won. Only love gives one the strength to struggle, and the love of my family was what fueled me and lighted my way in difficult moments, which were not a few. Thank you for being there. Thank you for being my refuge in stormy times.

Foreword

How many people do you know in modern life who have ended a war not on the battlefield but at the negotiating table?

Think about the long sweep of history. We revel in studies of the great generals, from Washington to Eisenhower; the world's enduring military academies study the battles from Bosworth to Midway; and NFL coaches and classics professors all assign as mandatory reading Sun Tzu's *Art of War*.

But what of the art of making peace? What do we know of the peacemakers? And of those we think we know, from Gandhi to Mandela, what can we say we learned *from* them *before* history put them on a pedestal, consigned them forever to the stuff of myth and allegory rather than real life flesh and blood?

President Santos's *The Battle for Peace* is a gift to those who will long want to study and understand how the world's longest-running war finally came to an end—in the words of the man himself who ended it, with the benefit of his fresh recollection of pivotal events. It is the definitive case study for conflict resolution in the modern era, an insider's journey through what the Kroc Institute for International Peace Studies called the most comprehensive peace agreement of the thirty-four post–World War II agreements it had studied.

Looking back, I'm reminded that this destination was far from preordained. I was in college when the war between the government of Colombia and the revolutionary guerrilla army known as the Farc began. I was first elected a United States senator when it had raged for more than twenty years. And I was America's secretary of state when finally, it came to an end: 52 years, 225,000 Colombian lives lost, 6 million Colombians forced from their homes, and Colombia's vast countryside strewn with more landmines per capita than any other country except for Afghanistan. One Colombian president after another tried to negotiate an end to the conflict. All came up short, some with disastrous political consequences.

When Juan Manuel Santos assumed the presidency in 2010, after a highly successful term as minister of defense in the previous government, conventional wisdom—and many of his own advisers—counseled the new president: "Husband your political capital, seek success on the battlefield, but do not start down the slippery slope of negotiations. It's full of risks and likely to end badly."

But President Santos was determined to "get caught trying," as some of us like to say.

The Irish poet Seamus Heaney, in his Nobel laureate address, said the secret to success is deciding to "walk on air against your better judgment." President Santos decided to walk on air. He bet his presidency on the peace process. He spent his political capital without fear or hesitation.

Santos set out not just to disarm and demobilize the Farc army but to eliminate the root causes of the war. He called for an end of the historic division between "the two Colombias": the modern Colombia of the cities and that of the vast, rural interior where there was virtually no government presence and no security, health services, justice, education, or economic infrastructure. Perhaps his boldest and most important decision was to place victims at the center of the peace process: to remind all sides that this agreement was not just about stilling the weapons of war but about justice, accountability, truth, reparations, and ultimately national reconciliation.

All told, counting the secret negotiations that preceded formal talks, the peace process took six years to reach a final agreement. There were ups and downs and crises along the path to success. Santos's political opponents vilified his efforts. A national referendum lost narrowly. Still, Santos persevered. Through a national dialogue with his critics Santos corrected misinformation and addressed legitimate concerns. The amended agreement was ratified overwhelmingly by the Congress of Colombia. For most Colombians it was the first time they lived in a nation at peace. Santos was rightly awarded the Nobel Peace Prize, but it was peace for his beloved country that was his true reward.

The Battle for Peace is a compelling political narrative, and a case study in conflict resolution—but most important, it is a portrait of leadership, and a tale told by a true leader who could have chosen the easier route but did what was right despite the risks.

On a visit to Capetown, South Africa, Robert Kennedy said, "Moral courage is a rarer commodity than bravery in battle or great intelligence. Yet it is the one essential, vital quality of those who seek to change a world which yields most painfully to change."

Juan Manuel Santos is a man of moral courage—and because he acted on it, he did change the world.

We're all lucky to relive his story—and to all the future peacemakers, I hope you find in Juan Manuel Santos the inspiration to cut your own path for peace and justice.

—John Kerry
Former US Secretary of State, 2013–2017

Prologue to the Spanish-Language Edition

In memory of Gabriel García Márquez and Belisario Betancur, two dear friends with whom, over the course of many years, I covered much ground in Colombia in the pursuit of peace.

I was writing a few words on this book by President Santos, *The Battle for Peace*, when I was shocked by the news of the criminal terrorist attack on the police academy in Bogotá that caused the death of twenty-two young cadets. Terror had returned to the streets, and my memory went back to Colombia's long conflict, reflected in the historic account contained in the book I was reading with enormous interest.

I wondered whether I should keep to the impressions I had gathered from what is written here, or if the aftermath of the attack was going to signify a setback in the process undertaken over so many years. Despite the pain and sadness this criminal act caused me, forty-eight hours later I came to the conclusion that the advance toward the conflict's solution is irreversible. My sorrow and my solidarity with the families, with the security forces, and with the Colombian people do not cloud my judgment of the process, nor diminish my conviction that the terrible events of the past will not be repeated in Colombia.

Those twenty-two young people, innocent victims of terror, not only demand justice but also deserve a tribute of hope that their death will not be in vain, will not deter anyone from the path undertaken, a path that leads to a shared life in peace and freedom. At this difficult moment, my wish is that all of Colombia's citizens will unite around the legitimate government of President Duque, his police force, and all those who fight against the atrocious crime that is terrorism.

This impressive story about the road to peace, which I have read with interest and passion, has led me, in each chapter, to a kind of dialogue with the account. I have personal knowledge of almost every one of the episodes which appear here, in some of them from positions which allowed me, or *obliged* me, to experience them from a different angle relative to that of President Santos, although I coincide with him in my appreciation of the historic significance of this sustained effort.

For many Colombians, above all the younger generations, a veil of shadow, even of forgetfulness, has been drawn over this long conflict. In my most recent visits to Bogotá, I was disconcerted to hear an account directly contrary to that described by Juan Manuel Santos. Some went as far as to deny the existence of an armed conflict, and discredited so many people's efforts to overcome it. Since there had never been a conflict, these people were saying, there is no need to reach an agreement to resolve it.

I cannot say that my vision of what has been happening over the past five decades, and particularly from the eighties of the last century until now, has been totally that of an outsider, although I would not presume to claim that I have lived through that period as if I were just one more Colombian. However, my closeness to Colombia and my interest in what has been occurring here since the mid-seventies made me available to collaborate, in whatever way I could, with those who legitimately asked me to do so—or, if you will, with those who had the moral authority to ask for my help from motives of personal friendship, as was the case with Gabriel García Márquez, Gabo. And this involvement was further enhanced when President Santos honored me with Colombian citizenship.

On reading this account—which combines excellent journalism and historical perspective with the author's outstanding personal role in the events—I have felt particularly involved in those episodes in which I was able to take part, both from outside Colombia and later from within, beginning with the time of the presidency of Belisario Betancur. In other words, from the moment when the Colombian state understood that it could, and should, open up a process of dialogue with the armed insurgents in search of a peace agreement.

Inevitably—or intentionally, rather—Juan Manuel Santos has described here his involvement in the process. First as a journalist but also as a committed citizen, above and beyond his professional obligations; later on, as part of various Colombian governments, especially when acting as minister of defense in the government of President Uribe. And then, of course, when he assumed the presidency from 2010 to 2018.

In the mid-eighties, I met Santos the journalist when he won the King of Spain International Award for Journalism and, simultaneously, the enmity of

Daniel Ortega for his reports on the situation in Nicaragua, which, in light of what is happening today, can be seen as a premonition. Around this same period, we had a meeting with the *El Tiempo* family at a hacienda near Bogotá at the invitation of President Betancur, who had worked as a journalist on this newspaper and was pained by what he saw as the paper's lack of understanding of his efforts to achieve dialogue in search of peace. Betancur felt that his friends did not understand him, while his friends complained that he had not sufficiently explained what he was trying to do. Both parties were right, but I don't wish to go off on a tangent about those dialogues that evoke so many memories. Stored on my mind's hard drive there are so many anecdotes, dating from the Betancur presidency up to the present time, that I am in danger of digressing.

Within what we call civil society, Juan Manuel Santos worked with politicians, businessmen, trade unions, universities, intellectuals, and actors in the complex network of the Colombian conflict. He knew, both of his own accord and also thanks to our mutual friendship with García Márquez, that I was available to lend a hand in Colombia, whether or not I was occupying positions of institutional power. His efforts from that stance were interrupted when he accepted responsibilities in government. This occurred when he became minister of foreign trade under President Gaviria, and as such I received him in 1992 at the Universal Exhibition in Seville, where he represented Colombia's president, who was unable to attend due to the situation brought about by Pablo Escobar's escape from the prison known as the Cathedral. We also met later, in the second half of President Pastrana's administration, when he acted as finance minister during that period's severe crisis.

In the mid-nineties, when I was out of government, I had a visit from Santos and García Márquez. This was during the turbulent presidency of Ernesto Samper, who was committed to the search for peace—as were all the governments that succeeded Betancur—but restricted by a narrow margin of operations for reasons clearly described in this book. The efforts for peace lost momentum at this time. Samper didn't know what was going on, and understandably, as I believe, felt denigrated as head of government. This is something he has made abundantly clear.

I have to state here that García Márquez was tireless in his permanent desire to find a road that might lead to peace and reconciliation between Colombians. His spirit, his hope, was reborn with each of Colombia's new presidencies, whether it was that of Betancur, or Gaviria's or Pastrana's, or that of Uribe, not to mention all the rest. Gabo spoke with all possible players on the conflict's board, and he urged me to do the same, however difficult and complicated it might seem. That is why, when the moment came to sign the peace agreement, I was saddened that he was not present to see it.

In the personal itinerary of Juan Manuel Santos one observes a notable continuity in his commitment to finding a way, even accepting that he was interrupting other concerns when he took on government responsibilities. This vital process explains his profound knowledge of all the conflict's complex aspects, as can be seen here. And of course, his role as defense minister during Uribe's second period immersed him in the terrible reality of a total confrontation.

At the time he was defense minister, and before his presidency, my personal relationship was with the president, and much less with the minister. When Juan Manuel came to power, I placed myself at his disposal and a bond was forged that went beyond politics and became one of personal friendship and familiarity. I have collaborated with all of Colombia's heads of government from Betancur to Santos, and with them all I have had a frank and open relationship enabling me to say exactly what I was thinking, always with the intention of helping. With Betancur, even before his presidency, I established a more intimate and friendly relationship, as happened later with Santos.

My ongoing presence in Colombia, unlike the perspective of distance of many of my international colleagues interested in the Colombian process, has led me to insist, repeatedly, that all of Colombia's presidents have attempted to achieve peace—whatever their attitudes may be as regards the present peace agreement signed with the Farc—and that Santos has made it irreversible, despite the immense difficulties in building peace after the signing of the agreement to end the conflict.

The book that you have in your hands explains clearly the origin of the conflict and the complications the past five decades have seen, including the worsening of the situation after Betancur's efforts, and the involvement of guerrillas, drug traffickers, and urban terrorist actions. Over the past forty years I have lived through these experiences directly, when in government and also as a committed Colombian citizen. I have followed events from that first process initiated by Betancur, marred by the terrible episode of the assault on the Palace of Justice and then by the tragedy of the Patriotic Union, up to the new Constitution under President Gaviria and the complex undertaking of Pastrana.

This brings me to the presidency of Álvaro Uribe, whom I met when he was candidate. I anticipated that the overwhelmingly negative public opinion of the Farc's behavior under Pastrana would place Uribe in the presidency of Colombia. This I told him on our first meeting, although he said he did not think so at the time. Álvaro Uribe, as president, has the merit of having led the insurgents to understand that by force of arms they would never come to power. Thus they began to see that the only solution was to exchange boots for votes.

As we know, and as Santos recounts here, he himself, as defense minister, led the harshest battle against the Farc leaders, while reforming and strengthening the capacity of the armed forces and the police. As president, taking as a starting point that change in the correlation of forces, Santos saw that continuing the war until his adversaries were exterminated was not a possibility, and that even if it were, it was not the road he wanted to take; namely, the road to peace, justice, and reparation, which was what Colombia needed.

Santos learned from other people's experience, and from his own. He was extremely cautious in discreetly negotiating a clearly defined agenda before beginning negotiations as such. He was adamant that there should be no agreement until everything was agreed. Despite incomprehension on the part of those who were not following the process, he resisted any false ceasefire that might have strengthened the guerrillas. And above all, he placed the victims at the center of the process to obtain reparation and reconciliation, and to advance in the future after the agreement had been signed.

He has led the most complex process I have known and, it must be said, the most successful. The world looked on with renewed hope. And specialists are analyzing the process with great interest, given the convulsive situation we are witnessing in other latitudes.

These are my words of gratitude to Juan Manuel Santos for his friendship and confidence which allowed me the impertinence of discussing some of his positions while maintaining my disposition to help in any way I could. That is how it was before he was president, and how it is now during the presidency of Duque. I am with Colombia, with its hopes and sorrows, if my services can be useful.

My final words go again to the victims of the horror of the attack on the police academy.

—Felipe González
Former Prime Minister of Spain
January 20, 2019

Letter to the Reader

I was president of Colombia for eight years, from August 2010 to August 2018, and received the Nobel Peace Prize in 2016. This prize was awarded for what the Norwegian Nobel Committee referred to as my "resolute efforts to bring the country's more than 50-year-long civil war to an end, a war that has cost the lives of at least 220,000 Colombians and displaced close to six million people."

The words of the committee are a faithful reflection of the reality. The Colombian people suffered for more than half a century the internal armed conflict between guerrillas known as the Farc, a subversive group of Marxist orientation, and the Colombian state. The social and political claims of the Farc have their origin in a fierce confrontation that affected above all the civilian population, especially in rural areas. Massacres, kidnappings, extortions, murders, the blowing up of oil pipelines and energy pylons, attacks on villages, the planting of illegal coca leaf crops, and drug trafficking were the items that dominated the Colombian news throughout this whole period and discredited Colombia's image around the world. We had become accustomed—or resigned—to the stigma of being a country at war.

My predecessors tried to defeat the guerrillas militarily, and several of them, in the last three decades, attempted to find a negotiated end to the conflict. Neither the one nor the other proved possible. And so, in 2010, when I assumed the presidency of Colombia—after having been defense minister and, as such, responsible for some of the most devastating military operations ever to weaken the guerrilla's strongholds—I set myself to learn from past errors and advance, prudently, but firmly and patiently, toward a negotiation, a peace process that might finally bring to an end the war with the oldest and most powerful guerrilla in my country, and on the Americas.

Almost two years of secret approaches and dialogue took place in order to arrive at an agenda for negotiations. We had to overcome all kinds of difficulties and incomprehension. But once the points of the agenda were agreed upon, in October 2012, we formally installed in Oslo the negotiating table that was then to be transferred to Havana, with the firm intention of achieving peace.

Four years later—in September 2016, in Cartagena—we signed the final agreement to end the conflict with the Farc in the presence of the secretary-general of the United Nations and heads of state and representatives from a number of countries around the world. The peace accord became our first positive news item for many years on the subject of peace.

Nonetheless, the way was not free of obstacles. In a plebiscite, which I myself convoked, a vote of approval for the agreement we had reached in Havana and signed in Cartagena was defeated by a very narrow margin. I therefore called for a national dialogue in order to hear the misgivings and critiques of those who had voted no. And finally, on November 24, 2016, in the Teatro Colón in Bogotá, we signed a new text that incorporated the great majority of the proposals and suggestions we had received.

Since then, Colombia has been moving forward—accompanied by the international community—in the implementation of the agreement. It's a complex task, and will take several years. Approximately thirteen thousand combatants and militia members from the Farc—a guerrilla force that, a few years before, had numbered twenty thousand members—came together in temporary camps to begin a process of reinsertion into civil society and to hand over their weapons to the United Nations in a gradual process that ended in June 2017.

A few years earlier, if you had asked any Colombian if he or she thought it possible to obtain a successful negotiation with the Farc, the great majority would have replied that it was impossible. It had been tried many times and had always failed. The differences were irreconcilable and there was little or no will to reach an agreement. But this time, in Colombia, we managed to make the impossible become possible. This is why the international community is following our process with interest and hope, since it may serve as a model for other conflicts as yet unresolved in many corners of the planet.

How was this achieved? What is the secret that explains why thousands of men and women who had taken up arms against the state now decided to renounce violent measures and realize their ideals by democratic means? The answer to these questions has a lot to do with what I have learned during the course of a life dedicated to journalism and public service.

I did not seek peace ingenuously. I knew that first I would have to ensure certain conditions to arrive at my goal, and that these would imply, for example, consolidating a military strength that would make armed rebellion less attractive. I had also to create an international opinion favorable to negotiation, and learn from diverse experiences in the search for peace in my own country and in the world.

There is no instruction manual on how to make peace. Each case is unique, and one learns as one goes along. But certain parameters do exist, certain principles, innovations, which become beacons that can illuminate every new effort at peace anywhere on earth.

This is both my story and the story of how Colombia managed to end an internal war that had lasted for half a century, overcoming one difficulty after another, one obstacle and then the next. It is an account of how we built up a process that would work, and that would be successful, in the complex context of the twenty-first century where the new era of international tribunals demands a minimum level of justice to sustain a peace process.

Here, then, are the lessons I learned about peace. And also about war, since one is intrinsically related to the other. Here you will find the lessons that convinced me I could hope for a better future, and that there exists a possible solution to any conflict. As I said in Oslo on December 10, 2016, on receiving the Nobel Prize: "The sun of peace finally shines in the heavens of Colombia. May its light shine upon the whole world."

—Juan Manuel Santos
Former President of Colombia
January 2021

The Battle for Peace

Two Centuries between War and Peace

A GUERRILLA IN MY BEDROOM

It's one of my earliest childhood memories. It happened toward the end of 1956 or early in 1957, when I was five years old, in the house of my paternal grandfather in Bogotá.

I sometimes slept at my grandfather's place since I was very attached to him, and on that particular night I was in a room with two beds. I was awoken from sleep by the sound of someone opening the door and saw the shadow of a man who silently went across the room and got into the bed beside mine. I didn't say anything or ask any questions. I just went back to sleep, and next day when I woke up he wasn't there.

Years later it was my grandfather himself, Enrique Santos Montejo, a journalist, free thinker and anticlerical, the country's most celebrated columnist, known by his nom de plume, Caliban, who told me who had shared the room with me that night. It was the famous Liberal guerrilla leader Guadalupe Salcedo, whom my grandfather sometimes had stay with him when he was in town.

Guadalupe was nothing short of a myth, a symbol of a terrible era of fierce armed battles between the followers of the two traditional political parties in Colombia, the Liberal and the Conservative.

Beginning with that far-off memory, all my life I was, like a lot of Colombians, often close to an experience of war—at times only centimeters away from it. When we traveled by car to my uncle's farm in the warm, humid climate of Ambalema in the department of Tolima, near the center of the country, I wondered why the roads and the countryside were so heavily patrolled by soldiers. "It's because of the violence," I was told. "To protect us from the bandits." There, in Tolima, the Liberal Party guerrilla groups were operating, several of which had turned into simple bands of marauding outlaws commanded by hardened, cruel men with aliases such as Black Blood, Sparks, Revenge, and Tarzan, who had become part of popular legend.

So it was that, hardly before I reached the age of reason, I knew I wasn't living in a normal country, and that war was a shadow that accompanied us all, one we had to get used to living with.

A NATION AT WAR

Colombia has been a nation marked by violence from the very birth of the republic over two centuries ago. We had scarcely raised our cry of independence from Spain in 1810 when our leaders were locked in wars over their different views on how the new state should be built, whether centralist or federalist.

In 1815, when the Spanish troops arrived back on our shores to reconquer us, they found a people divided into multiple regional governments, a fact that made it easy for them to force Colombians to submit to the colonials, and to subject them to a reign of terror.

Later, once we had won our independence definitively—sealed on August 7, 1819, at the Battle of Boyacá by troops fighting under orders from Simón Bolívar and Francisco de Paula Santander—the panorama didn't much change. The nineteenth century was typified by an almost uninterrupted succession of civil wars, which left us with an unenviable record as the century's Latin American nation with the greatest number of internal wars.

Any cause whatsoever provided incentive for a fight: followers of Bolívar against those of Santander, Centralists against Federalists, free traders against artisans, clericals against anticlericals. And so we passed the time in domestic quarrels that caused us to miss the train of progress and led only to the proclamation of new constitutions, constitutions that would last for only a few short years until the outbreak of another civil war.

In the transition from the nineteenth to the twentieth century, we were embroiled in the worst armed confrontation of all, the so-called War of a Thousand Days. The two traditional parties—the Liberal and the Conservative—embarked on a dispute that they attempted to settle by means of relentless military battles, leaving a hundred thousand dead—and that in a country whose population at the time was hardly more than four million. And it left us with something else: the cutting off of Panama in 1903, shamelessly engineered by Theodore Roosevelt, the president of the United States, in order to build the canal. Colombians scarcely put up a fight to prevent this, since the war had virtually reduced the country to ashes.

After this, Colombia, though sorely affected, entered a period of relative political calm and public order during which the Conservatives held power up until 1930, and the Liberals from then until 1946. In the course of the first half of the twentieth century, free at last from internal strife, Colombia began to develop its industry and modernize its infrastructure, and began to emerge as one of the world's most important producers and exporters of coffee.

This was the longest period of peace we have known since our country became a republic. But it was to be no more than an interregnum.

THE VIOLENCE

In 1946 a division in the ranks of the Liberal Party meant that the Conservatives returned to power under the presidency of Mariano Ospina Pérez. And with him four decades of relative tranquility came to an end. The armed forces, especially the government's police, wrought havoc on members of the Liberal Party around the country, and the Liberals reacted no less fiercely by attacking anyone who owed allegiance to the Conservative Party. For more than ten years, in towns and rural areas up and down the country, Conservatives and Liberals were killing one another simply for waving a red or, alternatively, a blue flag. These murders were carried out with a degree of savagery never before seen in Colombia.

One particular crime added further fuel to this unprecedented violence; namely, the assassination, in the center of Bogotá, of the populist Liberal leader Jorge Eliécer Gaitán, a caudillo who seemed likely to become Colombia's next president. His passionate rhetoric and emotional oratory against the oligarchs had won him hundreds of thousands of followers. And on the day he was murdered, April 9, 1948, people's hopes were frustrated and rage entered their hearts.

It was never known who ordered the murder of Gaitán, or whether it was a crime carried out for personal reasons. What is certain is that on the day of his assassination and during the days that followed, people rampaged through the streets of Bogotá, burning, shooting, and looting, until the city was half destroyed. From then on, virtually the whole country was caught up in a spiral of revenge against the Conservatives, who were seen as responsible for the

Liberal leader's murder. Many people point to this moment as the start of the *via crucis* of violence—later to be continued by the guerrillas with the internal armed conflict—a violence that has been raging in Colombia ever since.

This desolate period of our history, when Liberals and Conservatives treated one another as mortal enemies, is known simply as The Violence. It is estimated that, in just a decade, some two or three hundred thousand Colombians were slaughtered in Colombia's towns and countryside.

In 1953, under the Conservative regime of Roberto Urdaneta—who replaced Laureano Gómez in the presidency, due to the latter's failing health—Colombia continued to be consumed in the flames of partisan feuding. However, a military coup, backed by a broad section of society, returned things more or less to normal. General Gustavo Rojas Pinilla, accompanied by both Liberal and Conservative party leaders, began a process of pacification and amnesty that led to the dismantling of most of the Liberal guerrilla forces, including the most feared guerrilla group of them all, that of Guadalupe Salcedo (my accidental roommate) in the country's Eastern Plains.

Guadalupe and his men signed a peace agreement and were demobilized in 1953. He was already a free man thanks to the Rojas amnesty when he spent nights at my grandfather's home, as he did in that of other Liberal Party leaders who were glad to welcome him as a hero of resistance to the onslaught of the Conservatives. Others, however, especially those on the opposite side of the spectrum, saw him as nothing more than a bloodthirsty bandit. In June 1957 he was shot dead in Bogotá in circumstances that were never properly investigated nor explained. He had just left a dinner party organized in his honor in the Bella Suiza restaurant by a group of militant Liberal Party women known as Las Policarpas, whose members included my mother, my aunt Helena, and María Paulina Nieto, the grandmother of Sergio Jaramillo, who was to become my high commissioner for peace. The official version says that Guadalupe, in a drunken stupor, was firing pistol shots into the air when he was brought down by a policeman. But my mother never believed that story.

General Rojas, who led the military coup to bring peace to the nation, with the virtually unanimous support of all political leaders, was seduced, as so many caudillos are, by the damnable temptation to hold on to power forever. Like any other dictator, he resorted to repression and censorship. In fact, he closed down the country's most important newspaper, *El Tiempo*, which belonged to my family. Even the elite who had originally supported his takeover were appalled by such actions. In 1957 the leaders of both the Liberal and

Conservative Parties—who had been sworn enemies for half a century—now formed an alliance to overthrow Rojas and return to democratic government.

And so it was. Rojas was forced out of office by pressure from civil society. Then, after a plebiscite, a system known as the National Front was created and ushered in a period of sixteen years in which the two political parties took turns at government. This was due to a political treaty concerted by the Conservative leader Laureano Gómez, living in exile in Spain, and the Liberal Party leader Alberto Lleras Camargo. As a result, from 1958 to 1974, during four presidential periods, the head of state alternated between members of those two parties. This brought about stability and a certain political calm, and put a definitive end to interparty violence.

Nevertheless, the National Front had some adverse effects. By restricting access to power to Liberal and Conservative Party members only, it politically stifled other, minority political groups, among them the Communist Party. It was conducive, also, to a feeling of political immobility that, in the 1960s, was a breeding ground for student rebellion. This gave rise to new guerrilla groups, which were not political party oriented, but revolutionary.

THE BIRTH OF THE GUERRILLAS

The pacification process undertaken by Rojas brought about the dismantling of most of the Liberal and Conservative Party guerrillas. But not all. Some refused to hand over their weapons, and continued to maintain pockets of resistance in isolated rural areas.

In the early 1960s the peasant guerrillas discovered an ideological justification in the triumphant Cuban Revolution and the rampant Cold War, represented by the Berlin Wall and the missile crisis. As early as 1961, the Communist Party declared that it was ready to resort to a combination of all forms of struggle, including the taking up of arms.

In this context, a former Liberal Party guerrilla fighter, Pedro Antonio Marín, alias Manuel Marulanda or Tirofijo (Sure Shot), at the head of a sizable number of agricultural workers, established a kind of commune in a rugged mountain area called Marquetalia, to the south of the department of Tolima. These men and women set themselves up as an armed self-defense group, claiming their right as peasant families to the smallholdings from which they had been forcefully evicted during the violence of the preceding years. Marquetalia and other like areas in places far from the urban centers were denounced by the Conservative senator Álvaro Gómez Hurtado, son of Laureano Gómez, as "independent republics" over which the state had no control. They thus became military targets.

In May 1964, under the Conservative government of Guillermo León Valencia, the Colombian army launched an operation to wipe out this isolated revolutionary peasant rebellion. But the army's plan backfired. Despite the fact that they were numerically inferior, Marulanda and most of his followers escaped unharmed. And a few weeks later, they drew up an agrarian program and formed what was known as the Southern Block, soon to become Colombia's first revolutionary nonpartisan guerrilla army. Two years later, in 1966, this group set themselves up officially as the Fuerzas Armadas Revolucionarias de Colombia (Revolutionary Armed Forces of Colombia), known as the Farc. They trace their origin to the Colombian army's failed military operation in Marquetalia.

The Farc promptly adopted a Communist platform of Marxist-Leninist orientation headed by their ideologue Jacobo Arenas, who had strong links to Colombia's Communist Party. In the same period, fired up by the inflammatory revolutionary climate of the sixties, other guerrilla groups sprang up.

Also in 1964, a group of young men inspired by Che Guevara and the Cuban Revolution, founded the National Liberation Army (Ejército de Liberación Nacional, or ELN), which was later to adopt the postulates of liberation theology, a current of thought among some members of the Roman Catholic Church who proclaimed their preferential option for the poor and the need to take direct action, even armed action if necessary, to achieve their ends.

The ELN's most popular figure—though he spent only four months with the insurgents and was never a commandant—was the Bogotá priest and sociologist Camilo Torres Restrepo, to whom I am related on my mother's side. Torres embraced the revolutionary cause and was killed in action in a confrontation with Colombian army troops in February 1966. He was just thirty-seven years of age, and died in his first and only combat. When I was about eleven and Torres was chaplain at the National University of Colombia, I served as an altar boy—along with Luis Fernando Botero, a friend at the Anglo Colombian School—at the wedding mass of my cousin Marsha Wilkie Calderón and Edgar Gutiérrez, at which Torres officiated. Edgar was later to become finance minister in the government of Betancur. After Guadalupe Salcedo, Father Camilo was the second famous *guerrillero* with whom I had contact, although at this time Torres was far from being an armed revolutionary and my contact with him took place amid the odor of incense and to the sound of sacred music.

In early 1967 a third revolutionary guerrilla group sprang up, the so-called Popular Liberation Army (Ejército Popular de Liberación, or EPL), of Maoist orientation, which had a certain influence in some areas of the Caribbean and in the north of the department of Antioquia.

In 1970, when the deposed dictator General Gustavo Rojas Pinilla, having recovered his political rights as citizen, presented his candidacy for president of Colombia, he was defeated in the polls. When the votes were counted, the Conservative Party's National Front candidate, Misael Pastrana, was elected by a narrow margin. To many, Pastrana's victory seemed highly suspicious, and the possibility of fraud aroused the anger and indignation of the multitudinous followers of Rojas. As a result, a group of radical *rojistas* founded a fourth guerrilla group that, as distinct from the others, was both urban and nationalist. It took the name 19th of April Movement (M-19) in memory of the date of the 1970 elections, which they considered had been stolen from them.

Other small guerrilla groups were founded in the early years of the 1980s: the Quintin Lame Armed Movement, made up of rebels from some indigenous communities; and the Trotskyist Revolutionary Workers Party (Partido Revolucionario de Trabajadores, or PRT).

Of the revolutionary guerrilla organizations mentioned here, the Farc was not only the first but also the one that managed to gain the greatest number of adherents, and that represented the greatest threat to the country's institutional democracy. However, in their early years, up until 1980, they were little more than an isolated movement with fewer than one thousand combatants. Soon that situation was going to change.

THE SEVENTIES: A DECADE OF TRANSITION

At the end of the 1960s, when I was a student at the Colegio San Carlos in Bogotá, I decided I wanted to finish high school and graduate from the Admiral Padilla Naval Cadet School in Cartagena. The two long years that followed transformed my life. They taught me discipline and the mystique of military life, and they allowed me to get to know the intensity of our geography and the richness of our cultural diversity, represented in the regions from which the other cadets, my classmates, had come.

In the Naval Cadet School I learned to navigate, a very important lesson, because when you navigate you have to know exactly where you intend to go—you have to have a precise point of destination. There I also attained a certain proficiency in mathematics and studied the tactics and strategies of war. However, the subject of the recently formed guerrilla groups was not yet on the curriculum—at least, it was not mentioned in the classroom—even though it was beginning to present a serious threat to our institutions. We were concerned, rather, with defending our shores and our sovereignty in case of any hypothetical confrontation with a neighboring country.

While I was wearing a military uniform, my older brother Enrique, by way of contrast, had set off on an ideological course toward the left in the faculty of philosophy at Los Andes University, where he was to graduate. He then specialized in political science in Munich and spent time in Paris, where he took part in the stirring events of May 1968. In Europe he was further inculcated with the revolutionary and socialist ideas that were attracting so many students worldwide. And so, a few years later, he ended up founding the magazine *Alternativa*, along with Gabriel García Márquez and other left-wing intellectuals. This publication opposed not only the particular government in power but the system itself, in open contradiction with the moderate liberal ideas and the institutional structures defended by *El Tiempo*. Thus, in our own family, we experienced on a domestic level what the country as a whole was going through; some of us remained faithful to our traditions and defended the institutions and the established order, while others, in the spirit of the times, identified with movements of protest and rebellion.

Once I had graduated from the Naval Cadet School, I decided to study economy and business management at the University of Kansas. My brother Luis Fernando—the second of us four brothers; I was the third and Felipe the youngest—was studying at the famous William Allen White School of Journalism at that university, and he persuaded me to try it. "If you don't like it, you can go somewhere else," he said. However, I liked it and stayed, and graduated.

I returned to my country to work in the Colombian Coffee Growers Federation. I didn't want to work in my family's newspaper, as my father would have liked. I needed my independence and felt that if I wanted to become a good economist in Colombia I had to learn all I could about coffee, which at the time was our main export product.

My dream as an economist was to study at the famous London School of Economics, to which I applied with no great illusions about being accepted. To my surprise and delight, they admitted me. And this was followed by another stroke of good luck: the manager of the federation offered me a job in

London, which I could combine simultaneously with my studies. So I went to England, where I was to spend practically the whole of the seventies. I worked there as the federation's representative, while also representing Colombia at the International Coffee Organization and completing a postgraduate course at the London School of Economics. From England I went to Boston on a Fulbright scholarship, and obtained another postgraduate degree from the Kennedy School of Government at Harvard. I finally went back to Colombia in 1982 to take on the deputy direction of my family's business, the *El Tiempo* daily newspaper.

Meanwhile, the guerrilla groups in Colombia continued to wage war, although their field of action was still quite limited. The country's armed forces combated them as best they could with the meager resources at their disposal, while the guerrillas practiced their classic method of strike and retreat, financing their activities mainly by means of kidnappings and extortion.

In the years between 1978 and 1982, the Liberal Party government of Julio César Turbay opted for a politics of harsh repression of the guerrillas and their sympathizers. To do this, the government passed a draconian piece of legislation known as the Security Statute, which endowed the military and the police with broad faculties for persecuting illegal activists or suspects. It was an era of dictatorships in most Latin American countries. And although ours was a democracy, the methods employed by the armed forces were identical to those used by other colonels and generals from across the continent with whom they received training at the so-called School of the Americas in the United States. There they were indoctrinated within the parameters of the Cold War to fight the menace of communism and to combat—often with questionable means—not only subversives but any social movement with left-wing tendencies.

Paradoxically, in the final months of this hardline government, Colombia's first peace commission was set up to explore possible ways of ending the conflict with the guerrillas. The commission, officially installed in November 1981, was headed by ex-president Carlos Lleras Restrepo and composed of diverse personalities, including the then commander of the Colombian army and a prelate from the Catholic Church.

However, the commission was dissolved in the first months of 1982 when several of its members dropped out, including Lleras. They complained that their proposals had not met with the backing of the Turbay government.

This same commission was reconstituted by the president who followed Turbay; namely, Belisario Betancur, elected for the period 1982–1986.

Betancur aspired to go down in history as the president of peace, and very promptly his administration launched the first serious process of dialogue with the guerrillas. The guerrilla groups the government was addressing had been formed in the sixties, almost twenty years earlier.

But since then things had changed drastically. Drug traffic, a new and devastating phenomenon, had greatly increased the traffickers' capacity to amass immense fortunes and, as a result, they exerted enormous power. This illegal traffic, with its incalculable resources, appeared in Colombia in the late sixties. It is said that the first batch of marijuana from here was dispatched in 1968, on a Swedish boat, by ex-combatants from the Vietnam War. The drug trade grew exponentially in the eighties with disastrous consequences for our country. The traffickers realized that cocaine was a much more profitable business than marijuana. And since they already had control of the routes, they took over the market. Since then, Colombia has been the chief exporter of cocaine to the world's markets, at a tremendous cost in human lives, corruption, and weakening of our institutions.

BETANCUR'S PEACE PROCESS: FROM DOVES TO HOLOCAUST

Belisario Betancur was a humanist and intellectual of humble beginnings, one of twenty-two children fathered by a mule driver from Antioquia, who came to power promising he would do all he could to achieve peace. His campaign's slogan, "Yes, we can," inspired hope in a great many Colombians, and doves of peace appeared everywhere, painted on walls in public places up and down the country.

In the meantime, the Farc had begun a process of expansion that reached a turning point in 1982 at their Seventh Conference when the guerrilla's two leaders—Manuel Marulanda, the strategist, and Jacobo Arenas, the ideologue—traced a new line of attack for the organization, which had been gradually growing in numbers.

At that meeting, the Farc decided to strengthen their combat potential, doubling the number of fronts in the country's regions (from twenty-four to forty-eight) and setting as their goal the overthrow, in the course of eight years, of the present political regime and the establishment of a provisional government. As a clear sign of their determination, they added to their name the initials EP (Ejército del Pueblo, People's Army) and were subsequently known as Farc-EP.

The recent triumph of the Sandinista revolution in Nicaragua, which put an end to the Somoza dictatorship, gave new impetus to Colombia's guerrilla movements, reconfirming their belief that they could come to power by the use of arms.

Betancur set up the peace commission anew, and on a broader basis than that of Turbay. He also proposed a generous amnesty for members of the insurgent groups who returned to civilian life.

Thus there began a peace process that embraced the Farc, the EPL, and the M-19 organizations. Only the ELN refused to take part in dialogue, except for a few of its members who did agree to negotiate. In 1984 a ceasefire agreement was reached with the above organizations, albeit a precarious one, since there was no concentration of troops, nor were adequate mechanisms set up to ensure the agreement was respected. Nonetheless, for the first time in decades we Colombians began to believe that peace could really be achieved.

As always happens in these processes, the government's proposal to dialogue with the insurgents was openly attacked by part of Colombia's society, as well as by a considerable number of the clandestine obscure forces of the type that thrive on war. This opposition reached such a point that the commission's president, Otto Morales Benítez, felt obliged to resign because, as he said, "hidden enemies of peace" were undermining the process from both within and outside the government.

In April 1984, just as the Betancur government was agreeing on a ceasefire with various guerrilla groups, a hired gunman working for the drug traffickers assassinated the justice minister, Rodrigo Lara, who had been waging a valiant war on the drug trade's capos, especially on Pablo Escobar, the feared criminal at the head of the Medellín cartel.

President Betancur's response was to authorize the extradition of drug traffickers to the United States, a decision that unleashed an out-and-out war on the state by the drug cartels, a war in which Colombia lost many of its most illustrious citizens, including presidential candidates, politicians, judges, and journalists, not to mention soldiers and policemen and ordinary men and women, victims of indiscriminate terrorist attacks launched by the mafia.

This era of narco-terrorism left Colombia with an unenviable record as the country with the world's highest rate of homicide per capita, and converted cities like Medellín into symbols of crime, although fortunately Medellín now has become a tourist attraction and model of progress and modernity. War on the drug trade has cost Colombia more dearly than any other nation on earth. It is a war that was declared by the United Nations more than half a century ago, and unfortunately has not been won.

Drug traffickers' money, smeared with blood, ended up financing and increasing violence at both of its extremes. On the one hand, as the traffickers began to convert Colombia into the world's major producer and exporter of cocaine, they sought alliances with the guerrillas in the jungle and in areas with access to the country's frontiers, counting on the insurgents to protect their illegal crops. Thus they forged a link with the guerrillas, mainly with the Farc, whose resources thereby soared. As a result, their combat capacity also vastly improved. I have no doubt that, without drug money, the Farc would have been defeated, or would have negotiated peace long before they eventually did so.

On the other hand, some of the drug lords, whose family members had been kidnapped by the guerrillas, created and financed death squads known as self-defense groups, which quickly became commandos bent on exterminating not only the guerrillas but also democratic political leaders on the left. These groups sowed the seeds of paramilitary organizations that, with the pretext of defending society from subversion, resorted to extortion and massacres, driving millions of agricultural workers off their land.

This kind of confrontation between the state and the guerrillas, which had been maintained at a relatively moderate level from the sixties up until the eighties, now evolved into an immensely complex war due to these two new factors: drug traffic and paramilitarism.

Despite this increasingly difficult situation, President Betancur continued to promote his peace process. It collapsed, however, in the most appalling fashion on November 6, 1985, when the M-19 guerrilla group stormed the Justice Palace in a reckless action that concluded with the palace being recaptured by Colombian army troops, who left the building totally destroyed. In the holocaust more than one hundred people were killed, including most of the Supreme Court magistrates. Along with them, many important judicial documents indicting drug traffickers for extradition were reduced to ashes.

It was a catastrophe whose scenes of death and destruction will remain forever engraved on the nation's memory. Clearly we were not as close to achieving peace as we had hoped.

DARK TIMES, TIMES OF ANXIETY

To all of these phenomena I was a witness, and I analyzed them as both columnist and deputy director of *El Tiempo* at a time when it was particularly difficult for the press due to the threat that was hanging over anyone who dared to express an opinion in favor of the extradition of the drug traffickers. Guillermo Cano, director of the other large national newspaper, *El Espectador*, was murdered by the mafia toward the end of 1986. Other courageous journalists like him were assassinated for having defended the values of truth and freedom even at the risk of their lives.

I well remember the day a loquacious character by the name of Carlos Nader arrived at my office. He was a friend of Enrique, but also of the Ochoa brothers who belonged to the Medellín drug cartel, and he wanted to alert us to an air attack that was being planned on the headquarters of *El Tiempo*. It was going to be either a bomb, he said, or a kamikaze operation. He left my brother and me petrified, but apart from reporting the matter to the authorities, there was nothing much we could do.

These were dark times, without a doubt. Times of anxiety.

President Betancur had bequeathed to the country a fragile ceasefire with the Farc. This was ratified in March 1986 in a document signed, among other guerrilla commanders, by Timochenko, the very man with whom, thirty years later, I would sign an agreement that would put an end to the conflict with that same guerrilla organization. The ceasefire didn't last long, however. It was broken around the middle of the following year.

Betancur ended his term of office amid general unpopularity and the incomprehension that inevitably accompanies those who seek peace.* Not for nothing did Georges Clémenceau, prime minister of France during World War I, coin a phrase that many of us have attested to in our personal lives: "It's easier to make war than peace."

Betancur was followed by Virgilio Barco, a civil engineer and a member of the Liberal Party. Barco was a pragmatist under whose government (1986–1989) no new advances were made with the Farc, although a peace agreement was obtained with the M-19 guerrilla movement, whose members were demobilized and handed in their weapons in March 1990. This provided us with an example of reintegration into society in which former combatants returned to civilian life and took part in politics, immediately playing an essential and constructive role. The very year of the M-19's demobilization, their commander Carlos Pizarro presented his candidacy for the office of mayor of Bogotá, coming third at the polls. He then launched his candidacy

* Belisario Betancur died on December 7, 2019, at the age of ninety-five, acknowledged unanimously as having been Colombia's first head of government to attempt a negotiated solution to armed conflict with the guerrillas. He was a man of peace and a true humanist.

for president, but in April of that year was assassinated in an airplane by a paramilitary hired gunman.

The response to Pizarro's murder on the part of a broad section of Colombia's society was one of solidarity with the members of the group recently demobilized. So much so that, in 1990, the ex-guerrillas won one-third of the votes in the polls to elect a constituent assembly destined to provide the country with a new political constitution. One of M-19's former leaders, Antonio Navarro, acted as copresident of the assembly and went on to hold important public posts successively as minister of state, congressman, mayor, and departmental governor. Since then, other former members of M-19 have served in important regional and national capacities, including the office of mayor of Bogotá.

During President Barco's four-year term in office, the actions of drug traffickers and paramilitaries reached unprecedented levels of violence. They assassinated not only Pizarro but two other presidential candidates: the Liberal Party's Luis Carlos Galán and Bernardo Jaramillo, candidate for the Patriotic Union.

The case of the Patriotic Union (Unión Patriótica, UP) deserves special mention. In 1985, in the midst of the peace process carried out with the guerrillas by President Betancur, several groups on the left formed a party with the name Patriotic Union with a view to prepare the way for the Farc to eventually take part in democratic politics. Some Farc members who had been granted amnesty joined the party, along with unionists, Communists, and others with left-wing tendencies.

The Patriotic Union was a kind of laboratory to experiment with the possibility of the Farc's incorporation into political life. But it did not turn out well. At the beginning, members of the new party were elected as congressmen and women, mayors, deputies to departmental assemblies, and municipal councilors in different parts of the country. But almost at once there began a systematic process of assassination of the party's members, which led to its virtual extermination and a retreat, on the part of those who had begun to carry on political activities within the country's legal institutions, to rejoin the guerrillas in the jungle.

During the final years of the 1980s, obscure forces, led by drug traffickers and paramilitaries, occasionally with the complicity or indifference of state organs, carried out a campaign of selective assassinations perpetrated on members of the Patriotic Union. Among those murdered were Jaime Pardo Leal, the party's president and former presidential candidate, as well as Bernardo

Jaramillo, in turn candidate for the presidency, as well as congressmen and women, deputies, councilors, and mayors affiliated to this political organization, not to mention approximately three thousand of its militants.

The Patriotic Union's tragedy was also a tragedy and an immense setback for peace in Colombia, since it confirmed the Farc guerrillas in their conviction that there was no way they would be able to achieve their ends by political means.

Over a quarter of a century later, in September 2016, as president, I met with survivors of the Patriotic Union in the presidential palace, and the following was my message to them:

> We, as a government, are obliged to fulfill our commitment to ensuring that nobody who participates in politics falls victim to armed attack, and most especially that no member of any political party, including the new political movement which results from the incorporation of the Farc into civilian life, should be a victim of violence.
>
> It is in this historic moment for our country, when we face the future with such hope, that we should look back and remember and recognize the Patriotic Union's tragedy, which the Council of State has categorized as extermination.
>
> For the persecution of the Patriotic Union was exactly that: a tragedy that led to the disappearance of a political organization and caused unspeakable damage to thousands of families and to our democracy.
>
> . . . It is the responsibility of the state to offer all possible guarantees that this will never again occur, including the guarantee that the state's agents and society in general abstain from the stigmatization that contributed so much to the violence against the UP.
>
> I solemnly commit myself here before you to take all the necessary measures and give all the guarantees that never again in Colombia will a political organization face what the UP has suffered.

THE CONSTITUTION AS A PEACE TREATY

The Liberal Party economist César Gaviria, who became president in 1990, took up the cause of the assassinated presidential candidate Luis Carlos Galán after the leader's son, in the cemetery where the murdered man's funeral was taking place, indicated that Gaviria was the man who should assume the role of his father's successor. The new president inherited a country in disarray, and whose institutions were in need of structural changes. And this overhaul was brought about by a national constituent assembly that was convoked thanks to the pressure and initiatives of Colombia's young university students.

As deputy director of *El Tiempo,* I supported this process from the start through editorials and opinion columns, since I was aware that our country was in urgent need of a change of course that would steer it in the right direction; namely, the direction of hope, after the wave of violence that we had suffered during the difficult decade of the eighties. The student initiative became a reality thanks to the so-called seventh paper, an additional voting card that was introduced at the polls during the parliamentary elections of March 1990. A lot of these "papers," which were destined to change the course of our country's history, were printed with my authorization on our newspaper's presses.

Taking part in the constituent assembly were the traditional parties and the political organization created by demobilized M-19 guerrillas, as well as academics and representatives of many and varied sectors of society. It ended on July 4, 1991, with the promulgation of a new constitution to replace the former one, which had been in place since 1886.

The 1991 Constitution has been called a peace treaty. And no doubt it was. In it, peace with M-19 was sealed, and the new constitution prepared the way for other armed groups to hand in their weapons, renounce illegal activity, and return to civilian life. So much so that, apart from the seventy elected delegates, the assembly saw the participation—with a voice, although not a vote—of four delegates from each of the groups in the process of demobilization.

Colombia's 1991 Constitution represented a progressive political accord that declared Colombia to be a social state under the rule of law, broadening citizens' fundamental guarantees and establishing novel mechanisms such as the "tutelage action" by which citizens themselves can demand that the state respect their rights.

Article 22 consecrates an unquestionable right that has ever since been the support of all the country's efforts for peace. "Peace is a right and a duty of compulsory observance."

DIALOGUE WHILE THE FIGHTING GOES ON

The Gaviria administration not only promulgated a new constitution but also achieved the demobilization of the greater part of the EPL as well as that of other more recent guerrilla groups, such as the Quintin Lame Armed Movement, the PRT, and the Socialist Renovation Current, a dissident group from the ELN.

In this situation, practically the only groups still illegally combating the state were the Farc and the ELN, the largest and oldest guerrilla groups. These two organizations presented the country with an ever-increasing challenge. They had openly expressed their wish to participate in the constituent assembly, but this was never agreed upon due to the government's insistence that they first set free all those whom they had kidnapped and were holding in captivity, while at the same time ceasing in their war on the state and showing that they were ready to demobilize. In early November 1990, a commission made up of members of the Patriotic Union was authorized by Gaviria to meet with the Farc leaders in a last attempt at making their participation possible. The commission did not get a positive reply from the guerrillas, and on December 9, the very day Colombians went to the polls to elect delegates to the assembly, the government launched a surprise attack on the Farc's high command, bombing their legendary headquarters known as the Green House, located in the municipality of La Uribe in the region of the Eastern Plains.

The bombs destroyed the guerrilla camp, but the Farc's commanders escaped unharmed, as they had done at Marquetalia over a quarter of a century before. Colombian military forces had suffered a stunning defeat, the number of soldiers killed in the attack being far greater than was recognized by the army. And, as was to be expected, the incident only led to further igniting the war.

In the midst of this confrontation, and with deep distrust on both sides, the Gaviria government made an attempt at dialogue with the different guerrilla groups who, at this juncture, came together in what they called the Simon Bolívar Guerrilla Coordinating Board, composed of the Farc, the ELN, and the remnants of the EPL.

These conversations were conducted in three stages, carried out while the conflict continued; that is, with no ceasefire or any diminishing of hostilities. The first meeting, of an exploratory nature, took place in May 1991 in the municipality of Cravo Norte, in the department of Arauca, in Colombia's northeast, close to the Venezuelan border. The second stage was held in Caracas in June 1991, and the third in Tlaxcala, Mexico, early in 1992. This last meeting was broken off when a former minister of Colombia, Argelino Durán Quintero, was assassinated by the EPL, which had been holding him captive.

The dialogues thus came to an end in October of that year with no positive results.

The guerrillas had increased in strength, both in military and operational terms, thanks to the immense resources obtained from the drug trade. Their agreement to negotiate at this time was not due to pressure exerted on them by the Colombian army but rather because they saw how M-19 militants, now demobilized, were representing the Left and winning a degree of popular support.

M-19's move from waging war to taking part in politics was not an isolated case. The world had already seen how many illegal groups were playing a role in the political arena in the wake of various peace processes. Such was the case with the Mozambique National Resistance Movement (Renamo), the African National Congress in South Africa, the National Union for Total Independence of Angola (Unita), the Unified Communist Party in Nepal, the Guatemalan National Revolutionary Unity, the Farabundo Martí National Liberation Front (FMLN) in El Salvador, and Sinn Féin in Northern Ireland, among others.

In our country, however, in the early nineties, the possibility of negotiating with the guerrillas no longer seemed to be an option. The Colombians, who had applauded the decision of the M-19 and other groups to hand in their weapons, had lost patience with those who persisted in illegal activities. For their part, the Farc, in light of the extermination of thousands of members of the Patriotic Union, had special reasons for distrusting the government. And the state's natural reaction was to declare "total war" on the insurgents. The conflict deepened.

Nothing sums up the tragedy of war better than the words of Alfonso Cano when acting as Farc negotiator in Tlaxcala. When conversations broke down, he remarked: "We'll see each other ten thousand deaths from now." I don't know whether he said it out of cynicism or sadness, but he summed up the consequences of giving up on negotiations for peace: more people dead, a great many more people dead. Sad to say, he was right.

In April 1993, after the efforts to dialogue had proved unsuccessful, the Farc held its Eighth Conference, the first since 1982, and there they made two fundamental decisions: on the one hand, to increase their military capacity and their presence in the country by creating five regional block that would bring together the different fronts, each one under the command of the Farc Secretariat, the guerrilla army's maximum authority. On the other, they approved a political program: in a detailed agenda covering all aspects of Colombian society that they aspired to change if and when they came to power and could begin to install a government of "national reconstruction and reconciliation."

The search for peace had run into a dead end from which it was going to be very hard to find a way out.

PART ONE

Conspiring for Peace (1991–1998)

CHAPTER 1

A First Approach to Peace

ENTERING PUBLIC LIFE

Journalism is in my blood. I have always been passionate about it as a profession, and it has afforded me a great many satisfactions and challenges. In the 1980s I was a member of the Commission for Freedom of the Press at the Inter American Press Association, and as such visited El Salvador, where civil war was raging, and Nicaragua during the Ortega brothers' regime, and Chile under the Pinochet dictatorship, in each case to defend the fundamental right to a free press as one of a society's major guarantees of progress.

There was no political angle to this. Only one simple aim: to defend freedom of expression. Which is why I was as forceful in my criticism of censorship in Pinochet's Chile as I was of that exerted in Nicaragua by the triumphant Sandinista revolution, in particular its censorship of the daily paper *La Prensa* directed by Violeta Barrios de Chamorro, who was later to be elected the country's president. In 1985, the *Nicaragua Chronicles*, which my brother Enrique and I wrote on the new Sandinista regime, its unfulfilled promises, and its corruption, won us the King of Spain International Journalism Prize, the first time this award was given in the category of the press.

In the early nineties, my future seemed decided and seemed inexorably linked to my family's newspaper, *El Tiempo*, where I had already been working for several years as deputy director. When the generation of my father and my uncle—respectively editor and director—decided to step down, I was the candidate most likely to take on the paper's direction.

But life had other plans in store for me.

In 1991, the then president César Gaviria offered me the opportunity of entering public life as minister for foreign trade. It was a monumental challenge, since such a ministry had not hitherto existed and it would be my job to create and organize it, and from that position spearhead the opening up of our economy, a policy that would put an end to decades of protectionism.

It was not an easy decision. My family was opposed to mixing journalism with political activity, and they made it very clear that if I were to accept the ministry, I could not later go back and take up the paper's direction. I decided to consult some good and sensible friends, such as former president Belisario Betancur and former minister Alfonso Palacio Rudas, known as the Confrère. Both urged me to accept.

I well remember the words of Palacio, which remain engraved on my mind: "There's a great difference," he said,

> between having an influence and having power. During his lifetime, the director of *El Tiempo* will have a great influence on the country. But that is not the same as having power. He who has power can give an order and say, "Let it be made public and carried out," and so make sure that such a thing becomes reality. You are a man who doesn't want merely to influence; you want to get things done. It's in your temperament.

Curiously, it was a doctor's mistake that ended up confirming my decision. I had just undergone medical tests, having come back from Rio de Janeiro with a high fever that lasted for days. I had been there visiting an old school friend, Miguel Pires, whom I had known as son of his country's then military attaché in Bogotá, General Leônidas Pires. Miguel's father was later to become the powerful army minister of the government of President José Sarney in Brazil. My friend, for his part, had become the righthand man of Roberto Marinho, Brazil's king of communications, and my trip was to explore the possibility of an alliance between *El Tiempo* and the O Globo group, owned by Marinho.

Well, the doctor wrongly interpreted my tests and said he thought it possible I had cancer. A few days later he corrected his diagnosis, but the sole possibility of cancer made me reflect, and I recalled something I heard my grandfather say when I was still a boy: "My son, when you reach my age, it's better to repent for what you've done than to regret not having done it."

And so, having just turned forty, I took on the challenge of becoming Colombia's first foreign trade minister and turned my back on a safe and appealing career as director of *El Tiempo*. My life veered toward public service, where I encountered the fascination that power exerts, power rightly understood: as the ability to produce results, to make a difference. Which is what my wise mentor Palacio had been talking about.

I wasn't obsessed with the idea of one day becoming president. That was not among my goals—although many have said it was—not because I didn't want the presidency but because I thought it quite impossible. However, a fortuitous turn of events made me begin to consider it.

Colombia's recently promulgated 1991 Constitution had done away with the role of "the designee"—that is, the person called on to assume the presidency of the republic in the absence of the sitting president—and this office had been replaced by that of vice-president, making it clear, however, that the role of presidential designate would remain in place up until the end of President Gaviria's term of office in August of 1994.

Humberto de la Calle, who was interior minister at the time and presidential designate, resigned this post in order to run for president and left the position vacant. As foreign trade minister, only recently arrived on the public scene, I rather cheekily decided to put forward my name for the post. The other candidate was the minister of communications, William Jaramillo, who, unlike me, had spent his life in politics and was a success in the role of what is known in Colombia as "electoral baron," or kingmaker. President Gaviria, for his part, remained neutral. To everyone's surprise, I was elected by Congress by a wide margin over my competitor and thus became the last presidential designate in Colombia's history. This in a way catapulted me into the political arena and made me look like someone who one day might even attain the highest post of all, that of head of state. In the process, I also learned a good deal about how things work and about the way votes are cast in Congress.

This was the first time in my life that I had put my name up as a candidate for election, and I would not do so again until I postulated my candidacy for the presidency twenty years later, in 2010.

"CAPITAL IS NO FRIEND OF WAR"

As Colombia's first foreign trade minister, I faced a tremendous challenge: to open up the country's economy to international markets under the best possible conditions. And one of those conditions was to increase foreign investment, since that was the only way we could grow and be competitive on the open market. You could say that my task was to sell our country to large companies and foreign multinationals so they might bring capital investment to Colombia and thus generate employment and the transfer of technologies.

In developing this mission, the Chemical Bank—which no longer exists but was then very important and had many interests in Colombia—organized a meeting in New York for the finance minister, Rudolf Hommes, and me to introduce the country to a select group of presidents of US companies, potential investors in Colombia. I could not have imagined it, but this conference was going to mean the start of my commitment to peace.

We were in the middle of our pitch when we learned that a bomb had blown up in Bogotá, causing numerous deaths. The news virtually put an end to our meeting since, given the terrorism rampant in our country, how were we going to convince our listeners of the benefits of investing there?

Later on, in conversation with several of the presidents of industry who had attended the event, one of them said to me with disarming frankness: "Minister, your plan to open up Colombia's economy is very interesting. But as long as you have a war going on in your country, it's going to be very difficult for you to attract important investments, I mean really substantial ones. Capital," he concluded sententiously, "is no friend of war. Capital is no friend of violence and insecurity, whether physical or juridical."

He could not have put it more bluntly, and his words made a deep impression on me. For decades, since early childhood, like most Colombians I had been used to living in the midst of violence and confrontation and to accept them as practically normal. But the rest of the world doesn't see things that way. Perhaps it was then that I understood that the effort to achieve peace was not just advisable but absolutely indispensable if Colombia was to know real progress—in other words, if we were ever to advance toward the goal of economic development and the reduction of poverty and inequality.

One clear idea became fixed in my mind: if Colombia was to someday become a developed country with a better quality of life, then its first and most urgent task would have to be the achievement of peace.

GOOD GOVERNMENT AND THE THIRD WAY

When Gaviria's government came to an end, and with it my first experience as a public servant, I returned to journalism, not this time as director—that was not to happen, given the restrictions imposed on me by the family—but as columnist, with the discipline and the responsibility of voicing my opinion on national affairs from the editorial pages of a daily paper.

I also decided to create a think tank to promote debate and research on a subject that had engaged me passionately from my student days at the John F. Kennedy School of Government at Harvard University; namely, good government.

At the time, the British sociologist Anthony Giddens—who was later to become director of my alma mater, the London School of Economics—had started to circulate among academics a concept that I found deeply attractive: the doctrine of the Third Way. This was a kind of modern version of British Labour Party politics and a subject on which, some years later—in 1999, to be precise—I published a book cowritten with Tony Blair, at that time prime minister of the United Kingdom.

The Third Way conceives the role of the state in search of an intermediate path, a pragmatic one, between the two principal currents of thought that held sway worldwide during the twentieth century: classical liberalism, which promoted economic and individual freedom in a system based on private property, and "statism," or intervention, which defends the property and control of the means of production by the state and the preponderance of collective rights over individual ones.

The Third Way does not consider the state and the private sector as mutual antagonists, but rather sees them as allies that can work together to achieve social prosperity. This idea has been summed up in a simple but telling phrase: "The market as far as is possible; the state as far as is necessary."

And so, between my columns and my newly created Good Government Foundation, I set off on a new stage of my life in the midst of one of the most serious political crises in recent history to affect Colombia and its institutions: I refer to what became known as "Proceso ocho mil" (8,000 Process).

CHAPTER 2

Destination Colombia

THE MEETING AT MONSERRAT ABBEY

In the aftermath of the dreadful decade of narco-terrorism, Colombians faced three principal threats to their security: the drug trade, the guerrillas, and the illegal self-defense groups known as paramilitaries. Following on the death of Pablo Escobar in 1993, other cartels and drug-trafficking organizations grew in importance, the strongest of which—Escobar's rival—was the Cali cartel headed by Miguel Rodríguez Orejuela and his brother, Gilberto Rodríguez Orejuela.

It was in this complex scenario that two men appeared as favorites in the forthcoming elections for president from 1994 to 1998: the Liberal Party candidate Ernesto Samper, and the Conservative Andrés Pastrana. After a virtual draw in the first round of voting, both campaigns strove even harder to win adherents and in the end Samper was elected in the second round. But as it turned out, his victory was to be bittersweet.

A few days after the election certain recordings came to light—they would go down in history as the narco-cassettes—consisting of telephone conversations in which people were heard talking about the important financial backing of the Cali cartel in favor of the winner, the Liberal Party candidate and newly elected president, Samper.

Needless to say, the discovery of these tapes caused a tremendous scandal and led to a legal process identified with the number 8,000, in which it was shown that drug money had indeed infiltrated the Samper campaign. The president alleged that if mafia money had been used to finance his campaign, it had occurred "behind his back." In the end, the congressional investigation into the matter came to nothing and was filed away.

Samper, however, found he had to spend the better part of his term of government defending himself from these accusations, and news of the scandal led the international community to look upon Colombia as a nonviable country virtually wallowing in drugs. The United States went so far as to rescind the president's entry visa.

In Colombia, the 8,000 Process became the main topic of conversation and the subject of peace was one among many that were put on the back burner to be addressed some other time. Through his peace advisers, Samper attempted to send out feelers to the insurgents, but the guerrillas replied, no doubt with a degree of cynicism, that they were not interested in dialogue with a government that was in itself illegitimate.

In this atmosphere of stagnation, with the government's hands practically tied as far as peace was concerned, it fell to us ordinary citizens to take upon ourselves a commitment to the constitution's article on peace as "a duty of compulsory observance" and to ensure, if possible, that this constitutional right be complied with.

In 1996, at a dinner with the president of the National Association of Industrialists, Carlos Arturo Ángel, and the Spanish ambassador Yago Pico de Coaña, we discussed the country's worrying situation and the need to make progress in search of peace in whatever way possible.

It occurred to Ángel that we might invite to Colombia a guru in the matter who could provide us with new ideas, and he mentioned the name of a Canadian, Adam Kahane, a former Shell Oil Company executive and an expert in conflict resolution who had played an important role in South Africa's process of reconciliation after the elimination of apartheid.

This seemed to me an excellent idea and I got to work to make it happen. The Carvajal Foundation agreed to underwrite the expenses involved in bringing the expert to Colombia, and I was able to make contact with him thanks to my erstwhile professor at Harvard Roger Fisher, himself a renowned expert in negotiations.

Kahane told me he had no time available on his agenda for the next year and a half at least, due to commitments in his own country, Canada, related to the independence movement in Quebec, and also with events in Northern Ireland and South Africa. However, a few days later he phoned me to say that an opportunity had arisen after all. He would be in Brazil and from there would be traveling to South Africa, and could make a stopover in Colombia in between his commitments in these two countries. The only problem was that it would have to take place just three weeks hence, and Kahane did not think that at such short notice we would be able to bring together enough actors in Colombia's conflict to make the exercise truly worthwhile.

Nonetheless, working with the Good Government Foundation we set about making the congress become a reality. And great was our guest speaker's surprise on arriving in Bogotá on March 29, 1996, and entering the conference hall in what was called the Monserrat Abbey, to discover that we had brought together representatives of nearly all of the country's social and political organizations.

"You have achieved in three weeks," said Kahane, "what in South Africa took fifteen years; namely, getting all the participants in the conflict to sit down at the same table."

Those present included ex-president Alfonso López Michelsen; the foreign affairs minister, Rodrigo Pardo; and the minister of defense, Juan Carlos Esguerra. Among other key figures in attendance were two former foreign affairs ministers, Augusto Ramírez and Luis Fernando Jaramillo; a former finance minister, Rudolf Hommes; the president of Congress's Chamber of Representatives, Rodrigo Rivera; members of the highest echelons of the Catholic Church and of the Colombian army, and the mayor of Bogotá, Antanas Mockus.

Also present were members of both the government and the government's fiercest opponents, as well as representatives of agricultural workers' associations and of rural industrialists, company heads and union bosses, academics, politicians, and retired army officers. Even more striking was the participation of representatives of the self-defense groups and—via telephone—Felipe Torres and Francisco Galán of the ELN, who at the time were prisoners in the Itagui jail, and Raúl Reyes and Olga Marín of the Farc, communicating with us from Costa Rica.

Never before had Colombia seen a meeting so broadly based and so diverse, bringing together different sectors of society, many of whom were declared enemies of one another. All had come with the avowed intention of trying to find a way to bring the conflict to an end.

I particularly recall an incident with Aída Avella, a well-known and combative leader from the Left and survivor of the Patriotic Union's virtual extermination, who, after decades in exile, would be elected to the Senate at the polls in March 2018. Avella threatened to leave the meeting when she was seated at the same table as Víctor Carranza, a notorious emerald dealer whom many saw as linked to the paramilitaries. "Doctor Santos," she said, evidently alarmed, "do you expect me to sit beside the man who, on five different occasions, ordered his men to murder me?" My answer was: "Aída, precisely to prevent him from ordering your murder a sixth time, go and sit beside him."

And so she did.

The meeting was extremely interesting, firstly because of its broad representation but also because at last we could have an open debate between all the parties in the conflict. Not to reach an agreement necessarily, but to get to know what each one was thinking.

ADVICE FROM MANDELA

Chance would have it that, in my capacity as foreign trade minister, I was to preside at the United Nations Conference on Trade and Development, the UNCTAD, and as such, exactly a month after the Monserrat Abbey meeting, I traveled to South Africa where I would hand over the presidency to Nelson Mandela. I had met him a few years before in Davos, Switzerland, and our present meeting offered me a golden opportunity to ask him what he thought of Kahane.

For me it was a very emotional moment. Mandela was, without a doubt, the world's most important living symbol of peace. After twenty-seven years in prison, he came out of captivity with no hate in his heart, and with a commitment to unite his nation. And he had done so. He had received the Nobel Peace Prize in 1993, and had become the first Black president in the history of South Africa.

At the time of my visit, the South African Commission for Truth and Reconciliation was in full swing, headed by Archbishop Desmond Tutu, who had also been awarded the Nobel Peace Prize, in 1984. I was impressed watching on television the public hearings in which victims and perpetrators recounted, each one from his or her particular perspective, the atrocities that had been committed during the long years of violence and discrimination. It was certainly a difficult exercise in confrontation, but an indispensable one if genuine reconciliation was to be achieved. I never imagined then that twenty years later, in April 2017, as president, I would be signing a decree to create a similar commission—the Commission for Clarifying the Truth, Coexistence and Non-repetition—in Colombia.

After the ceremony of ceding the presidency of the UNCTAD to Mandela, which took place in the main auditorium, I met with him in a small room within the convention center. Our conversation was scheduled to last just fifteen minutes. In reality, we talked for several hours.

I told him about the meeting we had held in Bogotá with Kahane and asked him to tell me what the Canadian expert's contribution to the process in South Africa had been. Mandela confirmed for me that Kahane's work had been important in bringing together former antagonists in the conflict and setting up scenarios for reconciliation. Furthermore, he told me, this exercise had afforded him a chance to meet a lot of people, some of whom he had later appointed to ministries in his cabinet.

Mandela, in his opening address to the UNCTAD Congress, had made a very simple but powerful statement: "Peace and development are indivisible." He repeated this idea in the course of our conversation, making a remark that echoed in my mind recalling the words of that company manager years before in New York: "Peace," said Mandela, "is an indispensable condition for development. Without peace, Colombia will never get off the ground." That was the moment when I began to suspect where my destiny might lie.

A PROPHETIC EXERCISE

On returning from South Africa, I decided not to continue involving myself in the technical exercises we had begun with Kahane. I did not want our efforts to become politicized, and at the time my name was being mentioned as a possible presidential candidate for the Liberal Party; or to be more exact, I was dreaming of the candidacy, for which I had really no chance of being nominated. So I passed the baton on to Augusto Ramírez, former foreign affairs minister, and Mario Suárez Melo, then president of the Bogotá Chamber of Commerce.

And the exercises continued. The following year, 1997, a meeting was held at the Recinto Quirama in Antioquia, sticking to the Kahane methodology that he called "transformative scenario planning." This consists of integrating working groups, preferably made up of people who have conflicting views of reality and of the problem to be solved, so that the collaborative exercise can imagine diverse scenarios for a possible future outcome. In this way, without anyone imposing his or her views on anyone else, imaginative and novel agreements can be reached and possible paths toward a solution visualized, keeping in mind the different points of view of everyone, while overcoming prejudices, obstacles, and setbacks that before had seemed insoluble.

The Recinto Quirama workshop, which was called "Destination Colombia," brought together about fifty men and women, representing all possible sectors of society. They discussed and imagined four possible scenarios for

Colombia's future over the coming sixteen years. Their conclusions, seen today in retrospect, were surprisingly prophetic, for the four scenarios unwittingly described exactly what the next four governments would do, beginning with that of Ernesto Samper, followed by the administrations of Andrés Pastrana and Álvaro Uribe, and finishing with mine.

The first scenario, "We'll wake up tomorrow and see," proposed that we should think of what would happen if, instead of intervening in a specific way, we let the country's problems simply solve themselves. This would lead to the state's authority being weakened, the violence growing even more fierce, the breakup of territories, and a dramatic increase in the conditions that produce poverty and inequality.

The second scenario, "A bird in the hand," referred to concessions made to the armed groups in order to begin immediately to rebuild democracy and put a brake on the increasing spiral of death and violence. We were to see how this scenario would fail in the Caguán peace process carried out by the Pastrana administration.

In the third scenario, "Everyone marches together," political leadership responds to the popular demand for a return to security and takes on the task with firm measures to combat the perpetrators of violence. This was doubtless a premonition of what was to happen under the government of Álvaro Uribe.

One cannot but be impressed by how this hypothetical exercise, practiced back in 1997, predicted exactly what was going to happen: "The measures taken to stimulate the economy and the productive sector, accompanied by military victories, will assure the president of a second term of office, authorized by an appropriate reform of the constitution."

The fourth scenario, "Strength in Unity," spoke of a legitimate government and an empowered society who, together, will finally achieve the desired result: an end to the armed conflict and the beginning of national reconciliation.

As in a kind of magic circle, life led me to be the one responsible for beginning this process and bringing it to an end. We, who in 1996 began to think about how to achieve peace, were the ones destined to sign a peace agreement with the Farc twenty years later, in 2016.

CHAPTER 3

The Story of My Conspiracy

CIVIL SOCIETY RESPONDS TO THE CHALLENGE OF PEACE

After the Monserrat Abbey meeting, I talked with Álvaro Leyva, a Conservative former minister, but a progressive person, who had long maintained open channels of dialogue with the Farc. He let me know that the guerrilla leaders, having noted our ability to bring together such a varied group of people, were interested in continuing to explore possible paths that might lead to peace.

And so we began a series of conversations and discreet contacts with a view to achieving a viable proposal that, at the appropriate moment, we might be able to present to the national government, whose bridges for dialogue with the insurgents had virtually broken down.

Working with several personalities who had taken part in the Monserrat Abbey meeting, and with others interested in ending the armed conflict, we began to design a critical path that would keep in mind the particular meeting, and with others interested in ending the armed conflict, we began to design a critical path that would keep in mind the particular aims of each of the various armed groups and would facilitate a way for the state to approach them in order to create conditions that might lead to a peace process. Given the fragile circumstances in which President Samper's government was laboring, we felt that it would be best to proceed with our approaches, working gradually without drawing attention to ourselves until we had come up with a proposal sufficiently mature to present to the government.

It was the first time civil society, independent of official channels, had begun an approach to all actors in the conflict: the guerrillas, the paramilitaries, and, finally, the government itself.

Among the personalities who knew of this proposal and took part in it were the archbishop of Bogotá, Pedro Rubiano; the then union leader and later vice-president Angelino Garzón; other leaders of diverse sectors such as Nicanor Restrepo, Luis Fernando Jaramillo, Juan Manuel Ospina, Fabio Valencia Cossio, Antonio Gómez Hermida, Luis Carlos Villegas, my brother Enrique Santos Calderón, and, naturally, Álvaro Leyva. Others who were informed of the plan, and who indicated their total approval, were former presidents Alfonso López Michelsen and Belisario Betancur.

We decided, too, that it would be important to count on the support of world figures. Immediately two names came up as the most suitable candidates to act as guarantors of a peace process: our Nobel laureate Gabriel García Márquez, and the former prime minister of the Spanish government Felipe González.

Gabo (as García Márquez was called by his friends) had always been a tireless and discreet worker for peace. He responded with enthusiasm. González also indicated his willingness to accept, but only on certain conditions. First—and in this his logic was impeccable—we should begin by talking to the different unlawful actors to obtain their approval of the plan, so as to ensure we were on firm ground and not basing our expectations on mere guesswork. Secondly, in his opinion, we should seek the participation of other Latin American governments, as well as the backing of the United States and members of the European Union, specifically Spain.

CONVERSING WITH THE ENEMY

Thus I set out on an intense round of visits that led me to arrange personal meetings with Carlos Castaño, the fearsome commander of the paramilitaries, and also with Farc guerrilla leaders at the highest level of command, and with leaders of the ELN. In other words, as a private citizen I threw myself into the task of seeking peace, never imagining that I was going to spend the next twenty years on that same path.

I met with Castaño on two occasions at a farm in the mountains of the department of Córdoba, where he had his headquarters. Castaño, whose father had been kidnapped and murdered by the Farc, had founded, along with his brothers Fidel and Vicente, groups of self-defense in the department of Córdoba and the region of Urabá in the north of Antioquia, in Colombia's Caribbean area. Like other criminal leaders, he had struck up alliances with the drug traffickers. As part of his war on the insurgents, and on the left in general, he had given orders to carry out innumerable massacres and the murder of political and social leaders such as the directors and candidates of the Patriotic Union and the humorist Jaime Garzón. In his criminal delirium, he saw himself as a patriot fighting to free the country from the plague of the guerrillas and from communism.

When I met him in 1997, Castaño was commander-in-chief of the United Self-Defense Group of Colombia. In other words, he was the undisputed head of the paramilitaries. Our first meeting was merely an exploratory one, to see if he and his followers would be interested in taking part in a peace process that would involve all illegal armed groups. I reached his headquarters in a helicopter owned by the emerald king and friend of the paramilitaries Víctor Carranza, who had participated in the Monserrat Abbey meeting. On this occasion I was accompanied by the journalist and chronicler Germán Santamaría, We found Castaño surrounded by the majority of members of his paramilitary high command, including his second-in-command, Salvatore Mancuso. It was a brief encounter in which I scarcely had a chance to explain our hopes for creating a proposal for peace with the participation of all actors in the conflict that we would then present to the national government. He said he would think about it.

Our second meeting was longer, and we advanced further regarding the details of how the process was meant to work. A massacre by paramilitaries had just occurred and I showed Castaño the headlines of the press reports. As long as they continued to act in that way, I said, it was going to be very difficult to start a peace process. He claimed that the massacre had been carried out without his authorization and said, finally, that he was ready to participate in the framework for dialogue that we were proposing.

This time I was accompanied by Álvaro Leyva, who had long been seen as a facilitator with the top-level guerrillas of the Farc. It was the first time he had come face to face with the paramilitaries. However, despite initial tension, the meeting went ahead without any major hitches.

It is worth mentioning that Leyva has been a key figure in the search for peace in Colombia, a man who has never given up on his conviction that peace can be attained through dialogue. He has participated in practically all efforts at negotiation, beginning with President Betancur's process initiated in 1982 and continuing right up to the final agreement signed with the Farc in 2016. Due to his experience and his knowledge of the main actors in the conflict, he has more than once been the person most qualified to reignite a process when obstacles and difficulties have arisen that seemed insurmountable.

Indeed, it was Leyva who helped me make contact with leaders of the Farc. Acting as intermediary, he set up my meeting in Costa Rica with Raúl Reyes, the member of the Farc secretariat in charge of international relations, and with his companion, Olga Marín. They listened to my proposal with interest, and it was agreed that I should have a personal meeting with Manuel Marulanda, the commander-in-chief of the Farc, in the Colombian jungle in order to make concrete arrangements for his guerrilla group to participate in our plan.

In the end, I was unable to see Marulanda, since military operations were being carried out near the place where we were scheduled to meet, and in addition I had planned an urgent visit to Spain to meet with González and ensure we could count on his support. In the event, Leyva took me to a house in the central Bogotá barrio La Perseverancia, where we met with the Jesuit priest Gabriel Izquierdo, director of the Center of Investigations and Popular Education, who was able to communicate directly with the guerrilla leader. Via radiotelephone we were in touch with Marulanda's camp and again spoke to Reyes and Marín, who had returned to Colombia. They assured us of the guerrilla's approval of the plan.

In my conversation with Reyes, I made a joking reference to our meeting in Costa Rica. "I hope next time you'll serve better wine," I said. This offhand comment, spoken in jest, was to come back and haunt me. It seems our communication was being tapped by military intelligence and led to the rumor that I was conspiring with the guerrillas to overthrow the government of Ernesto Samper.

The other outlawed participant in the conflict was the ELN. In this case I counted on a businessman from Cali of Jewish extraction, Morris Ackerman, to act as intermediary. Ackerman played a role similar to Leyva's; he had access to communication with the ELN leadership and had long taken part in their process of dialogue. Thanks to him, I was able to interview two important leaders of that guerrilla group, who were acting as ELN spokesmen while serving prison sentences in Itagui, near Medellín. Their assumed names were Felipe Torres and Francisco Galán, and they had participated by telephone in the meeting at Monserrat Abbey. They expressed their group's willingness to advance in the building of a proposal that could lead to dialogues in favor of peace.

THE PLAN FLOUNDERS

Having completed the task—that is, having been assured of interest in the proposed plan on the part of the paramilitaries, the Farc and the ELN—I flew to Spain to meet with Felipe González and Gabriel García Márquez.

The three of us were lunching at Casa Lucio, a traditional Madrid restaurant, when Lucio, the owner, told me I was wanted on the phone. It was an urgent call from Bogotá. On the line was Julio Sánchez Cristo, director and announcer of one of Colombia's most popular morning radio programs, who told me that President Samper's close advisers had denounced a supposed conspiracy headed by me to topple the government. The radio personality wanted to know if I had anything to say on the matter.

I went back to our table and told my two fellow diners. Gabo's immediate reaction was, "We're screwed!" (or words to that effect), while González was adamant that I should return to Colombia at once to clarify the situation. Without further ado, Gabo and I between us produced and signed a communiqué, letting it be known that what we were concocting was a constitutional formula to achieve peace and that "in no way was it a scheme to produce short-term political effects, but rather the only viable way put forward so far for terminating the bloodbath." Our document included an assurance from Spain's former prime minister that he was ready and willing to act as guarantor of this incipient project.

Back in Bogotá I called for a meeting with the other prime movers of our proposal, including spokespersons from political parties, representatives of businessmen's associations, and trade union leaders. We decided to call for a press conference to explain what we had achieved so far and to make it clear that we were working within the framework of Colombia's constitution. Unfortunately, an enthusiastic comment by Álvaro Leyva caused me to say something I later regretted: that "peace was just around the corner."

Following the press conference, President Samper and I engaged in an exchange of letters, a correspondence that received wide coverage in the press. My statement on the subject provided a résumé of the fundamental points of our process and explained that we had made direct contact with the Farc, the ELN, and the paramilitaries, and that all of them had expressed interest in the plan. I added the following:

> As regards myself, for peace I am prepared to take all necessary risks. Fortunately, I have made it clear from the start that I am prepared to make whatever sacrifice the success of this process may require, even to renouncing my aspirations to the presidency. Peace in Colombia is more important, very much more important, than any personal aspiration, any dignity, or any individual person. I am sure you feel the same as I do. Which is why I am optimistic. I pray to God I am not mistaken.

Mister President, the way has been cleared for us to build a country at peace, the peace we all hope for. For the thousands upon thousands of potential widows and orphans whose tragedy we could prevent, and for the future of your children and mine, and of all Colombians, I beg you with all my heart not to stand in our way.

As was to be expected, President Samper made it clear that my activities did not meet with official approval since they had been undertaken—and in this he was right—"without informing or calling upon the government and Colombia's armed forces." This was a natural reaction, even more so if you take into account the fragility of his government, which had attempted, unsuccessfully, what we as private citizens had achieved in just a few months. From this point forward, a fierce campaign was waged to discredit us, during which, among other things, my telephone conversation with Raúl Reyes in the guerrilla camp was leaked to the press. It was evident that our proposal was in its death throes.

García Márquez published a communiqué in which he reiterated that, in presenting our proposal, far from conspiring against the government, we were exercising "the right and the duty of every Colombian to seek peace at all costs." Archbishop Pedro Rubiano made the following public statement: "I don't know why it is that every time someone presents a serious and objective plan to promote peace, the authorities react with the foolish accusation that it's a conspiracy to overthrow the government."

Under the circumstances, the best I could do was to provide an account of what we had attained. Which is what I did. In October 1997, in a letter I addressed to the National Commission for Reconciliation, I declared that the substance of our proposal was destined to be put into practice not during Samper's term of office, which was drawing to a close, but in that of the next president, whoever he or she might happen to be.

In my statement I summed up the five central points of our proposal. First, that the new president create a cabinet of national unity, appointing ministers who would represent a broad political and social spectrum of the population. Second, that the government order an area of the country's territory to be cleared of military presence and converted into a zone of dialogue without interference. Third, that there be established an agenda that would include, among other things, the call for a constituent assembly and that would establish a true agrarian reform in the context of a comprehensive agrarian policy. Fourth, that once the clearance of a territory had been verified, a bilateral agreement on a ceasefire be agreed upon between the insurgents and the government. And fifth, that friendly countries be invited to participate in the process, as well as national and international personalities who would serve as facilitators and guarantors.

Later—in view of the disorganization and excesses of the peace process carried out by the government of Andrés Pastrana in Caguán—I changed my opinion regarding the advisability of establishing a demilitarized zone and a bilateral ceasefire at the very beginning of the peace talks. This touches on what the process of seeking peace is all about: a method of trial and error that gets perfected little by little. What we proposed years later, in the Havana negotiations, was to learn lessons from the past, redesign schematic plans, and correct our mistakes.

The time was not yet ripe. The understandable paranoia of a government that was under scrutiny from the very day the president was elected, and that imagined conspiracy where in fact there was a serious and concerted labor in favor of peace, made it impossible for us to go ahead. Sadly, we were unable to put a stop to the bloodbath that continued to envelop the country for many more years.

I should acknowledge, however, that President Samper and his interior minister, Horacio Serpa, had every reason to be annoyed with us. No head of state likes to have people carrying on such far-reaching activities without his consent. My mistake was not to have told Samper what I was doing from the start.

But not all was lost. The seed of peace had been sown, and the day would come to reap the harvest.

PART TWO

Creating Conditions for Peace (1998–2009)

CHAPTER 4

The Start of the Caguán Process

THE MANDATE FOR PEACE

It wasn't just a handful of Colombians who were calling for an end to violence. Peace had become a national priority. This became abundantly clear in October 1997 at the time of the elections for governors and mayors, when social and humanitarian organizations insisted on introducing into the ballot box an additional card. They called it "a vote for peace, life and freedom."

Through this innovative card, citizens voted for building peace and social justice, to protect life and reject all violent action, and—most important of all—to demand that the actors in the armed conflict resolve their disputes peacefully.

This initiative, known as the Mandate for Peace, was supported by millions of Colombians who placed the card in the ballot boxes.

What did this imply? That the next president of Colombia, no matter who he or she might be, would be obliged to respond to the citizens' mandate and commit to seeking peace through dialogue.

In 1998 the race for president was fought out between the Liberal Party candidate Horacio Serpa—I had abandoned my aspiration to be the party's candidate, since I had not the slightest chance of winning—and the Conservative Andrés Pastrana, who ran as a super-party candidate, with the support of those Liberal Party members who had not stood by President Samper during his controversial term of office.

Both candidates, Serpa and Pastrana, were in favor of beginning peace talks with the Farc and ELN guerrillas. However, Pastrana—having run second in the first round of voting—made a move that enormously enhanced his public image. One of his campaign managers, Víctor G. Ricardo, in response to a suggestion by Álvaro Leyva, paid a visit in the jungle to Manuel Marulanda, commander-in-chief of the Farc guerrillas, and so let it be seen that Pastrana was more likely than his competitor to bring the guerrillas to the negotiating table.

Ricardo was shown placing a political campaign watch on the wrist of the wily old guerrilla leader Marulanda as a gift from the presidential candidate Pastrana. A photo of Marulanda wearing the watch in company of Ricardo and Mono Jojoy, the Farc's military chief, became overnight a symbol of the Pastrana campaign. The message was clear: Pastrana, not Serpa, was the man who was going to achieve peace.

As a result, in the second electoral round, Pastrana was elected president for the period 1998 to 2002. His mandate was to make peace. And that was how he understood it.

Even before he was installed officially as president, he had taken a step in this direction with a bold—one could almost say reckless—gesture. Managing to elude the vigilance of his bodyguards, he traveled secretly to the guerrilla camp in the jungle where he had himself photographed with Marulanda and other guerrilla leaders. At this meeting, the president-elect and the guerrilla commander laid the basis for what was going to be a new peace process, the most ambitious one since that tried by Belisario Betancur in the 1980s. It was the first time a president, albeit still only president-elect, had met face to face with the highest-level commander of a guerrilla army.

The Colombians wanted peace, and these first approaches filled them with hope.

THE UN SITUATION ROOM

The Mandate for Peace, which won votes in October 1997, produced another interesting result. It inspired the resident coordinator of the United Nations Development Programme (UNDP)—a live-wire Italian by the name of Francesco Vincenti—to create a kind of think tank he dubbed the Situation Room, a space where people might meet and come up with ideas to help the mandate become a reality.

In a way similar to the workshops coordinated by Adam Kahane, people from different walks of life—me among them—would get together at the local UN headquarters to toss around ideas on how we might find a remedy for the political, economic, and social chaos in which the country found itself. There we met up with the same crowd as before: Augusto Ramírez, Angelino Garzón, industrialist Nicanor Restrepo, plus a select group of intellectuals, political scientists, journalists, and economists, all ready to devote hours of their time to analyzing and proposing suggestions that might be useful for the incoming president, including proposals on the peace process. High-ranking military officers were also invited to take part and give their opinions.

After several meetings in the first half of 1998, we produced a document that we informally called a Marshall Plan for Colombia. I was chosen to be the one who would present it personally to the president-elect, Andrés Pastrana. And I did so at the UNDP office in Bogotá, in the presence of the working team from the Situation Room. Pastrana received the document with great interest, referring to it as his "road map."

It was a comprehensive proposal to meet the country's problems—not only as regards seeking a solution to the armed conflict—and at least partly inspired the way the peace talks in Caguán were organized, as well as influencing Plan Colombia, which were to be the two most significant platforms in Pastrana's program of government.

DISCREPANCY WITH THE CAGUÁN PROCESS

Once I had presented the document, I went back to my work at the Good Government Foundation, and as a columnist in various media outlets. I was getting ready for a trip to Rome with my parents to attend an audience with Pope John Paul II when a phone call from Ricardo—now high commissioner for peace—obliged me to change my plans. President Pastrana, who had taken office a few weeks before, required my presence "most urgently" at the presidential palace.

Pastrana had already set in motion the process of withdrawing all members of the armed forces from five municipalities in the region of Colombia's Eastern Plains and Orinoquia with a view to holding peace talks with the Farc. Four of these municipalities in the department of Meta—and another, San Vicente de Caguán, in the department of Caquetá—accounted for a total of forty-two square kilometers, an area larger than Switzerland or the Netherlands. It was to be known as the Zona de Distensión (Demilitarized Zone): that is, a zone where military operations against the insurgents were relaxed—or rather, suspended altogether in the demilitarized area.

President Pastrana asked me to take part in an international commission to verify conditions in the zone. The commission was to consist of the following: James LeMoyne, a UN official who had spent several years in Colombia as correspondent for the *New York Times*; Costa Rica's foreign minister; the Mexican senator Gustavo Carvajal; Juan Gabriel Uribe of the Conservative Party, and myself, supposedly representing the Liberal Party.

This international commission was never officially installed nor did we ever get to operate in an official capacity, since the Farc and the government could not agree on what we were actually supposed to be doing. Nonetheless, I did go to Caguán, along with Uribe, to informally initiate our mission of verification. However, before leaving for Caguán, we made calls on different official bodies to find out what part they were going to play and to solicit their opinion on the existence of the demilitarized zone. I confess that my first impressions were not good. What I found was a totally improvised withdrawal of troops, carried out in a hurry, with no planning or coordination, and lacking the requisite participation of both the attorney general and the prosecutor general. Not even the army's high command was involved. It was no surprise that the generals, in their hearts, did not feel at ease with the government's plan.

It is true that the proposal we had discreetly worked on during the final years of the Samper administration, and then later in the UN Situation Room, included the option of an area free from military presence in some part of the national territory where peace talks could be held. But we never imagined this would encompass an area of such immense proportions, and that not only would the armed forces be withdrawn but also all civilian officials, such as judges, plus members of the Office of the Attorney General and the Office of the Prosecutor General. Not a vestige of the state's presence would remain. In other words, the demilitarized zone was handed over totally to control by the Farc.

I visited the Red Cross offices to inquire whether there was any precedent for a zone of this kind, and was told that no such situation had been known before. The Caguán experiment of giving up any presence of the state in a large part of a nation's territory and leaving its administration in the hands of the insurgents was, to say the least, an exotic ploy, and one fraught with risk.

In any case, I visited Caguán a couple of times in compliance with the verification task the president had asked me to perform, and there I again met with Raúl Reyes, member of the Farc secretariat, whom I had known in Costa Rica. I conversed with him this time at a farm some fifty minutes from the center of San Vicente de Caguán, traveling on a dirt road. I remember the fright I got when, as we were talking, Reyes silently crept up behind me and put a knife against my cheek. My blood ran cold. But then I realized what he was doing. He was using the point of the knife to shoo away an insect that had landed on my face, to make sure it didn't bite me.

It was October 1998 and the army had not yet withdrawn from their last stronghold in the area; namely, the Cazadores Battalion. As a result, a heated discussion was going on about what use should be made of the battalion's headquarters. I had in my possession a copy of a document Leyva had given me in which the peace commissioner, Ricardo, had promised the guerrillas they would be in charge of the battalion's buildings. Nevertheless, Ricardo was saying that the way the battalion's facilities were to be employed was still open for debate. This, of course, led the Farc to protest, alleging that an agreement on the matter had already been reached.

Uribe and I agreed to broach the matter with President Pastrana, since it had become a major bone of contention and would prevent the talks from getting under way. To this end we met with the president and Ricardo at the palace. But when the subject of the battalion headquarters came up, Ricardo was evasive. So I took out the document and handed it to the president, who was both surprised and annoyed. Naturally, the fact of having shown up the commissioner in this fashion led to a cooling of our relations, making it virtually impossible for me to continue with my task of verification. So I resigned. In any case, at this point that mission seemed to me totally useless. After many meetings and two visits to the zone, I had come to the conclusion that the state had left itself in a weak position vis-à-vis the Farc, and under those conditions would get nowhere.

In the end, the army handed the battalion headquarters over to the Catholic Church, who would run it for the time being with the technical support of the National Apprenticeship Service. In fact, the battalion's buildings became the headquarters of the government negotiators, and housed special guests during the course of the peace process.

WHAT GETS OFF ON THE WRONG FOOT . . .

What begins badly finishes badly. And sadly this was the case with the Pastrana process. The guerrilla organization that occupied the Caguán zone to negotiate with the government was a military force of considerable strength and confidence, comprising more than twenty thousand men and women in arms. In the final months of Samper's administration, they had changed their strategy. They no longer practiced the classic guerrilla tactic of attacking in small groups and withdrawing immediately. Now they were waging a war of maneuver, operating in much larger contingents, carrying out devastating strikes and inflicting serious harm on the armed forces.

They had their sights set on a superior form of conflict, what is known as the war of position, to which end they had to gain control of more territory, especially in the urban centers. With this in mind, in November 1998 the guerrillas launched a bloody attack on Mitú, the capital of one of Colombia's departments located in the country's remote eastern corner, in a jungle area near the Brazilian border. They held the town for three days, until they were finally driven out by the army. But not before they had captured dozens of police officers, whom they would hold for ransom.

At the time the Caguán talks began, hundreds of soldiers and policemen, including some high-ranking officers, were being held prisoner by the Farc, who kept them caged up in concentration camps in subhuman conditions.

The Farc had arrived at the negotiating table with no real intention of giving up armed insurgency. Their hidden agenda was to take advantage of the talks to gain greater strength. This became evident on January 7, 1999. On that day, in the main square of San Vicente de Caguán, a ceremony was held to officially inaugurate the peace talks in the presence of several hundred national and international personalities invited as witnesses. It was a solemn occasion in which the Farc, for the first time, played hosts to a distinguished audience. The guerrillas strolled confidently around the town, sporting smart new uniforms and highly polished weaponry.

Everything was in place and an atmosphere of hope prevailed at the start of this new road to peace. However, Manuel Marulanda, the guerrilla leader, didn't turn up. He declined Pastrana's invitation, alleging security reasons to explain his absence. He stayed at his rural property not far from the town, while his prepared speech was read by Joaquín Gómez, one of his lieutenants. This was no surprise for the president. He had been warned that the guerrilla chief did not intend to appear. In fact, he took two speeches with him: one in case Marulanda showed, and the other if he didn't. In the event, he read the second one.

The photo of President Pastrana, seated on the main platform looking extremely annoyed by the affront, as he stares at a vacant chair placed there for Marulanda, was published in the press and seen by people all around the world.

What begins badly ends badly. Only after three years—years in which the number of attacks and kidnappings soared to record heights—did the government finally understand that, given the irresponsible way it had been conceived, the process had no future.

GAMES OF WAR AND PEACE

Two weeks after the peace talks had officially begun, the Good Government Foundation, of which I was director, and the Iberoamerican New Journalism Foundation, created by Gabriel García Márquez and directed by the journalist Jaime Abello, held a workshop for journalists with the support of a team of experts in conflict resolution from Harvard University. Their leader was Professor Donna Hicks. And we christened the event with a catchy name: Games of War and Peace.

Besides those already mentioned, the workshop was attended by some thirty communicators, mostly directors of important national and regional media outlets. The workshop's aim was to analyze the way the media covers internal conflicts and how the incipient peace talks should best be reported.

I know from experience that, in reporting on a conflict, or in this case a peace process, the media—due to the role it plays as intermediary between the events and public opinion—is decisive in gaining the popular support required for the success of a negotiated settlement to end a war.

The exercises we practiced in our workshop were interesting in that we played different roles, each of the participants taking on that of guerrilla, or government army officer, or mediator. And we were able to base our games on a real case, that of Sri Lanka, in which the Harvard experts had participated directly.

It is often said that the press should be objective and not get involved in the news it is transmitting to the public. And this is true. But it is no less true that, to cover with impartiality a complex situation like war, or a negotiation to end it, a journalist should be equipped to understand the inner motivations, and justifying arguments, of each of the parties. And that was what this exercise attempted: to put us for a few days in the other person's shoes in order to understand the basic reasons that explain our opponent's position. In this way we would not only report more accurately but also be better negotiators.

This workshop reminded me of lessons I learned from Roger Fisher, an expert in negotiation and conflict management, whose classes I had the opportunity to attend when I was studying at Harvard, and also when I returned to that university on a scholarship to the Nieman Foundation for Journalism.

Professor Fisher was a veritable master, and also my friend. His teaching on the importance of seeing the other person's viewpoint in negotiations was crucial for me, and I have employed it not only in seeking an end to the conflict in Colombia but also when exercising the complex art of governing. A similar lesson—putting oneself in the other person's shoes—was one I had been taught years before by the manager of the Colombian Coffee Growers Federation, Arturo Gómez, when he appointed me to represent the federation in London at the International Coffee Organization. Every year, the organization negotiated the price and volume of coffee each country would be permitted to put on the world market. For Colombia this negotiation was of prime importance, not only because coffee sales constituted our main source of foreign currency but also because we were the chief exporters after Brazil.

Nobody, not even the most hardened criminal, does something without having an ulterior motive. That being so, faced with any situation I always want to understand the motivation, the inspirations, and concerns or sufferings of my counterpart, even when his actions are frightful and seem inexcusable. Behind every act, there is a human being, and behind every human being there's a reason that compels him or her to act. Once we know what this is—and this is something I learned from Fisher—we're halfway on the road to finding a solution.

The Games of War and Peace, played in Gabo's stimulating presence, left an impression on us all, providing us with a new focus on the role played by the media in covering and resolving internal conflicts.

García Márquez arrived in Cartagena on a direct flight from Havana, where—with great discretion, as always—he had facilitated a meeting between Fidel Castro, Pastrana, and the newly elected president of Venezuela, Hugo Chávez, to support the peace process that had just begun in Colombia.

We will never know how much, and in how many different ways, in silence and without drawing attention to himself, our Nobel winner collaborated in efforts to end our internal conflict. We owe García Márquez for a lot more than his books and his glory as a writer. We are indebted to him for his permanent and effective commitment to peace.

A few days after the workshop, I published a column on the experience. The following was my conclusion:

> The message is that a conflict like the one we are dealing with is much more complex than is usually realized, and to resolve it we must submit it to a

thorough analysis, looking at it from different angles. If we put ourselves in the position of just one of the parties and wait to see at what moment the other will cede a point or, as in a football match, will score a goal, we can be assured negotiations will be fruitless. This is a lesson for both negotiators and journalists.

CHAPTER 5

Plan Colombia

I RETURN TO PUBLIC LIFE

During the months that followed, in my newspaper columns and elsewhere, I continued to analyze and comment on the way the peace process was going, with considerable concern at how little progress was being made. Which, of course, was foreseeable. Excessive haste and improvisation had led the government to accept the agenda and procedural methods dictated by the Farc. To give an example: the guerrillas sat down to negotiate dressed in full combat uniforms with short-range weapons tucked under their belts and their intimidating machine guns laid out on the table in front of them.

Early in the year 2000, Colombians were appalled by scandals of corruption and the squandering of public money by certain members of congress. Taking advantage of public outrage, President Pastrana proposed a referendum to reform the constitution, including the closing down of the existing congress and the election of a new one. The plan backfired on him, however, when his opponents said that if he were to revoke the mandate of the parliamentarians, his own should be revoked too. The result was a general crisis, with political and economic repercussions. Uncertainty is never a friend of investment, even less so at this time when our economy was going through one of its worst moments.

In the end, although Pastrana withdrew his proposal for a referendum, the country's governability was adversely affected. Given this situation, in an attempt to improve his relations with the Liberal Party, which was the chief force of opposition, he sent me a commission made up of several of his cabinet ministers to invite me to join his government in the ministry of my choice. I told them to tell the president I would give it some thought.

I had a conversation with my good friend the businessman Samuel Yohai, who made a few comments that helped me make up my mind: "You're an economist, aren't you?" he said. "And what's in trouble at this moment? The economy." It was true. In 1999, the economy had experienced a negative growth rate, the worst in at least seventy years. "You're a gambler," Samuel said, "and any gambler knows that high risks bring high rewards. I recommend that you choose the finance ministry."

Julio César Sánchez, a wily politician and also a good friend of mine, was present during this conversation. He put his head in his hands and said he thought it would be political suicide, since I would have to make some very difficult decisions.

Other friends were of the opinion that if I aspired to a future in politics, I should choose any other ministry but that one. In a time of crisis, no one is as unpopular as the finance minister, since he is the one responsible for budget cuts and for taking austerity measures that win few plaudits in the gallery. Nonetheless, I decided to take it on because of the challenge it implied and because it would give me an opportunity to prove myself in the most complex scenario. It also provided me, in a sense, with a way to free myself, once and for all, from a secret hankering after the presidency.

I had planned a trip to London to see the Wimbledon tennis finals. So I took it, and witnessed the emotional semifinal between the sisters Venus and Serena Williams, the first time they played against one another in this tournament, of which they were to become the almost undisputed champions for the next seventeen years. But most of all, I took advantage of my stay in London to consult one other person.

I well understood I could make a success of my performance as finance minister only if I could count on the support of both the Liberal Party and the media. I knew I had the first. But I had to be sure of the second, since I was going to have to introduce some extremely unpopular reforms and was going to need all the help I could get. However, I had some misgivings about my relations with the one of the country's media magnates, Julio Mario Santo Domingo, who I knew was in London, as I was, for the Wimbledon finals. Santo Domingo was one of Colombia's wealthiest industrialists, the owner of the country's largest brewery and of some of its most influential media outlets. Unfortunately, I had fallen foul of him a few years earlier because of some columns I published criticizing his monopoly on brewing. Nonetheless, I made an appointment and called on him at Claridge's Hotel to seek his support in getting Colombia out of the quagmire in which it was floundering. He promised me his backing. And with that, I finally decided to take on the ministry.

From London, I phoned Pastrana to convey my decision, and he was amazed that I should have chosen such an unpopular and thankless ministry. And so it was that, in midyear 2000, I returned to public life. I was replacing Juan Camilo Restrepo, a Conservative Party lawyer and economist who had been my boss in London in the early seventies, when I was working with the coffee growers' association, and with whom I had become friends.

The reader might be wondering what exactly were the problems I had to deal with. Well, in 1999 Colombia suffered its worst economic crisis since the 1929 Wall Street crash and the ensuing Great Depression in world markets. The country's GNP fell 4.2 percent; private investment contracted 66 percent; per capita household consumption fell back to the levels of ten years before; eight hundred thousand people were unable to pay off their mortgages and were on the verge of losing their dwellings; and between 1998 and 2000, five million Colombians fell below the poverty line.

This required drastic measures. So, once I had taken up my post as finance minister, I reminded my fellow citizens of Churchill when he said all he could promise his compatriots was "sweat and tears."

I explained this in August 2000 in the course of an interview with the weekly magazine *Semana*:

> Colombians can rest assured I'm not going to make use of public money to promote an eventual presidential candidacy. On the contrary, I am aware of the enormous risks involved, and of the unpopularity that may make inroads on my prestige due to the measures I am going to have to take. Over the course of the next six months, all I can promise is sweat and tears. Because I'm going to make some drastic announcements, since adjustments have not been made and we cannot give up the fight, which will mean all of us fighting together. Otherwise, it will not be possible to get our economy afloat and truly attain sustainable development and ensure a decent growth rate. I expect that, by merely tackling the problem, my popularity will go down the drain. But if that's what it will cost to get the country back on its feet, I am prepared to pay the price.

And so it was. I had to make unpopular decisions and stand up to powerful adversaries, such as the teachers and health workers unions. My children asked me why almost every night they had to watch television news broadcasts showing cardboard cartoons of their father being set alight in public places. They were very young, and I told them people were paying me homage, since the smoke rose to heaven, where God was. My popularity hit rock bottom. That is to say, whatever degree of popularity I might have had ceased to exist. But we saved the economy.

PLAN COLOMBIA AND THE STRENGTHENING OF THE ARMED FORCES

On February 4, 2016, as president, I accepted an invitation from President Barack Obama—along with several of my cabinet ministers and a distinguished delegation of Colombians—to a reception in the East Room of the White House to commemorate fifteen years of Plan Colombia, a bilateral cooperation scheme supported by both Democrats and Republicans to combat drug traffic in Colombia, which had been established by agreement between Presidents Pastrana and Bill Clinton in the year 2000. In the following words, President Obama summed up what Plan Colombia had achieved:

> We all remember a time, not long ago, when Colombia was torn apart by terrible violence—plagued by insurgency and civil war. Many of you who are here have lived through those times. Some of you have lost loved ones or friends, colleagues.
>
> And that's why the United States and Colombia forged what became Plan Colombia—starting with President Pastrana and transcending administrations in both our countries. We were proud to support Colombia and its people as you strengthened your security forces, as you reformed land laws, and bolstered economic institutions. So Plan Colombia has been a tribute to the people of Colombia and their efforts to overcome so many challenges. And after fifteen years of sacrifice and determination, a tipping point has been reached. The tide has turned.

Many people agree that Plan Colombia was the most successful bipartisan international cooperation plan undertaken by the United States in recent decades. And I underline the word *bipartisan*, since that is what explains its continuity. Although the plan was launched under the Clinton presidency, it had the support of a broad section of both Republicans and Democrats in the US Congress. Thanks to this support, aid from the United States continued under the umbrella of Plan Colombia during the administrations of both George W. Bush and Obama.

Between the years 2000 and 2016, Colombia received a total of almost $10 billion through Plan Colombia, becoming the third country, after Israel and Egypt, that received the most aid from the United States.

How, you might ask, was this aid employed? The answer is that the money was mainly used to strengthen the fight against the drug traffic in Colombia by supplying planes, military equipment, radars, consultants, and training, in order to optimize the spraying of illegal crops and the interception of planes and boats transporting cargoes of cocaine.

Also, though to a lesser degree, these resources were used in the substitution of crops and social programs in zones where coca plantations were ubiquitous, offering legal alternatives for employment and income for agricultural workers. Another aim was the strengthening of Colombia's justice system.

There can be no doubt that Plan Colombia represented a fundamental and positive turning point in the struggle against drug trafficking and terrorism.

But not everything was due to foreign aid. I was very much aware of the precarious situation in which Colombia's armed forces found themselves. If they were not strengthened, we would never bring the guerrillas to a point where they would be convinced they had no chance of taking power by force of arms. As finance minister, even in the midst of the difficult fiscal crisis in which we were laboring, I decided that an indispensable minimum of the national budget should be allotted to increasing and professionalizing the number of men and women on the ground, acquiring arms and equipment, improving conditions and weaponry in the battalions and, in short, providing everything required to ensure that the correlation of strength and ability to wage war would begin to lean in favor of the state.

I held several meetings with Luis Fernando Ramírez, the defense minister, and with the commander-in-chief of the armed forces, General Fernando Tapias, and the commander of the army, General Jorge Enrique Mora. With them we studied the defense budget, item by item, to increase it and invest the money in the most effective way possible.

This considerably taxed the national budget. But, added to resources from Plan Colombia, it enabled us to begin to strengthen the armed forces in a process that would be continued in the administration of Álvaro Uribe and my own.

One especially important achievement was the modernization of the air fleet of the military and the police force. Between 2000 and 2012 their aerial potential went from four to sixteen artillery combat helicopters, while they acquired, in addition, one hundred new helicopters for transport.

Unfortunately, however, there existed a restriction that conspired against their effective use by the troops: the US government had given strict instructions that planes acquired with funds from Plan Colombia could not be employed in military operations against the insurgents, but only to combat the drug traffickers. This led to situations that were not only absurd but quite frankly painful. There were moments when the guerrillas attacked positions just half an hour's flight from the Larandia military base in Caquetá, where helicopters were parked to be used exclusively in the antidrug war. Our soldiers and policemen were frustrated at not being able to give their comrades support in repelling the guerrilla attack for the simple reason that these helicopters had to remain grounded. They were not to be used for sending help or military reinforcements.

Fortunately, this was to change once the Caguán peace talks broke down.

CHAPTER 6

The End of the Caguán Process

"YOU HAVE ASSAULTED ME IN MY GOOD FAITH"

When I agreed to form part of the Pastrana government as finance minister, I did so only after the president had understood and accepted my one condition: that, unlike the rest of the ministers and dozens of directors of trade associations, businessmen, and many other national and international personalities, I would not be expected to travel to the Caguán zone and take part in the interminable discussion sessions on the country's economy or render accounts to members of the Farc. It was obvious to me that such talk would lead nowhere.

In 1998, after I had carried out the first task of informal verification in the demilitarized zone, I remained convinced that the process was wrongly oriented. And the way it developed, day after day—slowly, and as if in a labyrinth—only served to confirm that conviction.

Not only had the government left an immense terrain in the hands of the guerrillas, with no control or official presence on the part of the state, but it had accepted a broad agenda for negotiation that covered every possible aspect of reform, an agenda that had more to do with the guerrillas' ambitions than with the need to put an end to the armed conflict.

In the course of the three years the Caguán peace talks lasted, the parties did not come to an agreement on a single one of the twelve points that made up the so-called Common Agenda for Change towards a New Colombia. In point of fact, the conversations had centered on just one point in the agenda that related to the country's economic model, about which no agreement was ever reached.

The process had experienced and overcome all kinds of difficulties. On several occasions, talks were suspended due to demands by the guerrillas of greater action by the state against the paramilitaries. In February 2001, in the midst of one such suspension, Pastrana traveled to the Caguán zone to meet with Marulanda. The president stayed the night, sleeping in the guerrilla camp, and returned to the capital the next day after having reached an agreement—the Los Pozos Accord—that gave the process some breathing space. But it was like giving oxygen to someone with a terminal illness.

The Colombians were tired of all this and skeptical of dialogues that showed no sign of arriving at concrete results, even partial ones. It was clear the Farc were not interested in arriving at concrete conclusions. But Pastrana never accepted that fact. He suffered from a certain defect: never to accept a reality if it were contrary to his desires.

The straw that broke the camel's back as far as the government's patience was concerned—the general populace had lost patience long before—was what happened on February 20, 2002. That day, members of the Farc commandeered an airplane on a commercial flight, forcing the pilot to land on a country roadway and taking hostage one of the passengers, Senator Jorge Géchem.

President Pastrana's only possible response was to call off the peace talks and order the armed forces to retake control of the Caguán area. He announced this to Colombians in a televised speech in which he addressed Marulanda in the following terms of reproach and disillusionment:

> Manuel Marulanda, I gave you my word and I kept it, I never failed to keep it, but you have assaulted me in my good faith, and not only me, but all Colombians. From the very first moment, you left the seat of dialogue vacant when I was there, surrounded by your own men, ready to begin talks. We decreed a zone to carry on negotiations, we complied with our agreement to free the zone of military presence, and you converted it into a lair of kidnappers, a laboratory for illegal drugs, a depository for weapons, dynamite, and stolen vehicles. I offered you—and complied with—a forty-eight-hour respite, but you and your men have just mocked Colombians to their faces. Therefore it's now up to you to answer, before Colombia and the world, for your arrogance and your lies.

Thus came to an end the most ambitious effort at peace talks with the Farc that had ever been attempted up to that point. Its conclusion was a great letdown for Colombia. But it also taught us a number of important lessons that one day, almost fifteen years later, would enable us to sign a peace agreement with this very guerrilla group.

WHAT THE CAGUÁN PROCESS LEFT US

As a Colombian, I always hoped for the success of the peace talks carried out by Pastrana government, a government of which I was part. Nothing would have pleased me more, and I can now say that we would have saved the country from fifteen years more of war, deaths, victims, and pain. However, my desire for peace did not blind me to the fact—a fact patently clear to me from the outset—that the way the process was designed and the negotiations focused made it difficult to arrive at the desired conclusion.

By the same token, it must be admitted that the process was not a waste of time. Thanks to Caguán, advances were made and lessons learned that would later be very useful when it came to attempting a new cycle of talks.

In the first place, the process served to demythologize the Farc and its leaders. Up to that time, they had been a totally clandestine guerrilla organization, whose chiefs had become legendary figures, with names or aliases that inspired fear, men whose faces were rarely seen. After the Caguán process, Colombians had gotten to know what they looked like, had heard their arguments, had seen how they behaved. And this helped humanize them, and demythologize them, too. They stopped being legends and became just other Colombians, ordinary men and women who were fighting against the state, who erroneously had taken to arms, but with whom one could sit down and debate and discuss.

Secondly, although it is true that the Farc gained in strength during the three years they were able to use the demilitarized zone as a terrain for practicing military exercises and recruiting personnel, as well as a hiding place for people they had kidnapped and were holding up for ransom, while at the same time establishing contacts with all kinds of personalities, both national and international, it must be said that the Colombian state also benefited from the experience.

Thanks to the resources from Plan Colombia, plus the effort we made at the finance ministry to improve the military budget—and this despite the objections of ministers whose budgets in other areas were diminished—while the peace talks were going on, the armed forces became much stronger as far as equipment and technology were concerned, and increased greatly in the number of men and women in active service. It was a much-fortified army that President Álvaro Uribe received on coming to power. And it served him well in combating the guerrillas with his policy of Democratic Security.

On top of that, there was a notable increase in the degree of unpopularity of the Farc. Colombians, who had been watching the guerrillas every day talking and preening themselves in front of the television cameras without making any serious advance on the points of the agenda, felt they had been betrayed. Ten million people had voted in favor of the Mandate for Peace in 1997 in the hope that the government and the guerrillas might sit down and talk. And now, more than four years later, they felt the guerrillas had no intention of giving up their weapons, that their participation in the process had been a farce.

Among the many lessons left by the process, I would call attention to two. First, that it is not a good idea to carry out peace talks under the floodlights of cameras and the permanent focus of the media and public opinion. This leads the negotiators to concentrate more on producing declarations that will favor their positions than on making serious progress at the negotiating table. The process often came to a halt when a public declaration did not coincide with what was being discussed in private.

The second lesson, which we will deal with more fully later on, is the need of an agenda designed and focused exclusively on matters strictly to do with the conflict, and not to try to embrace all the country's problems. Half the success of a peace process depends on a successful negotiation of the agenda. And the failure of the Caguán process can be attributed, at least in part, to a poorly negotiated agenda.

THE FARC ON THE WORLD'S TERRORISM LIST

Once the peace process had broken down, the Pastrana government's diplomacy, which had been dedicated to fomenting the support of the international community in the effort to achieve peace—the so-called peace diplomacy—changed emphasis and set about explaining to the world the reasons why the process had been called off, and to denouncing the Farc for its failure to fulfill its commitment and for its terrorist activities.

The world scenario had also veered in a new direction in its attitude to terrorism. In 2001, after the 9/11 attacks in the United States, tolerance of this kind of activity came to an end and all efforts converged in a new direction: a global war on terrorism.

Since 1997, during Bill Clinton's administration, the US State Department had included the Farc and the ELN on the list of terrorist organizations that are a threat to that country's interests. Now Colombian diplomacy was aimed in a new direction: to convince the European Union to include not just the paramilitaries but also the guerrillas on their list of terrorist groups.

On May 2, 2002, President Pastrana wrote a letter to José María Aznar, prime minister of Spain, who at the time was taking his turn as president of the European Union, with the following considerations:

> To doubt that the Farc are acting as terrorists when, day after day, their actions violate and terrify the Colombian population; have kidnapped and hold in captivity hundreds of our citizens, including one presidential candidate, a departmental governor in office, two ex-ministers of state, five congressmen and twelve members of a departmental assembly; who place car bombs, bicycle bombs, even corpse bombs to attack the population; who dynamite power stations, oil pipelines, and aqueducts; who blow up bridges that are necessary for communication: who attack and destroy entire towns of the most vulnerable; who commandeer airplanes in flight to kidnap passengers; who continually commit acts of extortion against businessmen and commercial enterprises; who plant personnel mines, causing the death or mutilation of children and rural workers; who foment and protect the drug traffic among many other vile actions, constitutes a painful message not only for my government but for all Colombian people, who daily suffer the disastrous consequences of these activities.

As if these arguments were not enough, on that same day, May 2, 2002, the Farc perpetrated an act that left no doubt they should be described as terrorists: in the midst of combat against the paramilitaries, they fired a cylinder charged with dynamite into the church of Bojayá, a small town in the department of Chocó, where three hundred villagers had sought shelter. This brutal action left the macabre spectacle of eighty dead bodies, most of them children, and at least one hundred wounded.

In June, in the face of such painful facts, the European Union included the Farc in its list of terrorist organizations, where it would remain for the following fifteen years or more. In June 2002, the Farc—along with Al-Qaeda and other equally dangerous organizations—formed part of a group known as humanity's worst enemies.

This had a consequence that had to be multiplied exponentially: the state's capacity to combat them. In July 2002, an important lobby by the Colombian government convinced the US Congress that military equipment donated by the United States under Plan Colombia might be employed not only in anti-drug-traffic operations but also in combating terrorists; that is, all illegal armed groups in the country, including the Farc, the ELN, and the paramilitaries.

This decision, known as a "change of authorizations," greatly improved the efficiency of air attacks, since we could now make use of dozens of aircrafts and helicopters with state-of-the-art technology in the fight against the guerrillas. The most successful operations against the Farc—that it was my lot to wage, years later as defense minister—could be summed up from then on by a common denominator: first, the location of the target through intelligence information; second, precise and effective bombing by air force bombers; and third, consolidating the terrain with troops on the ground. This simple formula was what changed the war's equation.

ROCKETS AGAINST THE PRESIDENTIAL PALACE

The failure of the Caguán talks had other political consequences. Colombians, fed up with the guerrillas, their arrogance, and their terrorist acts, voted for a candidate who promised a firm hand and strong military action against the illegal armed groups.

Five years earlier, millions had voted enthusiastically for a mandate to promote dialogue. This time the voters, on going to the ballot boxes to choose Pastrana's successor, elected a former senator and provincial governor from Antioquia who had been one of the most voluble critics of the peace talks: Álvaro Uribe Vélez.

The popular mandate had undergone a change and had swung to the other extreme of the pendulum. While before they had hoped for a president who would lead the guerrillas to the negotiating table, now public opinion demanded they be combated with all available force. And that was precisely what Uribe promised with his slogan, "Firm hand, big heart."

Thanks to Plan Colombia and the recent change of authorizations and immense efforts to provide a sufficient military budget, the new president was to receive an armed forces not only fortified and more professional but also in possession of modern and effective military equipment. In addition, internationally he would be given the green light to enter combat against the guerrillas with all his might, and paramilitary groups included on the lists of global terrorism.

The date he took office, August 7, 2002, would go down as a day that ushered in a new period in our history, one characterized by bombs and bloodshed.

That day, President Pastrana invited his ministers and chief government officials to a farewell luncheon at the presidential palace, Casa de Nariño, while at the capitol, seat of congress, just three hundred meters away, his successor was being sworn in as the new president.

Before lunch, the outgoing president decorated several of us who had been his cabinet ministers with the Boyacá Cross, Colombia's highest distinction. I attended with my wife, María Clemencia, enjoying the satisfaction of having done the best job I could as finance minister. On taking office, I had received an economy with a negative growth rate and worrying signs of alarm in several sectors, and I had ended my term by handing over an economy in a positive process of renewal that had won the confidence of investors and of the multilateral banking system, with a finance sector fortified after having been in intensive care. Unemployment figures and inflation were on the decline.

We lunched in one of the salons of the presidential palace in a relaxed and pleasant atmosphere. Then, before three o'clock, the president got up and went off to retrieve a few last things from his office. The rest of us stayed drinking coffee and chatting in small groups. Suddenly we heard a powerful explosion. It sounded like a bomb going off nearby. We held our breath, and a few minutes later we felt another explosion, this time on the roof of the palace.

In the midst of the general consternation—some were frankly terrified—we were ushered down to the president's theater in the basement, the safest place in case of danger, where we were apprised of what had occurred: the Farc had fired rockets into the presidential palace!

Later we were told that the attack had been launched from the back yard of a house some two kilometers away, that most of the rockets in readiness had not actually been fired, and that some of them had fallen in a marginal area some blocks from the presidential palace, causing the deaths of twenty pedestrians and wounding more than seventy.

Meanwhile, at the capitol, the president-elect was giving his inaugural address before members of congress and important international guests, including the presidents Eduardo Dubalde, of Argentina; Gustavo Noboa, of Ecuador; Ricardo Maduro, of Honduras; Mireya Moscoso, of Panama; and Hugo Chávez, of Venezuela; as well as the then Prince of Asturias—now King of Spain—Felipe de Borbón. At that moment, nobody was aware of how close we had been to a tragedy. Because, just as several mortars had gone astray and fallen hundreds of meters from the palace, others could very well have hit the capitol, with consequences no one could imagine.

In this dramatic fashion, Colombia witnessed the transmission of power from President Pastrana, who had sought peace through dialogue, to President Uribe, who promised to win the war by force of arms. The Farc, with their bombs, supplied the background music, underlining—in case anyone hadn't gotten the message—their decision to resort to terrorist actions to make their presence felt. No one could now doubt that, after the failed Caguán process, this guerrilla group had become a major factor in the country's instability.

CHAPTER 7

First a Hawk, Then a Dove

MAKE WAR TO WIN PEACE

In my address of acceptance of the Nobel Peace Prize in Oslo on December 10, 2016, I quoted the great Swedish inventor Alfred Nobel, the man who created this award. "War is the horror of horrors," he said, "the greatest of all crimes." And I followed up with a further reflection:

> War must never be considered, under any circumstance, an end in itself. It is merely a means, but a means that we must always strive to avert.
>
> I have served as a leader in times of war—to defend the freedom and the rights of the Colombian people—and I have served as a leader in times of making peace. Allow me to tell you, from my own experience, that it is much harder to make peace than to wage war.
>
> When it is absolutely necessary, we must be prepared to fight, and it was my duty—as defense minister and as president—to fight illegal armed groups in my country. When the roads to peace were closed, I fought these groups with effectiveness and determination. But it is foolish to believe that the end of any conflict must be the elimination of the enemy.

I quote these words because some people have thought it paradoxical that the world's highest tribute to a worker for peace was being awarded to someone like me, who waged the greatest military offensive against the very illegal armed group with whom he then negotiated a peace deal.

Mine, however, is not an isolated case. On studying the careers and background of the men and women who preceded me in receiving the Nobel Peace Prize, I find that not all were born pacifists, nor humanitarian workers, nor champions in the fight against the arms race. Some—and I was one of them—have had to wage cruel wars and make tough and complex decisions that implied the death of human beings. In other words, they had been hawks before they became doves.

One of the earliest examples of this was Elihu Root, awarded the prize in 1912. He had been the United States' secretary of war—under presidents William McKinley and Theodore Roosevelt—and as such had given greater scope to West Point, the US military academy, and established the US Army War College. Then, as Roosevelt' secretary of state, and in his activities in the law, he was a proponent of a better understanding between the countries of North and South America, a policy that later would be known, under Franklin D. Roosevelt's administration, as the Good Neighbor Policy. Root also insisted on the importance of arbitration tribunals and international courts as institutions suitable for resolving conflicts.

A similar case is that of the US general George Marshall, awarded the Nobel Peace Prize in 1953, who was also defense secretary. He took part as an army officer in the twentieth century's two world wars. In the second, as army chief of staff, he coordinated military operations that led to the triumph of the allies in Europe. Not for nothing did Winston Churchill refer to him as "the true organizer of victory."

Marshall was a great soldier who fought for the freedom of his country and that of the whole of Europe. He was called upon to lead a "good" war—if any war can rightly be so called—to confront oppression and the threat of Nazism. After retiring from the army, he labored as secretary of state in the economic reconstruction of Europe, which came to be known by his name: the Marshall Plan. It was for that achievement above all that he earned the Nobel Peace Prize.

Another outstanding example is that of Israel's first prime minister, Yitzhak Rabin, awarded the prize in 1994 along with Israel's foreign affairs minister Shimon Peres and the Palestinian leader Yasser Arafat because of their signing of the Oslo Agreement, which opened up a horizon for peace—one that sadly was destined to fail—to solve the long Arab-Israeli conflict.

Rabin had been an uncompromising military commander—a veritable hawk—responsible for nothing less than the triumph of the Israel army against Egypt and its allies in the Six Days War in 1967. In his address of acceptance of the Nobel Peace Prize, Rabin spoke of his military experience and what it had meant for him to make decisions that implied the death of his own people as well as people on the side of his enemy. Nonetheless, the Nobel

Committee acknowledged in him not the combatant but the political leader who, fully aware of the horrors of war from the inside, made courageous efforts to achieve peace.

The fact is that pacifism, pure and simple, rarely achieves peace. In a world so full of violent threats, with a high degree of intolerance, it is often necessary to combine the art of war with the art of peace. In other words—to borrow the phrase someone used to describe Root—you have to be "a realist with a healthy dose of idealism."*

The president of the United States Barack Obama, on receiving the Nobel Peace Prize in 2009, summed up this dilemma: "To say that force may sometimes be necessary is not a call to cynicism—it is a recognition of history; the imperfections of man and the limits of reason."

A NEW PARTY AND A NEW MISSION

Once President Uribe had taken office, under a shower of rockets from the Farc, Colombia saw the start of a new era, that of Democratic Security, the name the new head of state gave to his principal government policy. This policy's aim was to improve citizens' conditions of security and confront the guerrillas and the drug traffickers with all available might. To do so, he counted on broad popular support.

As for me, I returned to my activity as opinion columnist and director of the Good Government Foundation. In my columns I wrote on all kinds of subjects, and analyzed the political and economic state of the country and of the world. But there was one personality in particular, the Venezuelan president Hugo Chávez, to whom I dedicated several of my texts. As a result, I became the object—as I well deserved—of his most acrimonious hostility.

Highly reliable sources in Venezuela supplied me with documents and confidential information that showed how Chávez was plotting against democracy and human rights, with the intention of expanding his power and influence to other Latin American countries. I repeatedly denounced the threat that the Chavista regime represented for Venezuelans themselves and for the region. So much so that I became Chávez's principal adversary in Colombia. At that time I never imagined that, years later, in the interest of peace

* Jay Nordlinger, *Peace, They Say: A History of the Nobel Peace Prize, the Most Famous and Controversial Prize in the World* (New York: Encounter Books, 2012), 81.

and well-being for our two countries, I was going to transform that enmity into a pragmatic and constructive relationship of collaboration.

At first, Uribe differentiated in his approach to confrontation with illegal armed groups. To deal with the guerrillas, who had grown in strength under the Pastrana administration, he employed a firm hand and military force. By way of contrast, with the paramilitaries he initiated a process of dialogue and submission that culminated in the demobilization of the main paramilitary structures. More than thirty thousand members of these groups of private justice, which were nothing more than bands at the service of the drug traffickers and large landowners, handed in their weapons and became beneficiaries of the government's reintegration program.

To achieve this demobilization, the Uribe government presented Congress with a project he called the Law of Justice and Peace, which would benefit the paramilitary commanders. These were men who had been guilty of massacres, kidnappings, and rape, men who had driven people off their land and stolen their property, not to mention the crimes they committed related to the drug trade. The projected law would ensure they would get prison sentences of no more than eight years, so long as they collaborated with the justice system. This aspect—collaboration with the justice system in exchange for benefits—would be a key component of the transitional justice system that we were to agree upon with the Farc in Havana.

This demobilization of the paramilitaries was an important achievement. However, it had three serious defects. In the first place, several drug lords, attracted by the promise of short sentences, invented ploys to appear as paramilitaries, or acquired a kind of franchise that allowed them to present themselves as paramilitaries and obtain benefits that did not correspond to their real situation.

In the second place, thousands of demobilized paramilitaries went back to a life of crime, teaming up with mafia groups and spawning a multiplicity of lawless bandits whose criminal activities are still wreaking havoc in extensive rural areas of our country.

Lastly, the judicial processes and the reparation to victims contemplated in the Law of Justice and Peace were clearly ineffective. In 2017, when this law had been in operation for ten years, the general comptroller of the republic released a study that came to some worrying conclusions. Even after the law had been in force for ten decades, only 47 sentences had been passed condemning 195 former members of the paramilitary groups, a mere 8 percent of those who aspired to benefit from this special legislation. As for reparation, the figures were no better: only 6 percent of the amount of money paid for reparation to victims had been covered by amounts provided by those responsible for the crimes; that is to say, the paramilitaries who had applied for the benefits offered by the demobilization program.

Nonetheless, President Uribe's popularity was undeniable. For a start, his fight against the guerrillas was showing results. So much so that Colombians gradually began to travel again on the country's roads that before had been largely deserted because of the danger lurking on most highways. Even so, some still only traveled in convoys with a military escort. Uribe's popularity was also due to the fact that his government had put an end—at least on paper—to one of the most savage and dangerous of the illegal armed groups: the paramilitaries.

A lot of people wanted Uribe to remain in office after his four-year term. However, the Colombian constitution did not allow reelection. And so, to make it possible for Uribe to serve a second term as president, Congress set in motion a process that would permit a president to be reelected for one more four-year period. The law that introduced this constitutional reform was finally passed in 2005.

Uribe came from the Liberal Party, but had been elected president with the endorsement of an independent political movement. The Liberals opposed the reform that allowed for a reelection. They felt so strongly about this that fifteen Liberal members of Congress who voted for the measure were expelled from the party.

In the midst of this party split, I joined forces with other dissident Liberals such as Luis Guillermo Vélez, Aurelio Iragorri Hormaza, and Oscar Iván Zuluaga to create a new party that would back not only the reelection but also the policies being executed at the time by President Uribe's government. Thus was born the Social Party of National Unity, from then on known as the Party of the U.

The new party began with an unprecedented success. Not only was Uribe reelected for the period 2006–2010 but the Party of the U—the first time it presented candidates at the ballot box, and having been in existence a mere four months—won twenty seats in the Senate, equivalent to one-fifth of the Upper House, plus twenty-nine in the Chamber of Representatives. It was the first time in more than a century and a half that a party other than the two traditional political parties—the Liberal and the Conservative—had gained a majority in the Congress of the Republic.

Extraordinary times often reveal the inability of traditional parties to confront a crisis and solve a nation's problems. Thus paradigmatic changes tend to occur in politics. In France, President Emmanuel Macron's party, the Republic on the move, virtually swept the traditional parties off the political map; in Israel, Prime Minister Ariel Sharon created a new center party from nothing and with it came to power, since the party he belonged to, the Likud, could come up with no acceptable solution to the critical situation the country was going through at the time. In Italy, Brazil, and Mexico, winning candidates have come from recently created parties that have distanced themselves from the traditional ones.

The political victory we achieved with the Party of the U was the occasion for my return to a position in government. President Uribe, newly elected for a second term, invited me to accompany him as defense minister, which would be the third ministry of my public life. Once again I accepted, for it represented an immense challenge, nothing less than that of heading the Uribe administration's flagship policy: national security.

The president knew he was entrusting the execution of his principal policy to someone who not only had an intimate knowledge of the armed forces but had actually worn a military uniform and, on top of that, was experienced in handling matters to do with the budget. All of these factors doubtless influenced his decision.

I had three predecessors as defense ministers during Uribe's first term of government. One of these was Marta Lucía Ramírez, a lawyer who had served as my first vice-minister in the Ministry of Foreign Trade and was later to occupy that same ministry herself. In 2018 she was to become Colombia's vice-president. The other two were Jorge Alberto Uribe, a businessman from Antioquia, and Camilo Ospina, a lawyer who had worked as legal secretary to the presidency. Between them, they had set in motion the policy of Democratic Security. It fell to me to take a further step and build on what had gone before.

CHANGES IN MILITARY INTELLIGENCE

In assigning me to the Defense Ministry, President Uribe issued me with very clear instructions. As he often said when referring to the terrorists, "the viper is still alive." Despite the fact that the government had dealt serious blows to the guerrillas and the paramilitaries, the armed forces had been unable to bring down the principal leaders and capos. They seemed to be untouchable.

“It is now time,” the president said to me, “that members of the Farc secretariat should start to fall. I haven’t been able to get them. I hope you will. That will be your chief responsibility.” Up to that moment, even though the Farc had been in existence for forty-two years, not one of its secretariat’s members had fallen.

With that task ahead of me, I took a trip with my family before taking up my post at the ministry. We went to China, and on the way back to Colombia, I made a point of stopping over in London to talk with Prime Minister Tony Blair. I had had a close relationship with him since 1999, when we jointly published a book on the Third Way. Now I told him we would be grateful for advice from the United Kingdom, whose intelligence organs were famous the world over for their professionalism and effectiveness. They could help us to be more effective in our fight against terrorism. Blair sent me to talk to Sir John Scarlett, general director of the British Service of Secret Intelligence, the celebrated MI6 of the James Bond movies.

The MI6 building on Vauxhall Cross on the River Thames is a most original construction that seems to be made of Lego blocks. In fact, its nickname is Legoland. Sir John told me I was right in placing capital importance on intelligence and counterintelligence. He recommended we change our intelligence system, which was based on the United States’ concept of putting different agencies to compete with one another. In Colombia’s case, the Administrative Department of Security operated independently from the others, and other agencies carried out their own particular intelligence operations separately. The British expert advised me to centralize and oblige all intelligence bodies to share their information. Which is what we did.

I also spoke to my good friend Shlomo Ben-Ami, former foreign minister and public security minister of Israel, as well as vice-president of the Toledo Center for Peace, of which I am a member. Ben-Ami recommended I consult with an intelligence firm formed by former generals and members of Mossad, the well-known Israeli intelligence service. We consulted with this firm in 2007, and their advice proved fundamental in developing the concept of joint operations at the highest level, producing formidable results in our fight against illegal armed groups.

In addition to British and Israeli cooperation, we continued to count on the support of intelligence, technology, and training provided by the security and defense forces of the United States in the context of Plan Colombia.

I returned to Colombia and took possession as defense minister on July 20, 2006, National Independence Day, with the imposing military parade that is a highlight of the commemoration ceremony. Uribe was in the final days of his first presidency. The rest of the ministers took possession of their ministries on August 7, the day Uribe was sworn in for his second term, 2006–2010.

In order to carry out my mission of dealing mortal blows to the leaders of the illegal armed groups, I had to do three things: first, improve our intelligence; second, guarantee adequate teamwork by coordinating the different bodies that made up the military forces and the national police force; and third, obtain the resources required to keep on strengthening the operative and offensive capacity of our troops.

When I took over the ministry, the military had an organization known as Cancerbero (Watchdog), whose job was to gather high-level intelligence information and use it to ensure the success of operations aimed at hitting highly prized targets. However, it soon became evident—and my foreign consultants let me know it—that our so-called Watchdog had a serious problem: somehow it was letting information leak out and therefore could not be relied on by those who were putting their lives on the line in operations or on the battlefield. As a result, the men on the ground preferred to get their own intelligence. But this only duplicated efforts and led to a significant time lag between the receipt of the information and the particular military operation. So by the time the troops were ready to go into action, their targets had moved to somewhere else, often because they had been warned of the attack being prepared against them.

With the support of Israeli experts and the advice of British and US intelligence consultants, we completely transformed our system. We created a centralized planning group—the Headquarters of Special Joint Operations (Jefatura de Operaciones Especiales Conjuntas, JOEC), now known as the Joint Command of Special Operations (Comando Conjunto de Operaciones Especiales, CCOES)—to process intelligence gathered by different entities and coordinate the operations that these sources suggested. This group reported directly to me and to the commander of military forces, and had as its exclusive mission to concentrate on the main targets, such as members of the Farc secretariat and other strategic heads of the guerrillas, as well as on capos of the drug trade. An officer from one of the forces—the army, the navy, the air force, or the police force—was assigned as commander responsible for each target and would receive more information. All the rest would report back to him.

Resistance to change is part of human nature and we felt it during the first months of this new system. I recall a meeting we held at the Air Force Club with commanders, secondary commanders, and heads of operations and of intelligence in each of the three military forces, where several men expressed their concern and reticence to cooperate in the project. With some of them I had to put my foot down. "If you don't work together," I said, "you're out! And if any intelligence chief refuses to share information, he's out too!" I had no more problems. Fortunately, results soon began to be seen, since the lag between the moment information became available and the operation of attack no longer took weeks. Now it was a matter of hours, or maybe a couple of days.

The first success on the ground that demonstrated the effectiveness of the joint system of intelligence and operations was an offensive in September 2007 that put out of action a high-level drug trafficker by the name of Negro Acacio, the man responsible for drug trafficking business and supplying the Farc with weapons in the country's southeastern region. At last, we had begun to catch some of the big fish.

A WARTIME BUDGET

During President Uribe's first term in office, the government established a "tax for preserving democratic security" designed to continue strengthening the armed forces. The amount one was liable to pay depended on the value of your assets; only those whose assets were worth upward of 169.5 million pesos (equivalent to US$75,000 at the time) were liable to pay this tax.

Given the warlike spirit that prevailed among Colombians after the failure of the Caguán process, this new tax was for the most part well received by the population. People were ready to pay so long as they could see results. Even so, the funds raised were not sufficient. We needed to triple them if we were to guarantee a real improvement in equipment, technology, training and increase of numbers.

So one of my principal aims as minister was to get approval for a new tax on assets that would really serve to consolidate a more effective development of democratic security. But it would have an essential difference: a levy would be made only on large fortunes, not on the main bulk of the population. From now on, only those whose assets exceeded three billion pesos (that is, more than US$1.3 million) would be liable to pay.

I met with the heads of the country's principal commercial associations and industrialists to explain the situation. They were ready to cooperate, but they wanted to be sure the resources were properly used; that is to say, effectively and free from corruption. So I created a consultancy body for the defense ministry named the Commission of Ethics and Transparency, made up of the main leaders in the economy's private sector together with the state's control organs. We also included the technical secretariat of Fedesarrollo, a highly regarded center for economic analysis. Our aim was clear: to accompany and supervise the process of decisions made to execute these special resources for the strengthening of the armed forces.

The equivalent to around US$3 billion was raised—and no shadow of doubt ever arose about how these funds were spent. With them—plus the progress made in matters of intelligence and work undertaken jointly in coordination with the different armed forces—we were able to hit the guerrillas, especially the Farc, with a debilitating force such as they had never experienced before.

CHAPTER 8

A Team for War and Peace

WATER AND OIL

I have always been in favor of teamwork. I believe in collective intelligence and the need to delegate. And I have put that conviction into practice in all the posts I have held. The best intentions can be frustrated by competition between individual egos, people looking for acknowledgment and praise, who tend to underestimate the contribution of others. In contrast, when everyone puts their efforts and talent at the service of a cause, without egoism or attempts to be the sole protagonist, any goal can be achieved, no matter how daunting it may seem to be.

The success of any manager—and every public mission needs a manager—can be attributed to forming a team and knowing how to lead his team members, getting them to act together like clockwork, where every part of the machinery is indispensable for the successful achievement of the task in hand.

That's why, from my very first day at the ministry, with responsibility for nearly half a million men and women who make up not only the military forces and the police but all the entities that participate in the defense sector, I was determined to surround myself with the best, and so implement a system of teamwork that would produce results.

A key section was that of my vice-ministers. At the beginning only two vice-ministries existed, and I appointed to those positions two men who—and this is no exaggeration—were like oil and water: Juan Carlos Pinzón and Sergio Jaramillo. It was a decision I made deliberately, for thanks to that duo, I had access at all times to two different but complementary perspectives on security. And that helped us reach a balanced opinion.

Pinzón was a young economist who had worked with me in the Good Government Foundation from the time he was still a student, and had later been my private secretary at the Finance Ministry. He had also represented Colombia at the World Bank in Washington. He is of a practical turn of mind, and though dressed as a civilian, he seemed more like an army officer in the way he talked and walked, even down to the way he combed his hair. He was born in the military hospital, studied at a military school, is the son and grandson of army officers, and his wife is also the daughter of a military man. As such, he was in his element among the men in uniform. And like any true soldier, he was good at obeying orders.

With him, we planned the restructuring of the defense sector. Also, he helped me secure the new patrimony tax and design the procedure for investing the funds in the most efficient and transparent manner.

Jaramillo, on the other hand, is the prototype of the intellectual and academic, possessed of a theoretical intelligence that contrasted with the practicality of his colleague. He is a philosopher and philologist, with degrees from the Universities of Toronto and Oxford respectively, plus university studies at Cambridge and Heidelberg. He is also a polyglot, with fluency not only in modern languages but also in ancient Greek. In an interesting combination, he had spent several years as director of the foundation Ideas for Peace, and then, under the ministry of Marta Lucía Ramírez, had designed the policy of defense and Democratic Security at the start of the Uribe administration.

The fundamental condition required of a victorious army is its legitimacy. That's why I entrusted Jaramillo with the task of leading a group of experts—made up of civilians and members of the army and the police force—to produce a policy on human rights for the armed forces. The result was the Comprehensive Policy on Human Rights and International Humanitarian Law of the defense sector, which we launched early in the year 2008. At the present time, it would be hard to find anywhere in the world a public defense force better prepared than that of Colombia as regards training and awareness in the field of human rights, or one that acquired those skills in such a short lapse of time. It was precisely in matters to do with human rights that, with Jaramillo's support, I had to deal with the biggest and most serious scandal of the armed forces in the country's recent history: the so-called false positives.

THE "FALSE POSITIVES"

My stance on the legitimate use of force by the state and respect for human rights and international humanitarian law was consistent and unchanging during my time at the Defense Ministry and later as president of the republic. I summed it up in a speech I gave in February 2009:

> If we failed to respect human rights, if we were to behave like the drug traffickers and the terrorists who have no consideration for the life of others, we would be giving up our principal operational asset, which does not consist of the equipment we have, nor our troops and our strategy, but the support and confidence of the population.
>
> The army that does not win the support and confidence of the people by its correct behavior and its respect for the community is an army that has been defeated from the start, that has no longer a reason for existing. On the contrary, an army that obeys the law and respects human rights enjoys the greatest possible strategic advantage: legitimacy.
>
> Only with legitimacy and morally impeccable actions can we beat the peddlers of violence, the terrorists and drug traffickers, who mock humanitarian principles and tread mercilessly underfoot the most basic human rights of their fellow citizens. That's where we are different. Therein lies the legitimacy that gives strength to our actions.

A most painful episode, which brought shame on our military forces, was one I had to face as minister. It was given the name of "false positives" and motivated me even further to insist on a policy of human rights and international humanitarian law in the armed forces.

When I came to the ministry, I found there had been established a system of recompense paid for the killing of guerrilla leaders or simple guerrilla fighters, combined with a special incentive for those military commanders who showed the most results in combating the enemy. This was known as a "corpse count," and had been practiced in Vietnam with appalling consequences. It ended up becoming a perverse incentive that people with no morals used to gain personal rewards.

Reports began to come in of possible situations in which the military had gone beyond their remit and were executing civilians who were not in combat. In some cases these executions were called "false positives" because the men responsible for these murders pretended their victims were the result of positive operational successes. They presented them as if they were members of terrorist groups legitimately killed in action. This was a total aberration, which flew in the face not only of military honor but of the most basic notions of human dignity.

I set up a committee to follow up on these reports and ordered that all available resources be used to ensure that, in case of deaths in combat, the examination of the body and the gathering of all preliminary evidence should be carried out by judiciary police, not by the troops.

When the press denounced the disappearance of young men from the town of Soacha on the outskirts of Bogotá, we became even more thoroughgoing in our efforts to combat this inhumane practice. I set up a special commission to investigate the matter, headed by the general who commanded the JOEC. Once we had reached conclusions, with President Uribe's approval, I ordered the retirement of twenty-seven members of the army, among them three generals. They were not to be the last.

Since then, dozens of officers of different ranks and common soldiers have been sentenced or are on trial for participating in these atrocious acts. Some of them have been condemned to over fifty years in prison. Many of them are now seeking to benefit from the Special Justice for Peace set up as part of the peace agreement, in the hope of receiving some reduction of their sentences in exchange for their account of what really occurred and a promise of reparation to the families of the victims.

These were difficult months, and hard ones. But they were necessary in that we had to conduct a thorough cleanup of our military forces. I devoted my best energies to changing our soldiers' way of thinking, trying to make them get their priorities right. Every time I addressed the troops, they would have to listen to me repeating the same lesson, like some sort of mantra. From now on, I told them, our slogan will be: "Better a demobilized man than a prisoner; better a prisoner than a corpse."

I announced this new doctrine in the speech I gave at the Junior Officers Club, and I backed it up with the argument that a demobilized guerrilla brings information with him and leaves the enemy concerned and demoralized, whereas a dead man becomes a martyr. Besides, from a humanitarian point of view, we would be saving lives. That way I put an end to the deplorable "Vietnam doctrine" that measured the success of the war by the number of corpses.

Naturally, this didn't go down well with the president. However, it did bring about an abrupt but necessary change of attitude in the mental makeup of the militaries. Now the major triumph would not be the death of the enemy, but something very much greater: converting the former adversary into someone useful in society.

A PROFOUND DISAPPOINTMENT

Pinzón and Jaramillo were two collaborators who, despite—or rather because of—their differences, complemented one another and helped me to carry forward the ministry's commission. Then, in the context of the ministry's restructuring, a third vice-ministry was created, charged with coordinating the different entities that made up the Social Business Group of the Defense. To manage this group, I appointed the retired general Fernando Tapias, the same high-ranking officer with whom I had worked hand in hand—when he was commander-in-chief of the military forces and I was finance minister—to endow the country's security and defense with a greater proportion of the budget.

Later, in 2010, when I became president, I again put my trust in the work and the human qualities of my two original vice-ministers, whose personalities were poles apart. I appointed Jaramillo to be consultant on national security and later high commissioner for peace. From this latter position he would coordinate nothing less than the peace talks with the Farc in Havana that were to culminate in an agreement to end the conflict.

As for Pinzón, I first appointed him chief of staff of the presidency, and later minister of defense, an office he held for almost four years, from mid-2011 to mid-2015. He was a disciplined minister who supported me in the war effort, and also supported me unreservedly—at least that was what I believed—in the search for peace. The last office he held under my administration was that of ambassador to the United States in Washington.

The relation between the two men was respectful, though not always harmonious, due precisely to the difference in style of each one and their way of seeing things. Often I had to act as a kind of mediator between them. It was the price I paid for having contracted two very different kinds of intelligences, two different but equally valuable perspectives that, taken together, provided a necessary balance.

Sad to say, my relation with Pinzón deteriorated toward the end of my administration. As defense minister, he was always forthright, both in his language and his attitude, against the guerrillas, and I understood he should be so. But it was also true that he formed part of a government that was placing its bets on a peaceful and dialogued solution to the conflict, and clearly understood that our efforts were geared to end in a peace agreement, not with impunity, but with certain benefits for those who would lay down arms, benefits that are inherent to this kind of agreement. Several people drew my attention to the fact that, in private and in military circles, he was speaking against the process. But I didn't believe it. He never told me he had reservations about it. I asked the military commanders if Pinzón had spoken to them about his objections to the peace process, and they said no.

Pinzón served as ambassador to the United States for close to two years, and then told me he was thinking of putting up his name as candidate for the presidency for the Party of the U, in which case, if he did not wish to invalidate his candidacy, he would have to resign from the ambassadorship by May 25, 2017, at the latest. I understood his reasons and told him I had no objection. We agreed that he would remain in the embassy until after I had made my official visit to President Trump on May 18, and then he would resign. After I had completed my official agenda in Washington, I visited the University of Virginia in Charlottesville, where I had been invited to give the commencement speech to the students, one of whom was my son Esteban. I invited ambassador Pinzón to accompany me, as a gesture of personal affection. But he declined, saying that his official business had concluded with my visit to the White House. Only after my personal secretary called him up and remonstrated with him did he finally decide to attend. On May 19 in Charlottesville, in a press conference, I referred to his imminent departure from the embassy, a comment to which he strongly objected, even though it was exactly what we had agreed upon. General Jorge Enrique Maldonado, military chief of staff for the presidency, told me later that Pinzón, on learning of my declaration to the press, had exclaimed angrily: "That is going to cost the president blood."

A few days after he had resigned from the embassy, Pinzón's first declarations were criticisms of the administration of which he had been part for over seven years, especially during the years of the peace process. In his messages on Twitter, he claimed we were making perverse concessions to the terrorists, and he threw doubt on the handing over of weapons by the Farc, even though this was being supervised and approved by no less an authority than the United Nations. So finally I understood, with deep disillusionment, that what I had been so often warned of was a fact, and that as a candidate for the presidency, Pinzón preferred to play the card of criticism, rather than that of loyalty. No doubt he felt it would bring him more votes.

As it turned out, the Party of the U did not run a candidate for president. This was partly my suggestion, on seeing that the party members did not agree on which of the two main candidates, Pinzón and Senator Roy Barreras, would have the better chance. Pinzón, for his part, began collecting signatures to ensure his candidacy, but finally desisted and ran as vice-presidential candidate to Germán Vargas Lleras, with poor results at the polls.

This left me—and still leaves me—with the bitter taste caused by a person so close to my affections, in whom I placed my confidence and friendship for more than twenty years, who took up a stance on the opposite shore and joined his voice to the strident chorus of my most voluble critics. I was reminded of a classical warning on the struggle for power: it brings out the worst in the human condition.

A SHAKEUP IN THE TOP ECHELONS OF THE POLICE FORCE

In the military terrain, during my time as minister for defense, I was accompanied by General Freddy Padilla de León in his capacity as commander of the military forces. Padilla de León, from the country's Caribbean region, was a specialist in intelligence with a long record of operational successes. A few years later, when I was in the final months of my second term in the presidency and General Padilla de León in retirement, he took part, along with other officers aware of the need for peace, in a team that attempted to negotiate with the ELN guerrilla group.

In the role as director-general of the national police force, I was accompanied initially by General Jorge Daniel Castro, and later by General Óscar Naranjo, an exceptional person who has played, and will continue to play, a positive role in our country's history.

Naranjo was appointed director-general in May 2007 in extraordinary circumstances that obliged me to bring about nothing less than a shakeup in the highest spheres of the police force. The magazine *Semana* revealed that illegal phone tapping, carried out with no judicial order, had recorded thousands of hours of police intelligence on members of the government, the opposition, public figures, and journalists. These tapes included information on the former magistrate and presidential candidate Carlos Gaviria, an important political opponent of President Uribe, and also on the journalist Claudia Gurisatti.

Alarmed and indignant, I immediately accepted the resignation of General Castro, director-general of the police force, and of General Guillermo Chávez, chief director of central intelligence. Aside from the personal responsibility of these officers, which I discovered thanks to the collaboration of certain journalists, conduct of this kind had no place in an institution that should guarantee, not violate, the rights of Colombia's citizens.

In designating the man to replace General Castro, I made a difficult decision, but one that would prove to be fortunate: I passed over eleven generals who were on the list of hierarchical succession, and appointed General Naranjo. As director of criminal investigations, Naranjo had been producing outstanding results in the fight against organized crime.

At first President Uribe did not approve of my provoking a shakeup of these dimensions, which meant that thirteen generals were to leave the police force: the two who had handed in their resignation, and another eleven who had a longer record of service than Naranjo. I reminded the president that he used to quote Napoleon, who appointed his generals according to their results, their talents, and above all their luck. And I told him Naranjo possessed all three—an argument that finally convinced him. Naranjo's appointment brought with it a generational relay and introduced a breath of fresh air into the police force. Under his direction, and often in coordination with the military, he increased the force's effectiveness and dealt heavy blows against the subversives, and in particular against the drug trade mafias.

General Naranjo, an extremely well-prepared officer and a great humanist, is an even-tempered man and a conciliator, but at the same time does not hesitate to act with a firm hand against crime and corruption. He was the right man at the right moment. He served as director of the institution for over five years, and in 2010 the International Police Association proclaimed him as the world's most outstanding policeman.

After he retired from active service, I included Naranjo as plenipotentiary negotiator in peace talks with the Farc in Havana, where his calm and his ability to relate to people played a fundamental role. Early in 2017, I appointed him vice-president of the republic, replacing Germán Vargas Lleras, who resigned to run for the presidency as my successor. Naranjo served as vice-president right to the end of my term of office. As such, he carried out tasks as important as the implementation of the peace agreement with the Farc, the protection of ex–guerrilla fighters and of social leaders and human rights activists, coordinating teams of citizen security and applying the government's antidrug policy.

I will never tire of underlining the importance of teamwork to achieve complex goals. And that was what I counted on in the Ministry of Defense. With commanders like Padilla de León and Naranjo, we made notable advances in consolidating democratic security. It was no coincidence, then, that these same men would later be by my side in the search for peace.

THE LESSON OF GENERAL VALENCIA TOVAR

After the failure of the Caguán dialogues, and during the following years, the Farc continued to wreak havoc on the population, above all in rural areas—attacking towns and blowing up power stations, kidnapping indiscriminately and holding their victims for ransom. They had become public enemy number one. Especially once the paramilitaries had been demobilized.

Perhaps the most powerful symbol of how defiantly the Colombians opposed the Farc was the citizens' march, which took place on February 4, 2008. This multitudinous event was not sponsored by the government, nor by social organizations, but was a response by the Colombians to a call to action by a group of Facebook users identified as "One Million Voices against the Farc."

Spontaneously, millions of men and women, entire families with their children, marched through the country's streets and gathered in city squares and public places in the towns—as well as in cities overseas—to let it be known, with posters and white flags, that they were fed up with the guerrillas' violent actions and their kidnappings.

With the support, professionalism, and sacrifice of our armed forces, we at the Defense Ministry reacted to this nationwide clamor for peace by combating the Farc with more serious and debilitating attacks than they had ever suffered since they came into existence in the 1960s.

However, our war against the Farc—at least as I understood it—was not inspired by hate. It was not a war of extermination but a war geared toward obtaining the only noble result of any armed confrontation: peace.

I recall with particular affection the philosophy I learned from General Álvaro Valencia Tovar, a military officer who did sterling service in the Korean War and became the commander-in-chief of the National Army of Colombia. After this, as author and academic, he was finally able to give free rein to his overriding passion, that of historian. General Valencia said he did not consider the guerrillas enemies, though he had fought them for years, but simply adversaries. He explained that the term *enemy* implies that one is motivated by passion and hate, attitudes foreign to military honor.

This is fundamental: to understand that one's opponent, no matter who he or she may be, is someone like you, another human being, and not just a digit to be counted among the number of those brought down in military operations. This is a first step to humanizing a war, and eventually finishing it. A true soldier, a soldier of honor, does not combat out of hate, but to see peace triumphant.

THE CONDITIONS REQUIRED FOR A SUCCESSFUL PEACE PROCESS

During the more than ten years in which I made every effort to find a way out of the armed conflict by means of negotiation, and after studying other peace processes—both those that succeeded and those that failed—in different countries around the world, I came to the conclusion that if we were ever to gain peace in Colombia, we would do so only when we had established four indispensable conditions:

- The first was to produce a change in the correlation of strength between the guerrillas and the state—in the state's favor. So long as the guerrillas were able to successfully attack our soldiers and our police force, procure weapons and resources with relative ease, kidnap and hold in captivity hundreds of Colombians and some foreigners, too—and so long as they still believed in the possibility, however remote, of their ultimate victory—the state would have no chance of arriving at a fair agreement to end the conflict. We could not sit down to negotiate until the state's legitimate forces had achieved military and strategic strength superior to that of the guerrillas.
- The second condition would be a genuine intention on the part of the guerrillas to make peace. And this could be attained only when the guerrillas' commanders—who had so arrogantly driven their four-wheel-drive trucks around the Caguán—had come to understand, thanks to devastating blows inflicted on them by our public forces, that for them personally, and for their armed organization, it would be better to sign a peace treaty than to keep on waging a war they simply had no chance of winning. To put it bluntly, they should be brought to see clearly they had only two options to choose from: the negotiating table, on the one hand, or prison—or a grave—on the other.
- The third condition is to ensure international—and above all, regional—support. In today's asymmetrical wars it is impossible to think of victory or a fair negotiated solution if one does not count on

the participation and the support of the region. This was something we lacked during the Uribe administration, and that I, as president, set about obtaining.

- The fourth condition consists of acknowledging the existence of an internal armed conflict so as to be able to apply international humanitarian law and negotiate within the parameters of international justice, as authorized by the Statute of Rome.

However, each new day brings its own particular problems. Between the years 2006 and 2009, my period as minister for defense, I could see the moment had not come for dialogue. To attempt it, with neither a correlation of strength in the state's favor nor any indication at all that the guerrillas might be interested in peace talks, we would have been wasting our time. What we needed to do at this juncture was combat them, hit them hard, inflict damage on them with millimetric precision, so long as they continued to threaten and attack the Colombian population. The time had come for me to assume the role of what some began calling me: the Farc's executioner.

Thanks to the changes and improvements achieved in matters of intelligence, and with teamwork and the coordination of our forces, coupled with new resources obtained by means of the patrimony tax, it was not long before we began to get results.

CHAPTER 9

Checkmate for Terror

THE FALL OF HIGH-LEVEL TARGETS

This is a book about peace. I have already written one about this stage in the war,* so I won't go into too much detail here about the military strikes that changed the correlation of forces in the state's favor. One of the factors that produced this effect was a sophisticated and opportune military intelligence, employing elements such as microchips placed in clothing or other items worn by the guerrilla commanders in order to locate and attack them with absolute precision. Most operations were conducted jointly in coordination with the different forces that make up the military forces and the police. Another common factor was air strikes, which were what the guerrillas mostly feared.

The neutralization of high-value targets began, as already stated, in September 2007, when we brought down Negro Acacio in the jungle to Colombia's southeast. Acacio was the Farc's major supplier of monetary resources, explosives, and weapons, all in exchange for cocaine. In other words, he was the guerrilla capo of the drug trade.

Acacio was the man who headed negotiations with the Peruvian criminal network coordinated by Vladimiro Montesinos, intelligence chief under the Alberto Fujimori government, providing the Farc with a cargo of ten thousand AK-17 rifles that the Peruvian government had acquired in Jordan, valued at over US$11 million. The weapons were dropped, toward the end of the year 2000, in parachutes from planes flying over the jungle area where Acacio was operating. It was the largest shipment of weapons ever smuggled into the country.

---

* See Juan Manuel Santos, *Jaque al terror* [Checkmate for terror] (Bogotá: Planeta, 2009).

The Acacio operation was the first coordinated by the new Conjoint Headquarters of Special Operations (JOEC), which we had designed and created with the help of the Israelis. It concluded with the accurate bombing of the guerrilla camp. Acacio's body was not found; his own men had removed it. Days later, however, in an episode that only highlights the inhumanity of war, his intestines were discovered in the jungle. They had been cut out of his corpse so as to prevent it from decomposing, and we carried out a DNA test on them to identify the body.

A month later, in another part of the country, this time to the north in the Caribbean region, we brought down another historic leader of the Farc, Martín Caballero, who had been terrorizing the inhabitants of this beautiful and fertile region known as the Montes de María. Not only was Caballero responsible for a multitude of kidnappings and extortions, he had even had in his sights a target no other guerrilla commander had even imagined. That was in May 2002, when he planned an attempt on the life of the US president Bill Clinton during his visit to Cartagena. Fortunately, the plan was detected in time.

Accompanying the high commands of the military and the police, I myself traveled to Carmen de Bolívar, a town in the center of the Montes de María, to show the results of the operation, because people were refusing to believe that Martín Caballero had actually been eliminated. There, at the aerodrome, were the black bags containing the bodies of twenty guerrillas killed in action, among them that of their nefarious leader. The most impressive proof of how degrading the war had become was the relief and delight of the population who reacted with applause and shouts of approval when we put Caballero's corpse on display. After many years of violence and intimidation, the region of the Montes de María began to become an example of economic recovery, reconciliation, and peace.

Other commanders of guerrilla fronts began to fall like a house of cards. One of them was alias JJ, the scourge of the Pacific Ocean region, who had been the brains behind (and the person to carry out) the kidnapping of twelve deputies from the Valle del Cauca Departmental Assembly. We also captured Martín Sombra, one of the guerrilla's historic leaders, who had been with Manuel Marulanda since 1966, and more recently had been in charge of the Farc's concentration camps, where hundreds of kidnapped civilians and members of the armed forces had been kept locked up for years. Sombra was known as the Jailer. We also achieved the demobilization of Karina, a bloodthirsty guerrilla who operated in Antioquia and the departments of

Colombia's coffee-growing region. These are just a few among many guerrilla commanders and subcommanders who were put out of action in the course of just three years.

However, the most important aspect of all this, the mission that took priority for President Uribe and for me, was that of demoralizing the guerrillas as much as we possibly could. This meant getting at the guerrilla leaders, the members of their high command—what they called their secretariat—which consisted of Marulanda and another six commanders.

We got our chance on March 1, 2008, with the high-precision bombing of a camp that housed Raúl Reyes, the Farc's foreign affairs man. His international contacts were what helped us locate him. He was responsible for multiple attacks and kidnappings and was wanted for extradition to the United States for his drug trade activities. As I said earlier, I met Reyes in Costa Rica in 1997, when conversing with different illegal groups in search of a formula that might enable us to begin peace negotiations. I caught up with him again at Caguán in 1998, when I visited the demilitarized zone while engaged in the thankless task entrusted to me by President Pastrana.

Operation Phoenix, which put an end to Reyes and some of his men, and in which we confiscated computers full of valuable information on the guerrillas' financial operations and their contacts with the governments of Venezuela and Ecuador, was a combined operation of the air force, the army, and the police. Another aspect of the operation was to cause us serious diplomatic problems: the guerrilla chief's camp we bombed was inside Ecuador, less than two kilometers from the Colombian border.

On the subject of how exactly that operation was carried out and how we handled the ensuing problems with Ecuador, I'll give more details later, when I refer to our complex relations with Venezuela and Ecuador, with their leaders Hugo Chávez and Rafael Correa, and what effect these had on the peace process. For the moment, it is sufficient to highlight the fact that the death of Reyes, the first member of the Farc's secretariat we had brought down, was a milestone in our conflict with that guerrilla organization. It showed, for the first time in four decades, that the guerrilla's top commanders were not untouchable, that we were capable of reaching them.

Just three days after this operation, another member of the secretariat died. This time it was Iván Ríos, who met his end in strange and macabre circumstances. He was marauding with a group of combatants in the coffee-growing region. He had asked Karina, who commanded a different group in the same area, to send him a man whom she trusted to take charge of his personal bodyguards. This special envoy Karina sent was a man called Rojas, who had no qualms when it came to killing. From that moment on, he was constantly beside his new chief. He became Ríos's shadow.

Ríos and his men were under great pressure, and when they heard of the bombing of Reyes's camp, their morale was at an all-time low. That was the moment when Rojas, Ríos's right-hand man, decided to murder Ríos and then give himself up. And this he did, on the night of March 3. While Ríos and his companion, Andrea, were asleep in their tent, Rojas crept up silently and shot them at close range. The most disgusting part of the story is that Rojas, to prove he had killed his chief, cut off Ríos's hand and gave it, wrapped in a handkerchief, to the army colonel who demobilized him. That shows how cruel and absurd war can be.

But that was not the end of bad news for the Farc. In late March 2008, while the air force was engaged in continual bombing of the guerrillas' security rings, Marulanda, their founder and top leader, died of a heart attack. Marulanda was seventy-seven years old, and most of those years he had spent in combat against the state. In May, the Farc announced the name of their new supreme leader: Alfonso Cano, a member of the secretariat.

So, in less than one month, the Farc, whose principal leaders had for decades evaded the guns of the armed forces, had lost three of the seven members of their secretariat: Manuel Marulanda, their founder; Raúl Reyes, their foreign affairs representative, and Iván Ríos. All we needed now was to deal a deathblow. What followed was perhaps the most spectacular and devastating operation on record in Colombia's military history: Operation Checkmate.

OPERATION CHECKMATE: OBJECT OF NATIONAL PRIDE

For me there's one special day, among more than one thousand I spent at the defense ministry. It's a day I'll never forget because of what it meant for fifteen human beings and for the country. And for me, too, who had put my political capital on the line in taking a very risky bet. That day was July 2, 2008, when Operation Checkmate was carried out with outstanding success.

On that unforgettable Wednesday, an elite command made up of officers from military intelligence experts, civilian intelligence agents, pilots and air technicians from the army, and also one demobilized former guerrilla fighter, put down their helicopter in a remote region of the jungle in the department of Guaviare, near the Inírida River. In the guise of an international humanitarian mission and without firing a single shot, they snatched from the Farc's clutches fifteen kidnapped men and women being held captive, including the former presidential candidate Ingrid Betancourt, three US contractors, and eight Colombian soldiers and policemen who had been languishing half-dead in the jungle.

It was a masterstroke, a perfectly executed operation, as Betancourt called it in one of her first statements after being freed. And it was a tremendous relief, an injection of hope and joy for all Colombians who had lived in expectation of what might be the final outcome for these and other victims of kidnapping.

A great deal has been written about Operation Checkmate, and a lot of people have spoken of it and seen videos of what took place. It has been the subject of several books, of national and international documentaries, and even a television series.* That is my excuse for not giving an exhaustive account here of how our forces planned and executed what military intelligence worldwide looked on as a model operation.

No sooner did news get out on the operation than tongues began wagging about how it must have been planned and executed by foreign intelligence agencies, since a lot of people did not believe it possible that such an extraordinary result could be achieved solely with our own Colombian resources and technical ability.

On this subject we should make a distinction. In general, Colombian military intelligence owes a great deal, in training and technical contributions, to the support and consultancy of countries such as Israel, the United Kingdom, and especially the United States. Thanks to them, we achieved levels of precision and sophistication in matters of intelligence that would have been unthinkable a few years earlier. Without those years of training and cooperation, it would not have been possible to carry out an operation like the one we executed to free those victims. Having said that, it must be understood that, in the concrete case of Operation Checkmate, the planning and gestation—plus the execution of electronic deception that enabled us to infiltrate and supplant Farc's communication system, coupled with the preparation and realization of the rescue mission on the ground—were all activities carried out exclusively by Colombian personnel.

---

* The most detailed account of this operation, including testimonies of those involved, can be found in Juan Carlos Torres, *Operación Jaque: la verdadera historia* (Bogotá: Planeta, 2008).

At a certain moment, just a week before we carried out the operation, I invited the US ambassador William Brownfield to my apartment to tell him what we had planned. President Uribe had promised President George W. Bush that he would advise him of any operation that might involve the three Americans being held hostage. So I was complying with the president's promise. Also present at that meeting were General Freddy Padilla de León and two embassy officials, the local CIA agent, and an expert in military operations.

The ambassador's immediate reaction was one of incredulity and skepticism. However, he offered to consult with experts on the matter and report back to us in twenty-four hours. By contrast, the CIA man was optimistic. "If what you're telling me is true," he said, "then I take my hat off to Colombian intelligence. Wow! It's incredible!"

After consulting with people at the White House, Ambassador Brownfield offered us whatever help we might think necessary. This assistance was given concrete form in two ways: first, the US experts helped us install sophisticated components that made it possible for the helicopter's pilots to communicate with the men on the ground, who would pass themselves off as officials of an international agency for cooperation; secondly, the United States provided an airplane that served as intelligence platform. Keeping itself out of sight of the guerrillas, this plane monitored communications and served as a bridge between the helicopter and the command centers.

This highly technical assistance was approved, two days before the operation, in an extraordinary meeting of the US National Security Council at the White House. The following were present: Vice-President Dick Cheney; Defense Secretary Robert Gates; the chairman of the joint chiefs of staff, Admiral Mike Mullen; the director of the Central Intelligence Agency, General Michael Hayden; the secretary of homeland security, Michael Chertoff; the deputy secretary of state, John Negroponte; and the national security adviser, Stephen J. Hadley. Another official who took part via telephone was the US southern commander, Admiral James Stavidris.

One other important US politician who was informed of the operation just a few hours before we went into action was Senator John McCain, who was at the time running for president as the Republican Party candidate, competing against the Democratic Party candidate, Barack Obama. McCain had arrived in Cartagena on July 1 on a lightning tour that took in Colombia and Mexico. That night he met with President Uribe at the Colombian presidential guesthouse in Cartagena. Among those present were Colombia's foreign affairs minister, Fernando Araujo; our ambassador in Washington, Carolina Barco; and myself. Senator McCain was accompanied by his wife Cindy, the Democratic senator Joe Lieberman, and the Republican senator Lindsey Graham, as well as Ambassador Brownfield.

I had a good relationship with McCain. I had met him on several visits to Washington and we had coincided at the International Conference on Security in Munich in February 2007, where we both insisted on the importance of the fight against the drug trade as a means of cutting off resources that were fueling terrorism.

That night my mind was somewhere else; I could think of nothing but the extremely risky rescue operation we had planned for the following day. After a working meeting, when we got up to go to dinner, I asked President Uribe if he thought it a good idea to tell McCain of the operation, given that he was the possible next president of the United States. Uribe agreed, and so it was that, on our way to the dining room, I said to McCain that I had something important to tell him. He called to his colleagues Lieberman and Graham, and I gave the three of them an idea, in general terms, of the operation we were about to launch. "My God!" exclaimed McCain. "This is spectacular! I wish you every success!" I insisted on confidentiality regarding what I had just told them, and we went on to dinner amid expressions of support and good wishes from the senators.

The next day, in the late afternoon, when McCain was on a flight from Cartagena to Mexico, he got a call from President Uribe to let him know that those kidnapped by the guerrillas, including the three Americans, had been set free. If he had delayed a few hours more in Colombia, McCain could have gone back to the states with his liberated compatriots, which no doubt would have bolstered his presidential campaign.

So that was the extent of foreign participation. Operation Checkmate was carried out by a combination of creativity, talent, and courage on the part of officers and junior officers working with army intelligence agents under the leadership of their commanders, Generals Montoya and Padilla de León, plus my political decision as minister and the support of President Uribe. It was a proudly Colombian operation, up there with the most sophisticated and daring rescue operations undertaken anywhere in the world. And with a component almost never seen in such an event: there were no victims, and the rescue was carried out without a single shot being fired. It was a genuine intelligence operation.

THE LONGEST MINUTES OF MY LIFE

The operation was planned in a way that did not put at risk the lives of those we intended to rescue. But there were certain elements involved that easily could have failed. It was far from being a safe bet, but rather a daring and complex adventure. But we had to give it a try. The ones who did risk their lives were the men and women who took part in the mission of deceit and rescue. And that was something that never ceased to worry me. Besides, I was very aware that if the mission were to fail, I would have to accept full responsibility and hand in my resignation. But at that moment my political capital was the least of my concerns. I was engaged in trying to save fifteen people from a nightmare that had lasted for years, and at the same time deprive the guerrillas of their most precious bounty.

Wednesday, July 2, 2008, was a day that began with the utmost tension and ended in jubilant celebration. From six o'clock in the morning, I was in touch with General Montoya, who was in control of the operation from Guaviare, and with General Padilla de León, commander of the military forces. I stayed in my office at the ministry, called off all appointments, and continually received coded messages informing me of what was going on. I remember that very early in the day I spoke on the phone with my wife, María Clemencia, who was in Paris with our daughter María Antonia. Of course, she had no idea of what we were up to. I just told her that something very big was going to happen and that I wanted her to go to the Church of the Miraculous Virgin in the Rue de Bac and pray that everything would turn out for the best.

The operation was such a carefully guarded secret that only on that morning did I call up Admiral David René Moreno, joint chief of staff of the military forces, and General Óscar Naranjo, director of the police force, to tell them of the operation. We had lunch together in my office, waiting for news of the outcome. Without giving any explanation, I ordered my head of communications to organize a press conference. Whatever the outcome might be, I would have to face the nation and give a report. At half past one in the afternoon, General Padilla informed me that the helicopter had landed at the place in the jungle where the kidnap victims were to be picked up. If everything went as planned, it would be on the ground for not more than ten minutes. So when more than twenty minutes had gone by, our anxiety had reached breaking point. They were the longest minutes of my life. Finally, just before two o'clock, Padilla called me and said: "They're off!" Three minutes later, he gave me the good news with just one word: "Neutralized."

I rang the president at once to report the mission's success. He only managed to say, "Thank God! That's wonderful! Congratulations!" before he got cut off. My second phone call was to his wife, First Lady Lina Moreno, since I had promised to let her know as soon as I had good news; and the third was to Yolanda Pulecio, Ingrid Betancourt's mother, who had been planning to leave for France that day, though we had managed to dissuade her from traveling without being able to tell her exactly why. I sent María Clemencia a text message: "Total success. The kidnapped are free." Now she knew why I had her praying to the Miraculous Virgin.

On the afternoon of that July 2, I announced to the Colombian people the news we had all been waiting on for four years: "I am pleased to be able to make the following announcement to public opinion, both national and international: In a special intelligence operation, planned and executed by our military intelligence, fifteen of the prisoners being held captive by the Farc have been set free and are safe and sound. Among them are Ingrid Betancourt, three American citizens, and eleven members of our armed forces."

In a gesture I had never seen before at a press conference, the journalists applauded every time I mentioned the names of those who had been rescued. I went on:

> They were rescued in an operation in which we managed to infiltrate the Farc's number one front commanded by alias César, the same band of felons who for years has held a numerous group of kidnap victims in its power.
>
> Through various procedures, we also managed to infiltrate the secretariat. Although the kidnap victims were divided into three groups, we managed to get them together in one place and then facilitated their being removed to the south, where they were supposedly to be placed under the direct orders of Alfonso Cano.
>
> The helicopter, in fact, belonged to the Colombian army, and its crew members were highly qualified members of our intelligence. They picked up the victims near the department of Guaviare a few minutes ago and are now flying free, safe and sound, to San José del Guaviare. There they will board a plane that will take them to the military base at Tolemaida.
>
> Alias César and other members of his band of outlaws were neutralized in the helicopter and will be handed over to the judicial authorities to be tried for their criminal acts. As for the other members of the band who accompanied César in handing over the prisoners, . . . and others who were a few kilometers away, we decided not to attack them and to respect their

lives in the hope that the Farc will make a reciprocal gesture and release the rest of the kidnap victims they are holding.

The operation, which we called Operation Checkmate, has no precedent and will go down in history because of its daring and its effectiveness, which demonstrate the high quality and professionalism of the Colombian Armed Forces.

Fifteen kidnap victims rescued without a single shot being fired.

My most sincere congratulations go to our army's intelligence men, to General Mario Montoya, their commander, and to General Freddy Padilla, who was at the head of the operation from beginning to end. The country, the world and the loved ones of the victims will never be able to adequately thank those generals and their men for having carried out such an outstanding rescue operation.

We will continue to work night and day to free the remaining hostages, Once again we call on the new leaders of the Farc to lay down their weapons and not continue to let themselves be killed nor sacrifice their men. Let them demobilize.

THE EFFECTS OF OPERATION CHECKMATE

The kidnapping of Ingrid Betancourt, which occurred on February 23, 2002, three days after President Pastrana called off the peace talks in Caguán, had special repercussions overseas. Betancourt was not only a presidential candidate in Colombia, she was also a French citizen, celebrated for her publications and her unremitting fight against corruption. She had worked with me at the Foreign Trade Ministry and was a close personal friend.

News of her liberation, after more than six years of despicable captivity, had moved not only Colombia but France also, and the international community as a whole. I spoke by telephone with the French president Nicolas Sarkozy from the tarmac of the military airport where the freed hostages touched down, to give him the good news. There was great rejoicing, too, in the United States for the rescue of the three American contractors who had been prisoners in the jungle for almost five years.

After a press conference in which the liberated prisoners, the commanders of the military forces and the army, and I myself had a few words to say, I went from the Catam military airport in Bogotá to the ministry, where an invitation was waiting for me to appear live on the Larry King show on the US channel CNN. Larry King was on air communicating with the plane on which Ambassador Brownfield and the three liberated Americans were flying to San Antonio, Texas. I got to my office just in time to take part in the program.

The famous interviewer asked me if I thought the rescue operation could compare with the famous rescue carried out by Israeli forces at Entebbe, Uganda, in 1976. I said ours had been much better, because not a drop of blood had been shed. King hesitated a moment, and then said: "You're quite right." At the end of the program he concluded: "It's a great day for the Americans." And so it was. But not just for them. It was a day of celebration for the Colombians and for defenders of freedom everywhere.

King commented to me later, when we were off the air, that all his life he had studied military intelligence operations—it was a kind of hobby—and that this one was perhaps the most spectacular of all, precisely because it was done without weapons and without the loss of a single human life. That gave me great satisfaction, because it showed what a great and positive change the culture of our armed forces had undergone in matters of human rights. It was our own commanders—Generals Padilla and Montoya—who suggested that we should not attack the three hundred or more guerrilla combatants who remained on the ground when the helicopter took off. "They'll feel it all the more," said General Padilla. "And we'll be better—and *feel* better—for it."

Operation Checkmate delivered a lethal blow to the Farc, probably more debilitating than the deaths of Reyes, Ríos, and Marulanda—all of which occurred in March of the same year, 2008—and worse than Karina's demobilization in May. It was the turning point, which would eventually bring them to the negotiating table four years later, no longer exhibiting the arrogance of men who believe they are invincible.

On the one hand, the Farc realized that their communications system, their codes and their frequencies, which they had been developing and perfecting over many years, were vulnerable and were being monitored by our intelligence corps. After the bombing of the Reyes camp, they had ceased to make use of satellite telephones to communicate among themselves; now they could not even trust their own radio communications. This meant they had to go back to the old-fashioned human courier system that might not reach their destination, or might arrive too late. This situation aggravated a problem they had already been facing: a loss of command and control over their own men.

In the field of political blackmail that the Farc had presumed to exert by holding kidnap victims they considered "exchangeable," this loss left them immeasurably weakened. Of the approximately sixty hostages who had once been held under these conditions, they had lost eleven deputies from the Valle del Cauca Assembly—assassinated by the guerrillas themselves—plus others they released as a unilateral concession to strengthen the role as intermediaries played by President Chávez and Senator Piedad Córdoba. With Operation Checkmate they lost fifteen more, including four whom the guerrillas considered to be their most valuable playing cards because of their resonance internationally: the Colombo-French citizen Ingrid Betancourt, and the three Americans.

The guerrillas had achieved a certain notoriety and an international profile thanks to their dealing directly with heads of state of such countries as France, Venezuela, and Ecuador mediating in the efforts of these governments to free the hostages. The guerrilla leaders were convinced that in this way they would gain the status of belligerents, a kind of juridical recognition by the international community. But this hope was dashed also with the July 2 successful rescue mission.

France's celebrated citizen was now enjoying her freedom, the United States had retrieved its three citizens, and Venezuela and Ecuador—after the emails found on Reyes's computer became known and were authenticated by Interpol—began to distance themselves from the Colombian guerrillas, at least in their official declarations.

The Farc guerrillas' intention of being recognized as belligerents was not really a viable proposition, since they did not occupy a territory nor did they respect the norms of international humanitarian law, which were indispensable requisites for obtaining this status. The matter was filed away. And their proposal to demand a demilitarized zone of almost eight hundred square kilometers in municipalities near Cali where they would negotiate a humanitarian agreement to free their kidnap victims was simply forgotten.

In fact, in 2007, President Uribe had offered the Farc, in exchange for the liberation of the hostages, a terrain where they could gather and negotiate over a period of ninety days. None of this was necessary now, thanks to Operation Checkmate.

THE WAR I WAGED, I WAGED FOR PEACE

In the book I published in 2009, where I described the blows we dealt to the Farc in the course of the three years I was at the head of the Defense Ministry, I ended with the following conclusion:

The horrible years of the Farc, the annus horribilis that I have recounted in these pages, began toward the end of 2006 and, it is to be expected, will not end until the moment when this organization comes to its senses—after being debilitated militarily and by the pressure of the national and international communities—and decides to initiate a sincere process, with no marked cards, with the intention of definitively renouncing weapons, kidnappings, terrorist acts, and violence aimed at their compatriots and at the nation's infrastructure.

It is some time since Colombia's democracy became mature enough to incorporate into its system all those who have paid their dues to society and are ready to participate in political debate and in the building of a country at peace. Constituents, ministers, governors, mayors, congressmen and women, directors of public entities, diplomats, and presidential candidates who once took up arms against the state and later decided to return to civilian life are the best example of how this is possible.

I have already quoted some paragraphs from my December 2016 Nobel Prize address in Oslo, where I explained that it is sometimes necessary to make war, but I also say that war cannot be an end in itself, but a means. A means for what? There's only one answer: for obtaining peace.

The war that does not lead to peace, although you may win it, is really lost. That's why my period as a "hawk," when I confronted with determination and a firm hand those who were attacking the Colombian people and damaging their resources, the era in which I was known as "Farc's executioner," does not contradict my lifelong conviction that true peace, stable and lasting peace, can be achieved only through dialogue.

As minister for defense, I managed to make progress in the two first conditions that can lead to a successful peace negotiation: that the correlation of strength inclines in favor of the state, and the guerrilla commanders realize they will never achieve their aims by the use of weapons.

The war I waged, I waged for peace. After years of accompanying the widows and orphans of my soldiers and policemen as they bid farewell to their loved ones fallen in combat, and after witnessing in every corner of Colombia the pain and misery caused by violence, I could not pretend that war would be the ultimate solution and bring the guerrilla conflict to an end.

It is true that we had weakened them, that we had reduced more than twenty thousand men in arms to less than ten thousand. But to extinguish them entirely, to bring them to surrender, would take many years, maybe decades, and that would mean more years of death, pain, and poverty and a lack of opportunities for millions of compatriots in the country, the jungles, the frontier zones of our country.

My time at the Defense Ministry brought me a good deal of popularity among Colombians, because there's nothing as popular as showing the trophies of war, of holding up and exhibiting the enemy's bloody head. But this in no way led me to the conclusion that I should continue the war to its ultimate consequences. On the contrary, it only confirmed to me my decision to search for peace through negotiation, even more so when the conditions for a fruitful dialogue began to appear.

Some years later, when peace with the Farc was an accomplished fact, I restated this personal conviction in my speech at Oslo: "A final victory through force—when nonviolent alternatives exist—is none other than the defeat of the human spirit."

LESSON 1

To Achieve a Favorable Correlation of Strength

The Farc were never so strong, nor believed themselves to be so strong, as when the Caguán peace talks began in the first days of 1999. They could boast the greatest number of combatants ever, while money from kidnappings, extortion, and the drug trade poured into the coffers; their members proudly displayed modern weapons and spanking new uniforms, and they had successfully moved from guerrilla warfare tactics to a war of positions, holding in their power, for three days, the city of Mitú, capital of a Colombian department. In addition, they had the upper hand as far as hostages went, since in their most recent armed incursions they had taken prisoner hundreds of soldiers and policemen, including military officers of various rankings.

Colombia's armed forces, on their side, were acting more on the defensive than the offensive. They were operating under the restrictions imposed by the national budget, and kept to their traditional mode of operations with the soldiers cooped up in army quarters and battalions while the guerrillas moved around the country at will. The guerrilla leaders felt they were untouchable.

In these conditions, it is not surprising that peace talks had failed. A guerrilla group that is arrogant and sure of itself, and has more triumphs than defeats to show in its recent history, does not sit down at the negotiating table to seriously discuss its demobilization, disarmament, and reincorporation into civil society. If it agrees to dialogue, it does so under its own conditions, imposing the agenda and almost certainly taking advantage of the state's willingness to make peace as an opportunity to grow in strengthen militarily and to gain notoriety among the public, and internationally too.

The following clear lesson was to be learned from the Caguán process: that when the correlation of forces between the guerrillas and the state does not incline in the state's favor, any peace talks are fruitless. And why is this so? Because the guerrillas—or any other illegal armed group—so long as it is convinced it will be able, at least in the long run, to achieve its objective by force of arms, is not going to progress toward a negotiated settlement that would imply making concessions such as giving up its weapons, being placed on trial, and paying an indemnity to its victims. This is a perfectly obvious truth.

One essential difference between the Caguán process (1999–2002) and the Havana peace talks (2012–2016) can be seen in the fact that, when this latter process began, the state was in a position of clear advantage in the correlation of forces vis-à-vis the guerrillas.

To reach this point, it had been necessary to endow the armed forces with a bigger budget, and this was achieved thanks to resources supplied by the United States through Plan Colombia plus a considerable slice of the national budget that I, as finance minister, was able to assign to the armed forces, enhanced by a tax to finance the Democratic Security program during President Uribe's first term of office, and the patrimony tax that we had approved in his second term, and which was prolonged into my own administration. With these increased resources, the army grew in numbers and professional training, military and police facilities were improved, and the military acquired the most up-to-date technology in weaponry and equipment.

In addition, political will is needed to combat the guerrillas confrontationally and with decision, and this was sustained throughout the two presidential terms of Uribe, and also during mine, even while peace talks were being held. In fact, the greater part of the peace process was carried out as the conflict continued.

Finally, we needed a total restructuring of intelligence and of the operational strength of the armed forces so as to become more effective and able to attack at last the targets of greatest strategic importance. This was achieved thanks to consultation with the world's most expert intelligence corps, and by applying a centralized system of coordination against the said targets that guaranteed harmonious collaboration between the military and the police force. All of this, plus the Comprehensive Policy on Human Rights and International Humanitarian Law, was my main legacy from my time at the Ministry of Defense.

By combining all these elements over a sufficient lapse of time, the balance of correlation of forces inclined in favor of the state.

In short, it is not a matter of winning the war by exterminating the enemy or taking prisoners down to the very last member of your enemy's organization. This could take decades and would lead to an infinite number of victims, and to human suffering that any head of state is obliged to avoid. It is simply a question of inclining the balance so that the insurgency's commanders come to understand that their best way out—in fact their *only* way out—is by means of negotiation.

PART THREE

The Secret Phase (2010–2012)

CHAPTER 10

"Betrayal"

THAT DAMNABLE TEMPTATION

The problem with caudillos—and I mentioned this earlier when referring to the dictatorship of General Gustavo Rojas Pinilla in the mid-twentieth century—is that they always end up surrendering to the temptation of wanting to hold on to power forever. Somewhere along the line, they begin to feel they are indispensable and they make people believe it, and so they come to the messianic and antidemocratic conclusion that there is only one person capable of running the state.

In Africa, quite a few nations have endured, and some still continue to endure, a sole leader in power over periods of two, three, or even more decades in regimes almost invariably characterized by corruption and the violation of basic human rights. But this is not an exclusively African phenomenon. Today we see some of the world's great powers affected by the same syndrome. Vladimir Putin has been at the head of government in Russia since 2002, and was reelected for a new term that will keep him in office until 2024. Now, thanks to the referendum voted in July 2020, he is allowed to run again for president for two more terms, so he could remain in power until 2036. And in China, they have done away with the limitation of two consecutive periods for a president, which would seem to suggest that Xi Jinping will stay at the helm for a very long time to come.

Latin America is no exception. In recent times, Cuba has led the way in this regard, with two brothers, Fidel and Raúl Castro, holding on to power for almost six decades, beginning in 1959. In a sense, Raúl is still holding the reins despite the fact that Miguel Díaz-Canel was appointed president in 2019. Other Latin American countries are going down the same track, beginning with Venezuela, where the Chavista regime has been in power since 1999, and President Nicolás Maduro, in government since 2013, organized blatantly manipulated elections to get himself reinstated for another term that will not end until the year 2025. Something similar is occuring in Nicaragua with the disgraceful regime of Daniel Ortega, who, having been president from 1985 to 1990, contrived to get himself elected again in 2007, sharing power this time with his wife as vice-president. In Bolivia, Evo Morales, who had been in the presidency since 2006, tried to get a fourth term in office and ended up resigning in November 2019. Ecuador had to call for a referendum to do away with indefinite reelection in order to frustrate Rafael Correa's hopes of returning to the Carondelet Palace after having been in power for over ten years.

Colombia has not been fertile ground for caudillos. Our fundamental tendency toward democracy combined with the multiplicity of leaders with both the ability and the possibility of directing the nation's fortunes has served as an antidote against this temptation. In the course of the twentieth century, under the 1886 constitution, only one nonconsecutive period was allowed to an elected president. And the only person to seek—and actually win—the presidency a second time was Alfonso López Pumarejo who had been president from 1934 to 1938 and was reelected for the period 1942–1946, although he did not complete this second presidency. Alberto Lleras Camargo, in his capacity as presidential designate, replaced him and governed for a year, and then later was elected at the ballot box to serve as first president of the National Front from 1958 to 1962. Others, such as Carlos Lleras Restrepo and Alfonso López Michelsen, of unquestioned merits both political and intellectual, made unsuccessful bids to return to power. Finally, the 1991 Constitution roundly forbad any reelection.

As has already said, President Álvaro Uribe, elected initially for the period 2002–2006, managed to get Congress to reform the constitution—by simply altering one little article—to get himself reelected for another four-year period. I myself, from my position in the Party of the U, agreed with this initiative because, like a lot of Colombians, I was convinced that the policy of Democratic Security that Uribe was carrying out merited another four years to consolidate the necessary correlation of forces, which was beginning to incline in the state's favor.

However, the caudillo virus is contagious, and so Uribe—like other presidents in the neighborhood—decided to look for a way to get himself reelected for a third term. He had already once said, in a meeting with those members of Congress who formed part of his government's coalition, that he did not think it appropriate that a president should hold on to power and that reelection should only be necessary in case of an imminent catastrophe.

Well, it seems he thought a catastrophe was pending. That is the usual pretext of a caudillo: to convince people the country will collapse if his leadership is not prolonged. Uribe, therefore, gave his approval to a plan, proposed by the Party of the U, to collect signatures of citizens in favor of calling for a referendum to change the constitution and allow for a second reelection. The referendum project was voted for in Congress and sent to the Constitutional Court for its rubber stamp. However, on February 26, 2010, the court denied the measure its approval.

The court considered that doubts about the way the campaign for signatures had been conducted and the manner in which the process was pushed through parliament amounted to serious irregularities. But even further, the court found that a second reelection would violate principles such as the separation of powers, equality, and the democratic practice of alternation in power, as well as endangering the system of political weights and counterweights established in the 1991 Constitution.

That, among other things, is why the division of powers exists: to avoid the situation where one of the constituted powers claims excessive prerogatives and puts at risk the indispensable democratic equilibrium. Luckily, the Constitutional Court saved Colombia from the contagious effects produced by caudillos in the region.

In 2014, I presented a constitutional reform—which was approved in 2015—to eliminate again the reelection of presidents, and thus we went back to what had existed as of the 1991 Constitution. And to make it even more watertight, this prohibition could be lifted only by means of a referendum on popular demand or a constituent assembly, but never by Congress.

Perhaps from a historical viewpoint—and this has been the opinion of certain analysts—the reelection of Uribe in 2006 was necessary because of exceptional circumstances, as was mine in 2014. In the first case, a lapse of eight years was required to ensure the continuance of Uribe's priority policy of Democratic Security that debilitated the guerrillas; and in the second, without abandoning the practice of Democratic Security, eight years more were needed to arrive at the negotiating table and get peace talks under way with the Farc. Once we had completed this task, essential for the country's future, I was convinced we should return the waters of democracy to their normal riverbed, with different and alternative governments succeeding one another, based on institutions and not on individuals. That is what guarantees an efficient system of weights and counterweights and the healthy rotation of political leadership.

I confess I would have preferred that the presidential period, now with reelection excluded, should be of five years rather than four, so that each president would have a slightly greater margin in which to maneuver. But this idea did not find acceptance in Congress, so, in the matter of reelection—or better said, of nonreelection—we ended up returning to things as they were in 1991.

AT THE SEAFRONT IN CARTAGENA

As for me, after thirty-four months as defense minister, I resigned in May 2009 in order to be eligible to run for president in the 2010 elections. I was very well aware that if Uribe managed to get his way and reform the constitution with an eye to getting himself elected for the third time running, no other candidate would really have a chance. His popularity was still very high, in great measure due to the damage he had inflicted on the guerrillas and the drug traffickers, thanks to our improvement in matters of intelligence and military operations.

However, I knew it would not be easy for him to get approval for a second reelection; a great many signatures had to be gathered, Congress had to give its approval, and, again, the Constitutional Court would have to validate the proposal. I knew, too, that if Uribe did not run, the way would be open for other candidates, and I could be among them.

I spent my time writing a book on the strategic strikes with which we had hit the Farc during my time at the Defense Ministry. The book was launched in December 2009, and I waited patiently for destiny to play its cards. Meanwhile, on January 26, 2010, I assumed the leadership of the Party of the U, which I had founded four and a half years previously. Journalists constantly asked me if I was going to run for president, and I invariably gave them the same answer: if Uribe is not going to be in the race, then I'll give it serious thought. Contrary to what many people have suggested, I was not ever totally convinced, in my heart of hearts, that I really wanted the presidency. Or to put it another way: if things didn't turn out that way, I was not going to feel frustrated or give myself over to tears and lamentations.

Exactly one month later, on February 29, 2010, when it was announced that the Constitutional Court had declared unconstitutional the law calling the referendum to approve the second reelection, I was attending an event at the convention center in Cartagena. When I heard the news, I withdrew from the meeting and spent some time contemplating the waters of the bay, lost in thought. That was the moment when, for the first time, I really felt it might be possible that I could become the president of Colombia.

Up to that moment, I had played with the idea; I had dreamed of seeing my name on one of those lists of presidential hopefuls or precandidates the media likes to present to the public. But I had never seriously believed that I would attain such an exalted post. I had been minister three times but I had never submitted my name as a candidate for the popular vote. The only electoral process I had been part of was when Congress chose me as presidential designate. Furthermore, I often thought that my surname and my relationship with President Eduardo Santos, a well-remembered head of government in the mid-twentieth century, plus my belonging to the family that owned the country's most influential and widely read daily paper, would be seen as a handicap, not an advantage, when it came to winning popular support at the ballot box. For a lot of people, despite anything I might have achieved personally, I represented the elite who had never ceased to hold power in Colombia. My candidacy smacked of nepotism.

Apropos, I recall an anecdote with my friend and professor Carlos Fuentes, who should have been awarded the Nobel Prize in Literature. Once, when we were dining with our wives at one of London's best restaurants, Simpson's in the Strand, enjoying their famous roast beef, I complained because in a futuristic novel, *La silla del águila* (*The Eagle's Throne*), published in 2003, Fuentes had written that I would be president of Colombia in 2020, and this had caused considerable laughter and leg-pulling among my friends. Fuentes stood up and said: "How old do you think I am?" He certainly looked to be in great shape. "I am older than you'll be in 2020. Don't you think that, at my age, I would be a better president than the clown we have right now in Mexico?" He was referring to Vicente Fox, not exactly his favorite.

"But that's not the point," he went on. "Tell your friends that when you're going to be president, everyone wants to invite you out. They coddle you, praise you. And when you do become president, they all criticize you and hit you over the head because you're not fulfilling your campaign promises. And when you leave the presidency, nobody even answers your telephone call. So what I'm doing is prolonging your happy life."

Maybe that's what I really wanted: to keep dreaming and hoping, but without having to take on such enormous responsibility. Nonetheless, at that moment, contemplating the majestic Caribbean Sea, I felt that the dream I had always thought of as something far away in the distance might, in fact, become a reality.

I recalled what my admired friend and counselor Alfonso Palacio Rudas had said to me twenty years ago when he pointed out the difference between people who have influence—such as the director of a newspaper—and people who have power—like those who sign decrees—and told me that my vocation was to make things happen. I realized the time had come to attempt to get things done if I could attain to the nation's highest post.

THE PRESIDENTIAL CAMPAIGN

And it seemed to be written in the stars. On March 9, 2010, I was designated presidential candidate for the Party of the U, and on March 14, while I was still acting as the party's president, we obtained a resounding victory in legislative elections. The party was consolidated as the leading political force in Congress, rising from twenty to twenty-eight senators, and from twenty-eight to forty-eight members in the lower house.

We ran a lightning presidential campaign of just two and a half months, since we had lost time waiting for a decision by the Constitutional Court. My competitors were Antanas Mockus of the Green Party; Germán Vargas Lleras of Radical Change; Noemí Sanín of the Conservative Party; Gustavo Petro of Alternative Democratic Pole; and Rafael Pardo of the Liberal Party.

I ran my candidacy on a central platform—endorsed by the party that had promoted the reelection of Uribe and most hotly defended his legacy—namely, to continue Uribe's policies in matters of public security, the promoting of confidence for investors, and social inclusion. I was totally convinced that this was right. Because of my results as defense minister, I represented a firm hand in fighting illegal armed groups, beginning with the Farc. And in economic and social matters, I proposed progressive reforms that had their origin in a concept I have always considered responsible: to build on what already exists.

If there is one thing that causes harm to a society it is that each new head of government comes to power with what is called "the Adam complex," convinced he is beginning from scratch and that the country will really start to find its feet at last as of the moment he takes possession of the presidency. This is a mentality that does not allow long-range policies to take effect, when in reality those are the ones that can genuinely transform a nation. For my part, I was ready to carry on and improve the best policies and programs of the man who went before me, and to launch new ones that would leave my own personal stamp on the government.

As candidate for vice-president I chose Angelino Garzón, a social leader, ex-union organizer, and former governor of the department of Valle del Cauca, with whom I had shared a place in the Pastrana government's cabinet, when Garzón was minister for labor and I was minister for finance. Garzón had accompanied me, also, in several groups of analysis in search of a dialogued solution to the armed conflict. I chose him as running mate on the theory of complementary contraries since he, as a man of humble beginnings and a unionist, represented a different sector of society and might attract votes that I would find hard to win.

Not many people know that, before offering the vice-presidency to Garzón, I had suggested it to a businessman from Barranquilla, Antonio Celia, who had the advantage of being from the Caribbean coast—and therefore complementary to me, born and bred in the capital—and a manager of indisputable probity and efficacy, with notable social sensitivity, who had converted Promigás into the country's most important company in the gas business. Celia thanked me for the offer but did not accept, since he was committed to the development of his company. It was a shame, because as it turned out, Garzón was not up to the task expected of him.

As things went, on May 30 I won first place in the first round of elections, with 47 percent of the votes. If I had gained over 50 percent, a second round would not have been necessary. I was followed up by Mockus, the Green Party's candidate, who got 21.5 percent of the votes. Mockus is a mathematician and university professor of Lithuanian extraction who had been rector of Colombia's National University and twice elected mayor of Bogotá. He represented a breath of fresh air in politics, with innovative proposals based on respect for legality and the promotion of citizen culture. I respected him as my competitor, and I continue to respect and admire him even more as a man without guile, always well intentioned and committed to the defense of life and peace. He has been a great promoter of a better citizen culture, which the country so badly needs.

In the second round of elections, in which only Professor Mockus and I were candidates, I was able to count on the endorsement not only of the Party of the U but also the Conservative Party, Radical Change and that party's candidate, Germán Vargas Lleras, and many members of the Liberal Party.

With this broad spectrum of support, I called for a government of national unity to make progress in solving the country's principal problems. Finally, on June 20, 2010, I was elected president with more than nine million votes, the highest figure ever obtained by a candidate up to that moment in the history of Colombia.

"THE DOOR TO DIALOGUE HAS NOT BEEN CLOSED AND LOCKED"

I have to admit that the subject of an eventual dialogue with the guerrillas to attempt a new peace process was not one I mentioned in my debates and speeches during the campaign. I was elected, fundamentally, because the Colombians acknowledged my work as minister of defense—especially the resounding strikes we had made against the Farc—and they saw me as the person most likely and able to continue weakening the illegal armed groups militarily. Of course, my experience in the economic field as Colombia's first minister for foreign trade in charge of opening up our isolated economy to the world, and as the finance minister who had been given the task of confronting and overcoming the worst economic crisis the country had experienced in eighty years—together with my visible role in national affairs generally over the preceding three decades—had all been factors in my favor.

It is no wonder, then, that on the day I assumed the presidency, when in my inaugural address I referred to the possibility of opening a door to dialogue, a lot of people's eyes opened wide with surprise, not least those of my predecessor, the now ex-president Álvaro Uribe.

On that Saturday, August 7, 2010, I got up very early and flew to the Sierra Nevada de Santa Marta, where, in an act of respect for our indigenous communities—our older brothers—I asked the *mamas* of the Kogui, Arhuaco, Kankuamo, and Wiwas peoples for permission to take possession as president. They ceremoniously handed me the symbolic baton of command and said, "Seek after peace and reconciliation with Mother Earth, who is suffering." I will always try to be worthy of that charge.

That same afternoon, the Plaza de Bolívar in Bogotá was crowded with guests invited to my inauguration. What predominated was the festive atmosphere that invariably accompanies these events. Seated on the main platform were, among others, a dozen presidents of Latin American countries; the then Prince of Asturias, Felipe de Borbón; the former presidents of Colombia, and in a particularly visible spot behind me, the outgoing president

Álvaro Uribe Vélez. Not only my family but his also had been honored with a special place in the ceremony. This was something unusual, since normally the president who is leaving office does not participate in the inauguration of his successor. But I wanted to change this custom as a homage to the head of government with whom I had worked not only as minister but also in the task in which we had done so much together to recover the country's security. In my speech, I devoted several paragraphs to exalting his achievement and that of the outgoing First Lady, Lina Moreno de Uribe, a simple and discreet woman who had won the hearts of the Colombians.

I did this out of conviction, and I do not take any of it back now, despite the bitter and often unjust opposition I have suffered on the part of the ex-president. His principal lines of government—security, confidence for investment, and social inclusion—are ones I continued, while many of his programs I reinforced, in accordance with my maxim of building upon what already exists. Naturally, the government I began was mine, not a copy of his, and for that reason had my own unique personal seal on it. Perhaps that was why he could never forgive me.

He didn't forgive me, either, for having taken up the challenge of peace, which is not a choice for a Colombian president, but a constitutional mandate consecrated in Article 22 of our magna carta, where it says that "peace is a right and a duty of compulsory fulfillment."

What caused the greatest surprise in my inaugural address was the fact that I was contemplating the possibility of achieving peace through dialogue.

The paragraphs I devoted to this subject are of crucial importance. Which is why I transcribe them here:

> In the midst of the willpower and perseverance of more than forty-five million good Colombians, there exists a tiny minority who persist with acts of terrorism and drug trafficking, obstructing our path toward prosperity.
>
> We will continue to combat all illegal organizations unrelentingly and without respite. We will not rest until the rule of law prevails in every corner of our fatherland, down to the last village.
>
> With the consolidation of Democratic Security, we have made great strides in that direction, but there is still a long way to go. To reach that goal will be our priority, and as from now, I ask the new heads of our armed forces to continue producing results and resounding progress.
>
> At the same time, I reiterate: the door to dialogue is not closed and locked.

I aspire, during my government, to lay the foundations of a true reconciliation among Colombians. I am talking of a real disarmament of spirits, to build on lasting foundations that will not give rise to false hopes, will not allow for any further deceit, and will not lead to further frustration in a country that, from the bottom of its bloodied soul, above all else desires peace.

We have to take heed of the lessons from the past and learn from our mistakes in this task of overcoming a confrontation that has been for too long tearing us apart.

It is certain that those who do not learn from history are condemned to repeat it. But the Colombian people have profoundly assimilated their history. And that's why they express, every day and in every way, their rejection of those who persist in senseless and fratricidal violence.

To the illegal armed groups who invoke political reasons and today are talking once again of dialogue and negotiation, I say that my government will be open to any conversation that seeks to eradicate violence and to construct a more prosperous, equitable, and just society.

But I insist, only in accordance with unalterable premises: that they renounce the use of arms, kidnapping, drug traffic, extortion, and intimidation. This is not the capricious demand of a passing government. It is the clamor of a nation!

But so long as they do not liberate their captives, so long as they continue to commit acts of terrorism, so long as they refuse to restore children recruited under duress, so long as they keep planting mines and contaminating the Colombian countryside, we will continue to confront all the violent groups, without exception, with everything we've got. And you who are listening to me know how effective we are.

I have said, and I repeat: it is possible to have a Colombia at peace, a Colombia without guerrillas. And we're going to prove it! By reason or by force!

"BETRAYAL"

It didn't happen at once, but it was a subject that people began to talk about until, little by little, it became an almost unmovable conviction in the popular imagination: "Santos has betrayed Uribe and so, in some way, has betrayed his electors."

The title of traitor was used by the opposition directed by Uribe—very effectively, I have to admit—as a continuous and deliberate strategy of character assassination. This strategy was so obvious that, in 2014, one of the ex-president's sons, Tomás Uribe, published a tweet urging his followers to denigrate me: "I suggest we unify our technique so the message will stick. Let's change the adjective traitor to trickster. The first can be justified in the light of perceived benefits; but not the second." That was the kind of slur the implacable opposition resorted to and that I had to endure throughout my whole term in office.

So, what was the principal motive that prompted this talk about my supposed betrayal? It was said that, having been elected to continue the policy of Democratic Security and defeat the guerrillas militarily, I had opened the door to dialogue. Those who put forward this argument forget that the offensive I promised to launch against the practitioners of violence, I put into effect to the letter. So much so that, under my government, a lot more heavyweights of the Farc, commanders and leaders, were wiped out.

Was it betrayal, then, to attempt—and not only attempt, but achieve—a negotiated solution to the armed conflict with the guerrilla organization? Of course not. And here are two main reasons that refute that epithet used against me with such Machiavellian intent.

First, there was my track record. It was true that, as defense minister, I had just led heavier attacks on the guerrillas than anyone before me, but nobody could deny or ignore the fact that I had long been searching for a negotiated solution to the conflict.

In 1996, I invited Adam Kahane, the Canadian expert who had helped the reconciliation process in South Africa, and with him began a process of reflection by civil society that led to a workshop and the scenarios of exercises we called Destination Colombia. In 1997, for having attempted to arrive at a consensus among guerrilla leaders and paramilitaries to start a broad and integral peace process, I had ended up being accused of conspiracy. In mid-1998, I personally handed to Andrés Pastrana, when he was president-elect, a document that summed up the conclusions of the work of the so-called Situation Room that a number of Colombians had formed under the auspices of the United Nations representative in Colombia to look for a civilized solution to the armed conflict. Early in 1999, I organized an international workshop for journalists on how to cover the armed conflict and the peace process. And often in my opinion columns I had written on this very subject.

In light of all the above, nobody should have been surprised that, in addition to continuing with a military confrontation, I was contemplating the possibility of beginning a peace process in the hope of putting an end to half a century of a nightmare of violence. In a certain way, for the past fourteen years my efforts in the public sphere—whether it be in obtaining economic resources for the armed forces or leading a successful campaign to weaken the guerrillas—had all been focused on a single aim: to achieve peace in Colombia, a peace I very well knew would have to be won, sooner or later, at the negotiating table.

A second reason that gives the lie to accusations of betrayal is even more compelling: how can it be said that I betrayed the legacy of my predecessor when he himself, strenuously and on several occasions, had attempted to open up a space for dialogue with the guerrillas, and even to begin a peace process?

Like me, Uribe was not elected to dialogue with the insurgents. On the contrary, the overwhelming mandate of his electors—disillusioned as they were with the failure at Caguán—was to defeat the guerrillas on the battlefield. But that did not prevent him from trying to dialogue with them. And that's normal; it has to be that way. You don't have to be elected to make peace, nor do you have to promise to do so. It's a moral duty and a constitutional obligation for any political leader in Colombia.

From 2004, if not earlier, and through the first half of 2010, President Uribe, by means of his commissioners for peace—first Luis Carlos Restrepo and later Frank Pearl—sent messages to the Farc and received messages back from them, with the intention of arriving at a humanitarian agreement to exchange kidnap victims for imprisoned guerrillas. And not only that; he also sought the possibility of dialogue, with an open agenda, "in the hope of building trust between the parties . . . that might lead to a more detailed and deeper peace agenda for the future." This last proposal, sent on March 5, 2010, by the Uribe government's commissioner for peace to the head of the Farc, Alfonso Cano, and his second-in-command, Pablo Catatumbo, also suggested Brazil as a possible scenario for a "direct and secret meeting."

This proposal was followed up with another communication by Pearl to the same Farc commanders on April 8, 2010, attaching letters from the Swedish embassy in Bogotá and the International Committee of the Red Cross in which both the Swedish government and the international humanitarian organization expressed their readiness to accompany an encounter between the Colombian government and the Farc that would take place in a friendly country, in order to provide the parties with an atmosphere of trust and to serve as witnesses to the conversations. In the end, the Farc did not accept the proposal, alleging that it arrived too late seeing that in just over four months there would be a change of government.

The great majority of these approaches had been organized through the mediation of Henry Acosta, an economist native to Quindío but a resident of Cali, who had worked for years in the world of coffee cooperatives and, due to a variety of circumstances, struck up a friendly relationship with Catatumbo and thus became an ideal go-between for transmitting messages back and forth between the guerrillas and the government. Acosta never took a message to the Farc without first being authorized to do so by the government's high commissioner for peace, who in turn was authorized by the president of the republic to carry out tasks as facilitator aimed at achieving a humanitarian exchange of prisoners and advance in the search for peace.*

President Uribe went even further than simply sending or receiving proposals for a meeting with the Farc. He offered to not extradite Simón Trinidad and Sonia, two strategic guerrilla leaders, in exchange for the Farc's liberating their kidnap victims. Moreover, he unilaterally freed 150 guerrillas who were being held in Colombian jails and, in response to a petition by President Nicolas Sarkozy of France and without receiving any reciprocal compensation, he liberated Rodrigo Granda, a member of Farc's military command who had been captured in Venezuela and was being held in a Colombian prison.

I was with Uribe in his office when he took the call from Sarkozy. Also present was the president's private secretary, Alicia Arango. I remember Uribe bawling out Miguel Gómez, his ambassador in Paris, for not properly handling the matter of Ingrid Betancourt's kidnapping, and he told us that the French president issued the request in a harsh and aggressive manner. Uribe, on the contrary, was obsequious and even submissive in his reply, at least as far as we could hear. Perhaps it was more a problem of the language.

And there was something else: Farc's petition to withdraw police and military from an area of some eight hundred square kilometers in the municipalities of Pradera and Florida in the department of Valle del Cauca, in order to establish a zone of encounter where they could discuss an eventual humanitarian exchange of prisoners (what the Farc called a "swap"). In December 2005, Uribe had actually accepted a proposal by Spain, Switzerland,

---

* In his book *El hombre clave* (Bogotá: Penguin Random House, 2016), Acosta narrates in detail and with documentation his role as facilitator between the Farc and the Colombian government during the administration of President Uribe and the early stages of mine.

and France to demilitarize a smaller area of 180 square kilometers. In the end, the zone was not demilitarized, but not for lack of will on the government's part but because the Farc did not accept it. In fact, they responded with the following intemperate communiqué:

> With Uribe there'll be no humanitarian exchange. . . . We understand that in his eagerness to exploit electorally an initiative on the part of countries who wish to facilitate the swap of prisoners—a proposal we have not as yet received—he has thrown overboard an important diplomatic effort. While we lament this precipitated and frivolous attitude on the part of the president, we acknowledge the good intentions of the governments of France, Sweden and Spain. . . .

I have to say that, as minister of defense I was, along with the commanders of the military and the police, firmly opposed to this demilitarization, even though the president was inclined to concede it. The deplorable experience of Caguán had shown us that the clearance of a terrain only serves to strengthen the guerrillas, all the more so in municipalities that represented a strategic area for the Farc, since it would enable them to regain the control they had lost over drug trafficking corridors to the Pacific Ocean.

If the Farc had been offered all these concessions, approaches, and attempts at dialogue, with the ELN the Uribe government had made even greater efforts. Through his high commissioner, Restrepo, Uribe carried on conversations with this guerrilla group in Cuba and also in Venezuela, and in December 2007 they even came to the point of drawing up a proposal for a basic agreement that would include a ceasefire and the setting up of a table for dialogue between the government and the ELN, as well as holding a national convention in which civil society would participate. The crisis in relations with Venezuela, coupled with the government's nonnegotiable demand that the ELN concentrate their combatants in a defined area before formal talks could being, led to the freezing of these advances.

It is thus hard to understand why Uribe repeated over and over again that there could be no negotiating with terrorists.

On the question of the Uribe government's approaches to the Farc and the ELN, I had some knowledge as minister of defense, and was further informed by Acosta, and also by Pearl, the last commissioner for peace of the outgoing government. What I certainly was quite clear about when I gave my inaugural address on August 7, 2010, was that a number of previous efforts had been made and a path had been opened up toward dialogue with these two guerrilla groups—thanks to the initiatives of my predecessor—and that these avenues could be followed up to achieve a positive result for the Colombians.

Does openness to the possibility of dialogue with the guerrillas—without letting up on persecuting them with military force where necessary—deserve to be called betrayal? I leave it to history to decide.

A SURPRISE UP ONE'S SLEEVE

It seems worthwhile now to indulge in a moment of reflection on both politics and history. It's often good for a leader to have something up his sleeve, because you can't always let everyone know what you've got in mind for the good of the country. Charles de Gaulle was designated prime minister and defense minister of France in 1958, and then elected president in 1959, supposedly so that the French could be sure they would not lose Algeria. But in 1962, de Gaulle ended up giving that country its independence. In 1994, Israel's prime minister, Yitzhak Rabin, in the election campaign that brought him to power, declared that anyone who gave up the Golan Heights, even in exchange for peace, would be "out of his mind." Yet the first thing he did on assuming the government was to restore Golan to Syria in exchange for peace. Uribe was elected to make war on the guerrillas and defeat them, but that did not prevent him from talking to them and attempting to begin a peace process with both the ELN and the Farc. The fact that he didn't succeed is another matter.

In my case, peace was a vision and a goal I had been nurturing for years. However, there are circumstances that people don't even think of when you talk about a policy of peace—things like reestablishing good relations with Chávez, offering to shake hands with Timochenko, finding a way to ensure that guerrillas who tell the truth about what happened and make reparation to their victims will not go to jail. Your leadership is proven the moment you take the decision—not necessarily a popular one—to play your surprise card. De Gaulle once said that he preferred to betray the electorate rather than his country. That's a harsh thing to say, and I am convinced that to look for peace in a country immersed in war can hardly be considered betrayal. Nonetheless, there is always a gap between a leader's vision and the way people perceive his decisions.

Citizens often think that peace can be gotten for nothing, as if it were a matter of first annihilating the enemy and then making him sign an unconditional surrender. But when you begin to pay the price—because every peace has its price—the people think you've "betrayed" them.

Many of those who elected me in 2010 were frightened and indignant when they saw the surprise I had up my sleeve: nothing more than a search for peace through negotiation. Others, by contrast, understood the value of what I was attempting and felt represented by my ideal. That's why in 2010 I was elected on the basis of a center-right policy; and in 2014, reelected by the center-left.

THE CONDITIONS BEGIN TO BE FULFILLED

Perhaps you will be wondering why I included the possibility of peace talks in my inaugural address. Why did I say the door to dialogue was not locked? I could have not announced it and simply tried to put it into practice, as my predecessor had done. However, I decided that the moment had come to notify the country and the insurgents of my will to advance in that direction. In my speech, I said we were going to achieve peace "by reason or by force." My instinct, my heart, and my conscience were telling me that, after so many years of relying on force, the time had come to give reason a chance.

Two factors in particular—and I will refer to them later—showed me that the path to negotiation was viable: first, a few days before I assumed the presidency, a channel of communication had been opened with the Venezuelan president Hugo Chávez, who was my sworn enemy but also a fundamental actor when it came to establishing trust with the guerrillas; and second, I had firsthand knowledge of how far the Uribe government had advanced in their efforts to achieve dialogue with the guerrillas.

On April 7, 2010, the secretariat of the Farc, via their facilitator, Henry Acosta, sent a letter to the high commissioner Frank Pearl in which they declined the government's offer to hold "a direct and secret meeting" in Brazil. This letter was leaked and disseminated by Telesur, the Venezuelan pro-Chávez TV channel. In fact, it was in the news before Acosta had delivered the letter to Pearl. That was how the Colombians, myself included, heard about it. In it there was a paragraph of which, as candidate for the presidency, I took careful note: "We reiterate that the doors of Farc-EP remain open, we wish to insist on our opinion that dialogues such as those proposed by the government would be more appropriately held in Colombia, and with the country looking on."

What did this mean? That little by little we were arriving at the four conditions I always thought necessary if peace talks were to be attempted successfully: a correlation of strength in combat in the state's favor; the support of countries in the region; a real will to dialogue on the part of the adversary due to the guerrilla commanders being convinced that things would go better for them—personally, and from the viewpoint of their organization—if they opted for peace rather than war; and finally, recognition that an armed conflict did in fact exist.

CHAPTER 11

Hugo Chávez

Agreeing to Disagree

THE CHALLENGE OF CONVERTING AN ENEMY INTO AN ALLY

As I said in my address of acceptance of the Nobel Peace Prize, to achieve your final objective, peace, you have to be prepared to make difficult decisions—very often, unpopular ones. In my case, this entailed making approaches to the leaders of neighboring countries with whom I had maintained, and continue to maintain, profound ideological differences.

To advance toward peace is much more important than any personal or political dispute, not only at the international level but also in the domestic sphere. For Colombia, it would have been impossible to succeed in our efforts for peace without the support of our neighboring countries. In today's world, regional support is indispensable in resolving politically any asymmetric war. And regional support is precisely what was lacking when I assumed the presidency in August 2010.

At that time, we had broken off diplomatic relations with Venezuela and Ecuador, and in a certain way the majority of countries in the region looked on us as the black sheep, a country that seemed to prefer to be seen as an ally of the United States rather than as a partner of its neighbors. This opinion gained further credit when Colombia signed an agreement with the United States to increase cooperation in matters of security. Hugo Chávez went out of his way to exaggerate the scope of this agreement, repeating everywhere that it would allow unlimited use, by the US armed forces, of seven military bases on our soil. This was not true. The agreement focused on cooperation to confront the networks of organized crime, and was in no sense a threat to our neighbors. Nonetheless, Venezuela vehemently attacked this advance in bilateral military cooperation, and managed to mobilize other Latin American countries to unite in rejecting this measure.

I was the minister for defense who worked to improve links of military cooperation with our powerful neighbor to the north. I had strongly denounced the support Venezuela was giving to the Colombian guerrillas and the lack of cooperation from the government of Ecuador when it came to combating them. Furthermore, I was the one who had authorized the bombing of a Farc guerrilla camp located on Ecuadorian soil. No wonder those two leaders in particular—Hugo Chávez, president of Venezuela, and Rafael Correa, president of Ecuador—should hold me at the center of their hate and consider me one of their main enemies.

Will it be possible, I asked myself, to achieve peace in Colombia while these animosities are allowed to persist? The answer was no. Peace is not built in a vacuum. We are part of an international community; nations are interdependent, and I could not ignore the fact that Venezuela and Ecuador, our next-door neighbors, were key actors in the game of regional strategy. When you are after a larger goal, you have to work with people whom you may not like, and even further, it may be necessary to make your enemy become your friend, your ally.

That was my main challenge internationally. In this field—as in the process with the guerrillas—it was necessary to make the impossible become possible.

A STRANGE FUNERAL

On Friday March 8, 2013, at the military academy in Venezuela, in Caracas, in an atmosphere of grief and solemnity, I heard someone call my name. I stepped forward and took my place on the right-hand side at the head of the coffin that contained the remains of a man who in life had been my fierce adversary and, finally, my cordial ally: Lieutenant Colonel Hugo Chávez Frías, president of Venezuela, who had died three days before, while still at his post, after a battle of almost two years against cancer.

Beside me, in the second round of what was called the guard of honor, were other heads of state from Latin America and the Caribbean. During the two minutes of silence in homage to the memory of Chávez, I could not help thinking about the enormous paradox that was implied in the fact that I, as president of Colombia, should be accompanying the funeral of a popular and polemic leader, as Chávez had been, and above all the international personality with whom I had had the most severe confrontation in my whole career in public life, whether as journalist or politician.

In less than three years, our relationship had been turned upside down, and that was for one fundamental reason: peace in Colombia and the welfare of both our nations. Today I can say that, without the participation and the support given by Chávez and Venezuela to the peace process, it would have been very difficult—perhaps impossible—to achieve the guerrilla leaders' trust in the process and arrive at the successful outcome we obtained.

The fact is that Chávez had been my enemy, and before I assumed the presidency in August 2010, he had broken off diplomatic relations with Colombia. Besides, we were poles apart, both politically and ideologically. Two men could not have been more different, nor believe in such contrary concepts. Ideologically Chávez was on the left, promoting what he called his "Bolivarian revolution" based on a confrontation with foreign capital and distrust of the market and the private sector. As for me, I adopted a position somewhere near the center of the political spectrum, defending the doctrine of the Third Way according to which we should allow "the market to the degree it is possible, and the state where it is necessary." In other words, to achieve the right balance between a liberal economy and state intervention so as to ensure the fundamental rights of equality, security, and justice.

But it was not just a matter of ideological differences. Chávez and I had accused one another of just about everything. In the columns I published in *El Tiempo* at the turn of the century, I repeatedly expressed my concern over the politics and activities of Venezuela's president and their repercussions in Colombia. The implementation of his policies was especially painful to me since, as minister for foreign trade in the nineties, one of my major achievements had been to negotiate a free trade treaty with Venezuela and Mexico—the so-called G3—and an increase in commercial exchange with our neighboring country. Now I had to watch it all coming apart.

In one column from that era, I wrote the following:

> Colombia has a problem we cannot ignore, one we have the duty and the obligation to at least analyze dispassionately. Its name is Hugo Chávez and the project is called Bolivarianism. It is a problem because not only is it destroying an economic and commercial integration that until recently was considered an example for the rest of the world but there are too many indicators and signs, and often evidence, of President Chávez's sympathies with the Colombian guerrillas.

One article of mine made a special impression. It was titled "Venezuela is on Fire . . . and Colombia Might Get Burned," and I published it in a widely read magazine, *Diners*, in 2004. At the time, I was president of the Good Government Foundation and columnist in several papers, and I kept myself well informed about what was happening in Venezuela. So I felt I should organize with every passing day this information, analyze it and publish my conclusions.

In my *Diners* article, the terms I used to describe what was happening in Venezuela were no less critical than in my previous columns. I said that Venezuela's democracy had been sequestered by Chávez, that in its management of the economy his government was a dismal failure, that he was giving his support and friendship to the guerrillas of the Farc and the ELN. I also warned of the danger of his efforts to internationalize his Bolivarian revolution. In fact, I went even further: I described the Venezuelan president as "a professionally mediocre lieutenant colonel evidently inspired by social resentment," a populist and tyrant who "uses power in a typically autocratic manner and with every passing day is more and more removed from the State of Law."

So I became Colombia's most acerbic critic of Chávez and his regime, and naturally he did not spare epithets against me. That was why he took it as an act of animosity, or at best a provocation, when in mid-2006, President Uribe appointed me minister of defense. Chávez's misgivings were not without foundation, for as defense minister I was a thorn in his side, frustrating his hope of becoming an active promoter of Colombia's conflict, a kind of savior figure. This can be seen in a particular case: that of Emmanuel, a baby born in captivity.

DECEIT REVEALED IN THE CASE OF EMMANUEL

In the final months of 2007, President Uribe was worried and under pressure regarding the suffering of the number of people the Farc had kidnapped and were holding in captivity—including politicians, foreigners, and members of the armed forces. Knowing that his colleague, Chávez, had contacts with the Farc guerrillas and could influence them, he authorized the Venezuelan president to act as facilitator in the hope of achieving a humanitarian agreement that would lead to the liberation of the hostages.

This mediation did not produce results and Uribe withdrew his authorization, an act that infuriated Chávez. In mid-December 2007, when Chávez was no longer acting as intermediary, the Farc announced their intention of unilaterally liberating the following hostages: the former congressional representative Consuelo González, and the former director of the presidential campaign of Ingrid Betancourt, Clara Rojas, with her three-year-old son, Emmanuel, who had been born in captivity. The condition insisted on by the guerrillas was that they would hand over these hostages only to President Chávez or his representative, and to the Colombian senator Piedad Córdoba, sympathizer and friend of Chávez.

We—that is, the members of the government—received this news with prudent optimism and proceeded to do whatever was necessary to facilitate the freedom of the hostages. We authorized the entry of Venezuelan helicopters bearing the insignia of the International Red Cross and the presence of Venezuelan officials, as well as international guarantors from seven countries—Argentina, Bolivia, Brazil, Cuba, Ecuador, France, and Switzerland—plus Argentina's ex-president Néstor Kirchner, and Marco Aurélio Garcia, foreign affairs adviser and right-hand man of President Luiz Inácio Lula da Silva (better known as Lula), of Brazil. We also ordered the suspension of military operations in the area to avoid any possible upset at the moment the humanitarian operation was to be carried out.

But something didn't make sense. Military intelligence had detected signs that suggested it was going to be impossible for the Farc to keep their promise. According to our intelligence, in mid-2005 a baby of the age and characteristics of Emmanuel had been handed over to the protection of Colombia's Institute for Family Welfare at San José del Guaviare, a small town in the conflict area. The institute had sent the baby off to a foster home in Bogotá, where he was being cared for and had been given another name.

The commander of the army, General Mario Montoya, informed me of the case, which at first sight seemed farfetched. If the Farc didn't have Emmanuel in their power, why were they offering to liberate him?

But the fact was the little boy was not with the Farc. Almost two years before this, the guerrillas had left the baby in the care of a rural worker and his family. However, after a few months, since the baby showed symptoms of leishmaniasis and also had a fracture in his left arm, the head of the family took him to the local health center. The doctors who saw the child there were alarmed by his condition and, seeing that he was also suffering from malnutrition, decided to remit him to the Family Welfare Institute.

So when the guerrillas visited the rural family again and asked them to give them back the child so as to be able to hand him over, along with his mother, to the humanitarian mission, they ran up against a surprise: the baby was no longer there. Despite this, and while they were trying to find the little boy, they continued to promise they would restore him to his mother.

Our intelligence department showed us that the guerrillas were desperately trying to locate the foster family in Bogotá who had Emmanuel in their care. At this juncture, I gave orders that the child should be taken from the Welfare Institute and left in the care of specialized personnel in a secret place. Only two or three days were left before the Farc were scheduled to hand over the two kidnapped women and the child to the humanitarian commission headed by Chávez. On our side, we still were not certain that the little boy we had in our power was really Emmanuel.

On December 29, before traveling to Cartagena, where I planned to spend the New Year, I met with Barbara Hintermann, head of the International Red Cross in Bogotá, in her apartment, to tell her of our suspicions. I said that if the Farc did not liberate Emmanuel, it was highly likely that the child we had in our care was, in fact, the son of Clara Rojas. Hintermann was amazed by what I told her, and we agreed it should be kept strictly confidential.

Meanwhile, the international delegations were arriving from Venezuela and meeting at Villavicencio, capital of the department of Meta, an intermediate city that was chosen as the logistics headquarters of the operation, since it was Colombia's port of entry to the Eastern Plains. They were expecting to receive a hostage that the Farc did not actually have in their power. And if the situation had not already become sufficiently surreal, accompanying the delegations from the Venezuelan government was the famous US filmmaker Oliver Stone, who was preparing to film the liberation of the captives and so contribute to the legend of Venezuela's president. All that was still needed was for the Farc to inform Chávez of the coordinates and the exact time of the liberation, and the operation would be under way,

But hours went by, and nothing happened. In Villavicencio, the atmosphere was tense and rumors were spreading that the Colombian government was to blame for not having suspended military operations in the area, making it difficult for the liberation to take place. Of course, none of this was true.

When told of the situation, I called President Uribe at his farm in Córdoba, where he had gone to see in the new year with his family, and I suggested we both should fly to Villavicencio and tell what we knew before the defamatory campaign had gone any further. The president accepted unhesitatingly.

As I was boarding the presidential plane in Cartagena, I got a call from the director of the Family Welfare Institute, with whom we had coordinated everything with respect to the child, and she informed me that a very agitated man had shown up at the institute to reclaim the boy. With his voice trembling, he said that if they did not return the child, he and his family would all be killed. This phone call reassured me, for it confirmed our hypothesis: Emmanuel was not in the hands of the guerrillas. We had him ourselves!

In the afternoon, we arrived at the air force base in Meta and immediately met with the international delegates, who were coordinated by Kirchner. Among those present was the Venezuelan foreign affairs minister, Nicolás Maduro. At the time, we didn't imagine he was going to be Chávez's successor. Almost all voices claimed that the Colombian army had been responsible for the operation's failure. I asked the commander of the army to explain, with the use of a map, where his troops were concentrated so as to let it be clearly seen they were in no way interfering with the humanitarian operation.

While this meeting was still in progress, I was told that President Chávez had appeared on television disseminating the version of the supposed military operations that had impeded the liberation. I suggested to President Uribe that the time had come to reveal the truth about this farce, and he authorized me to do so. So I explained, to the astonishment of all present, the hypothesis that the Farc did not have Emmanuel, and that was the real reason for their not having proceeded with the liberation. I well remember the comment from Kirchner when he heard of the guerrillas' trickery: "If that's true, then they've made us all look like real idiots!"

Uribe immediately called for a press conference and declared: "The Farc have not ventured to fulfill their promise to liberate their captives because they do not have Emmanuel in their power." Journalists were left totally perplexed, as was the general public. What we were revealing to the world was one of the guerrillas' most grotesque lies, which also showed they had serious problems of communication. A few days later, DNA tests carried out in a specialized laboratory in Spain left no doubt that the child who had been handed in to the Welfare Institute's system of protection was, in fact, Emmanuel, the first baby born in captivity in Colombia's long history of kidnappings.

Finally, on January 10, 2008, in a region of the jungle, two women were liberated, with all guarantees given by the Colombian government and the air force. They were Emmanuel's mother, Clara Rojas, and Consuelo González, picked up by a delegation from Venezuela accompanied by members of the International Red Cross and flown to the neighboring country where Chávez was waiting to welcome them. This time there was no spectacle, no delegates from seven countries, and no Hollywood director.

While it is true that the deceit was the work of the guerrillas, there could be little doubt that Chávez did not harbor warm feelings toward Colombia's defense minister, who was not only his most acerbic critic but had stolen from him an opportunity to shine as an efficacious intermediary for peace. I should add that the sentiments were mutual.

WHEN GOVERNMENTS ARE IN DISPUTE, IT'S THE PEOPLE WHO SUFFER

During my time at the Ministry of Defense, 2006–2009, with the intelligence information I had at my command, I very well knew that the Venezuelan government, because of its ideological sympathies, was protecting and aiding the guerrillas, who found a secure refuge in the neighboring country. Of course, every time President Uribe and I denounced this publicly, we were inundated with insults from Chávez or his officials.

Some months after I had retired from the ministry, when my name began to be mentioned as a possible presidential candidate, Chávez came out with a threatening declaration: "If Juan Manuel Santos is president, there could be a war in the region." So great was his phobia of me. I was elected in June 2010, and while I was president-elect without yet having assumed power, a serious diplomatic crisis arose with our neighboring country.

Uribe's government, fed up with the connivance between the guerrillas and the Venezuelan authorities, put together a dossier of intelligence information, with videos and photographs of supposed Farc and ELN camps on Venezuelan territory, and denounced the Venezuelan government to the Permanent Council of the Organization of American States (OAS) in Washington for undue interference in the Colombian conflict. This denunciation, presented by our ambassador at the OAS, Luis Alfonso Hoyos, was lodged two weeks before my inauguration, without consultation with me or even my knowledge, and exacerbated the bad feeling between the two countries to the point that the Venezuelan government broke off diplomatic relations with Colombia. Chávez gave personnel at the Colombian embassy seventy-two hours to leave Venezuela, and announced he was sending troops to the border. And he topped it off with a not very reassuring comment: "If there's a war with Colombia, we'll be in tears, but we'll be there."

Thus was I faced with an imminent reality: I was going to assume the presidency in an atmosphere of bellicose animosity with Venezuela, a country that shares 2,200 kilometers of border with Colombia, and where millions of Colombians and their families were living. The official records talk of one million, but it is estimated they could be more than four million—although the number has diminished a lot in recent years with the exodus due to the social, economic, and political crisis Venezuela is facing. The scenario was immensely fragile; a single spark could ignite a war.

I remembered something I once read: a person may have his opinions and convictions, but if that person comes to a position of government, from then on those opinions and convictions should no longer be nurturing his own personality and prejudices, but placed at the service of the people he governs. I had certainly criticized Chávez in no uncertain terms, in my capacity as minister, and also when I was a journalist. But now, as president, I was obliged to calm the waters and avoid a confrontation that could only lead to a catastrophe for both nations.

I was aware—as was everybody else—that Chávez was nearer in his affections to the guerrillas than to Colombia's democratic institutions. In fact, the Farc and the ELN looked on Venezuela as a kind of sanctuary where they could rest, heal their wounds, and plan attacks on Colombia's armed forces, infrastructure, and transport system. But I also knew that an open confrontation with Venezuela would be not only useless but extremely dangerous and harmful for our people. So I had to be pragmatic. It would be better to build a constructive relationship with Chávez for the benefit of peace in Colombia than to have him attacking our government and our nation day after day in every possible scenario.

I was in Mexico when I heard the news that the Colombian government had denounced the Venezuelan government at the OAS. Accompanied by my future foreign affairs minister, María Ángela Holguín, I was on a round of friendly visits to Latin American countries before assuming the presidency.

A few days later, as part of that tour, I was in Argentina, where I enjoyed a very cordial luncheon with the president, Cristina Fernández de Kirchner, a friend and admirer of the Venezuelan regime. That same night, at the Colombian ambassador's residence, I dined with her husband, former president Néstor Kirchner, recently appointed secretary-general to the Union of South American Nations (UNASUR). I knew that Néstor Kirchner was a passionate fan of the soccer team Racing Club de Avellaneda, and since the Colombian soccer player Teo Gutiérrez was playing in that team, I asked him to send me a T-shirt with his signature, which I gave to the ex-president. That kind of gesture always helps break the ice.

Over dinner, Kirchner, as if he had read my mind and knew what I was thinking about, fired a question at me: "Have you thought about patching up your relations with Chávez?" My reply left him perplexed, since he wasn't expecting it. "Frankly, yes. The situation that exists between our two countries is not good for anyone." I told Kirchner he could pass on that message to Chávez. And a few hours later, he called me. "Chávez says he's ready to talk. And if you invite him to your inauguration, he'll go."

Given that we did not have diplomatic relations, and in light of Chávez's threats of war, it seemed to me exaggerated and inconvenient to have him present at the solemn act, which in the end his foreign affairs minister Nicolás Maduro attended. But I did make an alternative proposal: "Tell him," I said to Kirchner, "that instead I'll invite him, three days after my taking office, on August 10, to meet at a place I know he likes: the Quinta de San Pedro Alejandrino in Santa Marta." I knew that for Chávez the site would be symbolic, since it was where his personal hero, Simón Bolívar, died in 1830.

So that was how our next meeting was arranged. Meanwhile, on August 7, 2010, in the Plaza de Bolívar in Bogotá, I took office as president of Colombia. Among the invited guests, very serious and unsmiling, was the Venezuelan foreign minister Maduro, who gave not the slightest sign of whether he approved or disapproved of what I said in my inaugural address.

In that address, I sent Venezuela a clear message: "Just as I do not recognize enemies in national politics, I do not recognize them either when it comes to foreign governments. The word *war* is not in my vocabulary when I think of Colombia's relations with her neighbors or with any nation on the planet." Finally, I added:

> I thank all those people of goodwill who have offered to mediate in the situation with Venezuela, but I must honestly say that, given the circumstances and my nature, I prefer a direct and frank dialogue. And I hope it will be as soon as possible. But it has to be a dialogue in a context of mutual respect, reciprocal cooperation, and a firm hand against crime, and with a sincere and open communication.
>
> Good relations benefit us all, because when governments are in a dispute, it's the people who suffer.

"WE GOT OFF ON THE WRONG FOOT, PRESIDENT CHÁVEZ"

It was August 10, the day of the first encounter as colleagues between Chávez and myself, two men who had criticized one another in every conceivable way and were now coming together in an attempt to solve a crisis that had our two nations at loggerheads. And, coincidentally, it happened to be my birthday.

I waited with my foreign minister for Chávez to arrive at the Quinta de San Pedro Alejandrino. Kirchner was also there, as secretary-general of UNASUR and as facilitator of the meeting.

President Chávez arrived in Santa Marta surrounded by an impressive lineup of bodyguards. He made declarations at the airport, and on his way to the Quinta, ordered his convoy to stop in a popular barrio to greet the people. I was watching this cavalcade on television, wondering what our meeting was going to be like, and how I could break the ice. Then I heard Chávez, in his customary colloquial style, talking to the news cameras: "I am delighted to visit this sister country Colombia, and to meet with President Santos, especially today, a very special day for him, for today he will be 49." I took note of this and recalled a ploy that is useful for relieving the tension in any situation no matter how difficult: humor.

When Chávez arrived at the place we were to meet, he got out of his car and walked towards me and, consistent with his ever-expansive temperament, opened his arms to embrace me. I put out my hand in greeting and said, very seriously, as if annoyed: "President Chávez, I think we got off on the wrong foot." Chávez looked disconcerted. "Why? What's wrong?" he said, obviously puzzled. "When you arrived," I said, putting on my best poker face, "you made a declaration to the press that creates a serious problem for me."

"But, President Santos," he replied, "I only said I was coming in peace, to strengthen our relations. And I wished you well on your birthday."

"Precisely." I said. "You created a serious problem for me, because you said I was 49, when in fact I'm 59. And because of your statement, my wife's going to expect more from me!" Chávez threw back his head and laughed, and from that moment we got on fine and had a relaxed conversation full of good humor and understanding, without denying our profound differences.

We began to discuss just about everything, and our contrary positions soon became perfectly obvious. Going back over a bit of recent history, I said we should be like Ronald Reagan and Mikhail Gorbachev when they met for the first time to discuss nuclear disarmament. Reagan said to his Soviet colleague that neither was he going to become a Communist nor did he expect Gorbachev to embrace capitalism, but they could work together for a superior cause, such as saving the world from a nuclear disaster. I said something similar to my Venezuelan colleague: "I'm not going to become a Bolivarian revolutionary, and neither will you turn into a liberal democrat, but we can work together for a common goal, peace, for the benefit of both our people." And that is what we did.

We broke the ice with humor and maintained a cordial relationship right up to his last day, despite the fact that we were like oil and water. We were constantly pulling one another's leg over our differences. I told him repeatedly that the Bolivarian revolution was going to let Bolívar down, because it was going to fail. He would reply by denigrating Francisco de Paula Santander, the other great hero of our independence, born in what is present-day Colombia, unlike Bolívar, who was born a son of Caracas. Santander, he would say, was a neoliberal oligarch like me. But following the example of Reagan and Gorbachev, we decided not to criticize our respective economic models—twenty-first-century socialism versus the Third Way—leaving it to history to decide who was right. But one must admit that the Bolivarian experiment had not turned out at all well economically, socially, or politically. To be perfectly frank, it's been a catastrophe.

A few days later, diplomatic relations were restored, an agreement was signed regarding the payment of Venezuela's debt of more than 800 million dollars to Colombian exporters, and a process of respectful approaches was set in motion that would lead to improved relations with other countries in the region.

Very soon, the controversy over the agreement to cooperate in security with the United States by allowing the use of our military bases was no longer an obstacle. Ten days after my meeting with Chávez, Colombia's Constitutional Court decreed that the agreement could not take effect since it had not been voted by Congress. This was helpful to Chávez because it enabled him to justify, to his people and his allies in Latin America, his decision to reestablish and strengthen Venezuela's relations with Colombia.

It was a win-win situation. I got a key ally in the search for peace for my country, and he could say he had managed to avoid an increase in the United States military presence in the region—though in fact this was an internal matter in Colombia resolved by a Colombian court and, it should be said, with little practical effect, since cooperation went on as usual. In short, both of us gave a respite to our respective citizens, and calmed the waters.

"MY NEW BEST FRIEND"

A few weeks later, at an assembly of the Inter American Press Association in Mérida, Mexico, the well-known Uruguayan journalist Danilo Arbilla asked me a question about my restored relations with Chávez. My reply was not meant to be serious. I said: "Are you talking about my new best friend?"—an expression used jokingly in the United States. And of course, my critics, who can't tell the difference between a literal statement and a joke, soon reported it in Colombia as if it were a serious news item. What I had wanted to highlight was how exceptional it was that two such different people, who had confronted and insulted one another as Chávez and I had done, could work together harmoniously now as "good friends." But it was a joke for which my opponents never forgave me.

It was no secret that Chávez was greatly admired by other leaders who sympathized with his ideology and whose countries received economic benefits from Venezuela. And so the new relaxed relationship with Chávez served to strengthen Colombia's relations with President Lula in Brazil, President Fernández de Kirchner in Argentina, President Morales in Bolivia and President Correa in Ecuador, although in the case of Correa things were more difficult.

We also got better relations with UNASUR, an organization about which Colombia—and myself especially, for I had advised President Uribe not to join—initially had reservations, considering it to be unnecessary given the existence of the OAS. But the times and the circumstances had changed. So much so that, following on the unexpected death of Néstor Kirchner in October 2010—just two months after our meeting in Santa Marta—the position of secretary-general of UNASUR was shared by two candidates: María Emma Mejía for Colombia and Alí Rodríguez for Venezuela.

The passing of the years tends to surprise one with paradoxes. In the same way I had promoted Colombia's participation in UNASUR when it was necessary, I ended up pushing for its virtual demise. In the Summit of the Americas held in Lima in April 2018, and given the lack of transparency and operational effectiveness of UNASUR in recent times, I proposed—in an informal chat with presidents Michel Temer of Brazil, Sebastián Piñera of Chile, Mauricio Macri of Argentina, and our host president, Martín Vizcarra, who had just assumed the presidency of Peru after Pedro Pablo Kuczynski had resigned—that we should put an end once and for all to that useless invention called UNASUR. They all agreed. So we consulted with our foreign ministers and they thought we should dismantle UNASUR, but gradually.

So it was that on April 20, just a week after that conversation in Lima, the foreign ministers of our five countries, plus the foreign minister of Paraguay, sent a letter to their opposite number in Bolivia—since Bolivia was presiding the organization at the time—to give the following forceful notification:

"Given the present circumstances, the undersigned countries have decided not to participate in the activities of UNASUR from the present moment unless, in the course of the next few weeks, we can count on concrete results that will guarantee the adequate functioning of the organization." In accordance with this line of thought, my successor, Iván Duque, from the very start announced Colombia's decision to withdraw from the organization.

It must be said that the peace process with the Farc also served as a catalyst for uniting the solidarity and friendship of the Latin American countries around Colombia. Venezuela in particular was one of the four countries—with Cuba, Norway, and Chile—that accompanied the process from its beginnings and helped, thanks to its affinity with the guerrillas, to iron things out at difficult moments.

President Chávez, with whom I had had such difficult relations for many years, and then finally good ones, was a loyal ally in the peace process, in which he believed most deeply. Of that I am sure. That is why when, on March 8, 2013, I formed a guard of honor beside his coffin, I felt I was performing something more than an act of diplomacy, which is so often contaminated by hypocrisy. I was taking my leave of a complex and formidable adversary who knew how to be an ally for peace when the circumstances demanded it of him.

A DICTATORSHIP ON THE OTHER SIDE OF THE BORDER

What has occurred with his successor, President Nicolás Maduro, deserves a special chapter. My relations with him, as with Chávez, have had their ups and downs. Maduro, a devout disciple of Chávez, is loudly spoken and passionate like his predecessor, but with less charisma, little sense of humor, and a limited intellectual capacity. In the middle of the peace process, we clashed on several occasions, especially on border problems. Nevertheless, we kept intact our cooperation in search of peace for Colombia; on that subject Maduro was faithful to the legacy of Chávez and his commitment did not flag until the peace agreement was signed. That is something I have to recognize.

Our relationship broke down definitively when Maduro, after launching one attack after another on his country's institutional democracy, delivered the final blow in May 2017 when he convoked an illegitimate constituent assembly that he placed above all other constituted powers. In practice, what Maduro did was consolidate a dictatorship, very much in the style of the "democracies" of the former Soviet Union: with hungry people more desperate every day, victims of censure, and other abuses.

Neither my government nor I could remain silent. While thousands upon thousands of Venezuelans cross the border every day in search of a refuge and opportunities in Colombia—it is estimated that about two million have arrived so far—our country suffers from the instability of our neighboring nation. The position of the Colombian government—and that of most Latin American governments—has been to help find a nonviolent, peaceful solution to Venezuela's crisis. As I write these lines, Venezuela is still walking the tightrope, submitted to a regime that is repudiated by the greater part of the world's democracies. Until now, the Venezuelans have not been subjected to what was most to be feared: a bloodbath.

Of course, Maduro accused me of being a traitor and, in the final months of my government, could not find enough ways to insult and threaten me because Colombia denounced his country's increasing violations of human and democratic rights. He seems to have thought that because he helped us in the peace process, we were going to close our eyes and be accomplices to his arbitrary actions. But the necessary pragmatism in international relations doesn't go that far.

I have never ceased thanking Chávez, and Maduro too, for their contribution to my country's peace. The presence of Maduro in Havana on June 23, 2016, when the bilateral and definitive ceasefire agreement was signed, and in Cartagena on September 26 of the same year when we signed the final accord that put an end to the conflict with the Farc, was welcome and implied a well-earned acknowledgement for his support during the process. But I could never agree with the suspension of freedoms and the violation of citizens' rights in Venezuela, nor anywhere in the world.

The last time I spoke to Maduro was on March 23, 2017, apropos of the incursion of Venezuelan troops illegally into Colombian territory. Some sixty members of the Bolivarian Army had entered the department of Arauca, near the border, and had set up a provisional camp there. Once the details of this had been confirmed, I brought together the ministers of foreign affairs and defense and the high commanders of the Colombian army, and I asked the commander of the army, General Alberto Mejía, if he had sufficient troops in that area capable of dealing with the Venezuelan intruders. He assured me he did, so I ordered him to put them into action immediately. Then I called up my colleague and we had a very tense conversation in which I objected very strongly to the violation of our territory and demanded that he withdraw his troops at once.

Maduro tried to argue that his troops were on Venezuelan soil—which I refuted immediately, quoting the treaties on our border areas—and he replied that he would not withdraw the troops until a binational commission was set up to define limits and demarcation. And as if that weren't enough, he complained about the critical attitude of our ambassador at the OAS, Andrés González, regarding the serious state of democracy and human rights in his country. I told him that the commission would not be called for until his men, to the very last soldier, had abandoned Colombian soil, and that our position regarding the democratic crisis in Venezuela was not the subject of that conversation.

I am usually a very calm person, but for the first time in a communication of that kind, I got angry and shouted at Maduro. The commanders of the armed forces and the minister of foreign affairs, María Ángela Holguín, were astonished because they had never seen me so upset. I told Maduro that we had our army surrounding the zone of invasion and that if he did not withdraw his men within the next three hours, we would take them prisoners.

Just at that moment, when we had both angrily raised our voices and our positions seemed irreconcilable, the line went dead. Was it a technical failure? I doubt it. Those in the room suggested I should make another call, but I decided not to. I said to the generals, "If Maduro has a minimum of common sense, he will be the one to make the call." And so it was. A few minutes later, he was on the phone, very much calmed down. He assured me that Venezuela would always be in favor of peace and that he would order the immediate withdrawal of his troops. And he complied. Had he not done so, I was ready to order the arrest of the Venezuelan soldiers. Happily, diplomacy prevailed.

I never again spoke to the now Venezuelan dictator—because there is no other word for it, as is acknowledged by the immense majority of democratic nations worldwide. Maduro continued to insult me with more and more offensive and outlandish epithets, blaming Colombia for the general malaise affecting the Venezuelans and refusing to admit that he was the cause of it. I didn't fall into the trap of exchanging insults with him, but preferred to extend a helping hand, as far as possible, to the hundreds of thousands of Venezuelans flooding into Colombia to escape from the misery to which they had been submitted by an autistic and authoritarian regime.

The Bolivarian autocrat's final infamy was directed at me just three days before I finished my term of office. On August 4, 2018, he was victim of a peculiar and never clarified attempt on his life by drones in the middle of a military parade. No more than a few hours had gone by before Maduro was pointing to me as the intellectual author of the failed assassination attempt. No one with any sense at all took his accusation seriously, but it does reveal his lack of balance and his capacity for inventing falsehoods. I decided to respond with humor, publishing a tweet to say that on the day of the alleged attempt on his life I had more important things to do than conspire to murder my Venezuelan colleague: I was with my family celebrating the christening of our first granddaughter, Celeste.

In his eagerness to emulate Chávez—who introduced him into political life and raised him up to occupy posts of the greatest responsibility in the state—Maduro has performed in the exaggerated manner of all untalented impersonators. He roundly denies the frightful reality into which he has led his people, while his paranoia leads him to attribute all the problems to external factors. In his megalomania, he is convinced he is the very incarnation of the Venezuelan people, a kind of savior to whom his personal god, Chávez, in the form of a little bird, secretly whispers advice on how to run the country. As a result, he has become a grotesque and anachronistic reincarnation of the tropical dictatorships that were rife in Latin America and the Caribbean in the twentieth century. He would be laughable if it weren't for the real nightmare he has created for the Venezuelans and for the region. A nightmare that, like all bad dreams, sooner or later will come to an end.

CHAPTER 12

Rafael Correa

From Hostility to Cooperation

BOMBING ON ECUADORIAN TERRITORY

If my relationship with Hugo Chávez had been difficult because of our ideological differences, the situation with Ecuador's president, Rafael Correa, was no better. In fact, it suffered from a precedent that seemed to make reconciliation almost impossible. Luckily, it was once again the question of peace and the welfare of our respective nations that we put above any other consideration.

But why was our relationship so difficult? The reason could hardly be more cogent. Because on February 29, 2008, it was I who as minister of defense authorized an airstrike on a camp of one of the most important members of the Farc's secretariat, alias Raúl Reyes, on Ecuadorian soil just 1,800 meters from the Colombian border.

It was one of the most difficult decisions of my time at the ministry, and of my life, but I made it out of the conviction that it was necessary to strike the guerrillas in the head, delivering blows to their strategic leaders instead of limiting ourselves to combating, capturing, and eliminating guerrilla commanders of lesser rank who could easily be replaced. Reyes was the first member of the secretariat to be taken out by our armed forces. And he wasn't just one more guerrilla, but one of immense prestige in the Farc, only one step down in hierarchy from their top commander, Manuel Marulanda, and on the same level as the guerrilla's military chief, alias Mono Jojoy.

Reyes, whose real name was Luis Édgar Devia, had played a decisive role—and a very visible one—in the frustrated peace process at Caguán, and had then been put in charge of coordinating the activities of the Farc's Southern Block in the Colombian Amazon, and also of the guerrilla's international contacts. The Colombian justice system had issued innumerable warrants for his arrest for crimes of terrorism, kidnapping, rebellion, and other felonies, and he was wanted by the United States on charges of drug trafficking.

We knew where his zone of operations was located, but he had become a slippery customer for a reason that was out of our control: he was constantly crossing the Ecuadorian border, where he took refuge in a series of camps the guerrillas had established in that neighboring country.

The Colombian government had on several occasions alerted Ecuador's civilian and military authorities and police to the presence of Farc camps on their northern border. However, the actions of the Ecuadorian troops regarding those guerrilla settlements had not been particularly effective. And then we came to know that certain high-level officials of President Correa's government and some retired Ecuadorian military officers had been conducting clandestine meetings with Reyes.

Nonetheless, he was not an easy target. Between 2007 and February 2008, we launched at least four operations to capture him, which were thwarted, among other reasons, because he took refuge in the neighboring territory. Finally, toward the end of February 2008, the intelligence service of our police force, who had been tailing him for a very long time, obtained information that would be decisive. Reyes was in a base camp in Ecuador, less than two kilometers from the Colombian border, and it was expected that, on the night of February 29, he would cross the river that separated the two countries for a meeting with his contact in the drug trade, on Colombian soil.

With this information in hand, a sophisticated operation was planned—it was named Operation Phoenix—with the participation of special forces from the Colombian police, army, navy and air force. I was advised of the operation, naturally, as was President Uribe.

It so happened that on that day I was with members of the commission on ethics and transparency that accompanied and monitored the contracts and process of acquisition of military equipment with special funding. We were at the military base of Tres Esquinas (Three Corners) in Caquetá, from where the Super Tucano bombers would fly out on their mission to bomb the Reyes camp. We showed the Brazilian-made planes to the members of the commission—businessmen and industrialists that included Luis Carlos Sarmiento, José Alejandro Cortés, Gustavo Adolfo Carvajal, Luis Carlos Villegas, Carlos Angulo, and Juan Luis Mejía, along with the attorney general, Edgardo Maya, and the comptroller general, Julio César Turbay. Of course, they had no idea that these planes would be the same ones that, a few hours later, would cause the death, for the first time in the history of the war with the Farc, of one of the seven members of the guerrilla secretariat. To Villegas, president of the National Association of Industrialists, I said: "You will soon see results for the taxes you businesspeople are paying. Pray hard that tomorrow we'll be able to give you great news."

Around ten o'clock that night, when planes had left other bases farther away and were flying toward the border zone that separated Colombia from Ecuador, the center of intelligence received a call that changed our plans completely. "The guy didn't leave; he didn't cross the border. But we are absolutely certain he is at the camp."

Reyes's satellite telephone signal, which had been turned off for months, was now on again and left no doubt as to his whereabouts. At that moment, as minister of defense, I had to make a decision that, more than personal, was a decision of state. After years of pursuing him unsuccessfully, we at last knew the exact location of Reyes, a guerrilla leader who had orchestrated attack after attack on the Colombians and who right now was forging international links to continue his offensive actions against our nation. I had no option; the operation was to go ahead. At that moment I reflected that operations of this kind are not only to be seen in the context of the debated principle of self-defense, as some renowned jurists have insisted, but ought to be carried out in accordance with the norms of international humanitarian law, which provides the rules of the game in the case of an internal armed conflict.

Once they had my authorization, the pilots had only to alter very slightly the movement of their controls to make a change in the coordinates of their target. Two minutes after midnight, they dropped their precision bombs from Colombian air space, and without having to cross the border, hit the exact spot not just of the camp but of the bunk Reyes was sleeping on. We knew there were no civilians in the area. And no airplane with fixed wings crossed the border or flew over Ecuadorian territory.

The bombs were absolutely precise and hit the camp in the jungle area of Angostura in the Ecuadorian province of Sucumbíos. We sent special troops to close off the area, for we knew several guerrillas had survived and were attempting to hide Reyes's body. We also sent members of the police force to carry out judicial functions and guarantee the chain of custody of any items confiscated, and all legal proceedings.

After an arduous trek through the jungle in the darkness of the night, the military advance troops reported that they had recovered the bodies of Reyes and his companion, which other guerrillas had dragged some meters away in an effort to hide them. If the troops had taken a bit longer to get to the camp,

Reyes's men might have managed to abscond with his corpse, and without it we would be telling a very different story.

The army captain who directed the advance troops corroborated that Reyes had been killed and sent a simple radio message to his superior officer: "Viva Colombia! Viva Colombia!" This was the code phrase established to confirm the success of the operation. It was after three in the morning when I called President Uribe to give him the news that changed the military perspective of the internal conflict: it was the first time we had hit such a high-profile target. We had demolished the myth that the members of the Farc secretariat were invulnerable.

The president was euphoric. But he did not lose sight of the fact that we had broken only one link in the chain. So besides congratulating me, he set me a new challenge. "And Mono Jojoy? When are going to get him?"

CORREA'S INDIGNATION

Now came the most difficult part: to notify the Ecuadorian authorities that we had dropped bombs on their territory to eliminate a Farc guerrilla camp in the process of carrying out an attack that could also be typified as an antinarcotics operation.

The Colombian police communicated with their opposite numbers in Ecuador advising them of the operation and reporting that there were dead and wounded found in the camp, which the Colombian police would keep in their custody until the Ecuadorians arrived. At the same time, early that morning, President Uribe called President Correa and informed him of the incursion, explaining that the operation, as originally planned, was to have been carried out within Colombia's borders, but in the course of the operation, it had been found necessary to attack the guerrillas on Ecuadorian soil. Correa, who was in the middle of a radio broadcast, reacted calmly at first to Uribe's information and asked his police and army officials to verify what had occurred. After all, the attack had been on a camp of Colombian terrorists who had been violating Ecuadorian sovereignty. But a few hours later—and this was my impression, after discussing the matter with President Chávez—the Ecuadorian president flew into a fit of rage and indignation that led to the breaking off of diplomatic relations between our two countries.

The camp where we had located Reyes with the men and women under his command was not a makeshift temporary affair, as the Ecuadorian authorities tried to make out, beginning with President Correa, who stated that it was an "ambulatory camp improvised out of plastic sheets just for passing the night." No, it was a headquarters-type camp of a permanent nature, with timber and concrete buildings, places for meetings, and training grounds. On this site, the guerrillas planned kidnappings and attacks against the Colombian population and conspired internationally to overthrow our government and our democratic system. The secretary-general of the Organization of American States, the Chilean José Miguel Insulza, who visited the bombed camp a few days later on a mission of verification, declared that "this was not a recently installed camp, but had probably been there for several months."

And it was a hiding place for more than just the guerrilla chief and his cohorts. Reyes had three computers with him, and several external hard drives, which were captured and handed over to the police. They were a veritable treasure trove, containing nothing less than a record of all this guerrilla commander's goings-on in recent years, his communications with the other members of the secretariat and leaders of the guerrillas' various fronts, not to mention Colombian and foreign politicians, plus photographs and videos that linked a great many people with criminal activities.

This was Operation Phoenix's major success, even more important than having brought down, for the first time, a member of the secretariat. We had confiscated an arsenal of strategic information from which we extracted an enormous quantity of data with which we could combat the guerrillas and their connections, both in Colombia and internationally. The veracity and nonmanipulation or modification of the files found on the computers were certified by the secretary-general of Interpol, Ronald K. Noble.

Naturally, Ecuador's indignation did not take long in contaminating President Correa's allies on the Latin American continent, especially those who shared his left-wing ideology, such as the heads of state of Venezuela, Bolivia, and Nicaragua. On March 2, President Chávez, publicly and in a bombastic tone of voice, ordered ten battalions of troops to mobilize along the Colombian border, instructed all Venezuelan diplomats accredited in Bogotá to return at once to Caracas, and in what was evidently meant to be an act of provocation, called for a minute of silence in memory of Reyes. Chávez never lost an opportunity to present himself as the region's defender.

The situation become extremely dangerous and was not defused until March 7 when, in a meeting of the Group of Rio in the Dominican Republic, and thanks to the mediation of that country's president, Leonel Fernández, tensions were relaxed and the presidents of the two nations that were affected agreed to dialogue. When President Uribe stood up and approached President Correa with his hand outstretched in a gesture of peace, amid the applause of his colleagues in the region, Correa shook his hand but the cameras allowed everyone on the continent to see the severe look of defiance on his face, which sent an unmistakable message to Uribe and to Colombia: as far as Ecuador was concerned, the offense was not forgotten.

REPAIRING RELATIONS WITH ECUADOR

The target of President Correa's anger was not just President Uribe but also his defense minister who had authorized the attack on a guerrilla camp in the Ecuadorian jungle; namely, Juan Manuel Santos, about whom his colleague in Venezuela had confirmed his worst suspicions and put him on his guard.

A few days after the bombing, the highest tribunal of justice in the province of Sucumbíos instigated a criminal investigation involving me and the high commanders of Colombia's armed forces—General Freddy Padilla de León, commander of our military forces; and General Mario Montoya, commander of the army; General Jorge Ballesteros, commander of the air force; Admiral Guillermo Barrera, commander of the navy, and General Óscar Naranjo, director of the police force—for our part in the raid that led to the death of Reyes. I never hesitated in letting it be known that I was the person responsible for making the decision to go ahead with the bombing.

Finally, in the context of permanent tension still persisting between our two countries, I assumed the presidency in August 2010. President Correa attended the inauguration, a gesture of goodwill on his part that I greatly appreciated.

I have already quoted from my inaugural address. But here is another paragraph in which I spoke of Ecuador and Venezuela: "I am proud to have been the architect, as minister of foreign trade in the nineties, of the integration of Venezuela with Ecuador and many other countries around the world, an integration that generated hundreds of thousands of jobs and brought our people prosperity and welfare. One of my fundamental purposes was to reconstitute relations with Venezuela and Ecuador, rebuilding trust, with emphasis on diplomacy and prudence."

Just as I had done with Chávez, I was ready to improve, as far as lay in my power, relations with Correa and the Ecuadorian people, a nation with which Colombia had always maintained sentiments of friendship and solidarity.

The occasion to cement relations presented itself on November 28, 2010, when President Correa and I, along with six other heads of state from South America, including Hugo Chávez, attended the Fourth Summit of UNASUR in Georgetown, the capital of Guyana.

I should mention that the improvement of our relations with Chávez and the Venezuelan government was very well received by all other leaders in the region who were tired of tensions that only cause uncertainty and unease. Chávez and I greeted one another amiably, and our cordial relation had a positive impact on the summit meeting. Deep down we all knew that it would only be a question of time before an occasion arose that would lead to an approach to President Correa. If two sworn enemies like Chávez and me had found a way to put past rancor behind us, wasn't it logical that the same would happen with the president of a nation like Ecuador, with whom we had enjoyed so many historic bonds of friendship?

At the start, Correa and I saluted one another coldly and with our guard up. However, at a certain moment during the meeting we drew aside for a brief and frank exchange. It took only a few minutes, but they were immensely productive. I think we were both ready and willing to find a solution and to overcome angry reproaches in order to advance toward reestablishing relations between our two countries. It made no sense to remain stuck in a situation that had happened two years before. It was having a negative effect on both our economies, our border communities, and the—until then—close links between our people. Instead of which we could collaborate in our common fight against organized crime, revitalize investment and trade, improve the conditions of hundreds of thousands of people on both sides of the border, and all by simply sitting down to talk and coming to an agreement that would benefit both our nations.

In short, in those few minutes we agreed to work together as best we could for the good of our people. And I have to say we were faithful to that purpose during the time we both remained in power. I want to pay tribute to Correa's nobility in embracing reconciliation. After all, he was the offended party.

During the summit meeting, I was able to announce to the other heads of state that President Correa and I had decided to fully reestablish diplomatic relations and that we were committed to appoint our respective ambassadors at the latest by Christmas. It goes without saying that the salon resounded with jubilant expressions of relief and congratulations. President Correa also said a few words: "This is a joyful day for Latin America. We have decided to formalize and totally normalize the diplomatic relations that, as you know, were broken off in March 2008 for reasons everyone is aware of. . . . I want to acknowledge the openness of President Santos's government that, in a spirit of goodwill, has done everything possible to reestablish relations." And he added: "There are still certain things we will have to work on together, but we have taken the path that will lead us in the right direction."

President Lula of Brazil was very enthusiastic: "I am satisfied," he said. "I am convinced that we have managed to achieve, in these years, what many tried to do for decades without success: we have learned to respect one another and live together democratically in diversity." His words were met with a standing ovation. It was a very emotional moment for Colombia, a turning point in the normalization of relations between two neighbors.

FROM ANTAGONISM TO HARMONY

Rafael Correa is very different in personality from Hugo Chávez. The latter was an extrovert, full of that Caribbean warmth and sympathy that helps to quickly establish an atmosphere of trust. Correa by temperament is more reserved, but at the same time direct, and in that we are alike. However, Chávez and Correa had something in common: they both liked to sing! Whereas I never learned to sing, and have no ear for music.

After my conversation with Correa in Guyana, our relationship grew stronger and became more friendly, always characterized by mutual respect, frankness, and professionalism. Finally, the court in Sucumbíos lifted the warrants for arrest that had been issued against those Colombian military officers and police commanders who had taken part in Operation Phoenix. In 2016, another court in Ecuador closed a case that was still pending against me.

Unfortunately, in April 2018, when everything seemed to indicate that the judicial proceeding was a closed matter, the same court in Sucumbíos again called on the Colombian commanders to make declarations apropos the deaths of four Mexican citizens with links to the National Autonomous University of Mexico who had been visiting the Reyes camp and were killed in the raid. The commanders who were called by the Ecuadorian court included General Naranjo, who was director-general of the Colombian police force at the time, and was to become vice-president of the republic during the final sixteen months of my second term. I trust all will be eventually cleared up, on the understanding that the raid was a legitimate act of self-defense on the part of the Colombian government given the continued presence in the border zone of terrorists who were attacking our citizens and our infrastructure.

What we built with President Correa during what remained of our presidencies—after an incident as serious as the bombing of the Reyes camp—was a positive relationship that led to a level of cooperation between our two governments in economic, commercial, and security matters such as had never been seen before. We held bilateral cabinet meetings with relative frequency, in Ecuador or Colombia, to evaluate our coordination from all the relationship's aspects, with special emphasis on the welfare and progress of the border population.

And we achieved something more. Correa, like Chávez, became an ally and promoter of peace in Colombia. He determinedly supported the peace process with the Farc and was a facilitator of the process we initiated early in 2017 with the ELN, the last guerrilla group to still be operating in Colombia. The public phase of conversations with this subversive group was inaugurated in Quito in February 2017, with the first rounds of negotiation continuing up to April 2018, when Correa's successor, President Lenín Moreno announced Ecuador would not continue as guarantor for these dialogues.

This decision on the part of Ecuador was a consequence of the pain and commotion caused by the kidnapping and subsequent murders of three Ecuadorians, two journalists and their driver, in the border zone, a crime perpetrated by a dissident group from the Farc under the command of an Ecuadorian known as alias Guacho. The border area is an important corridor for the drug traffickers, with whom Guacho and his men were linked.

This kind of criminal activity is rare in Ecuador and for that reason caused enormous indignation and put pressure on President Moreno, who, surprisingly and with great haste, gave orders that Guacho should be captured in no more than ten days. This cost two of his ministers their jobs when the ten days were up and they had failed to comply with the president's peremptory command. You need time for these operations—as I know from experience—but sooner or later, they bear fruit. So I told my Ecuadorian colleague, "Don't worry, Lenín. Guacho will be caught before the year's out," And so it happened. Thanks to an operation set in motion by General Alberto Mejía, general commander of Colombia's military forces, and General Jorge Luis Vargas, director of criminal investigation of the national police force, the bloodthirsty guerrilla leader was finally killed in combat in the rural zone of Tumaco, department of Nariño, on December 21, 2018.

As I could well understand the motivation and sentiments of President

Moreno, we transferred the negotiating table with the ELN from Quito to Havana, where we had already experienced Cuba's capacity and willingness to house our efforts for peace.

With Hugo Chávez in Venezuela and Rafael Correa in Ecuador, I put into practice a principle that can be applied to every effort made to advance a superior aim: you must put aside any personal differences, any antagonism whatsoever, no matter how deep, to achieve peace. As long as differences are respected and the emphasis is placed on the concerns on which the parties coincide, it is possible, and indeed necessary, to work with one's rivals.

And this principle, which I found gave results on an international scale, was one I practiced, too, within my own government.

A TEAM OF RIVALS

I have always loved political biographies—the stories of men who have been decisive in world history, such as Benjamin Disraeli, Abraham Lincoln, Franklin D. Roosevelt, Winston Churchill, or John F. Kennedy—and during the months prior to my presidential campaign in 2010, I read one that certainly served me as an inspiration: *Team of Rivals: The Political Genius of Abraham Lincoln*, by the historian Doris Kearns Goodwin.

Anyone who knows the story, or has read the book or seen Steven Spielberg's magnificent film based on the book, will recall how Lincoln, after gaining the presidential nomination by the Republican Party in 1860, when he came to be president appointed the men who had been his rivals for the nomination to high posts in his cabinet. He appointed one of them as secretary of state, another as secretary of the treasury, and a third as attorney general. It was clear that his aim was to maintain his party's unity and gain something without which any presidential management is impossible: governability. In the film one sees how Lincoln had to compromise with congressmen and win their support by means of what is still called, in the United States, "pork barrel"—in Colombia the practice is derogitorily called "marmalade"—in order to ensure that he could obtain the most noble and most important of his objectives: the abolition of the hateful institution of slavery.

During my time as minister for foreign trade, and then as finance minister and minister of defense, I came to see that the success of a government depends to a great extent on governability vis-à-vis the legislative body. In each of these posts, I was required to push through Congress some crucial reforms and complex projects of law, and it was evident that, without an appropriate and constructive cooperation between the executive and the legislative branches of government, the priority aims of any administration can be frustrated. Among the hardest-fought battles I ever had to wage in Congress as finance minister was the constitutional reform on territorial transfers, Law 617 of the year 2000, which put a brake on the growing state bureaucracy.

Governability is what Lincoln needed to obtain the thirteenth amendment to the US Constitution that officially abolished slavery in the United States, and was invoked by Lyndon B. Johnson to win approval for the Civil Rights Law, to cite two well-known examples. And governability is what I was going to need to ensure votes for the Law of Victims and Restitution of Land, to reform and make more equitable the system of distributing royalties from oil wells and mining, and to guarantee the sustainability of the nation's finances, among other problems that required urgent attention.

When I won the presidential election, with the endorsement of the Party of the U, even though we were the principal presence in Congress, the party I represented did not have a sufficient majority to carry through the ambitious legislative agenda we had in mind to transform Colombia. So I saw the example of Lincoln as an inspiring precedent. Besides the Party of the U, I needed the collaboration of other parties that were different but had affinity with us, such as the Liberal Party, which is that of my political origins; the Conservative Party, and the party known as Radical Change, all of whom had competed with me in the presidential elections.

During the campaign, we had confronted one another with respect, but pulling no punches, as is normal in any electoral contest. Among my competitors there had been Rafael Pardo, the Liberal Party candidate, and Germán Vargas Lleras, candidate for Radical Change. After the first round, when the only two candidates left were myself and Antanas Mockus of the Green Party, I proposed a government of national unity and invited my erstwhile competitors, Vargas and Pardo, to accompany me in that effort for the good of the country. I also proposed to adopt some of the excellent initiatives they had presented on matters of employment and justice, for example. And they accepted, as did the Conservative Party.

In my first speech as president-elect, the day of my victory, June 20, 2010, I said: "Let's turn the page on hate. Let's turn the page on divisions. Colombia's hour has arrived, and it is the hour of unity." So, following the good example of Lincoln, I appointed Vargas minister for the interior and justice, a post of enormous political weight, and Pardo as minister for labor, a responsibility he took on only as of October 2011, because we had to reestablish that ministry, which had been abolished by President Uribe. From these posts, the two men had an opportunity to put into practice the most positive proposals they had made during their campaigns. I also appointed several members of the Conservative Party to key posts in the cabinet, such as the Ministries of Finance, Mining, and Agriculture.

Vargas Lleras later became minister for housing, and in the 2014 elections, when I was reelected for a second term, I had him as running mate for the vice-presidency, which post he held for three years before resigning to run for president again, in the hope of being my successor.

These appointments produced contrary effects. On the one hand, they contributed to generating governability in Congress, where we managed to win votes for some indispensable reforms that had been denied or postponed for years, or even decades. On the other hand, this brought down on me the ire of my predecessor, Álvaro Uribe, who considered several of the ministers I appointed—especially Vargas Lleras and the Conservative Juan Camilo Restrepo—his political enemies. Such was his loathing of Vargas Lleras that he sent me word via Gabriel Silva, a great friend who had followed me in the defense ministry, that if I were to appoint Vargas Lleras as minister of defense, he would seek asylum in another country.

I did not make these appointments with the intention of crossing my predecessor. But one thing had become very clear: the new president was acting with total autonomy. Exercising that autonomy, I decided to approach my former rivals—on the continent and in Colombia itself—and invite them to work together for superior goals. History was to show that I had chosen the right path.

LESSON 2

Make Allies out of Your Enemies

A recent film, *The Journey*, directed by Nick Hamm, tells a true story that occurred in 2006 and helped to get the peace process started in Northern Ireland. It deals with an event that involved two Irish leaders who represented diametrically opposed views and were considered to be sworn enemies: Ian Paisley, the Unionist leader, and Martin McGuinness, ex-militant of the IRA and a leader of the Sinn Féin party. Due to unusual circumstances, these two lifelong antagonists were forced to share a long journey by car, and their conversation along the way ended up bringing them together and making what years before had seemed impossible become a reality: the coexistence of the two parties in power. In the course of the journey, McGuinness says to Paisley: "We are on the verge of something the wider world will applaud, but our own people will hate." And they did it. A year later, in 2007, the Unionist party accepted to share power with Sinn Féin: Paisley as prime minister and McGuinness as vice-prime minister. Their relationship became so cordial that they were nicknamed the Chuckle Brothers, a reference to a comic duo who always appeared laughing and making jokes with one another.

This is just one example among many that illustrate a simple truth, but one that is certainly not easy to apply; namely, that when you pursue a superior goal—and what could be a greater goal than peace?—you should, and can, work even with those with whom you are separated by enormous differences and disputes. It is just a question of finding a common interest, of accepting that neither one is going to convince the other, but can respect the other while admitting the differences.

When I decided to seek pathways to approach Presidents Chávez and Correa, or my former rivals to the presidency, I did not have to renounce my principles or give up my ideals, and nor did they. What we sought—and achieved for the benefit of peace and progress in Colombia and also in Venezuela and Ecuador—was a harmonious cooperation on fundamental matters on which we agreed. In other areas—such as the economic and political model of each country—we were separated by a bottomless abyss, and in that we decided to treat our differences with respect. To put it very simply, and using a common turn of phrase: we focused on what united us, and not on what divided us.

Working with rivals or former enemies can be the object of misunderstandings and reproaches. Many people see it as an act of weakness and lack of consistency, or even as a betrayal. But what it implies, to put it plainly, is a pragmatic attitude adopted in order to obtain a superior goal. And besides—and this should not be forgotten—you make peace with your enemies, not with your friends.

It is hard to find greater opposites—to cite another historical example—than leaders such as Winston Churchill, Charles de Gaulle, Franklin Roosevelt, and Joseph Stalin, in both their personalities and their ideologies. But if these men had not formed an alliance to stem the tide of Nazism, Europe and the world might not have overcome the threat.

I will finish this reflection with another anecdote attributed to Abraham Lincoln. It is said that once somebody criticized him for the benevolent treatment he meted out, as president of the United States, to the Southern rebels in the midst of the cruel Civil War. Lincoln's reply left his critic speechless: "Do I not destroy my enemies when I make them my friends?"

CHAPTER 13

First Approach to the Farc

HENRY ACOSTA'S LETTER

Before assuming the presidency, I made two international trips to strengthen ties and exchange opinions with the heads of state of different countries, accompanied by María Ángela Holguín, who was to be my minister of foreign affairs during the eight years I was in government. My first itinerary included the United Kingdom, Germany, France, and Spain. Then I concentrated on Latin America, visiting Mexico, Panama, Costa Rica, Chile, Argentina, Peru, the Dominican Republic, and lastly Haiti, where I was shocked to see the devastating effects of the earthquake that had occurred in January, and noted that the impressive quantity of international aid that had been promised to that Caribbean country had not arrived, or at least I could see no sign of it. This prompted me to include in my government's international agenda a permanent commitment to the Haitian people, in accordance with which we proposed—and led—a session dedicated to the subject at the United Nations Security Council.

Back in Bogotá, on July 30, 2010, just a week before my inauguration, Lucía Jaramillo, a trusted collaborator who had worked with me at the Good Government Foundation and also in my presidential campaign, passed on to me a letter that Frank Pearl, the high commissioner for peace in the outgoing government, had asked her to deliver to me as soon as I returned from my travels.

It was a letter to me from Henry Acosta, the man who had acted as facilitator and intermediary between Álvaro Uribe's government and the Farc. The letter, dated July 12, contained a review of Acosta's activities over the past few years:

> In recent times, that is to say during the two presidential terms of Dr. Álvaro Uribe Vélez, I have taken on the responsibility to serve patriotically in

> helping to facilitate approaches between the national government and the Farc in search of peace, pardon, and reconciliation. During this period, and in my capacity as facilitator authorized in writing by President Uribe and by the Farc, I have been witness to the Farc's political willingness to look for a political negotiation to end the armed conflict that our country is going through. I have also seen how, intermittently, the national government varies between actions to defeat the insurgents by military force and the search for dialogue with the Farc. Meanwhile, blood continues to be shed. The nation's soldiers, and likewise the Farc guerrillas, belong to the poorest and most socioeconomically excluded sectors of the republic. It would be possible to negotiate politically so that these people in arms, on both sides, do not keep on killing one another. In fact, in the recent past we have been closer to that possibility than distant from it.

In this letter, Acosta proposed that we continue along the path on which the outgoing government had advanced, and that we should do so "by means of a secret meeting in another country, solely with the idea of establishing a road map for politically negotiating a solution to the internal armed conflict." And he ended with a concrete suggestion: "Dr. Juan Manuel Santos, my opinion is that neither will the government defeat the Farc militarily, nor will the Farc militarily defeat the government. All that is left is a political negotiation of the internal armed conflict, with dignity, equity and social justice. The alternative is more bloodshed and poverty taking root and growing in our homeland."

I had heard of Acosta and I was aware of the different approaches the Uribe government had made to the guerrillas through Pearl. The letter, therefore, fell on fertile soil.

WHAT FRANK PEARL TOLD ME

Frank Pearl, an economist with a long list of successes in the private sector, had been presidential adviser on social reintegration since the year 2006. As such, he had coordinated the reintegration into civil society of almost fifty thousand ex-combatants, including paramilitaries who had been demobilized collectively in the process carried out by President Uribe, and guerrillas, who had tired of fighting a war and demobilized individually or in small groups. At the start of 2009, Pearl became high commissioner for peace, replacing the psychiatrist Luis Carlos Restrepo, who occupied that post from the beginning of Uribe's government. Pearl inherited Acosta's contacts with the Farc and continued to advance in approaches to the guerrillas.

That is why Pearl was one of the first people I wanted to talk with as soon as I was elected, so that he could bring me up to date on progress in that area. He had worked with me in the Good Government Foundation, and his brother William had assisted me in my brief campaign as presidential precandidate for the Liberal Party in 1998. Frank and I had both participated in the same government and had a good relationship, cemented by his friendship with my brother-in-law Mauricio Rodríguez, with whom he had worked years before in Dow Chemical, the multinational pharmaceutical company. On Monday, June 21, the day after my win in the second round of voting, I called Frank and asked him if we could meet up. He consulted with President Uribe, who gave his consent for Pearl to inform me about his work.

It was interesting for me to find out what progress had been made in approaches between the government and the guerrillas. With the ELN, as I said before, the Uribe government had gotten as far as drawing up a preaccord to officially begin talks in 2007. And with the Farc, the same government had gone from messages on both sides to arrive at an eventual humanitarian exchange of kidnap victims for guerrilla prisoners, to a concrete invitation by Uribe to this insurgent group to hold a direct and secret meeting in Brazil "with an open agenda . . . that could lead to a more detailed and concrete agenda in the future."

Pearl told me that, although the guerrillas had declined this meeting via a communiqué on April 7, the content of which was leaked to Telesur, he had gone as far as meeting with the Brazilian minister of foreign relations, Celso Amorim, and had also talked to that country's defense minister, and had found the Brazilians ready and willing to host a discreet exploratory meeting between the Colombian government and the Farc. Furthermore, on May 24, 2010, the Brazilian embassy had given him a list of four possible sites for the meeting, with their respective maps. He added that a similar approach had been made to Sweden, and that country had also offered to host preliminary meetings intended to create an atmosphere conducive to peace talks. Pearl also insisted that, from his experience, it would be indispensable to restore relations with Chávez, since history has shown that internal conflicts cannot be resolved without a minimum of help from neighboring countries.

And he commented on something else that greatly surprised me; namely, that when the former commissioner for peace, Luis Carlos Restrepo—now a fugitive from justice due to having staged a false demobilization of a non-existent paramilitary group—resigned in February 2009, he took with him all the documents, files, and videos on the contacts for peace that he had promoted. The office Pearl inherited did not contain a single folder or any correspondence, neither on the attempts at contacts and negotiation with the guerrillas nor even on the process of demobilization of the paramilitaries and the negotiations carried out with them in the zone of Santa Fe de Ralito in the department of Córdoba. Everything was gone, and Pearl had to start from scratch.

It was with these elements in hand—the detailed information Pearl gave me on progress in the approaches to the guerrillas, Acosta's letter and the rendezvous with President Chávez to take place in Santa Marta on August 10, which had been arranged thanks to the mediation of the former Argentine president Néstor Kirchner—that I decided to openly announce in my inaugural address, to the surprise of many, that the door for dialogue was not closed and locked. The key to that door had been in the hands of President Uribe and his peace commissioners for eight years, and now I was preparing to use it when conditions were propitious.

MY MESSAGE TO THE FARC

At the start of my government, I did not appoint anyone to succeed Pearl as commissioner. At the time, no peace process was moving forward and I decided to take on personally the task of looking for a way to begin dialogue. In September, I appointed Sergio Jaramillo, my former vice-minister of defense, national security adviser, bearing in mind that he was the person who had all the necessary abilities and disposition to work on the subject of peace whenever required. Meanwhile, Pearl went to Harvard University to continue his studies, but not before letting me know he would be ready to work with me if and when I needed him.

Toward the end of August—in other words, less than a month after my inauguration—I called Acosta directly on my cell phone. I knew that any new approach to the Farc should be carried out with discretion, and I preferred to handle the matter without intermediaries. I told him I had received his letter and was interested in talking with him. A few days later, I called him again and invited him to the presidential palace, la Casa de Nariño, on Monday, September 6.

Acosta says that at first he doubted it was really me who was calling him, for he thought it odd that I had not phoned via the presidential switchboard. His wife, Julieta—who accompanies him in his exploits and to whom he lovingly refers as Dulcinea, a nickname given her by the guerrilla commander Pablo Catatumbo—called my office to confirm the appointment, and only then were they sure it was not a practical joke or some kind of trap.

Acosta arrived punctually and I received him in my office in company of Lucía Jaramillo. He told me he had met me thirty-five years ago—which I didn't remember—in the mid-seventies, when I was representing Colombia at the International Coffee Organization in London and he was managing a coffee cooperative. By now, he was a man who had seen a lot in life. He was sixty years of age, heavily built, round-bellied and slow in his movements. He gave me the impression of a sincere and good-humored man, committed to peace and to carrying out the role of emissary that had fallen to his lot.

We talked for a couple of hours, during which he recounted the different tasks he had been involved in as intermediary between Uribe and the Farc, and how things were at that moment, following on the government's proposal to hold a direct meeting in Brazil. He insisted emphatically that the guerrillas were ready and willing to find a path that might lead to a table for sitting down to talk.

That being the case, on that day, practically two years before I would be able to announce the beginning of formal peace talks with the Farc, I decided to send Alfonso Cano and Pablo Catatumbo a message via Henry Acosta, the intermediary in whom they most confided.

My message, transmitted verbally by Acosta, was more or less as follows:

> *I want to make peace with you, and I suggest we begin with a secret meeting, possibly in Brazil or in Sweden, between two high-level delegates on your side and two delegates appointed by me, to agree to a way of progressing toward a negotiated solution to the conflict. My delegates will be my brother Enrique, whom you already know, and the former commissioner for peace, Frank Pearl. There will be no intermediaries, because peace in Colombia can, and should, be made by Colombians. The meeting must be secret, and if you leak it, we will take that to mean there is no real willingness to dialogue on your side. Only when we think it convenient and the time is ripe will we make our conversations public.*

Acosta wrote a letter expressing the content of my message and handed it to Catatumbo. A week later, in some place in the mountainous area of

Valle del Cauca, Catatumbo said he would consult with Cano, the Farc's commander-in-chief, before giving a reply.

Now the ball was in the guerrillas' court. But the conflict did not let up, and the rules of war are hard. Nobody imagined that, within just a few days, on September 23, that subversive group was going to suffer one of the greatest losses in its history.

THERE'S NO BETTER AMBASSADOR THAN A BROTHER

One person who was important to me in those moments, for his advice and experience, was my brother Enrique. As I mentioned earlier, in 1968, that year of revolutions and utopias, while I was at the Naval Academy of Cadets, Enrique was doing a postgraduate course in Germany and imbibing the dreams and ideals expounded with proclamations, graffiti, demonstrations, and parades by students in Berlin, Paris, Chicago, Prague, London, and Mexico City. On returning from Europe, he had taken a stance politically on the left, and that was reflected in the chronicles and columns he published in *El Tiempo*.

Enrique became one of the country's most influential opinion makers through his column Contraescape. In 1974, he joined forces with Gabriel García Márquez, Orlando Fals Borda, Jorge Restrepo, Antonio Caballero, José Vicente Kataraín, Roberto Pombo, and Hernando Corral, among other left-wing journalists and intellectuals, to create the magazine *Alternativa*. This publication was critical of the National Front system of government that was coming to an end at that time, having been a political experiment conceived to put an end to partisan violence, but which, at the same time, stifled any other political initiatives. Until it closed down in 1980, *Alternativa* was the voice of the democratic Left in Colombia.

Enrique continued collaborating with *El Tiempo*, becoming deputy director when I resigned, and from 1999 to 2009, codirector jointly with our cousin Rafael Santos.

Like many of his generation, his ideology gradually veered from the left toward the center of the political spectrum, though he never abandoned his commitment to progressive ideas and freedoms—especially freedom of the press, which he vigorously defended as vice-president and later president of the Inter American Press Association. And he was no less committed to the cause of peace. In the eighties, he was a member of the peace commission during the administration of Belisario Betancur, and in that capacity visited the Green House (Casa Verde) in the municipality of Uribe, the Farc's headquarters, which would be bombed by the Gaviria government in December 1990. On his visit there in the mid-eighties, Enrique had long conversations with Jacobo Arenas, the ideologue and cofounder of the Farc, and with Alfonso Cano, at the time a young member of the Secretariat.

Enrique tells how Arenas said he had done his military service in the battalion in charge of security at the presidential palace, and how he served there on duty in the forties during the government of Eduardo Santos. "He was a true democrat," Arenas said. "Not a fascist, like your father and your uncle Hernando."*

Years later Enrique would meet Alfonso Cano again, in June 2000, this time in the demilitarized zone of Caguán during the Pastrana peace talks. One night Cano invited him to a glass of cognac or whiskey and a chat, and Enrique was up until dawn debating with him and his righthand man Pablo Catatumbo. Cano was an anthropologist and a radical, studious and intelligent but at the same time intransigent, who was to succeed Manuel Marulanda in the role of commander-in-chief of the Farc.

Given all these antecedents, Enrique was an obvious person to talk to whenever I needed an opinion or advice on how to handle approaches to the guerrilla and the search for peace. Temperamentally we are quite different and do not always agree. But Enrique's common sense and even his skepticism have often helped me focus my expectations when making crucial decisions.

Enrique had retired from *El Tiempo* not long before my presidential campaign, in which he did not take part, since he never liked the fact that his brother had gone into politics. At the moment I was elected, he and his wife Gina were living in Miami, and he came to Colombia only on short visits. Nonetheless, he made it clear that I could count on him and his experience in any way I thought he could be useful.

When he arrived in Bogotá early in August, in time for my inauguration, I asked him to jot down a few ideas on how I should handle the subject of the guerrillas, and I used several of them in my address.

In the first days of September, when I decided to call Henry Acosta, the Farc's facilitator, I told Enrique that, being my brother, I thought of naming

---

* This and other stories and reflections on the search for peace, especially on the exploratory phase of the dialogues with the Farc during my government are to be found in Enrique's book *Así empezó todo* (Bogotá: Intermedio Editores, 2014).

him as my personal delegate to the initial secret meeting in which we were going to try to find out whether the other party was really interested in making peace. Enrique accepted without thinking twice, and he agreed with me that the most important proof that the guerrillas were serious about making peace would be their observance of strict confidentiality with regard to the meeting, or any further progress we might make, until we decided it was time to go public. On former occasions, they had leaked to the press reports on attempts at an approach, causing them to fail before they got started. If they proved themselves capable of keeping things secret this time, it would probably indicate that we had arrived at the third condition for a successful peace process: a real will for peace on the part of the guerrilla leaders.

I have to say that the Farc received positively, and saw as a gesture that inspired confidence and ratified my commitment to dialogue, the fact that I had chosen my own brother as delegate to meet with them. I don't approve of nepotism, but in this case I had no doubt about what I was doing. What better ambassador could I have found for this task than my brother.

CHAPTER 14

The Fall of Number Two

THE POWER OF INTELLIGENCE

From my very first day as president, I assumed direct supervision of operations by the public forces against the guerrillas and the drug mafias. It was a kind of professional hazard since I had been doing it for three years as defense minister and so it seemed to me natural that I should keep working at the same job. To the Ministry of Defense, I appointed Rodrigo Rivera, a Liberal Party member and lawyer, former president of the Chamber of Representatives during the 8,000 Process, a well-mannered man, highly respected and an excellent politician. In fact, Rodrigo had been one of the coordinators of my campaign.

As I have already said in a previous chapter, from the year 2006 onward we had set in motion a profound transformation in the armed forces' mode of operating, based on two fundamental aspects: on the one hand, the strengthening and modernization of intelligence, as the principal weapon for hunting out elusive targets of high strategic value; and on the other, placing emphasis on joint and coordinated work between the different military forces and the police at the highest level.

This transformation had produced important results, like the death of Raúl Reyes, the first member of the Farc's secretariat to be wiped out by our public force, not to mention the killing or capture of a lot of other leaders of that guerrilla organization, such as Negro Acacio and Martín Caballero.

It is no wonder, then, that one of my priorities on assuming the presidency was to keep moving along the same lines of operational successes, to consolidate the conditions that I always felt were required to achieve peace: a correlation of forces in favor of the state that would convince the guerrilla chiefs—because we had shown we could get to them, something that no one had been able to do in forty years—that they would be better off personally by making peace than by continuing to make war.

At this point, as Manuel Marulanda had died in March 2008, the two main leaders of the Farc were Alfonso Cano, the new leader of the guerrilla group, who mostly operated in a mountainous region between Tolima and Cauca to the country's southwest, and alias Mono Jojoy, also known as Jorge Briceño, though his real name was Víctor Julio Suárez.

While Cano was the overall leader of the organization, and was considered to be their ideologue, Jojoy was their most outstanding military chief. With more than thirty-five years in the guerrilla, having entered as a boy of twelve, he had risen in the ranks under the tutelage of Marulanda and had become in the course of time the most powerful man in the organization. He was commander of the Eastern Block, which constituted the guerrillas' principal source of income since it operated in the area of the Eastern Plains and the Orinoquia where the major part of the drug trade was concentrated. In the era of the Caguán process, this block numbered five or six thousand men in arms.

Jojoy, a cold-blooded and bloodthirsty man who didn't hesitate to order the firing squad even for his own men, was responsible for the strategy of kidnappings and extortion. He ordered dozens of attacks on townships, firing gas cylinders at defenseless villagers, and at a certain moment attempted to mount a threatening guerrilla ring around Bogotá from his group's stronghold in the eastern mountain range. In practice, he behaved like an omnipotent authority in vast regions of Colombia where there was no presence of the state. One has to admit, however, that he was a great military strategist and a charismatic leader who won the respect and admiration of his men, and they protected him by means of concentric rings of security comprising between one and two thousand guerrilla combatants.

For over three decades Colombia's armed forces had pursued him in vain, for this experienced guerrilla chief was constantly changing his position and maintained a network of men so keenly on the alert that it was impossible to surprise him. Around him there had grown up a myth that he was untouchable.

This being the case, one of the first reports I requested from the commanders of the armed forces regarded how we were going to catch Jojoy. I especially consulted General Óscar Naranjo, who had been director of the police force during the former government—thanks to my recommendation,

Mandela told me: "Peace is an indispensable condition for development. Without peace, Colombia will never get off the ground." That's where I envisioned my destination port.

"I was a witness to the friendship between Fidel and Gabo in 1997 when I was trying to bring together the different actors in the armed conflict to dialogue and build a proposal for peace—the days of my 'conspiracy.'" (Havana, 1997)

Ever since the former British prime minister Tony Blair was in government, together we defended the thesis of the Third Way. Blair supported the process of modernizing our military intelligence and was a great ally of the peace process.

"Operation Checkmate was a masterstroke, a perfectly executed operation, as Ingrid Betancourt called it in one of her first statements after being freed. And it was a tremendous relief, an injection of hope and joy for all Colombians." (Bogotá, July 2, 2008. Photo: Fernando Vergara/AP)

"Chávez threw back his head and laughed, and from that moment we got on fine and had a relaxed conversation full of good humor and understanding, without denying our profound differences." (Santa Marta, Quinta de San Pedro Alejandrino, August 10, 2010)

Before we started the official meeting, we gave a joint press conference in which President Obama mentioned the results of Operation Sodoma, where the Farc military chief fell, which was the news of the moment, not only in Colombia but in the entire continent. (New York, September 24, 2010)

"If we have had victims, if we are still producing victims, we are going to locate them and take a stand where we ought to be, which is on their side, embracing them and understanding their suffering." (Sanction of the Law of Victims and Restitution of Land, with the presence of UN Secretary-General Ban Ki-moon. Bogotá, June 10, 2011)

"Today I want to announce that these exploratory meetings have culminated with the signing of an agreement between the national government and the Farc that establishes a procedure—a road map—to arrive at a final agreement that will put an end, once and for all, to this violence between children of the same nation." (Announcement to Colombians about the start of the peace process, surrounded by the dome of the armed forces and the ministerial cabinet. Bogotá, September 4, 2012)

"I could not help thinking about the enormous paradox that was implied in the fact that I, as president of Colombia, should be accompanying the funeral of a popular and polemic leader, as Chávez had been, and above all the international personality with whom I had had the most severe confrontation in my whole career in public life, whether as journalist or politician." (Caracas, March 8, 2013)

In a singular twist of history, in 2010 I was elected by the votes of the political right, and in 2014 I was reelected with the votes and support of the left, in addition to those in the center. Celebration of reelection for the second presidential term. *From left to right*: María Clemencia de Santos, María Antonia, Martín, Juan Manuel, and Esteban Santos. (Bogotá, June 15, 2014. Photo: León Darío Peláez/Semana)

The commission of lawyers that built the proposal for transitional justice, working in the apartment of Juan Carlos Henao. *From left to right*: Enrique Santiago, Manuel José Cepeda, Juan Carlos Henao, Douglass Cassel, Diego Martínez, and Álvaro Leyva. (Bogotá, September 2015)

As Timochenko stretched out his hand to me, President Raúl Castro approached us, laying his hands on ours to seal the importance of that moment. (Signature of the basis of the agreement on the subject of justice. Havana, September 23, 2015)

“We constituted a team of excellence whose dedicated work enabled us to achieve a final agreement to end the conflict with the Farc.” *From left to right*: Dudley Ankerson, Jonathan Powell, Frank Pearl, María Paulina Riveros, General Óscar Naranjo, María Ángela Holguín, Gonzalo Restrepo, Humberto de la Calle, President Santos, William Ury, Sergio Jaramillo, Joaquín Villalobos, Juan Fernando Cristo, Shlomo Ben-Ami, and General Jorge Enrique Mora. (Cartagena, January 8, 2016)

“María Ángela Holguín had given me the best news ever: negotiations with the Farc had been successfully concluded.” *From left to right*: Jesús Santrich, Iván Cepeda, Pastor Alape, María Ángela Holguín, Rafael Pardo, Sergio Jaramillo, Iván Márquez, Juan Fernando Cristo, Álvaro Leyva, Roy Barreras, Humberto de la Calle, Timochenko, Frank Pearl, General Óscar Naranjo, Rodrigo Granda, Joaquín Gómez, Pablo Catatumbo, and Enrique Santiago. (Havana, August 23, 2016)

“Perhaps the best summing up of the broad range of regional and world support we had received was seen on September 27, 2016, when the peace agreement with the Farc was signed in Cartagena in the presence of representatives from every corner of the planet.” Visible in the back, from left to right: Børge Brende, minister of foreign affairs of Norway; Ban Ki-moon, UN secretary-general; Enrique Peña Nieto, president of Mexico; Pedro Pablo Kuczynski, president of Peru; Raúl Castro, president of Cuba; and Juan Carlos I, king emeritus of Spain. (Cartagena, September 27, 2016)

“I prefer an imperfect agreement that saves lives to a perfect war that continues to sow death and suffering in our country, among our families.” President Santos and Timochenko, the top leader of the Farc, show the agreements signed. (Cartagena, September 27, 2016)

"Then I went upstairs to deliver my address. I spoke for just three minutes, doing my best to create an atmosphere of calm and confidence among all of my compatriots: those who had won a hairsbreadth victory with a no vote, the yes voters who had narrowly lost, and the great majority who had not voted at all." *From left to right*: Frank Pearl, María Ángela Holguín, General Óscar Naranjo, Humberto de la Calle, President Santos, Sergio Jaramillo, Gonzalo Restrepo, Juan Fernando Cristo, General Jorge Enrique Mora, and Roy Barreras. (Bogotá, October 2, 2016)

"Not since the time, years before, when he had decided to slander me, call me traitor, and convert himself into my most implacable opponent, had Uribe set foot in Casa de Nariño. After a formal handshake that was amicable enough, though cold, we conducted a meeting that lasted for about three hours." Looking on are Carlos Holmes Trujillo, who would be later minister of the Duque government, and Óscar Iván Zuluaga, my rival in the 2014 presidential elections. (Bogotá, October 5, 2016)

"The Nobel Prize arrived at just the right moment, like a gift from heaven, and made us feel as if the whole world was giving us a pat on the back and urging us to go ahead and bring the peace process to a successful conclusion." María Clemencia de Santos celebrates the news of the Nobel Peace Prize, together with President Santos and their daughter María Antonia. (Bogotá, October 7, 2016)

"The ceremony was a sober one, but no less emotional for that, especially since we had overcome one of the difficulties we had least expected and were signing an agreement that not long before had looked as if it were moribund." (Signature of new final agreement, Teatro Colón de Bogotá. November 24, 2016)

"There, in the solemn hall of the Norwegian capital, stood the representatives of eight million victims celebrating the end of a conflict that had robbed them of their loved ones or had stolen years from their lives." *Standing, from left to right*: Héctor Abad Faciolince, Pastora Mira, Liliana Pechené, Leyner Palacios, Clara Rojas, Fabiola Perdomo, and Ingrid Betancourt. (Oslo, December 10, 2016. Photo: Haakon Mosvold Larsen/AFP)

"The name of this one people is the world. The name of this one race is humanity." Nobel Peace Prize acceptance speech. (Oslo, December 10, 2016)

“Among the crowd there were a lot of Colombian flags waving, and when I heard cries of ‘Viva Colombia!’ my soul was filled with joy.” (Torchlight procession, Oslo, December 10, 2016)

“I was asked if I had any objection to Uribe joining me at the audience that I had scheduled with the pope. The request seemed odd, to say the least, but on the other hand I couldn’t say no to a petition from the Vatican, and maybe it could be an opportunity to smooth things over with Uribe and relieve the atmosphere of polarization that was so negatively affecting Colombia.” (Meeting of President Santos and former president Uribe with Pope Francis. The Vatican, December 16, 2016)

“Very discreetly, we played a part in helping those two sworn enemies, the United States and Cuba, to come closer. . . . I personally spoke about that matter with President Obama and President Castro, as well as with former president Clinton and the Democratic senator Patrick Leahy. My intention was to facilitate these approaches.” (Pictured with Bill Clinton at the World Coffee Producers Forum. Medellín, July 11, 2017)

“Even though Trump had congratulated us and expressed his praise for our peace process at a White House press conference, later, in his reelection campaign, that very process was to bear the brunt of his most fierce criticism.” (Meeting with President Donald Trump at the White House. Washington, DC, May 18, 2017)

"For verification, we also count on the support of a commission of notable personalities, comprising my good friend and fighter for peace at my side for over twenty years Felipe González, and Uruguay's ex-president José 'Pepe' Mujica." (Cali, June 13, 2017)

"Timochenko lifted the baby up while I took its hand. It was hard to believe that not long before we had been killing one another, and we had been doing so for fifty years, when we have so much in common: we are all Colombians and, above all, human beings." (Completion of the disarmament process. Mesetas, Meta, June 27, 2017)

“These arms, which had been hiding death and pain in their dark barrels, would now never be fired again.” (Closure and dispatch of the Farc’s last arms container for custody and destruction by the United Nations. Pondores, La Guajira, August 15, 2017)

“I met with the victims on countless occasions and in many parts of the country, in events where the government was providing free homes or some other kind of state assistance, and each time I was given proof of their courage, generosity, and solidarity. I was deeply moved by everything they told me.”

"In November 2016, in acknowledgement of his work for our country, at a ceremony in the Colombian embassy in Washington, I awarded Vice President Biden Colombia's most prestigious recognition, namely the Order of Boyacá." (Washington, DC, November 17, 2016)

Days after establishing the Compaz Foundation, dedicated to helping make reparation to victims, with funds from the Nobel Prize, I visited the monument *Fragmentos,* made by Doris Salcedo out of thirty-seven tons of weapons that belonged to the Farc. (Bogotá, December 14, 2018)

since I had total confidence in him—and was ratified in that post during my own government. Naranjo gave me details of the complex operation of infiltration that he had been carrying out ever since I first initiated it in my time as defense minister, and told me it would soon produce results.

Several members of the police force had infiltrated guerrilla structures near to Jojoy. One man, in particular, had gotten extremely close to the guerrilla leader. In August, he was just a few meters away from Jojoy's guerrilla camp and could furnish the armed forces with exact geographic coordinates to locate the spot. Once this data had been received by police intelligence, they worked with the other forces in what we called an "intelligence bubble"—something we had created when I was defense minister, where information obtained by different forces on any high-value target was shared, analyzed, and processed by a group of experts under the coordination of a high-ranking official. In that way the intelligence specialists reached a very high degree of certainty. Jojoy was in a locatable point in the jungle area of the Macarena mountain range in the department of Meta.

But the intelligence experts were not content with that. They knew the guerrilla commander was constantly on the move and they couldn't afford to make a mistake. Intelligence officers of the police force had already been in contact with a tradesman in the area who was contracted by the Eastern Block to provide the guerrillas with certain special items. Jojoy suffered from diabetes, so among the items were prescribed drugs as well as specially designed orthopedic army boots that enabled him to make long marches through the jungle. This tradesman was prepared to collaborate with the army in exchange for the 5 billion pesos (around US$1.5 million) that the government had offered as a reward to anyone who could help locate Jojoy. He gave the officers details on the items he was expected to deliver to the guerrillas in the following weeks.

The police acquired the necessary items, which included a pair of boots fabricated to the exact specifications of those worn by the guerrilla leader, and put them in the hands of the Farc's supplier, who delivered them to his clients on September 18. What the tradesman did not know was that in the heel of one of those boots there had been placed an electronic device—a microchip—with a GPS that would allow the police to detect Jojoy's location with absolute precision.

So, after patient infiltration into the guerrilla ranks, which took years to achieve, plus the use of the most sophisticated technology, everything was at last in place to ensure the undoing of the man who had commanded some of the Farc's most despicable and devastating attacks not only on the armed forces but also on the civilian population.

THE MOUSE THAT ROARED

On Friday, September 17, I held a meeting with high-ranking army and police officers at Larandia in the department of Caquetá, not far from where the Farc's Eastern Block was operating. Among those present were the minister of defense, Rodrigo Rivera, and the commanders of the military forces: Admiral Edgar Cely, commander general of the military forces; General Alejandro Navas, commander of the army; Admiral Álvaro Echandía, commander of the navy; General Julio Alberto González, commander of the air force; General Óscar Naranjo, director general of the police force; and the commanders of the Joint Task Force Omega, plus divisions of the army with influence in the area. The Omega force had been created precisely to strike blows at logistic targets at the Farc's center of operations in the Eastern Plains and the Orinoquia, and had more than twenty thousand combatants on that mission.

At Larandia, I was informed of the advances made to locate Jojoy and was given details of the joint operation planned to strike his camp in the coming days. I gave the commanders the green light to go ahead with the operation. In the press conference held the next day, naturally I made no reference to the matter. Instead I announced that I intended to create the National Security Council and the post of national security adviser, very much in the style of the national security adviser in the United States, and that the man I was appointing to that post was my former vice-minister of defense, Sergio Jaramillo. I added the following: "The Farc is a mouse that, with terrorism, attempts to roar like a lion. We're going to continue to pursue that mouse until it can no longer breathe. That is our watchword. The commanders have the unrestricted backing of the president of the republic. The military forces have my total support."

The following week I was scheduled to fly to New York, where, for the first time as president, I was to address the United Nations General Assembly, and I had a series of bilateral meetings on my agenda, including one with President Barack Obama. On the afternoon of September 20, a few hours before leaving Colombia, I invited the minister of defense and the military and police commanders to a meeting at the Casa de Nariño. There they informed me that everything was in place for the attack on Jojoy's camp, and that it would be carried out as soon as all the equipment and personnel involved were ready to go into action. It was going to be the biggest and best-coordinated military operation ever mounted against a guerrilla chief, and would entail the participation of troops and helicopters of the army, the navy and the police force, and of course Colombia's air force planes. On that same Tuesday, in the evening, just before boarding my flight to New York, I made communication again with the commanders and reiterated my order: Jojoy must fall.

OPERATION SODOMA

The operation against the Farc's number-two man was christened Operation Sodoma for two reasons: first, because it was to be carried out in September and the custom is to give an operation a name that begins with the first letter of the month in which it is to be executed; and secondly, it had as its goal the obliteration of one of the guerrillas' main strongholds that, like the Biblical cities of Sodom and Gomorrah, was a symbol of the great evils of mankind.

It was a joint and coordinated operation in which troops and planes left from different military bases: from San José del Guaviare, from Tolemaida (in Cundinamarca), Tres Esquinas (in Caquetá), and from La Macarena and Villavicencio (in Meta).

The first attack took place between one and two o'clock in the morning of Wednesday, September 22. Two groups of Super Tucano planes dropped intelligent high-precision bombs on the coordinates of the camp they had been given. Then Harpy helicopters flew in to secure the area and Black Hawk helicopters lowered assault commandos on ropes in the midst of volleys of bullets from the guerrillas. It was a fight to the death.

On the ground, there was man-to-man combat with the guerrillas that formed the security rings, fighting that became even more fierce by daylight. Finally, the special commandos entered the camp where they found material indicative of Jojoy's presence, such as documents, burned banknotes, M4 rifles, plus some fifteen portable computers and about seventy USB flash drives. The day was spent in an intense battle, guerrillas against soldiers, with the soldiers taking advantage of the trenches built by the guerrillas as barricades in their defense. At the end of the day, however, the troops still hadn't found Jojoy.

At eleven o'clock that night, planes flew over and bombed new coordinates some two hundred meters from the camp, and when a third air raid struck at five in the morning, more men from the special forces disembarked on the spot. At last, at dawn on Thursday, September 23, army commandos discovered the corpses of two guerrillas. One of them, complete with battle gear and rifle, was half-buried under a pile of earth. He had been crushed under the weight of a bunker that had been demolished by the bombs. At first they were not 100 percent sure, but after experts had examined the fingerprints, we could claim victory. Mono Jojoy was down!

It had been a pitched battle on land and in the air. Two soldiers were killed and several more wounded, and the anti-explosives dog, Sasha, also died in the operation. On the guerrillas' side, in addition to Jojoy, at least twenty other guerrilla fighters lost their lives. What was left, abandoned now by the guerrillas, was a vast camp that had housed eleven guerrilla structures, with tunnels, escape routes, and concrete bunkers. The camp complex had been established in a jungle area between two mountain ranges and occupied an area of 1,500 square meters. Without a doubt, of all the Farc refuges, this one had been their mother camp.

Finally Jojoy's body was lifted out of the area in a police helicopter—in recognition of the intelligence task carried out by members of the police force—and was escorted by a helicopter from the army and another from the air force. That was to symbolize the joint and coordinated effort of the combined military forces and the police force working together, which had been the key factor in the success of this operation.

IN THE STREETS OF MANHATTAN

At dawn on Thursday, September 23, I went jogging in Central Park, accompanied by a handful of men from among my security agents. I knew that at any minute I would be told how the operation went. All the previous day I'd been on tenterhooks, waiting for news. Once Jojoy's body had been identified, General Naranjo called General Luis Gilberto Ramírez, head of security of the presidency who had accompanied me to New York, and asked him to let me know at once. It was not yet seven o'clock when Ramírez, in an excess of zeal, took the elevator in the building that housed the Colombian mission to the United Nations, where we were staying, and pressed the button for the fifth floor. There the elevator door opens directly onto the living quarters, and when it opened, he found himself in front of my wife as naked as the day she was born. I don't know which of the two was more embarrassed, María Clemencia or Ramírez. In the end, someone went to look for me in Central Park, which is where I got the news I had been so long waiting for.

That Thursday, in the morning, President Obama was to address the United Nations General Assembly, as I would the following day. I wanted to hear his address. So I got myself ready as quickly as possible with the intention of making an announcement that would be broadcast to Colombia from the UN headquarters, to let our people know that we had eliminated the man considered to be public enemy number one.

We left the Colombian mission on 76th Street, between Fifth Avenue and Madison Avenue, in vehicles of the official convoy, following the usual route that took us along First Avenue to the UN building. But we were suddenly held up in a monumental traffic jam. As is normal when the US president is in Manhattan, they had closed all avenues where he would be traveling, making it impossible for a car to proceed. And there I was with this tremendous scoop that I was anxious to announce before it was leaked to the media, which sooner or later was bound to happen. I had no alternative but to jump out of the car with some of those who were with me, and walk—practically run—the few blocks that we still had to go to reach the UN building. There, in an open-air patio where the media were operating, I gave a press conference in which I told Colombia and the world that we had gotten Mono Jojoy.

That afternoon I recorded an address that was broadcast to Colombia on television and radio. In it, I said the following:

> Jojoy was a symbol of terror in Colombia. Jojoy symbolized the brutality, cruelty, and inhumanity of an organization that for almost half a century has been playing with the lives and freedoms of the Colombian people.
>
> The world remembers in horror the chilling images on television that showed this leading terrorist humiliating his defenseless kidnap victims incarcerated in atrocious concentration camps.
>
> This is how terrorists end up. Like Tirofijo, fleeing from the bombs, or Raúl Reyes, or Iván Ríos, betrayed by his own men, and so many others who died in accordance with the law they had lived by, the law of crime and violence.
>
> This is a victory for democratic security, which is not over, but on the contrary we are strengthening in order to continue on our path to democratic prosperity.
>
> Colombians can rest assured we will not drop our guard. We will not

> drop our guard against terrorism. I personally will be at the front of the strategy that will enable us to consolidate the security of all Colombians.

It was always clear to me that the ultimate objective was peace. That's why I added the following to my address:

> With heightened morale, more spirit, and greater determination will we keep seeking peace. That is our objective: a Colombia at peace so we can dedicate all our energies to seeking the welfare of all Colombians, especially those most in need. This operation has been a great victory. But it is not time for triumphalism. It is the moment to keep on fighting until all the perpetrators of violence understand that their only path is to demobilize, lay down their weapons and cease to terrorize.

FIRST MEETING WITH PRESIDENT OBAMA

The next day, Friday, September 24, I gave my address before the General Assembly and had a bilateral meeting—the first of several—with President Obama at the Waldorf Astoria Hotel. I had spoken with him on the phone, but we had never met face to face. My first impression was of a man full of energy, brimming with charisma, a man who acts and talks from the heart, genuinely, regardless of diplomatic formalities. In the daily round, a head of state meets a lot of world leaders, shares summit meetings with them, as well as lunches, dinners, and other gatherings. But only with a few is there immediate chemistry, a special connection. That happened with President Obama from the first moment, and that good chemistry was maintained from then on.

I congratulated him on the Nobel Peace Prize, which he had received in December of the preceding year, and before beginning our official meeting, we gave a joint press conference in which the result of Operation Sodoma was mentioned, as it was the news of the day in Colombia, and in the whole Latin American continent. On the topic, President Obama had these words to say:

> Yesterday was a big day for the people of Colombia and those who are seeking peace in the region; because of outstanding work by Colombian security forces, they were able to embark on a mission that resulted in the death of the leader of Farc.

> The people of Colombia have been plagued by this terrorist insurgency for a very long time, and as a consequence of the success of Colombian security forces, I think we now have the chance to see continued stability in Colombia and in the region. And that will create the prospects for peace and development under President Santos's leadership. So I congratulate him.

In that same press conference, President Obama recalled a joking exchange we had in a conversation by phone when he called to congratulate me on winning the presidential elections. During our conversation, Obama, who knew I had studied at the University of Kansas, famous for its basketball team, the Jayhawks, said to me: "I know you studied at Kansas and are a fan of the Jayhawks, but I should tell you I'm disappointed because last season I put good money on them and lost my bet. Next time, please let me know." And I replied: "I'm really sorry, Mister President. But now that you mention the matter of my education, did you know what the Republicans say about it?"

"No. What do they say?"

"That I was educated at Kansas, but corrupted at Harvard."

Obama, who is also a graduate of Harvard, broke into laughter because it's true; the University of Kansas has a reputation for being conservative, while Harvard is known for its liberal tendency.

When we recalled this anecdote during the press conference at the Waldorf Astoria, I added: "I'm sure that only the Republicans think that, not the Democrats." Obama concluded, jokingly: "Well, actually, they all think I was corrupted somewhere."

"BY REASON OR BY FORCE"

Seen in perspective, my government had gotten off to a good start, with promising advances on many fronts. In just a month and a half we had restored relations with Venezuela, we had also smoothed over the problem of relations between the executive and the judicial branches of government—which had been left seriously jeopardized by the end of the Uribe administration—and we were ready to present Congress with a "law of victims," a project that had been too long postponed and with which we hoped to pay Colombian society's moral debt to those who had most suffered the effects of the conflict.

With the Farc, there was news of peace and news of war. On the one hand, we had made an initial overture in an attempt to agree to a private meeting outside Colombia to look for a possible agenda that could lead to peace; and on the other, we had delivered the most devastating blow ever inflicted on that subversive group. It seemed like a contradiction, but it wasn't. As I said in my inaugural address, and reiterated in my broadcast on September 23, I had an objective that I intended to achieve in one way or in another: "Colombia can be a country without guerrillas, a country free from terrorism. And we're going to show it, by reason or by force."

CHAPTER 15

Admitting There Is an Armed Conflict

NO ONE IS AS FANATICAL AS A CONVERT

In 2005, President Álvaro Uribe, in the head of state's traditional address to the diplomatic corps at the start of each new year, outlined a thesis that defined what would be his attitude and his performance with regard to the guerrillas and any eventual attempt to make peace. His thesis, to state it broadly and in simple terms, was that in Colombia there was no internal armed conflict, but a terrorist threat, and that consequently the only way to deal with the Farc and the ELN was by military confrontation.

This thesis was the invention of José Obdulio Gaviria, Uribe's principal ideological adviser, and he spelled it out in his book *Sofismas del terrorismo en Colombia* (Sophisms of terrorism in Colombia), published that same year. Gaviria, who, like Uribe, has been since 2014 a senator for the Center Democratic Party, has been the brains behind what he himself calls the corpus of the Uribe doctrine, and is the chief proponent of denial of the conflict, a concept that characterized the government of President Uribe and continues to inspire his way of acting from his seat in Congress.

Gaviria is, to say the least, a paradoxical figure. Of the same age as the former president, and like him an Antioquian and a lawyer, he was in his youth a militant of the Communist Party and one of the founders, toward the end of the seventies, of the movement known as Firmes, of Marxist orientation, under the leadership of Gerardo Molina, one of the historical representatives of the Left in Colombia. He also collaborated in the magazine *Alternativa*, founded by Gabriel García Márquez, my brother Enrique Santos Calderón, and other intellectuals. And at a certain moment, he even helped me, from Medellín, when I was taking my first steps in politics with the Good

Government Foundation. He also bears the embarrassing stigma of being first cousin to Pablo Escobar Gaviria, the most despicable symbol of the drug trade in Colombia and in the world, something that of course is no more than an anecdote, since nobody can be held responsible for the crimes of their relations.

Given his left-wing past, it's interesting to see how Gaviria ended up a champion and ideologue of the Right, due to his linking up with Uribe in the mid-eighties. Gaviria—like Saint Paul on the road to Damascus—found in the then young Liberal Party leader his alter ego and the path to conversion. He was adviser to Uribe when the latter held the post of governor of Antioquia, and later his consultant in the presidency, with his own office in Casa de Nariño, where he drafted some of the president's speeches. But more than that, he became the creator, promoter, and guardian of the Uribe doctrine. They say there's no greater fanatic than a convert, and Gaviria's existential 180-degree about-face is a good example.

In fact, in 2006 he founded the think tank Primero Colombia (Colombia First) to ensure long-term validity for Uribe's doctrinaire proposals. Part of that doctrine is the creation of a "state of opinion" as the superior phase of the rule of law and, naturally, the denial of the internal armed conflict. Gaviria has even gone so far as to say that in Colombia there are no displaced people, just internal migrants.

If Uribism is, for many of Uribe's disciples, a kind of religion in which the ex-president plays the role of messiah and savior, then Gaviria is undoubtedly his Saint Paul.

REASONS FOR DENYING THE CONFLICT

Denial of the internal armed conflict in Colombia, conceived by Gaviria and practiced by Uribe, came into being at a most propitious moment; namely, during the global war on terrorism championed by the administration of George W. Bush in the United States after the September 11 attack on the Twin Towers in New York. This terrible event generated a reaction of fear and anxiety worldwide, and ended up reducing everything to terms of black and white, good and bad, terrorists and pacifists. It's a simplification produced by war. There are no half measures, and if you have to devastate a country in persecuting a terrorist group, as has happened in Iraq and Afghanistan, then go ahead, with no holds barred.

In this atmosphere of universal paranoia, and then after the failure of the Caguán talks with the Farc, which led to the guerrillas being included in the European Union's list of terrorists, encouraged in this by the very government that had negotiated with them for three years, the word *terrorist* became pretty well the norm when referring to the guerrillas. It was a kind of war of semantics in which you disqualify your opponent by means of the terms you use to describe him.

During the Uribe administration, it was virtually forbidden to talk of "guerrillas" or "subversives," terms that would suggest that the fight had a political connotation. The words formerly used to describe the guerrillas were replaced with a language more in keeping with the times: terms such as *terrorists* or *narco-terrorists*, or simply *bandits*. And that opened the door to denial of the conflict.

From this viewpoint, there was no internal armed conflict in Colombia for the following reasons: First, because Colombia is a solid democracy, enshrined in a rule of law, and not a dictatorship or any kind of tyrannical or de facto regime. Therefore, any armed revolt against the state is an act of terrorism and not an uprising with justifiable motives.

Second, because any justification of guerrillas who claim they are communists no longer has any political weight since the fall of the Berlin Wall in 1989; what's left are simply criminal groups dedicated to making money from kidnappings and drug traffic.

Third, because rather than being irregular armies fighting against the state's legitimate armed forces, the guerrillas have become the people's executioners, attacking and causing more harm to the civilian population than to the military. In other words, they're simply terrorists.

Starting from these premises, Uribe and his principal ideologue concluded that in Colombia there was no civil war—no one ever pretended there was, since a civil war implies that society is divided, which was not the case with the guerrillas*—nor an armed conflict, but a terrorist threat.

What is implied by talking of a terrorist threat instead of an armed conflict? Basically, that a terrorist threat is combated by the state with all possible legitimate force, without contemplating any possible negotiation, much less a

* A civil war almost always supposes the division of the army, not only of society, as occurred in Spain, the United States, and Syria. The Colombian army was never divided during the conflict nor during the peace process. On the contrary, it took part in the process and was one of the factors that made a difference.

peace process, apart from whatever dialogue may be necessary to agree to a surrender, the handing over of weapons and submission to justice.

If there is no armed conflict, any option that includes a political solution is out of the question. And worse still, there is no way to apply—or expect your adversary to apply—international humanitarian law, especially Protocol II Additional to the Geneva Conventions, whose norms are designed precisely to humanize a conflict. Neither would there be room for the Statute of Rome and international criminal jurisdiction.

Another consequence of denying the armed conflict is that it would make no sense to expect international humanitarian entities or human rights defenders to intervene or to apply international humanitarian law, and it would be understood that the population should take sides and could be expected to cooperate in fighting the terrorists.

That is in theory, because, despite the above, President Uribe negotiated with the paramilitaries, conceding them judicial benefits and even accepting, in Article 71 of the Law of Justice and Peace in 2005, that "to form or take part in paramilitary or self-defense groups whose activities interfere with the normal functioning of constitutional and legal order" is tantamount to sedition, which is a political offense, and thus would see to contradict the thesis on terrorism.

Furthermore, as we have already seen, in March 2010, the Uribe government proposed to the commanders of the Farc an informal meeting in Brazil that might lead to an agenda for peace. They also held conversations in Cuba for over a year with the ELN with the intention of beginning a peace process. None of this is consistent with the theory that no internal armed conflict exists, because a peace process is carried out to end a conflict, not to ward off a terrorist threat.

What happens, in the end, is that reality imposes itself. No matter how much you change the terms, you can't alter the truth. It's true—and nobody can deny it—that the Farc committed a great many terrorist actions, such as attacking townships, blowing up oil pipelines and power stations, and exploding bombs in public places, and the person who perpetrates terrorist acts is by definition a terrorist. But the Farc were something more than that. They were truly an irregular army, with thousands of men and women in arms, with an ideological substratum and a series of social and economic vindications that, realistic or otherwise, formed part of the essence of their organization.

Except for his overtures in the final months of his government, Uribe never wanted to advance toward a genuine peace agenda with the Farc, and for a long time all he offered them was to talk of an agreement to the terms of a unilateral ceasefire by the guerrillas, the liberation of their kidnap victims, the handing in of their weapons, and the demobilization of their troops. In practice, a surrender. For the state it was an ideal "agenda," but totally unworkable with an organization that had existed for fifty years, was present in a great part of the national territory, and whose members espoused revolutionary ideas and were not likely to give everything up in exchange for some vague benefit under the penal justice system. This is why these efforts never came to anything.

IF WE GET THAT LAW PASSED, BEING PRESIDENT WILL HAVE BEEN WORTHWHILE

In 2005, the presidency issued an express order to all members of the government and Colombia's diplomatic representatives overseas prohibiting the use of the term *armed conflict* when referring to the country's situation. It was as if, magically, we could make the conflict go away by refusing to call it by its name.

I confess that, in my years as defense minister during the Uribe government, from 2006 to 2009, I obeyed the order, and in none of my speeches or declarations did I refer to the conflict. And whenever I spoke about the guerrillas, I did what the military and the police and everyone in government were doing, and I called them terrorists or bandits. We were disqualifying them by our use of language.

Years later, as I said earlier on, a great military man and historian, General Álvaro Valencia Tovar, taught me to do the opposite: one's opponent should not be disqualified with words, he said, but treated as what he is, a human being. That is why, although he vigorously combated the guerrillas and the drug traffickers, Valencia Tovar never called them his enemies but rather his adversaries, on the understanding that there was no place in military honor for hate or unworthy passions.

Once I was in the presidency, even before I initiated the exploratory phase for peace, I understood that if we wanted to put an end to war in Colombia—and we would have to call the armed conflict war; after all, it had been responsible for hundreds of thousands of deaths and millions of victims—then I should admit that the conflict existed. You can't end something if you say it's not there. To make peace, you have to recognize your opponent.

And the opportunity presented itself with the Law of Victims and Restitution of Land. Between the years 2007 and 2009, the Liberal Party members in Congress—under the leadership of Senator Juan Fernando Cristo and Representative Guillermo Rivera, who would later be the last two interior ministers of my government—were pushing through Congress a project of law that established indemnity for the victims of the country's decades of violence. The project won the necessary votes in the Senate and in the Chamber of Representatives, but was defeated by votes against it on the part of the Uribe government's congressmembers when it came to the final vote of conciliation. The reason cited by the government for not supporting the law was that it would require too much of the national budget. Naturally, to indemnify the victims would be costly, extremely costly, but that, like everything else in the budget, is a matter of priorities.

With this antecedent, right at the start of my term of government, I set about mending this situation. On September 27, 2010, after less than two months in the presidency, I took advantage of the members of Congress who formed part of the coalition of national unity and presented the Law of Victims again. A few days earlier, we had presented the project of law on the restitution of land that favored rural workers and their families who had been violently forced to abandon their properties. Later the two projects were amalgamated and became just one law, the Law of Victims and Restitution of Land.

In an unprecedented act, I gave a speech in the Plaza de Armas of the Casa de Nariño in which I explained the reasons behind the Law of Victims, and then immediately walked in the company of some congressmembers and cabinet ministers to the national capitol, where I formally presented the project of law. I began my speech with the following words:

> How is it possible that we have caused such pain among our fellow Colombians? It is difficult to conceive that for decades there has existed such cruelty, such evil, among sons of the same nation. Even those of us who have never taken up arms against our brothers and sisters, have never participated in violent acts, have nonetheless contracted a debt with those who have lost everything: their lives, their health, their land, their love, and the company of their loved ones.

My next sentence summed up the significance of the step we were about to take: "If we manage to pass this law and carry it out, for the benefit of our victims—if we do no more than that!—for me, being president will have been worthwhile, and worthwhile also for you, members of Congress, to have been elected to parliament."

As of that moment, the breach with my predecessor in the presidency widened even more. If he didn't approve of my declaring open the door to dialogue in search of peace, if he had been annoyed at my appointing as cabinet ministers people whom he considered to be his political enemies, he took a dim view now of my insisting with such determination on a law to indemnify the victims and restore land to those of them who had been forced to flee—a law he had rejected. But he had yet another reason for disagreeing with me, perhaps the one that most infuriated him: my recognition of the armed conflict.

"FOR A LONG TIME NOW, THERE'S BEEN AN ARMED CONFLICT IN THIS COUNTRY"

During the debate in Congress on the project of the Law of Victims and the Restitution of Land, it soon became easy to see the inconsistency of on the one hand recognizing the harm caused by the violence against millions of Colombians and the need to indemnify them with the support of the state, and on the other, continue to deny the existence of an armed conflict. Because what history was showing us was a succession of violent acts committed, over the past several decades, by different guilty parties: guerrillas, paramilitaries, and, occasionally, agents of the state—in other words, members of the public force, either by act or by omission. If we were to keep insisting on the theory of a terrorist threat, we could only refer to victims of terrorism, excluding the immense number of Colombians who had suffered in the context of the conflict, while indemnifying victims of acts committed by ordinary delinquents.

As long as we refused to recognize the existence of the conflict, as I said before, we could not apply the Statute of Rome nor international humanitarian law, both fundamental elements, not only for the humanization of the war but also for recognizing the rights of the victims of that war.

On May 4, 2011, I called a meeting in the Casa de Nariño with parliamentarians of the coalition of national unity who were pushing the project of law through Congress, and we agreed that it would be necessary to include, in the terms of the law, a recognition of the fact that an armed conflict existed in our country. I had no doubt it was the right step to take, and that the time had come to stop trying to block out the light of the sun with the palm of one's hand, as we had been trying to do for years.

That same day, in Tumaco, where I had gone to put into effect a plan to combat bands of criminals in the region of the Pacific coast, a journalist put a question to me on the subject. My reply was simple and irrefutable: "For a long time now, there's been an armed conflict in this country."

Uribe's anger was not long in coming. That same day he launched several tweets, such as the following: "Democratic security: terrorists are not fit elements to be given the status of belligerents. Why are we opening the door for them?"; "Those who threaten the lives, honor and goods of the civilian population are not in conflict with the state. They are a criminal threat"; and "There is no legal reason for linking the indemnity of victims to recognizing terrorists."

However, despite the relentless opposition of Uribe and his supporters, the Law of Victims and Restitution of Land was passed by an immense majority of votes, and met with the approval not only of millions of victims who had hoped for this support but also of the international community and human rights organizations.

Such was the importance of this law that UN Secretary-General Ban Ki-moon came to Bogotá to be present at the act where the law was officially enacted with a well-attended and very emotional event on June 10, 2011. On that memorable occasion, in my speech, I expressed not only my own personal feelings but those of millions of Colombians who at last saw light on the horizon:

> If we have had victims, if we are still producing victims, we are going to locate them and take a stand where we ought to be, which is on their side, embracing them and understanding their suffering.
>
> Let us understand once and for all, and may those who insist on using the language of arms and violence also understand, that our country is not condemned—we are not condemned—to one hundred years of solitude, nor to one hundred years of violence.
>
> On August 7 I said that Colombia's hour had come; now more than ever we feel that hour is near. Because at last we look at ourselves and recognize one another, without masks, or euphemisms, or false consolations.

Because we are taking on our responsibility as a society. Because we have proposed that the sun of prosperity will shine on all, but first—before anyone else—may it will shine on the most forgotten, those who have suffered most, on the innocent who until now, alone, have borne the burden of their pain.

This is a historic moment; we all know it. Today is the day of national hope when not only Colombians but the whole world is witness to the fact that this state is proposing and showing that, in the name of society, it is prepared to pay a moral debt, a debt too long postponed, with the victims of a violence that must end—that we are going to end!

TO RECOGNIZE THE CONFLICT IS NOT TO GRANT THE STATUS OF BELLIGERENTS

One of the arguments of those who deny the existence of the armed conflict is that, if we admit it, we will be opening the door for other states and international bodies to grant the guerrillas the status of belligerents, which would give them an inappropriate political role, and would even allow them to set up offices, and means for disseminating their ideas, in other countries.

This status of belligerency was something the Farc had been aspiring to for a long time. In fact, they had only gotten one foreign government to concede it, and that was thanks to the Venezuelan president Hugo Chávez. The status of belligerence is an old international category no longer in use. It does not produce major effects, nor is it a corollary of admitting the existence of the conflict. That is why, in the same act in which the Law of Victims was officially enacted, I clarified this issue:

> We have achieved a definition of victim that does not discriminate about who was the guilty party. Accordingly, the beneficiaries will be all those who, whether individually or collectively, have suffered harm as a consequence of offenses against international humanitarian law or violations of human rights caused as a result of the internal armed conflict.
>
> And let no one be mistaken: recognition of the conflict we have been enduring for the past half century does not imply—and this is clear in the law itself—that we are conferring a political status on the illegal armed groups. We will continue to combat them as narco-terrorists so long as they keep undermining the peace and security of Colombians.

It was clear to me that admitting the existence of the armed conflict was not the same as conceding the status of belligerence to those who were causing the conflict. But it did open a door that allowed them to be seen as actors in the conflict, as an opponent with whom one could discuss conditions for a peace agreement. And that was a good thing. If you're going to talk to your adversary, you'd better first admit there's a conflict in which he's involved and then recognize that adversary as someone you can eventually converse with. The time had come for us to take off the blindfold and confront, realistically, the possibility of progressing toward peace through a negotiation that might put an end to the conflict. Yes, to the armed conflict.

It was in accordance with this same thesis—the need for the parties to recognize one another in order to resolve conflicts—that a few years later, just before I came to the end of my second term as president, I made the decision to recognize Palestine as a state. Many took this to be an affront against Israel, a country for which I have always felt—as my family has always felt—a great sense of solidarity. To call it an affront could not have been further from the truth. It was an act in favor of peace, which I hope will one day prevail in that conflictive region of the world.

THE DEBT WE ARE PAYING

The presentation, debate, and enactment of the Law of Victims and Restitution of Land occurred before we had initiated the peace process with the Farc, even before we had begun the exploratory stage in Havana. We didn't wait to see the process advance, let alone wait for us to achieve the final result, before we began to pay the country's historical debt to the unrecognized victims of a violence that had been suffocating the Colombians for decades. That is why, during the eventual Havana process, when the moment came for discussing the problem of the victims, the government could come to the table with proof that we had made considerable advance on that matter, and had created institutions that were in operation; namely, the Unity for Victims and the Unity for Restitution of Land.

When the time came to end my second term as president, in August 2018, we had achieved a historic record of 8.7 million victims of the armed conflict, of whom almost 7 million were receiving assistance and indemnity. We managed to give assistance and humanitarian aid to 4 million victims, and to indemnify economically almost nine hundred thousand. As for land, by means of judicial sentences, we had restored to agricultural workers and their families who had been forced off their land three hundred thousand hectares, while another seven hundred thousand hectares were in the hands of the judges waiting to be adjudicated.

CHAPTER 16

The Death of Alfonso Cano

THE RESPONSE OF THE FARC

The death of Mono Jojoy was a tremendous blow to the Farc, but it did not set back the peace talks, which were just beginning to get off the ground. The guerrillas—and you have to give them credit for this—accepted the logical consequences of the war they had been waging since 1964; they well understood that, so long as an armed conflict persists, all leaders and combatants, on both sides, are military targets and could fall at any moment. War is war.

On October 15, 2010—one month after receiving my message and just twenty-two days after the raid on Jojoy's camp—Pablo Catatumbo, who, since the death of Manuel Marulanda in March 2008, was a member of the Farc secretariat, replied to my proposal in a letter which he sent via the facilitator Henry Acosta.

In this communication, Catatumbo stated that the directors of the guerrilla group had approved the idea of a secret meeting outside Colombia between members of their high command and two delegates from the government. The aim of this first meeting would be to establish the way to proceed toward concrete plans for a second meeting—let's call it an exploratory meeting—between plenipotentiary delegates to discuss an agenda and the initiation of an eventual peace process. As for the country that would host this first meeting, the Farc proposed, instead of Brazil or Sweden, that the meeting take place in Venezuela or Cuba, countries that inspired them with greater confidence and the assurance they would not fall into some kind of trap.

When Acosta delivered the letter to me at my office in the Casa de Nariño, I knew there was a real possibility that we might eventually reach a dialogued solution to the conflict. Nonetheless, I was surprised that Catatumbo, in his letter, spoke of how the Farc appreciated the fact that I had expressed my agreement with the Farc's Bolivarian platform—which they had approved in the eighth conference in 1993—and that they considered this platform as a basis for negotiation. Nothing could have been more contrary to my way of thinking and my intentions. If there was one reason why Caguán process failed, it was for having adopted a maximalist agenda that coincided, point by point, with the Farc's platform. It was one of Pastrana's greatest mistakes, and I was not going to repeat it. I came to the conclusion that Acosta, in an excess of zeal, had gone further than I had told him to, in order to get an affirmative answer from the Farc. This is the sort of risk that's unavoidable when you work through emissaries.

But still, with little more than two months in government, and after having killed the guerrillas' chief military strategist, we had managed to rebuild contacts and open a path toward negotiation. Thanks to the thaw in relations with Chávez, Venezuela would prove to be a perfectly viable site for the first preliminary meetings. Cuba, also, was a good option, given the respect the guerrillas felt for the Castro brothers and the excellent relations Cuba maintained with Colombia, despite our profound ideological differences. Over the following months I met with Acosta several times at the presidential palace, and we discussed details of what the first meeting would be like. From November 2010, I invited to these meetings my former vice-minister and now national security adviser, Sergio Jaramillo, to whom I entrusted the functions of high commissioner for peace. In the small group that was informed of what was going on, I included Alejandro Éder, a young business executive from Valle del Cauca and an expert in the resolution of conflicts, who had worked with Frank Pearl in the counsel for reintegration and whom I appointed precisely to that office. To our meetings I also invited Jaime Avendaño, who had been working for eight years in the presidency directing efforts to bring the state's comprehensive action to areas affected by the armed conflict.

I decided that, for the first meetings with the Farc in which we were going to establish conditions for the meeting with plenipotentiaries in another country, the government would be represented by Éder and Avendaño. And as plenipotentiaries to agree on the bases for a new peace process, I chose Jaramillo, Pearl, and my brother Enrique. Only the abovementioned, and my private secretary, knew of these advances.

FIRST MEETINGS

Finally, and after having to postpone things several times for logistical problems, on March 2 and 3, 2011, the first preparatory meeting was held in a Farc guerrilla camp in a border zone between Colombia and Venezuela, near Río de Oro, a tiny village in the municipality of Tibú in North Santander, separated by a river from the neighboring country. The meeting was between my delegates, Éder and Avendaño, and two members of the Farc's high command, Andrés París and Rodrigo Granda, the man who had been liberated by President Uribe in mid-2007 by petition of President Nicolas Sarkozy of France.

The principal conclusion of that first meeting was that the meeting between the government's plenipotentiaries and the Farc to discuss terms and the agenda for an eventual peace process would be held in Cuba. I had already spoken to the Cuban president Raúl Castro, who expressed his readiness to host an exploratory dialogue. He had done so during the Uribe government for the conversations between the government and the ELN, and he told me he was more than willing to do the same on this occasion.

Cuba, which was the great exporter of the revolution in Latin America in the sixties and seventies, ended up becoming, in the course of time, a great facilitator for dialogues to end said revolutions.

In 1998, Fidel Castro—referring to the uprising of the Zapatista National Liberation Army in Mexico—had said he "did not recommend armed struggle" in the present circumstances. And he had added: "In Latin America, on ten occasions there had existed conditions like those of Cuba for making a revolution like Cuba's. . . . That is not what we preach today. The world has changed a lot in these times." Fidel was always attentive to peace dialogues in our country. So much so that in 2008 he published a book entitled *La paz en Colombia* (Peace in Colombia). He said he did not agree with the kidnapping of civilians, nor did he approve of the way the Farc treated their prisoners.

Another twist of fate: Fidel, an icon of the revolution, died in Havana on November 25, 2016, one day after we signed the definitive peace agreement with the Farc in Bogotá. In a tweet I wrote lamenting the news and extending my condolences to Fidel's brother Raúl and his family, I said: "At the end of his days, Fidel Castro recognized that armed struggle was not the way. Thus he contributed to putting an end to the Colombian conflict."

The other conclusion from the preparatory meeting on March 3 was that the plenipotentiaries and the Farc would travel to Cuba, either directly or through a neighboring country, in coordination between the government and the International Committee of the Red Cross, and with the accompaniment of officials from Cuba, Norway, and Colombia. It was also established that further meetings would be required to define details on exactly how the plenipotentiaries' meeting would work. And so those meetings were arranged.

Two new preparatory meetings were held to determine the security measures to be taken for the journey of the Farc representatives to Cuba. These meeting took place in July 2011 on the island of Orchila in the Venezuelan Caribbean, where there is a naval base and a house President Chávez used as an alternative presidential residence. Meetings were held in this house in which, in addition to the delegates from the first meeting in March—Éder and Avendaño for the government, and París and Granda for the Farc—there participated representatives of the governments of Cuba, Venezuela, and Norway, acting as international guarantors for these contacts.

For the exploratory meeting in Havana, the Farc chose as plenipotentiaries two members of the secretariat: Mauricio Jaramillo, who, because of his profession, went by the alias El Médico (The Doctor), and Timoleón Jiménez, or Timochenko, whose real name was Rodrigo Londoño. On the death of Mono Jojoy, El Médico had assumed the leadership of the Eastern Block, while Timochenko headed the Magdalena Medio Block, though he spent a good deal of time in Venezuela.

There was one thing that complicated matters, and on which both parties concentrated all their efforts from March to November 2011, and that was the question of how to transport El Médico from the jungles of Guaviare in eastern Colombia, along with Sandra Ramírez, Manuel Marulanda's widow, and get them to Cuba without putting their safety at risk nor revealing the preliminary meetings that were to take place. Many options were considered, including that of flying Ramírez and El Médico from Guaviare to Venezuela in a Red Cross helicopter, accompanied by delegates from Cuba, Norway, and the presidency of Colombia. From Venezuela, they would fly to Havana.

It seems unbelievable, but the decision on this route, due to logistical problems and wariness on the part of the guerrillas, consumed the best part of the year 2011. That gives you an idea of the complexities behind a peace process of this nature, where the simple mobilization of a delegate can turn into a major problem. During all this time, I met periodically with Sergio Jaramillo, Éder, and Avendaño for them to inform me on each step forward and every obstacle they encountered. At some meetings, Acosta was present, still acting as emissary between the government and the Farc through his contact with Catatumbo.

While we slowly advanced toward the start of dialogues, the war went on without a letup, and guerrilla leaders kept falling. In March, the public forces killed Oliver Solarte, a Farc link with the Mexican drug cartels, and Jerónimo Galeano, a member of the high command and the right-hand man of Alfonso Cano. In April we captured Alberto Martínez, director of the Farc's international news agency, and in May the army took prisoners Julián Conrado, also known as El Cantante (The Singer), one of the leaders of the Southern Block, and El Abuelo (The Grandfather), who had replaced Galeano.

Such were the rules of a bloody conflict that continued to claim Colombian lives, and in which we could not afford to drop our guard. My responsibility as president was to seek peace—which is what I was doing—and at the same time maintain public order and the safety of Colombia's citizens—and I was doing that, too, waging war permanently on the illegal armed groups.

I well knew that, so long as the war persisted, we had to confront the Farc with everything we had. And very soon I was going to have to make one of the hardest decisions not only of my time as president but of my life.

THE PERSECUTION OF ALFONSO CANO

After the fall of Mono Jojoy in September 2010, the most valuable strategic target was Alfonso Cano, the Farc's top leader. Cano—whose real name was Guillermo León Saenz—was different from Jojoy and Marulanda in that he was from not a rural background but an urban one. He was born in Bogotá into a middle-class family, studied anthropology at the National University of Colombia and while there made contact with the Colombian Communist Youth (Juventud Comunista Colombiana, JUCO) and gradually began to sympathize with the Farc. He was over thirty when he opted for the armed struggle and joined the rebels in the jungle. His academic training and his knowledge of Marxism were a guarantee that he would rise quickly in the organization, first in the shadow of Jacobo Arenas, the Farc's cofounder and ideologue, and later in that of Marulanda. He led the Farc's negotiators at the peace talks with the Gaviria government in Caracas and Tlaxcala in 1991 and 1992. During the Caguán process he preferred to keep a low profile. Nonetheless, his bearded countenance and thick spectacles were a familiar sight for Colombians, who saw him as the most intellectual of the subversives.

On the death of Marulanda, in March 2008, Cano, though more ideologue than guerrilla fighter, was elected as his successor and as such became the public forces' principal target. His center of operations was in an inaccessible mountain region in the canyon of Las Hermosas in the south of the department of Tolima. And that was where military operations were concentrated to counterattack him and his men. Little by little, though it cost the lives of many soldiers and guerrilla fighters, the army began to gain terrain, forcing Cano and his inner circle to keep moving until they found themselves in the department of Cauca, even further south.

These were years of a constant and implacable manhunt, during which the guerrilla leader kept losing more and more room to maneuver. I was kept informed of these operations, and frequently met with the commanders and generals and—just as before, in the Ministry of Defense—we reviewed the operations one by one, with the respective "intelligence bubbles," to see how close we were getting to the guerrilla leaders, or what we called our high-value targets.

In the case of Cano, as in that of many others, we combined the harassment by the military with finely calibrated labors on the part of police and military intelligence, who, over the years, managed to get a few men and women infiltrated into the area, passing themselves off as tradespeople, selling mobile phone minutes and such like. One even ran a brothel, because it is well known that some of the best-kept secrets are revealed under the sheets. We also got data from members of the guerrillas' security rings, who, feeling that the military were already breathing down their necks, took fright and demobilized. These ex-guerrillas told us, for example, that their chief, under harassment, had shaved off the beard he had worn for years. All this information was shared among the different forces, enabling us to get a fairly approximate idea about where we could locate the Farc's headman.

One of his closest collaborators was Pacho Chino, his head of security. Toward the end of October 2011, thanks to information from some of the undercover agents, we knew that Chino was in a house in the rural area of the Morales municipality, in Cauca. A military operation was mounted to find him and eliminate him, but what the advance group of commandos found was more than they expected: in a house beside the one Chino was in, there were two dogs, the very dogs that were always to be seen with Cano from the time of the Caguán peace talks. Better still, the commandos detected a woman who went by the name of Jennifer and who acted as Cano's nurse and personal cook. Jennifer made several calls to her brother on her cell phone, in which she spoke of Pirulo, one of the guerrilla commander's favorite dogs.

These calls were intercepted, and everything seemed to indicate that Pacho Chino was not alone; just a few meters away, hiding out in another peasant dwelling, was none other than Alfonso Cano.

I was informed of all this by the top military generals—General Alejandro Navas, commander of the military forces; General Santiago Mantilla, commander of the army; General Tito Pinilla, commander of the air force, and General Óscar Naranjo, who continued to be director-general of the police force. Practically no one else, apart from a few other army generals and my former vice-minister of defense Juan Carlos Pinzón—now himself minister of defense—knew about the real target of this operation.

I gave an order similar to the ones I had given when I was at the head of the Defense Ministry: "Do your best to capture Cano alive." I had in mind the case of Abimael Guzmán, the commander of the Peruvian guerrilla Sendero Luminoso, whose capture in 1992 demoralized the members of the group and led to its disintegration, and I imagined something like that might happen if we captured the leader of the Farc.

OPERATION ODYSSEY

The army and the air force mounted a joint operation that we called Operation Odyssey, beginning with the letter *O*, corresponding to the month of October, when we began to plan it. Taking precautions against any possible leak, we concentrated our men and airplanes at the military base in Palmira, Valle del Cauca, and not in Popayán, which would have been nearer. In charge of the operation was General Juan Pablo Rodríguez, at the time commander of the army's Fifth Division, who had been pursuing Cano for years. Later he would become commander of the Colombian army and also of the military forces.

On the morning of Friday, November 4, climatic conditions, up to then cloudy, finally permitted air force planes to leave Palmira and fly to the area where intelligence had located the presence of the guerrilla leader, his lieutenant Pacho Chino, and some of his inner circle. A little later, at eight in the morning, the bombing began. Military observers on the ground, about nine hundred meters from the site, detected a shadow that ran out of the house in which it was presumed Cano was hiding and disappeared into the dense foliage, toward the high ground. They also spotted Conan, Cano's other dog, running after him.

After the raid, helicopters flew special operations men to the area and let them down by ropes. They cordoned off the area, moving with caution, since they guessed the guerrillas might have planted antipersonnel landmines in the area. Guerrilla snipers shot at them from the mountains above, but our men fired back from air force Harpy helicopters and managed to hold them off. Once on the ground, the special forces men found two dead guerrillas—Jennifer and Daniel Zorro, Cano's radio operator—and captured others, including Indio Efraín, one of Cano's closest collaborators. Pacho Chino had fled, and no one knew where Cano might be. We risked losing him, because on several other occasions he had gotten away.

Accompanied by dogs that helped detect mines, the infantrymen searched in vain for over eleven hours, not stopping even when it was beginning to get dark. However, as the hours went by, their hopes began to decline.

That night I was in Cartagena at the government's presidential guesthouse, where I was offering a dinner for members of The Nature Conservancy, one of the world's most important environmental organizations, who had chosen Colombia as the site for the first meeting of their Conservation Council for Latin America. With me were Mark Tercek, president of The Nature Conservancy, and Luis Alberto Moreno, president of the International Development Bank. Others invited were members of the recently created council, among them Henry Paulson Jr., who had been executive president of Goldman Sachs and US secretary of the treasury in the administration of George W. Bush; Roberto Hernández Ramírez, an important Mexican business executive, formerly director of Mexico's National Bank; Alain Belda, director-general of the Warburg Pincus investment fund; and the Colombian Alejandro Santo Domingo, head of the Santo Domingo Group.

During this meeting, my mind was in the mountains of Cauca, where the action was happening. When night fell, I called General Rodríguez, who was directing the operation from the Codazzi battalion at Palmira. The general reported that, despite all their efforts and with hundreds of men covering the area, Cano had not appeared and, since it was getting dark, he had begun to withdraw the troops. I had a presentiment, and, I should add, a little supernatural assistance. After I had gotten that report from Rodríguez, I called up my sister-in-law, María Cecilia, my wife's sister, who had impressed me more than once by predicting something she had seen in the cards. When I spoke to La Mona, as she is known affectionately—I call her my Little Fortune Teller—she said she was completely certain that Cano was hiding near the area where we were looking, and that we ought to persevere.

So I told Rodríguez: "General, don't give up, keep at it, he's not going to get away from us this time."

And so it was. Rodríguez gave the order to keep searching in the half light. And his persistence bore fruit. At about eight o'clock, a good while after the whirring motors of helicopters could no longer be heard and all had gone silent, Cano, who had kept safely out of view among the dense foliage, came out from his hiding place. A soldier who was nearby heard someone moving among the bushes and the crackle of footsteps on dry leaves. He asked for the password agreed upon by the men in the operation. The guerrilla leader, instead of surrendering, ran back into the jungle with the soldier shouting after him, "Halt! Halt!" But as he didn't stop, the soldier fired. That young infantryman had no idea he had just brought down the most wanted man in Colombia, the number-one leader of the Farc.

"TODAY WE HAVE DEFEATED THE POLITICAL INTRANSIGENCE OF THE FARC"

In a matter of minutes experts from the prosecutor general's technical investigation unit, who had disembarked along with the special forces, reached the spot where Cano's body was lying and identified him. I immediately received a call from General Rodríguez, who, with not a little emotion, confirmed the military forces' most important operational victory in the fight against the Farc. From the time I took office at the Ministry of Defense in July 2008, five years had gone by in which the persecution of Cano had been at the center of my concerns. And that night, in Cartagena, as I received reports from the generals, my eyes filled with tears to think that the object so long pursued had at last been attained, and that this meant we were getting closer to ending the war.

In May of that year, 2011, the US Army Special Forces in Pakistan had killed Osama bin Laden, leader of the terrorist group Al-Qaeda, and now on November 4 of the same year, in a military operation of high complexity and precision, our special forces had brought down the leader of the guerrilla army that had caused most damage to public order and the tranquility of the Colombian people over the past forty-seven years.

I shared the news with my international guests, who were astonished, naturally, at the magnitude of what had occurred. And that same night, from the presidential guesthouse, I made an announcement to the press to let the Colombians know that Cano had fallen.

On Saturday, I flew to Popayán, capital of the department of Cauca, and there presided at a security council meeting and gave a press conference. From Popayán I spoke to the Colombians on television and gave an overall summary of the situation in which the guerrillas now found themselves:

> The Farc—which has been on its absurd trajectory of violence for almost half a century—has now reached its turning point. Martín Caballero has fallen, Negro Acacio has fallen, Martín Sombra has fallen, Raúl Reyes has fallen, Iván Ríos was killed by one of this own men, Tirofijo died under siege by our troops, César and El Paisa have gone down, Jojoy fell, too . . . and today we inform history that their number one, Alfonso Cano, has also fallen, because the high command of the Farc is crumbling like a house of cards.
>
> This unerring blow will not be the last, and is not a motive for triumphalism on the part of the government or the armed forces. The government will continue with its campaign to reestablish the state's authority in the whole of Colombia's territory. We will keep on until we reach the very last corner of our geography, and not just our armed forces but all of the state and its social services and its justice.
>
> There are still many in the corners of Colombia who insist on following the mistaken road of arms and terror, and they must know that we are going to reach them, also. I say this to the guerrillas: the government does not want any more Colombian blood to be shed on our soil.
>
> The Farc's time is running out. Don't keep offering your lives for a project that has failed, to defend a few intransigent chiefs. Demobilize!
>
> Because that is what we have eliminated today: intransigence. A year ago, we defeated the military intransigence of the Farc with the death of Mono Jojoy. Today we have defeated the political intransigence of the Farc with the death of their highest leader, Alfonso Cano.

THE HARDEST DECISION

In interviews I am often asked what was the hardest decision I had to make as president. There were a great many, of course. Governing often obliges one to make complex decisions with unforeseeable consequences. Charles de Gaulle once said that to govern is to be permanently forced to choose, among many evils, the lesser evil. A president can ask for advice and listen to an analysis, but in the end the decision and the responsibility are his, and his alone. In that consists the real solitude of power.

One of those decisions, if not the most difficult one, was the one I had to make when the minister of defense and the high military commanders informed me they had located Cano and that all was in readiness to launch an operation against him. At any other time I would not have hesitated for a moment. But just then I knew something that the generals and the minister did not know: that with Cano we were advancing, cautiously, in exploratory meetings to discuss the possibility of beginning a peace process. We had already held three meetings with his delegates—one in a border town, and two on the island of Orchila—in which representatives of guarantor countries also participated, and we were about to coordinate a possible meeting between the Farc and our plenipotentiaries in Havana.

It was in those circumstances that they informed me they had located Cano—a target we had been pursuing for years—and that was when I alone, completely alone, had to make a crucial decision. It wasn't easy. I was aware that I could be putting at risk all we had done to advance along the path toward a negotiated peace. But in the end I gave the order to carry on with Operation Odyssey. And I did so serenely and with a clear conscience, based on a rational analysis of costs and benefits. Several reasons influenced my decision.

The first had to do with the morale of the troops. That is to say, with that intangible stimulus the military and the police need to carry out, day after day, their dangerous tasks. I knew them well, I had worked with them and had witnessed the long labor of intelligence and infiltration they had devoted themselves to for years, at a high cost in human lives, in maimed soldiers, to discover the whereabouts of Cano. Now that they finally had him in their sights, there was no way I could cancel the mission without it having disastrous effects on their will to fight. We were progressing secretly toward a negotiated peace, and I knew that a lot of military men, who had suffered the Caguán process, were not going to feel happy about a new attempt. That is why it would have been a mistake to restrain them when they had their most strategically valuable target within their reach.

The second reason had to do with the characteristics of Cano himself. Many people questioned the fact that we had taken out the best-educated commander the Farc had ever had, believing that as an intellectual and ideologue he would be someone easier to negotiate with. But that is not necessarily so, as the magazine *Semana* had anticipated in its cover article for May 2008, titled "The Radical."

If Tirofijo was a wily peasant, pragmatic and not a convinced Marxist, Cano is a man of doctrine, inflexible and dogmatic, well educated but with more answers than questions. A man who has not modified his ideas or his discourse, whose reading of reality is the same today as it was twenty years ago. What everybody in the Communist movement admires in him is exactly what outside is seen as a defect: he's a man who does not change. An immovable object.

I had the same impression from many people who knew him. Héctor Riveros, for example, who was vice-minister of the interior in the Gaviria government and who had to negotiate with Cano in the rounds of dialogue in Caracas and Tlaxcala in 1991, described him in a column in the press:

> Alfonso Cano studied anthropology at the National University, which converted him into being the most literate man in a guerrilla that was fundamentally peasant in its origins, but it is evident that he stopped reading years ago and his thought never evolved, and that would make him an obstacle at a negotiating table.
>
> Cano was profoundly distrustful and absolutely skeptical about the Colombian "establishment" ever being ready to make the necessary concessions to facilitate an agreement that would permit the Farc to give up the use of arms to impose their interpretation of society and accept discussion of other people's view by democratic means.*

Perhaps Cano would have been the most difficult leader to bring negotiations to a fruitful conclusion. Others think the opposite. The truth will have to remain in the realm of hypothesis. Insofar, as it concerns me, it's a question I'll take with me to the grave.

There was one final reason that helped me justify my decision. Both the Farc and the government knew the rules of the game. We were advancing in an exploration that could possibly lead to negotiation, but until a ceasefire had been agreed on, it was clear that the war continued and that everyone, absolutely everyone, was a target—including the president, for I knew of several plans by the guerrilla to take my life. Those are the dynamics of war, and

---

* Héctor Riveros Serrato, "Alfonso Cano, delirio mortal," *El Espectador,* November 5, 2011.

it was precisely to leave those dynamics behind us that we had to sit down and talk, no matter who the leader might be. If the Farc were really looking for peace, they would have to continue with the process of dialogue in which we were involved. This would be the greatest proof of their will to negotiate.

I can't deny there was a moment when I feared the worst; namely, that they would throw everything overboard and the efforts we had made up to this point would be lost. It was a risky bet, riskier than most, but maybe what saved me was my reputation as a poker player. What I have proven in life is this: that it's only when you take a risk that you get the best results.

A few days after Operation Odyssey, the journalist Claudia Palacios, in an interview at the Casa de Nariño for CNN, asked me this question: "President, now that you've got the Farc's maximum leader, what's next?"

My reply contained the road map of what was going to happen over the following years: "What's next? On the military side, perseverance. We can't drop our guard. And on the political side, a possible dialogue if they show they effectively want to reach an agreement."

LESSON 3

Sometimes You Have to Negotiate in the Middle of the Conflict

I never met the Israeli leader Yitzhak Rabin, but his story has always moved me. Before he became prime minister of Israel, a post he held on two occasions, Rabin was a general in the Israeli army and commanded his nation's troops in the Six-Day War in 1967. Later, in 1994, he was awarded the Nobel Peace Prize in recognition of his role in signing the Oslo agreement that sought a permanent solution to the Arab-Israeli conflict. He also signed a peace treaty between his country and the Kingdom of Jordan. He was a hawk and a dove, as some of us have had to be: a warrior and, at the same time, an architect of peace.

He acknowledged this in a public square in Tel Aviv on November 4, 1995, just a few minutes before he was assassinated by a fanatic: "I was a man of arms for twenty-seven years. While there was no chance of peace, we had a lot of wars. Today I am convinced that we have a great opportunity for peace. Pains and hardships are intrinsic to the process of obtaining peace. But there is no road to peace without them."

It was my good friend Shlomo Ben-Ami, former foreign minister of Israel and vice-president of the International Center for Peace at Toledo, who drew my attention to one of Rabin's most famous quotes, a phrase I immediately assimilated for its practical philosophy, and have referred to in my speeches as the "Rabin doctrine." The great Israeli leader, when he sat down to negotiate with Yasser Arafat, made the following statement: "We must fight terrorism as if there's no peace process, and work to achieve peace as if there's no terror."

How many times have I recalled this maxim during the years of the peace process! It was what enabled us to persevere in our efforts at dialogue when the realities of war were battering our spirits.

The ideal, certainly, is to negotiate in an atmosphere of nonconfrontation, but that is not always realistic, and although it sounds paradoxical it is sometimes counterproductive. In several peace processes, the efforts to reach a ceasefire while negotiating fundamental issues has been the cause of greater distraction, and resulted in achieving neither the one nor the other. That was what occurred in the Caguán process; during the more than three years that attempt at peace lasted, while discussing the first point on the agenda, simultaneously the parties were trying to agree to a ceasefire. In February 2002, when the process was brought to a halt, no agreement had been reached on any of the issues.

On the other hand, a ceasefire agreed upon at the outset of a peace process can have unfavorable effects: it can lead to a prolongation of the process, since there is no great incentive to reach a final agreement if no military pressure is being exerted; and it could allow the opponent to gain in strength, taking advantage of the truce to obtain and train new recruits, acquire new weapons, and generally renew his forces and his strategy.

It is never easy to explain to the public why it is sometimes preferable to dialogue in the middle of war rather than embark prematurely on a quest for a ceasefire, which would imply complex debates about areas for concentrating troops and mechanisms for verification. The fact is that, in accordance with the logic of an armed conflict, it is often necessary, as Rabin said, to fight as if you weren't talking, and talk as if you weren't fighting.

This was agreed upon right from the start between the Farc and the government, and it helped us to fortify the negotiating table in Havana in the face of the vicissitudes of the war that was still being waged in Colombia. If the negotiators had been obliged to render accounts to one another for every death or wounded in combat, for every attack, every violent action, whether on the guerrillas' side or that of the armed forces, we simply would not have been able to negotiate anything at all. No matter how upsetting the news that reached us of the conflict in Colombia, our obligation was to disregard those facts and advance on the issues on the agenda. When all is said and done, the final objective of the negotiation was to end the war, and we could not allow the war itself to stop us from reaching that goal.

As dialogue proceeded, the armed forces continued to fight the guerrilla with all their might. Those were my orders as president and commander-in-chief of the armed forces: so long as no peace treaty has been signed nor any ceasefire agreed to, the military and the police should confront any group or person who threatens the security, tranquility, and welfare of the Colombians, independent of whether or not we are sitting at a negotiating table. No minister of defense, commander, or general can say we had asked them to put a stop to their fight against those who were causing violence in our country.

I have to say that the Farc understood this perfectly well. Despite our having taken out their principal leaders—Mono Jojoy in 2010 and Alfonso Cano in 2011—the exploratory dialogues continued. And Jojoy and Cano were not the only ones; over sixty leaders of guerrilla fronts or columns were neutralized during the time peace talks were going on. And our armed forces also suffered losses.

CHAPTER 17

First Meeting in Havana

CHANGES AND READJUSTMENTS

On November 5, 2011, the day after the death of Alfonso Cano, the secretariat of the Farc issued a public declaration in which they announced that they were going to continue in their fight. In one sentence they summed up their revolutionary obstinacy: "Peace in Colombia will not be the result of any demobilization on the guerrillas' part but of the definitive abolition of the causes that gave rise to the insurgency."

A few days later, I got a call from the facilitator Henry Acosta, who said he had a message for me from the Farc. I received him at Casa de Nariño on November 9, and he told me that Pablo Catatumbo had sent word that they were serious and had not varied in their decision to continue in the process of approaches in which we were engaged.

It was a great relief, and yet at the same time something I expected. The guerrilla commanders knew, as we did, that Cano's death had occurred in accordance with the rules of war, which would continue to be in force until we had agreed on something different.

I asked Acosta to let them know that the government also maintained its decision to advance toward a peace process, and that we were ready to hold the exploratory meeting in Havana between our plenipotentiaries and those of the guerrillas, just as had been planned.

On November 15 the Farc issued a communiqué announcing that Timoleón Jiménez, better known as Timochenko, would replace Cano as commander-in-chief of the organization. Timochenko, whose real name was Rodrigo Londoño, was born in Quindío in 1959. His parents, who ran a small shop in the town of La Tebaida, were convinced communists, so their son imbibed that ideology practically from the cradle. He was an avid reader, and while still quite young he, like Cano, joined JUCO and got training in Cuba. At twenty-three, he joined the Farc in 1982 and was to become the youngest member of the general staff. He held various posts in the organization, performing both military and administrative functions, and was finally promoted to the secretariat. The general public became aware of him in May 2008 when he was seen on camera confirming the death of the Farc's founder and top leader Manuel Marulanda. At the time of these meetings, he had been named the third commander-in-chief in the Farc's history—following on Marulanda and Cano—and would take on the responsibility of carrying through the peace process with my government.

In early December, I attended the Summit of the Community of Latin American and Caribbean States (CELAC) in Caracas and while there, I spoke with President Chávez, who was informed of our contacts with the guerrillas and asked if I would authorize him to talk to Timochenko. I did so, and that same month he met with the guerrilla leader in Caracas. As a result, Timochenko felt much more confident after Chávez had assured him that Venezuela supported the path we were taking.

As was to be expected, the changes that followed on the death of Cano led to delays in the timeline we had planned for the exploratory meeting. This I learned from Catatumbo, who sent me word with Acosta in a message dated December 23, 2011, in which he reiterated the guerrillas' commitment to seeking a political solution to the conflict and explained that recent events implied certain readjustments that required time. Timochenko sent me a similar message via President Chávez.

And so we came to the year 2012 and, between January 22 and 23, a final preparatory meeting was held to define details for the plenipotentiaries' meeting in Havana. This final encounter took place at Barinas, in Venezuela's eastern plains, at the home of Ramón Rodríguez Chacín, a retired naval captain who had been Chávez's interior minister and enjoyed the confidence of both Chávez himself and the Farc. The meeting went ahead in the presence of representatives from Norway, Cuba, and Venezuela, plus delegates from the International Committee of the Red Cross.

It was agreed that the exploratory meeting would take place in Havana beginning on February 23. The Farc's plenipotentiaries would be Mauricio Jaramillo, alias The Doctor; Rodrigo Granda, and Andrés París, accompanied by Marcos Calarcá and Sandra Ramírez, Marulanda's widow. The government would be represented, as we had said from the start, by the plenipotentiaries, the high commissioner for peace, Sergio Jaramillo, and Frank Pearl, whom I had appointed just four months previously to the Ministry for the Environment and Sustainable Development—a ministry the Uribe government had abolished. Also present would be Enrique, as my personal delegate, accompanied by Alejandro Éder, Jaime Avendaño, and Lucía Jaramillo, all of whom had participated in the first contacts.

Almost a year had gone by in preparation for this exploratory meeting, but now finally all was in readiness for us to begin, in Cuba, the definitive stage that would determine whether or not we were going to advance. The meeting would be held amid great expectations for the peace process.

TWO OBJECTIVES

Throughout the whole of 2011 and up to February 2012, I met on innumerable occasions with the team led by Sergio Jaramillo and with a group of international advisers—about whom I will have more to say further on—to decide on the strategy we should follow in this first phase of approach to the Farc. We decided on a first concrete objective, and a second long-term one.

The concrete aim of the dialogues was to achieve the end of the armed conflict with the Farc; that is to say, their demobilization and disarmament and the incorporation of their members into society. But we had to go further than that. Already in the nineties, other guerrillas had been demobilized, like the M-19 and the greater part of the EPL, and yet this had not brought with it a real pacification of the country. That is why we proposed a broader aim: not only to end the conflict with the Farc but to end the whole cycle of internal violence, with ideological and political foundations, that Colombia had been suffering since 1948, or even earlier.

To achieve that, we had to concentrate on guaranteeing the rights of the victims not only to truth, justice, and reparation but also to nonrepetition. In other words, we needed to ensure that violent victimization would not continue to occur. That implied that if we managed to end the conflict with the Farc—and let's hope with the ELN in the near future—then no other group would again be recognized as an opponent in a peace process. We wanted to sever, once and for all, the perverse link that existed in Colombia between politics and violence.

BREAKING THE ICE

The transportation of alias The Doctor and Ramírez from the Guaviare jungle to Havana—the planning of which had taken so long due to logistic difficulties combined with mistrust on the part of the guerrillas—was finally achieved on schedule. With the help of the Red Cross International Committee and using their insignia, these two members of the Farc were flown first by helicopter from a prearranged meeting place in jungle area near San José del Guaviare and then by plane to Caracas. There they met up with other members of the Farc delegation and were ready to travel to Cuba, in the company of delegates from the governments of Venezuela, Cuba, and Norway. From this point on, Venezuela would act as an accompanying country and as facilitator—in which capacity Chile would also participate, something we proposed to counteract the risk of too much emphasis on the left, which Venezuela represented. Cuba and Norway would be the guarantors and would be present at the negotiating table.

On February 23, 2012, the government's delegation flew to Havana, where most of the Farc counterparts had already assembled. Each delegation was lodged in the housing estate El Laguito, which consisted of 120 residences and mansions built in the first half of the twentieth century by North American magnates and Cuban millionaires, expropriated by the Cuban government after the triumph of the revolution. Ever since then, it is where the Cuban authorities lodge their special guests. Fidel Castro allotted one of these houses—number 6—permanently to his friend Gabriel García Márquez, Colombia's Nobel Prize–winning author, who was accustomed to spending a good deal of time there.

I was a witness to the friendship between Fidel and Gabo in 1997 when I was trying to bring together the different actors in the armed conflict to dialogue and build a proposal for peace—the days of my "conspiracy." I went to Havana to meet up with Gabo and a delegation from the ELN. In fact, the ELN delegates never arrived, but thanks to a suggestion by Fidel, I ended up spending most of the evening chatting and dancing with their partners, two very attractive guerrilla women. When I got back to Gabo's house well after midnight, I joined in a very agreeable conversation that went on until dawn between Gabo, Fidel, and Mexico's former president Carlos Salinas de Gortari, who was living in Cuba at the time. There's no doubt Fidel was a magical conversationalist.

But to get back to February 23, in the afternoon the two delegations met in a building called Casa de Piedra within the same housing estate, which was later to become the headquarters of future negotiations. The Norwegians had organized an informal evening with white wine and salmon imported from remote Nordic regions so that the plenipotentiaries and other delegates could get to know one another and break the ice before formal sessions began.

It was the first time since the Caguán process broke down in February 2002 that members of the Farc secretariat had met with government authorities of ministerial level. Exactly ten years had gone by—ten years of military confrontation—and everyone understood that this could be the last chance to end a war that had caused the Colombians nothing but poverty and pain.

That first meeting was tense, but cordial, and was useful to begin to establish the most basic requirement for any conversation: a recognition of the other, with his differences and particularities, but with the essential factor that we all have in common and that unites us as belonging to a common humanity, and in this case to a common country. For decades we had been killing one another, despite being children of a single nation. And that afternoon, under the evening sky of Havana, upon shaking hands, even though there was a certain guardedness noticeable in people's facial expression and in the words they used, they were opening a window of hope for Colombia.

THE EXPLORATORY MEETING

The next day, February 24, in the same Casa de Piedra, the long-awaited exploratory meeting took place. We had been preparing it almost from the day I took office as president. Sitting at the same table, face to face, were the delegations of the Farc and of the government, and at the end of the table the guarantors from Norway—Dag Nylander and Elisabeth Slåttum—and from Cuba—Carlos Fernández de Cossio and Abel García.

The meeting began with words from the host country's delegate, Fernández de Cossio, who welcomed everyone and ratified the Cuban government's support for this new effort at peace. Then the Norwegian delegate spoke, emphasizing his country's role as an impartial guarantor, with the understating that Colombia's conflict could only be resolved by Colombians. Norway, as is well known, has converted support for peace in the world into a veritable state policy, following in that the legacy of Alfred Nobel, who entrusted in that nation the task of annually acknowledging work for peace. This Scandinavian country with a population of scarcely more than five million has managed to accumulate experience, and even a methodology, for generating confidence and facilitating approaches between opposed parties, and has placed this capacity at the service of humanity. This is something the world must be thankful for, as Colombia is.

Next to speak was my brother and personal delegate Enrique, who took the occasion to place the armed conflict in context and to mention the different attempts that had been made to sit down and dialogue, and he pleaded with the Farc to commit themselves to finally reaching a "civilized solution"—a term that had been used by Alfonso Cano. Sergio Jaramillo, for his part, gave a complete exposition on the favorable conditions that existed for advancing toward an agreement, including the regional support and the governability that had been strengthened thanks to the coalition of national unity. He emphasized my government's readiness to initiate a serious, worthy, realistic, and efficacious process of conversations, indicating with those four adjectives the way in which the negotiations would be conducted. He also made it clear that, until a final agreement was reached to put an end to the armed conflict, the armed forces would continue to confront the practitioners of violence as they had been doing up to that moment. He also insisted, as I had instructed him, that nothing would be agreed upon until everything had been agreed upon.

On the Farc's side, two delegates addressed the meeting: first Mauricio Jaramillo, commander of the Eastern Block, who headed the delegation, and then the other plenipotentiary, Rodrigo Granda. They spoke of their organization's will to advance toward a process of negotiation, but at the same time, as was to be expected, they vindicated and justified their struggle, making it clear that they were there to talk not just about demobilizing but also—and mainly—about how to solve the country's major problems and injustices.

After these initial addresses, the rest of the day, and the day after, were dedicated to a frank and open discussion by plenipotentiaries and delegates on what each party hoped to obtain from the process, and on what would be the best way to proceed. They also aired some initial ideas on how to construct an agenda for negotiations. While the Farc proposed an agenda of twelve points—the very same agenda they had agreed upon with the Pastrana government during the Caguán process, based on the platform approved at their eighth conference in 1993—the government insisted on the elaboration of a concrete agenda, limited and realistic, that might lead to the end of the armed conflict.

None of these issues was resolved at that first meeting. It was, rather, a matter of listening to each side's arguments, and establishing the mechanisms and procedures to be followed. And that was what was done. It remained clear that this exploratory phase would continue to be developed in Cuba in total secrecy to avoid interferences that might lead to the process being aborted before it had begun. It was agreed that a new meeting would be held on March 17.

In the course of the following six months—that is, up to August 26—nine more rounds of an exploratory nature took place. In them, the delegates discussed—at times serenely, at other times with raised voices, and finally with results—what would be the agenda for negotiations to put an end to the armed conflict between the Farc and the Colombian state.

The guerrillas' representatives and my delegates concurred on the need for an agenda that would meet with popular approval and would, therefore, provide a firm basis for what was agreed upon. I understood that, to generate confidence, Colombians should feel confident that the government wasn't going to negotiate anything foolish, and that the Colombian people would have the final say. In that consisted the seed of the October 2016 plebiscite, with its consequences both negative and positive.

To sum up, in those final days of February 2012 in Havana, we inaugurated a high-level, face-to-face dialogue between the government and the insurgents, without knowing how long it would last nor if it would lead to a successful outcome. What we did know was that it was our moral and constitutional obligation to attempt it, and that we had at all costs to avoid repeating the mistakes of previous efforts.

Something very important in these processes is the building of confidence with regard to the people, because talk about peace that is not accompanied by acts of peace is of no use whatsoever. That's why the Colombians—and the government in particular—received as good news the communiqué the Farc secretariat released "from the mountains of Colombia" on February 26, the very day the first meeting in Havana had concluded. The statement announced the liberation of ten members of the public force who had been in the Farc's power, and the end of kidnapping for extortion. That was the first concrete fruit of the incipient process. What follows is the text of the communiqué that began to alleviate the pressure the conflict had been exerting on the civilian population:

> A lot has been said about the retention of persons, men and women from the civilian population, which with financial intentions the Farc has effected to sustain our struggle. With the same will indicated above, we also announce that as of today we forbid this practice as part of our revolutionary activity. The pertinent passage of Law 002 passed by our plenary chief of staff in the year 2000 is therefore repealed. The time has come to begin to clarify who is kidnapping today in Colombia, and with what intentions.

CHAPTER 18

The Importance of the Agenda

CAGUÁN: STICKING TO THE AGENDA OF THE FARC

In a peace process, half the success depends on agreeing to an agenda that is viable, limited, and reasonable, an agenda that concentrates on subjects directly related to ending the armed conflict and does not attempt to solve all the country's problems. One of the principal defects of the failed peace process at Caguán was the agenda. It was an obstacle of such dimensions that, after three years of negotiations, not one of its points had been resolved. By contrast, one of the main reasons for the success of the process in Havana was precisely to have agreed upon a manageable agenda.

Something quite strange occurred in the Caguán process: the government ordered the public force to evacuate an area as big as Switzerland and officially inaugurated the dialogues—including the episode of the empty chair—without having first discussed or approved the agenda that was to be negotiated. That is what is known as putting the cart before the horse. Not until four months after having installed the negotiating table was the agenda finally decided on. And then only after Víctor G. Ricardo, the government's peace commissioner, and other official representatives—including the former minister of foreign affairs, María Emma Mejía; the Conservative senator and president of Congress Fabio Valencia Cossio; the industrialist and head of the Antioquia Business Group (also known as Antioquia's Syndicate), Nicanor Restrepo; and the governor of Atlántico, Rodolfo Espinosa—had held lengthy, and sometimes stormy, discussions with the Farc's spokesmen, Raúl Reyes and Fabián Ramírez.

Even so, the result was not encouraging. What the discussions ended up with—a document they called "A Common Agenda for Change toward a New Colombia"—was nothing more or less, despite slight changes in the order and title of some items, than the "platform of a government for national reconstruction and reconciliation" approved by the Farc in their eighth conference in 1993. One by one, the ten points in the guerrillas' platform were recapitulated in the twelve-point agenda announced on May 6, 1999, in La Machaca, a town within the demilitarized zone. Some were almost exact copies of the original platform. For example, the first point on the agenda, "Political solution to the serious conflict leading to a new Colombia," was taken from the 1993 platform's opening item, titled "Political solution for the serious conflict the country is engaged in."

The most serious defect of the Caguán negotiating agenda was that it was a product of a moment in time when the Colombian state was at its weakest in the face of the Farc's threats and recent military strikes. This explains why the agenda included, among subjects to be debated with the guerrillas, so many broad aspects of national life that went far beyond the search for an end to the conflict. The following, for example, were among the principal points for discussion: the country's economic and social structure, with subsections such as "Review of the model of economic development" or "Policies on distribution of income," not to mention the reform of the justice system, the fight against corruption and drug trafficking, reforms of the state, including the reform of Congress and public administration, the military forces, and international relations.

This was a typical case of a maximalist agenda in which the government agrees to sit down and debate with the guerrilla not just how to end the war but the state's political and economic model, and even subjects like foreign and defense policies. In other words, the government was accepting the Farc's proposal to negotiate practically all crucial aspects of national life.

An agenda like this is not only unworthy of the country but it makes it absolutely impossible to reach a final agreement. To do so, the government and the guerrillas would have to agree not just on how to end the conflict—something in itself both complex and hard to achieve—but also on enormous questions and dilemmas that embrace the economy, policies, security and diplomacy. A pretension that is both absurd and unrealistic.

LESSONS ON CAPITALISM FOR THE GUERRILLAS

At a certain moment in Caguán, the first subject for discussion was one that appeared as point number five on the agenda: Colombia's economic and social structure. This entailed a debate so broad in scope that, as was to be expected, no agreement was reached on the subject in a process that lasted for more than three years.

Over that period, innumerable discussions were held, some with the participation of Colombian citizens who visited the demilitarized zone. Outstanding economists and other academics were invited to present their reflections, and a delegation of guerrilla leaders was taken on a three-week trip to Europe, which included the Scandinavian countries, so they could witness other political and economic models firsthand.

Things went even further. The government went to the extreme of inviting international personalities such as Richard Grasso, president of the New York Stock Exchange, with two of its vice-presidents, accompanied by Colombia's then minister for finance, Juan Camilo Restrepo, to try to convince Marulanda and other Farc leaders of the benefits of the capitalist system. Others who visited Caguán to converse with Marulanda and Reyes were people like Jim Kimsey, the founder of AOL (America Online), and Joe Robert, president of the J. E. Robert Companies, a gigantic real estate business, who had made his fortune during the mortgage crisis in the United States, by buying up family mortgages cheap and then selling them off at high prices. This is described in the autobiography of Alan Greenspan, the former president of the Federal Reserve Bank.

Because of all of the above, when President Andrés Pastrana invited me to form part of his cabinet in 2000, and I accepted the Ministry of Finance, I made it clear that I was not prepared to go to Caguán to explain what I was doing or render accounts to the Farc. To me, it was obvious from the very first months of the process that this attempt at peace, though praiseworthy as such, would not be viable because of the way it was set up.

If the discussion of point number five, about Colombia's social and economic structure, took three years and did not arrive at even a partial agreement, how much longer would it take to agree on the other eleven points on the agenda, which included reforms of the justice system, Congress and public administration, as well as fundamental changes in the armed forces and foreign relations? Ten years? Twenty years? And when would they finally begin to discuss the guerrillas' demobilization? The "Common Agenda for Change toward a New Colombia" presented to the public in May 1999—an agenda accepted by the government, but constructed by the Farc to suit the guerrillas' requirements—was largely responsible for the failure of the Caguán peace process.

THE RED LINES

In June 1998, during an event at the Hotel Tequendama in Bogotá, the then presidential candidate Pastrana—who was about to compete, in a second election round, with the Liberal Party candidate Horacio Serpa—gave an address in which he outlined his policy for obtaining peace. In reference to the agenda, he said: "The government will come to the negotiating table with an open agenda and without any prior conditions. The subjects to be discussed will be decided on jointly."

More than twelve years later, when it fell to me as president to attempt a new peace process, I set myself the task of learning from earlier mistakes, and one of the principal lessons had to do precisely with how best negotiate the agenda for the ensuing dialogues. There was no way we were going to arrive at the talks, as Pastrana had done, with "an open agenda and no prior conditions."

So, in October 2010, when Henry Acosta presented me with a letter from Pablo Catatumbo in which he said how pleased he was that I "had found satisfactory the proposals of the Bolivarian platform," I replied that I had said no such thing. How could I be expected to commit the very mistake that had been responsible for the abysmal failure at Caguán?

In the course of several meetings with Sergio Jaramillo and other delegates, including Enrique, during the secret phase of conversations, I made it perfectly clear—almost to the point of an obsession—that we could not and should not negotiate about everything, that we would have to draw some red lines that no one could cross in the process of dialogue.

What were these red lines?

We were not going to discuss the country's political and economic model. In other words, questions like the rule of law, democratic principles, and the market economy would not be on the table. Nor would we be negotiating matters to do with the present and future of the armed forces and their members, or international relations.

Very often, in all kinds of auditoriums, speaking to businesspeople and business associations, as well as in military events or when addressing the police, I reminded them of the red lines we had drawn in negotiating with the Farc. Whenever certain enemies of the process said, for example, that in Havana we were talking about reducing the number of members of the armed forces or eliminating of some of their benefits, we reminded the men in uniform that the future of our democracy and economy were not under discussion. For me, that was an inviolable principle.

What, then, were we ready to negotiate? Fundamentally, the best way to end the conflict and ensure that a group that had spent half a century at war with the state should be given a space in the political arena.

Naturally, we could not reduce everything to the guerrillas' demobilization and entrance into politics. We had to understand that their decades-long struggle had its roots in political and economic claims, especially those concerning land and its exploitation, and that was something we had to take into account. That is why, in the agenda that was finally decided upon, we included more than the obvious subjects such as the Farc's future participation in politics and their disarmament, demobilization, and reintegration—the so-called DDR. Of the other items that we included, three were of special importance: first, the agrarian question, which was the reason the Farc had come into existence in the first place; secondly, the problem of illegal drugs, a subject I personally asked to be included, since I was aware of the Farc's involvement in producing and trafficking in narcotic substances and required that they commit to putting an end to this practice; and thirdly, a guarantee that the victims' rights to truth, justice, reparation, and nonrepetition should be respected.

My position initially was that nothing related to public policy should be a subject of debate at the negotiating table, precisely because I was convinced that the agenda should be limited to aspects intimately linked to the conflict and its termination. However, given that the land problem and rural development generally were at the heart of the Farc's conflict with the state, we accepted they should be included for two reasons: on the one hand, after analyzing the guerrillas' general proposals with Juan Camilo Restrepo, the minister for agriculture, we saw that what the guerrillas were proposing was not much different from what the country had been postponing for decades, and that the proposed reforms would bring greater equity and more productivity to Colombia's rural community. In that sense, we could take advantage of our negotiation with the Farc to accelerate changes that the country badly needed. On the other hand, we understood that the guerrilla leaders, after half a century of fighting and living clandestinely, were not going to demobilize and disarm without achieving some of their goals and so feel vindicated, and let their troops feel the same. All of us, as human beings, need to justify things we do in our lives. An agreement on the agrarian question would be useful to the guerrillas, at least to save face. They said so themselves.

As for the last point—that of the victims—this ended up being the backbone of the peace agreement, and turned Colombia's process into a unique case. It was the first time in the world that the parties in a conflict went further than simply deciding to end the war; both sides committed themselves to creating an integral system to compensate the victims and guarantee that their rights would be respected. Thus, the eight million victims of the internal armed conflict became the protagonists and the center of said conflict's solution.

SIX MONTHS NEGOTIATING THE AGENDA

With express instructions not to cross any red line, the Colombian delegation spent six months in Havana discussing with the Farc, in ten rounds of several days each, what was going to be the negotiation's agenda and compass. Naturally, as was only to be expected, the Farc wanted to take as their point of departure the maximalist agenda they used at Caguán, which fully embraced all of their proposals. The government, on its side, proposed a much shorter, more concrete and realistic agenda, focused exclusively on subjects that were directly related to the conflict.

During this stage, the initial teams of each party were expanded with reinforcements. On the government's side, a new delegate was introduced: Elena Ambrosi, a lawyer who had worked with Jaramillo in the vice-ministry of defense, and had expertise in matters of international humanitarian law and human rights. Another person who entered the government's team as a technical support was Juanita Goebertus, also a young lawyer, trained in political science who had been in the team Jaramillo had put together in the vice-ministry. Goebertus was an expert in transitional justice, and is at present a member of Congress. Mónica Cifuentes, another excellent lawyer, also joined the team. She had worked with me at the Ministry of Defense and would from now on coordinate all juridical matters that would arise in the course of the process. We also added Gerson Arias, a political scientist who possessed a wide experience in investigating issues of armed conflict and peace processes, and had worked in the Ideas for Peace Foundation. Ambrosi and Goebertus, together with Cifuentes and Arias, were Commissioner Jaramillo's right hands during the whole course of the process, right down to the end. Ambrosi and Cifuentes were later delegates in the Office of the Attorney General of the nation. On the Farc's side, their team was reinforced with the presence of Hermes Aguilar, who had been the guerrilla's spokesman during the Tlaxcala dialogues in 1992.

It was not at all easy to convince the Farc that they should give up the broad agenda they had put into practice at Caguán and accept an agenda of just five points related to the conflict and its termination. Endless debates went on, often tense and exhausting, around a dining room table with the walls covered in white panels on which were gradually composed, word by word, the texts that would eventually result in a general agreement. Despite all the difficulties, however, there persisted a will on both sides to reach a consensus and a solution.

At this stage—which was kept confidential; that is to say, unknown to the general public and the media—our greatest moment of crisis came in the third round, between April 11 and 15, 2012, when the point about disarmament was being debated. The government proposed, as one of the natural subjects on the agenda, the handing over of arms by the Farc. However, the Farc delegates roundly refused to include this term. They considered that handing over their arms would be tantamount to surrender, and that was not what we were about. "We're not going to be like a *guara*,"* said Rodrigo Granda most emphatically. "Giving up our weapons and hiding behind a bush. Don't think we're that crazy!"

However, my instructions to the delegates had been very precise. "If the giving up of arms is not on the agenda, there'll be no peace process." Therefore, faced with the Farc's intransigence, our delegates got up from the table and left the room. Jaramillo, Pearl, and Éder were crestfallen, sweating it out under the inclement midday Caribbean sun, convinced that all was lost.

Fortunately, the guarantor countries were present. The representatives of Norway and Cuba did their best to hit on a formula that would be acceptable to both parties. And so it was they decided on the expression "leaving off of arms" instead of "handing over arms." It may seem a merely semantic point, but for the guerrillas it was a question of honor; it was to be clear they were not handing over their weapons to the state they had so long been combating. With the term "leaving off" it was clear they would abandon their weapons, but it implied that they would do so in presence of a neutral agent—as happened, in effect, when eventually they placed their weapons in the hands of delegates from the United Nations.

* An animal similar to the capybara, but smaller, also known as *lapa* or *guartinaja*, to be found in the Vaupés jungle. It is an endangered species, and its flesh is very much appreciated by consumers.

Once this impasse had been overcome, negotiations continued, round after round, up until August 8, when a draft text of a general agreement was drawn up, about which the Farc delegates would consult with their superiors, and the government's delegates would consult with me. The push-and-pull between the two parties had been long and hard, but the result was what we had been hoping for: a limited agenda that at no point crossed the red lines we had imposed.

By contrast, on the guerrilla side there were serious objections. The guerrilla leaders felt that too many concessions had been made compared to the Caguán agenda, and that what was lacking were precisely the issues that our government refused to discuss, such as the economic model and the political model. Finally, they decided to continue in the process, convinced that the introduction to the general agenda, which acknowledged the importance of objectives such as economic development and social justice, would allow them to include new material.

THE TRIUMPH OF COMMON SENSE

If you simply compare the agenda the Farc wanted—which was virtually the same as the nonviable one employed at Caguán—with that which was finally approved in Havana, you will appreciate the ability of the government's negotiators in circumscribing and limiting the issues to be discussed during the peace talks.

In their initial proposal, the Farc had presented the following points for discussion: (1) Political solution to the social and armed conflict; (2) Protection of human rights as a responsibility of the state; (3) Comprehensive agrarian policy; (4) Exploitation and conservation of natural resources; (5) Economic and social structure; (6) Reform of the justice system, fight against corruption, and drug trafficking; (7) Political reform for broadening democracy; (8) Reform of the state; (9) Agreements on international humanitarian law; (10) Military forces; (11) International relations; (12) Formalization of the agreements.

In the end, thanks to hard work on the part of the government's delegates, who were adamant about not letting any red lines be crossed, the agenda was circumscribed to five issues that were to be negotiated: (1) Policy of integral agrarian development; (2) Political participation; (3) End of the conflict; (4) Solution to the problem of illegal drugs; (5) Victims. To which would be added a sixth point of a procedural nature on how the agreement would be implemented, verified, and endorsed. This first exploratory exercise entailed six months of arduous negotiations and was not so much a victory for the government as for common sense.

On August 26, 2012, in the presence of the Cuban minister of foreign affairs Bruno Rodríguez, and in the Casa de Piedra, the very place where the first exploratory meeting had been held, the negotiators signed the general agreement for ending the conflict and building a stable and durable peace.

It was agreed that the public announcement would be made on September 4 and that the negotiating table would be officially installed in Oslo in October.

In paragraph 1 of point 3 of the agenda—the point that deals with the end of the conflict—it was clearly stipulated that arms would be "left off." It was the first time in the history of this long confrontation that the Farc had expressed their commitment to discussing disarmament. It was also the first time compensation for the victims of the conflict had been stipulated as a principal point, central to the agreement.

We had achieved our objective: a concrete, realistic, and viable agenda. Now would come the second part of our effort: to negotiate in the open—with Colombia and the whole world looking on—a final agreement that would put an end once and for all to the biggest armed conflict that existed in the American hemisphere.

LESSON 4

It's the Peace, Stupid!

In the course of the 1992 presidential election in the United States, which was being fought between the sitting president George Bush and the governor of Arkansas Bill Clinton, the Democratic Party's campaign adviser, James Carville—whose advice I also had the privilege of receiving in my 2014 campaign, completely *ad honorem*, for he is a good friend—coined a phrase that ended up being a symbol of the winning strategy that brought Clinton to the presidency. The phrase was "It's the economy, stupid!" This catchphrase served to remind Clinton and his campaign team, and his opponent too, that over and above ideological discussions or debates on foreign policy, the population's main concern was economic, since this was a time when the pockets of American families had been hard hit by the 1991 recession, a fact that had a negative effect on the popularity of President Bush. In other words, the message is: focus on what's really important.

This recommendation can be applied to the agenda of a peace process. When negotiating and designing the agenda, you must keep in mind that the objective is to end the armed conflict and to establish the rules and conditions that will make that possible. That's how clear and simple it is. A peace process cannot pretend to change a country's political and economic paradigms or modify its system of security, because if you do that, you will have brought about not a peace process but a revolution by decree.

It is to achieve profound changes of that kind that democratic processes exist. The essence of a peace process is to lead a group that has illegally taken up arms against the state to demobilize, put aside their weapons, and be incorporated into democracy, where they can defend their ideas and proposals in the political arena on a par with any other legal party or movement. It's a question of exchanging bullets for votes, of replacing the brutal power of arms with the peaceful force of the word.

And so, whenever someone wants to include in the agenda for negotiations the big questions of the economy, politics, security, or international relations, it's a good idea to bring that person down to earth by insisting, "It's the peace, stupid! Let's concentrate on stopping the war, and then, in democratic forums, we'll begin to debate the other problems."

There's a lot of wisdom in popular sayings. And one very common saying is "Don't bite off more than you can chew."

What must be avoided are maximalist agendas that, more than an agenda for negotiating the end of a conflict, seem like a government program. In fact, the agenda for the Caguán process was based on a program for government approved by the Farc in 1993. It encompassed so much, it achieved nothing.

To expect to include all the country's problems in an agenda is a perfect recipe for failure, for the negotiations become nebulous and interminable. That is not what a peace negotiation is about. It's about coming to an agreement on subjects directly related to the conflict and the demobilization of the illegal armed group. No more than that. Everything else, all the reforms the insurgents are pursuing, can be sought later, within democracy and by peaceful channels.

That is the very definition of a peace process: that those who have pursued change by taking up arms should now seek to achieve change in the bosom of democracy.

PART FOUR

The Table in Havana (2012–2016)

CHAPTER 19

Colombia Is Informed of the Process

THE SECRET IS REVEALED

Seen in retrospect, it's noteworthy that we had managed to avoid a leak to the media, and to public opinion generally, about all we had been up to between September 2010 and January 2012. In that time, the first contacts with the Farc by the government had taken place, including several preparatory meetings in Venezuela, and these had been followed by the exploratory phase in Havana during which the plenipotentiaries of both parties had discussed the agenda for negotiations in ten rounds between February and August 2012, when the agenda was finally approved.

The government had decided that one of the proofs that there existed a real will to dialogue on the part of the guerrilla commanders would be their ability to maintain confidentiality regarding the preliminary approaches. And it must be admitted they passed the test satisfactorily. There was no leak on either side about the steps we had been taking—the trips, the meetings, the discussions—in search of a peace process, and that allowed us to move forward without being under pressure or creating expectations. It also helped prevent interference from those who might be interested in keeping the war going.

This delicate bubble of confidentiality was maintained in spite of journalists with their natural eagerness for news. The bubble burst, however, on August 26, 2012, when the general agreement on the agenda for negotiations was signed in Havana. That day, the Colombian radio network RCN, and the Venezuelan television channel Telesur, broke the news that the government and the Farc had reached an agreement to begin formal peace talks, and that these would be inaugurated in Oslo in October.

Once the news was out, and given that we had agreed not to make an official announcement until September 4, I decided to anticipate speculations, and on Monday, August 27, I gave the following brief address on television:

> From my first day in government I have fulfilled the constitutional obligation to look for peace. In that line of action, we have held exploratory conversations with the Farc in search of an end to the conflict.
>
> I wish to make it clear to the Colombian people that the approaches we have made, and those we will make in the future, will be ruled by the following principles as guidelines:
>
> First: we are going to learn from past mistakes so as not to repeat them.
>
> Second: Any process has to lead to the end of the conflict, not to its continuance.
>
> Third: Military operations and presence will be maintained in every centimeter of the national territory.
>
> * * *
>
> In the next few days we will publish the results of our approaches to the Farc.
>
> The Colombian people can rest assured that the government is acting with prudence, serenity, and a firm hand, putting above everything else the welfare and the tranquility of all our country's inhabitants.

Naturally, reactions were not long in coming. Some were hopeful, others destructive, and still others in expectation of what was to follow. Former president Uribe was among the second group. Although he was busy launching a proposal for a new party that he intended to call the Pure Democratic Center—though finally it was named simply the Democratic Center—he did not hesitate to come out in full battle cry, denouncing what he called "the legitimization of terrorism." In an address to his followers, he asserted that "the only way to negotiate with the Farc is by submitting them to justice." And with reference to our dialogues with the guerrilla, he said: "This was something we already knew about. And that's why I announced it a week ago, with profound sorrow and the hope that it wasn't true."

In a declaration that was disconcerting to say the least, the man who as president had held peace talks with the ELN in Cuba and Venezuela; who had agreed to demilitarize a territory to negotiate a humanitarian agreement; who had authorized—in March 2010, a few months before he left office, after the Constitutional Court had barred his way to a second reelection—

a message to the Farc via his peace commissioner inviting the guerrilla to a "direct and secret" meeting in Brazil with an "open agenda" to advance toward "a more detailed and profound agenda for peace in the future"—this same ex-president now proclaimed his sorrow and indignation at the news that the government of his successor had held exploratory conversations with the Farc in search of an end to the conflict.

Other reactions were more reasonable. Camilo Gómez, who had been the last peace commissioner under the government of Andrés Pastrana, published a column in *El Tiempo* in which, based on his experience, he celebrated the fact that this first stage of the process had been handled with prudence and discretion. He added the following:

> We who have always favored a political solution ought to act with prudence and not speculate about what might occur without proper knowledge of the pieces that make up this difficult jigsaw puzzle.
>
> Colombia today is in a much more solid position than it was twelve years ago, when the Caguán peace process took place; the economy is in much better shape, international relations are at a high point, the military forces and the police force are much stronger than they were at that time. There's no doubt we're in a much better situation.
>
> But that is not enough. It is fundamental that society believes the process is possible. We Colombians have a lot of reasons for mistrusting the Farc and doubting their genuine intentions in a peace process. Nobody believes them or trusts them. But that is not sufficient reason for disqualifying the efforts of a government that is constitutionally obliged to seek peace.
>
> The critics resort to all kinds of arguments to disqualify the government's efforts. They claim, for instance, that if there's a peace process, the military forces will be weakened. Nothing could be further from the truth.
>
> * * *
>
> It's not a case of asking the critics to remain silent, but it would be more patriotic if those who devote their efforts to criticize, criticize and criticize the government, were to work, work and work for peace, prudently and with discretion.

It's a shame the former peace commissioner did not maintain that sensible attitude. Later, Pastrana, his friend and political boss, brought him into line, and he ended up aligned with those who opposed the peace process.

"DON'T GET MIXED UP IN THAT, PRESIDENT"

Something worth telling, perhaps, is that during the weeks and months prior to making the announcement, many people close to me and whose opinion I respected were advising me, even pleading with me, not to embark on a new peace process. They felt it was too risky and could end up badly—as had happened with earlier attempts. They also thought it might prejudice the progress we were making in social and economic matters and that, in any case, we were striking severe blows against the guerrillas and the drug traffickers, and that was enough to ensure my government's peace and popularity.

Their frank and emphatic pleas for caution could be summed up in a phrase: "Don't get mixed up in that, President. It could turn out badly for you."

I listened to their advice, since I knew they genuinely intended to help me, and also because I understood their reasonable fears, anxieties, and skepticism. But I remained convinced that if the exploratory dialogues produced results, it would be my duty not only as president but as a Colombian—and above all, as a human being—to keep on trying.

As defense minister, I had begun the most successful offensive against the Farc and had continued with this offensive during my government to the point that, in the course of my presidency, we had taken out the Farc's two principal commanders and neutralized a good many other leaders of their organization. That ensured my popularity; the majority of my compatriots appreciated and applauded these achievements. It's always easier, and certainly will win you more applause, if you hold up to a frightened population the bleeding head of their enemy, rather than sit down with him at a negotiating table.

In matters of war, leadership is vertical. In that sense, it's relatively simple: you divide the scenario between the good guys and the bad guys, and after every victory, every trophy, you win applause. By contrast, leadership for peace is horizontal, since it implies negotiation between groups and individuals where no one can consider himself to be superior to any other. And it presupposes something else, much more complex and ambitious: the combating of prejudices, the overcoming of a fear disguised as hate, and of a hate that can quickly turn into a thirst for vengeance. It also implies opening hearts and minds to the possibility of coming to an agreement with one's adversary.

Another thing: the search for peace is not nearly as spectacular as war. The search for peace is a meticulous and difficult task that demands prudence, silence, patience—a great deal of patience!—and an unshakable determination to persevere so long as there exists the possibility of attaining one's objective. And even when that is attained, there will always be critics who don't understand the difference between a negotiation and a surrender, and therefore believe that one has conceded too much, or that they, in one's place, would have handled things much better.

Shlomo Ben-Ami, my good friend and mentor from Israel, warned me of this from the start. "The search for peace," he said, "will cost you your political capital." To see the truth of that, you only have to look at examples around the world: the leaders of the opposing groups in Northern Ireland who agreed to share government were seen as traitors by a lot of their fellow countrymen; even Nelson Mandela was criticized by many of his own party in Africa's National Congress for having begun to negotiate with the South African government while still in prison. And that's without mentioning Mohandas Gandhi, Anwar Sadat, or Yitzhak Rabin, who paid with their lives the price of having placed their bets on peace.

In my case, I could have simply done nothing. It would have been so much easier. I could have just kept waging a war in which I was achieving visible results, though not definitive ones. But there was one thing I was absolutely clear about: if I had done so, I would not have been at peace with myself.

If there was any chance, any chance at all, of stopping the bloodletting and the absurd confrontation between Colombians and I did not take it, I would have to answer to history. I would also have had to answer to an even more implacable judge than that: my own conscience.

And so, fully aware of the risks I was running, but with a profound conviction that this was the path I had to take, I approved the general agreement my delegates had reached with the guerrilla's delegates in Havana and decided to notify the public, and the world, that my government was going to attempt a new peace process with the Farc, one that we hoped would be definitive. I recalled what my grandfather Caliban said to me when I was still just a boy, advice that helped confirm me in my decision: "It's better to repent for what you've done than to regret not having done it."

"THE RESPONSIBILITY FOR THIS DECISION RESTS ON MY SHOULDERS"

At last, it was September 4, 2012, the day both parties had settled on as the moment for letting the country—and the world—know that we had agreed to officially begin a peace process between the government and the Farc with one clear goal: to end the conflict.

That night I addressed the Colombian people on television and explained that we had reached this agreement because conditions existed that made it possible to attempt a new process with the guerrillas. I also spoke of the principal points on the agenda for the negotiations we were about to undertake.

It was a transcendental moment. I was notifying my compatriots that ten and a half years after the Caguán process had come to an end, leaving behind it a bitter taste of frustration, we were prepared to make another effort, with every reason to think we could carry it through.

My speech, which was listened to with interest by millions of Colombians, began as follows:

> A few days ago, I confirmed that we had advanced in exploratory meetings outside of Colombia with representatives of the Farc. . . . Today I want to announce that these exploratory meetings have culminated with the signing of an agreement between the national government and the Farc that establishes a procedure—a road map—to arrive at a final agreement that will put an end, once and for all, to this violence between sons of the same nation.
>
> The agreement is called "General Agreement for the Termination of the Conflict" and has its origin in certain channels the previous government had explored, and that we have taken up and continued.

At this point, I gave an account of what had been achieved during the secret phase, and then continued: "After these exploratory conversations, I am convinced that we have a real chance of bringing the internal armed conflict definitively to an end. It will no doubt be difficult—very difficult—but it is the path we must explore. Any responsible government knows it cannot let slip by a possibility like this to end the conflict. And that is something millions of victims can understand."

Further in the speech, I described how the negotiations would be carried out, and above all, why this process would be different from previous ones, assimilating the lessons we had learned.

> Why is this process different? Why are we not repeating past mistakes? Because this is an agreement to end the conflict.
>
> It contains the conditions the government considers necessary to begin

a process with sufficient guarantees, although, of course, we cannot take success for granted.

* * *

This agreement does not mean peace has been achieved, nor is it a final agreement. As I said before, it is a road map that defines with precision the terms of the discussion to reach a final agreement.

This agreement is different because it does not include a demilitarized zone or a halt of military operations. It is different because the conversations will be held outside of Colombia, to keep on working seriously and with discretion. It will begin in Oslo in the first two weeks of October, and then will continue in Havana.

It is different because the conversations will not have an unlimited timetable. They will be measured in months, not years. In any case, we have agreed that the duration will be subject to a review of progress at certain intervals, and if there is no progress, then, quite simply, we will not proceed any further.

It is different because the agreement establishes a process with a clear structure, divided into three stages: the first stage—the exploratory stage—defined a closed agenda and procedural rules to ensure its compliance. This has already been signed. The second stage will consist of working sessions that will be reserved and direct. These will entail a discussion, uninterrupted and without intermediaries, of the points agreed upon in order to reach a final agreement. And with that final agreement, the conflict will have formally ended. The third stage will be the simultaneous implementation of all that has been agreed upon, with the corresponding guarantees and verification mechanisms and citizen participation.

I followed up with a brief exposition of the agenda's five thematic points, and explained that Cuba and Norway would act as host countries and guarantors, and that Venezuela and Chile would accompany the process. I also made it clear that until a final agreement had been reached, we would make no concessions in the military terrain.

Military operations—Minister [Juan Carlos] Pinzón, General [Alejandro] Navas, commanders of the armed forces—will continue with the same intensity. We will not be intimidated by extremists or threats of sabotage from any sector, threats that are likely to appear at moments like these.

I ask the Colombians to show fortitude, patience, and strength if eventually faced with new attacks by the Farc or an increase in violence, which in any case will be met with all necessary force by the armed forces and the justice system.

Toward the end of the speech, I concluded with the following reflections:

> There are moments in history when a leader has to decide to take a risk and strike out on a new path to solve the nation's fundamental problems. This is one of those moments.
>
> Undoubtedly, there are risks, but I believe history would judge us much more severely if we did not avail ourselves of the opportunity that presents itself to us today. In any case, the responsibility for this decision rests on my shoulders, and on nobody else's.
>
> Above all I want my compatriots to know that, if we do not succeed, we will accept it calmly in the knowledge that we did what was right, that we made no concessions, nor did we cede a single centimeter of territory, or neglect to carry out the tasks of government.
>
> We have proceeded and will continue to proceed with all due caution, but also with determination. I invite you, therefore, to look upon this process with circumspection, but also with optimism. If we succeed, we will have put an end to that dark night of half a century of violence.

CHAPTER 20

The Human Factor

THE NEGOTIATING TEAM

Now that we were entering the public and definitive stage of the peace negotiation, we had to select a team of negotiators that would be capable of achieving an agreement that was best for the country, a team that would embody representatives of diverse sectors of Colombian society. On the selection of its members would depend, to a large extent, the success of the process. That is why I chose the members of the team following a double criterion: excellence and degree of representation.

As was natural, the coordinator of this peace effort on the government's side would be the peace commissioner, Sergio Jaramillo. But we also needed a figurehead, someone who would direct and orient the conversations as head of the negotiating team. This would have to be a personality with intellectual and didactic abilities, plus a good knowledge of the country and of Colombia's complex juridical labyrinths, and above all a person who would not meet with resistance but would be received favorably and with respect by the Colombians, and by the guerrillas.

After having gone over a list of people who might fit this profile, I finally chose a man who, for me, possessed those precise qualities: Humberto de la Calle, a lawyer from Caldas and not only a member of the Liberal Party but a liberal ideologically and out of conviction. He was a man with a long track record of service to the country and enjoyed a well-deserved prestige among the Colombians.

De la Calle had been on the cabinet with me in the government of César Gaviria—when de la Calle was minister of government and I was minister of foreign trade—and in that of Andrés Pastrana—when I was finance minister and he was minister of the interior—and we had a good personal relationship. He was vice-president of the republic during the presidency of Ernesto

Samper, but resigned when it was proven that the presidential campaign had been partly funded by drug money—a resignation that speaks well of de la Calle's moral tone. As minister in Gaviria's cabinet, he was the government's spokesman in the Constituent Assembly that produced the 1991 Constitution, our country's greatest advance in matters of law in recent times. In addition, de la Calle had experience in dealing with the guerrillas; in 1991 and 1992, he led the government team in dialogues with the Farc in Caracas and Tlaxcala. In 1993, having decided to run for president, he renounced the role of presidential designate—a post that existed before the vice-presidency was instituted. De la Calle's withdrawal from that honorific title sparked my being put up as candidate and elected by Congress to that post, the last Colombian citizen to occupy it. He had also served on three occasions as Colombia's ambassador, to Spain, the United Kingdom, and the Organization of American States.

Following that long career of service to his country, de la Calle had retired from public life and was having professional success in his legal firm. He was surprised, then, when I invited him to Casa de Nariño and suggested he lead the negotiating team at the Havana peace talks. It was not an easy decision for him, since it implied suspending his private activities and devoting his energies full-time for an indefinite period of months or years—in fact, it ended up being more than four years—to head a difficult negotiation with the guerrillas' representatives in Cuba. Also, it would mean sacrificing time with his family. Nevertheless, he accepted unhesitatingly. In the event, he gave himself up fully to the task, with unshakable commitment and conviction.

Jaramillo and de la Calle were the great architects of the peace agreement and were accompanied by a group of plenipotentiaries and advisers who contributed experience, ideas, and diversity. My aim in selecting the negotiating team was that it should be composed of a variety of people who represented Colombian society as a whole.

It occurred to me, also, to introduce an innovation that proved to be crucial: I included in the team two retired generals from our armed forces, officers who had spent many years combating the guerrillas and yet were now ready to sit down with them and negotiate peace.

The men I chose as plenipotentiaries were General Óscar Naranjo and General Jorge Enrique Mora. Naranjo had been a successful director-general of the police force for more than five years, first during the government of President Uribe and then in mine. General Mora had been commander of the army in the Pastrana administration during the years of the Caguán process, and later was commander of the military forces during the Uribe government.

With General Naranjo, I have always had an excellent relationship, both personally and as a colleague. When serving as minister of defense, I proposed him—in a sense, *imposed* him—as director-general of the police force, where he did outstanding work against criminality. Not only was he recognized as the world's best policeman but, even after his retirement, he was invited to countries like Mexico as an adviser on matters of security and the fight against drug trafficking.

Beyond the fact that I trusted him entirely, Naranjo possesses other qualities that made him an ideal man to participate in the negotiation table: he is calm and conciliatory, a true humanist with an enormous ability to put himself in the other person's shoes and understand his or her point of view, while also knowing how to defend his own positions with solid arguments. It was for good reason that I selected him as vice-president of the republic, when Germán Vargas Lleras resigned from the post to run for president. Naranjo was vice-president from March 30, 2017, to the last day of my presidency, August 7, 2018.

With regard to General Mora, my choice of him as negotiator had a special symbolism. He was someone who, even after he had retired from the armed forces, was held in enormous esteem by the troops; they respected him as a great military man. He had accepted with stoicism and discipline the withdrawal of the public force from the five municipalities that formed the demilitarized zone of Caguán, although he never agreed with the abandonment of sovereignty that implied. For that reason, he never had a smooth relationship with President Pastrana or his peace commissioners. Nonetheless, despite the restrictions placed on him at that time, he combated the guerrillas effectively and worked hand in hand with me when I was minister of finance, and with General Fernando Tapias, commander of the military forces, to begin the process of strengthening the armed forces.

When I spoke to General Mora to invite him to join the negotiating team, I knew he would have certain misgivings, precisely because of what had happened at Caguán. That is why I made it very clear to him that in this case there were considerable differences: there would be no demilitarized zone, nor would we negotiate the status or the future of the armed forces. The best guarantee the soldiers of Colombia could have that this would not occur would be his presence at the negotiating table. And I said something else: "General, you combated the guerrillas to weaken them, and now you have the opportunity to obtain the final victory. And you as a military man know very well that the final victory is peace." Faced with these arguments, the veteran warrior accepted and joined the team.

Generals Naranjo and Mora were plenipotentiary negotiators throughout the whole process, and were able to conduct respectful and cordial conversations with the negotiators on the guerrillas' side, against whom they had fought on the battlefield. Their presence was welcome and underlined the great difference between this process and earlier ones from which the military and the police were excluded. Yet the truth is that they were the ones who had been confronting the dangers of war. When addressing members of the public force on occasions such as military parades, I would frequently quote the words of General Douglas MacArthur, who succinctly summed up this reality. "The soldier above all others prays for peace," he said, "for it is the soldier who must suffer and bear the deepest wounds and scars of war." In fact, Manuel Marulanda himself, the historical head and founder of the Farc, at one time called for the participation of the military and the police in the peace talks. As he expressed it, "a real negotiation has to be with those who are involved."

Another person who acted as plenipotentiary during the whole process was Frank Pearl, who had the not-inconsiderable experience of being the last peace commissioner during the government of President Uribe when a process with the Farc was attempted. He had also taken part in the exploratory phase that concluded with the general agreement on the agenda for negotiations.

In accordance with my idea of including the views of those sectors of society whose support would be a key factor in the success of the process, I felt it was necessary to complete the initial group of negotiators with the presence of someone who enjoyed the respect of business people and investors. With that in mind, I selected the president of the National Association of Industrialists, Luis Carlos Villegas, who had been fifteen years at the head of the country's principal association of people in the world of business.

Villegas has other qualities, too. He is of an expansive and amiable temperament and quickly wins the trust of his opponents, although he can be adamant when the occasion demands it. He has a profound knowledge of the country and has always been ready to support social causes when required. He was at the head of the fund for the recovery of a wide area in the coffee-growing region of Colombia after the devastating earthquake that occurred there in 1999. He made a great contribution, too, in his capacity as director of the business association, in confronting the tragedy caused by the wave of extraordinarily excessive rainfall the country suffered in 2010 and 2011 due to the climatic phenomenon known as El Niño. In addition, he had been vice-minister of foreign affairs and had been a member, along with other leaders from the private sector, of the commission for ethics and transparency that helped to supervise the proper use of extraordinary resources designed to strengthen and modernize the armed forces during my time as minister of defense.

As regards the Farc, his situation was very particular: he and his family had been victims of that guerrilla group, and had suffered cruelly. On November 28, 2000, an urban guerrilla commando, under orders from alias Romaña, kidnapped their seventeen-year-old daughter Juliana on the steps of the Javeriana University in Bogotá. They held her in captivity for one hundred seemingly interminable days, during which the family had no news of her whereabouts. In fact, the guerrillas had forced her to walk for twelve nights on an exhausting trek through the mountains, from Bogotá, across the chilly highlands of Sumapaz, to the demilitarized zone at Caguán. Finally, they handed her over to the peace commissioner Camilo Gómez on March 2, 2001.

Despite having lived through that personal drama, Villegas accepted my invitation to take part as a negotiator, thanks to the fact that the Farc had committed their organization to give up kidnapping as a weapon of war. I remember what he said: "If my contribution to the table of negotiations serves to prevent in the future that someone suffer the torture of kidnapping my family went through, and that so many others have suffered also, then it will be worth trying." Villegas acted as plenipotentiary negotiator for one year, up to November 2013, when I named him Colombian ambassador in Washington. In May 2015, I appointed him minister of defense, in which capacity he accompanied me for the rest of my presidency.

The presence of a business leader at the negotiating table was, of course, essential. And so, after Villegas had left, I chose Gonzalo Restrepo to replace him. Restrepo had been president of the Éxito group, an important supermarket chain, and represented Antioquia's Syndicate, whose members were delighted that Restrepo should participate in the negotiations. They took it as a show of confidence. In fact, they were the ones who suggested it.

Further reinforcements arrived at the table at different moments in the course of the process, mostly women. In November 2013 I designated María Paulina Riveros and Nigeria Rentería as plenipotentiaries.

María Paulina Riveros is a lawyer with an important career in the public sector, specializing in human rights and in setting up communication channels for communities and minority groups. She participated in the talks until just a few weeks before the signing of the final agreement. Her contribution was fundamental in such matters as the substitution of illicit crops and the guarantees for the rights of victims, in which she had wide experience. From August 2016 until May 2019, she was deputy prosecutor general of the nation.

Nigeria Rentería is also a lawyer and had been working with me as presidential adviser on women's equality. At the negotiating table, she also represented the Afro-Colombian heritage. Her presence in Havana helped to maintain the gender equality focus in the conversations. She represented the government on the subcommission on gender equality at the negotiating table, an innovation in a Colombian peace process, the first to include the gender issue in the final agreement to end the conflict. In October 2014, she resigned to run as candidate for the governorship of El Chocó.

In May 2015 I also designated, along with Gonzalo Restrepo, María Ángela Holguín, the foreign affairs minister, as plenipotentiary. I felt that her experience as a diplomat, her ability to negotiate in the most demanding international forums, and her singular character that enables her to be respected and at the same time liked, would be of special value in the final stages. Besides, in the last year of the process, subjects were being discussed that were concerned with the validation and verification of commitments on the part of international organisms, and in all of this, the foreign affairs minister's contribution would be essential.

It should be understood that the situation of the negotiators in a process such as this one is not easy; they are confined for months in a house and in a process of permanent coexistence with their team members and employed in discussions with their counterparts. In a certain way it's like being in a television reality show, where the days go by in the midst of tensions and monotony, varying between two locations: on the one hand, the house where they sleep and conduct their internal discussions among the members of the team—which are almost as arduous as the discussions they have with their counterparts—and on the other, they're at the convention center where they meet with the Farc delegates to discuss the subjects that are on the agenda in order to move forward toward an agreement. Day after day, week after week, month after month, for four years.

From a human point of view, it is a very complex and exhausting situation, so the arrival of new negotiators such as the minister of foreign affairs brought a breath of fresh air as well as new ideas and new ways of interacting. On more than one occasion, I myself had to calm the troubled waters when things flared up between members of the delegation, whose widely dissimilar personalities sometimes clashed. This is natural and understandable, and not necessarily a bad thing. Any discussion is enriched by different ways of looking at things and by differences of opinion.

The last plenipotentiary I appointed, in April 2016, to accompany the negotiations in the final stage of the process, was Roy Barreras, a senator for the Party of the U, who presided over the Senate's peace commission. He was one of the most active members of Congress and the one best acquainted with the subject of peace. He not only supported the government's efforts to end the conflict but proposed projects of law and constitutional reforms aimed at achieving a peaceful settlement.

Senator Barrera's presence was most useful as negotiations drew to a close, since his experience in legislative procedures and the way the institutions work enabled him to explain to the Farc's delegates, and to ours, the best way to ensure the implementation of the agreement, which would necessarily have to go through Congress and be approved by the courts. Later, Senator Barrera would present Congress, and the media, with a highly articulate and effective defense of the agreement.

To sum up: with the high commissioner for peace, Sergio Jaramillo; the head of the negotiating team, Humberto de la Calle; the plenipotentiaries who acted throughout the whole process—generals Óscar Naranjo and Jorge Enrique Mora, and the ex-commissioner Frank Pearl—along with those plenipotentiaries who were active in part of the process—Luis Carlos Villegas, Gonzalo Restrepo, María Paulina Riveros, Nigeria Rentería, María Ángela Holguín, and Senator Roy Barreras—we constituted a team of excellence, representative of the diverse sectors of Colombian society, whose dedicated work enabled us to achieve a final agreement to end the conflict with the Farc.

THE SUPPORT TEAM

To the work of the plenipotentiary negotiators must be added the dedicated labors of the minister for the interior, Juan Fernando Cristo, who not only battled in Congress to get votes for the different laws and reforms required to implement the agreement but also traveled to Havana several times, as did the former minister and presidential adviser on the postconflict Rafael

Pardo. They both worked—especially in the final months—as the government's special delegates. Another special delegate, as well as tireless host, was our ambassador in Cuba, Gustavo Bell, a historian from Barranquilla who had been vice-president and minister of defense in the administration of Andrés Pastrana, and later, toward the end of 2017 and up until the end of my government, head of the negotiating team in the peace talks with the ELN.

During either part of the process or the whole of it, Jaime Avendaño and Alejandro Éder acted as alternating negotiators to support the plenipotentiaries. They had also been my delegates in the preparatory meetings in 2011 and January 2012, which made possible the exploratory meeting in Havana. Elena Ambrosi and Lucía Jaramillo were also involved from the start.

The technical support, from the peace commissioner's office, included the outstanding work of Juanita Goebertus, an expert in transitional justice, and Mónica Cifuentes, juridical director. Gerson Arias, with his unparalleled knowledge of the guerrillas' history and particular traits, was part of the technical support team, as was Mónica Durán, an experienced journalist who handled questions of communication on the peace process, among dozens of advisers, mostly young people, who were deeply committed to this task.

Finally, I must highlight the role of the facilitators: Colombians of good faith who served as intermediaries between the government and the Farc at different moments in the process, helping with their informal suggestions to disentangle vexed questions or simply making communication flow more easily. The first of the facilitators was Henry Acosta, who had carried so many messages back and forth between the guerrillas and the Uribe government. Others who were immensely helpful at the most difficult moments in the process were the ex-minister Álvaro Leyva and the senator of Alternative Democratic Pole, Iván Cepeda. Discreetly, but effectively, they brought the parties together and helped reconcile contrary positions.

Deserving of very special mention is the team of experts in jurisprudence who, from the viewpoint of the state, helped design the model of transitional justice that was given concrete institutional form in the Special Justice for Peace. This team comprised the ex-magistrates and ex-presidents of the Constitutional Court Manuel José Cepeda and Juan Carlos Henao, and the American professor Douglass Cassel, with the support and illuminating advice of the minister of justice Yesid Reyes. Especially valuable, too, was the contribution of high-ranking military and police officers in active service who, under the coordination of General Javier Flórez, constituted the subcommission for the end of the conflict.

Any process, no matter how well conceived, depends in the final analysis on those who carry it out. And I can truthfully say—because I know their worth and shared their efforts, their moments of discouragement and their achievements—that in the peace negotiations with the Farc, what was definitive was the human factor. To all of the members of the team Colombians owe their recognition and their gratitude.

THOSE ON THE OTHER SIDE

The Farc, for their part, reconstituted their negotiating team for the public phase, and in the course of the four years the talks lasted, they rotated commanders from different guerrilla fronts and geographic regions, incorporating them into the process in diverse capacities or as members of subcommittees.

The head of the guerrillas' team—with a role equivalent to that of Humberto de la Calle for the government—was Iván Márquez, whose real name is Luciano Marín. He was a member of the Farc's secretariat and commander of their Caribbean Block, and led their team throughout the whole process.

Márquez, like many of the guerrilla chiefs, began his political career with the Colombian Communist Youth organization, and studied in the Soviet Union. He joined the Farc in the mid-1980s, and in the middle of the peace process carried out by the Betancur government, was a militant member of the left-wing party Patriotic Union, and was elected member of the Congress's lower house in 1998. He was active in Congress for two years, but in light of the brutal persecution of members of the Patriotic Union by obscure forces of the extreme right and the paramilitaries, he went back to a clandestine existence and was reincorporated into the ranks of the Farc, where he soon rose to become a member of the secretariat and frequent spokesman for the guerrillas. He was negotiator in the Caracas and Tlaxcala talks during the Gaviria government, and also in the Caguán process. Given his considerable experience, Timochenko and his colleagues in the secretariat designated him to lead their negotiating team in Havana.*

* Márquez, who, as head of the Farc's negotiating team, signed the peace agreement in November 2016, announced in August 2019, along with a handful of midlevel commanders from the former Farc guerrilla—including Jesús Santrich, El Paisa, and Romaña—his decision to take up arms again. The vast majority of his former comrades, who expelled him and his partners from the Farc political party, expressed their total inconformity with this decision.

At his side inseparably was Jesús Santrich (his real name being Seusis Pausias Hernández), member of the guerrilla high command and second-in-command, under Márquez, of the Caribbean Block. Santrich, who has a degree in social sciences, is practically blind; he can only see partially by the left eye, due to a degenerative disease. In negotiations, he was apt to be intransigent and dogmatic, but is at the same time mentally agile and astute. They say he would spend hours locked in debate with commissioner Jaramillo over the use of one word, or the insertion of a comma. Both men are perfectionists in matters of language.*

In the course of the process, several other Farc commanders, the majority members of the secretariat, played a part in the table of negotiations. Of these, the most significant, apart from Márquez and Santrich, were Mauricio Jaramillo (The Doctor), Rodrigo Granda, Andrés París, and Marcos Calarcá, who had participated in the secret phase. Others who took part were Joaquín Gómez, Pastor Alape, Carlos Antonio Lozada, and Pablo Catatumbo. Besides the above named, some dozens of guerrilla fighters alternated in the different subcommissions or support teams. This was due to an intelligent strategy on the part of the Farc leader Timochenko, who wanted to give a voice to members of the organization from different regions. Among those were Bernardo Salcedo, Rubén Zamora, Hermes Aguilar, Olmedo Ruiz, Jairo Quintero, Benkos Biohó, Sergio Marín, and Sargento Pascuas, among many others who traveled back and forth between the jungles of Colombia and Havana, thanks to the ever-efficient services of the International Red Cross.

At certain moments in the negotiations, other guerrilla leaders known for their cruelty and terrorist acts were incorporated into the table of negotiations—people like Romaña, guilty of innumerable kidnappings, including the collective kidnapping of groups of unarmed citizens captured on Colombia's highways, a practice the guerrillas referred to as a "miraculous draught" (after the miraculous draught of fishes in the Gospel). Another was El Paisa, for many years commander of a mobile column called Teófilo Forero. This column was the most unscrupulously savage of all, responsible among other

---

* Jesús Santrich was arrested by order of the prosecutor general's office on April 9, 2018, on drug trafficking charges by the justice department of the United States, following on a covert operation by the Drug Enforcement Agency. Santrich and his accomplices are charged with having negotiated the dispatch of ten tons of cocaine to the United States, a crime that allegedly was committed after the signing of the peace agreement, and therefore the accused should be tried by the normal justice system. Taking advantage of a period of provisional release, he fled the country in July 2019 and later appeared among the group of dissidents commanded by Iván Márquez.

actions for the car bomb attack on the Nogal Club in Bogotá that killed thirty-six innocent people, and another car bomb in a barrio in the city of Neiva, causing eighteen fatalities.

For Colombians, it was not easy—and this is understandable—to see guerrilla chiefs, who have been the cause of such pain and suffering, now strolling freely about Havana and discussing points on the agenda. I myself, who as minister of defense had firsthand knowledge of the guerrilla chiefs' profiles and their felonies, and had pursued them as high-value targets, found this new situation hard to swallow. But there is one thing one must understand: just as we brought to the negotiating table the most unremitting military commander of recent times and the police commander who had obtained the most remarkable successes in the fight against the guerrillas and the drug traffickers, it was natural that the Farc should involve men who represented the fiercest or most extreme elements in their organization. They would have been wrong to negotiate an agreement that could later be questioned by their most battle-hardened fighters. Those also had to be present at the table.

We have to remind ourselves continually that you don't make peace with your friends, or with angels or saints. You make peace with your enemies, your adversaries, with those who have harmed you, people you have been combating. The victory of peace, the victory of the human spirit, consists in creating conditions where confrontation will cease, where opponents will be able to coexist within a space of justice, civility, and democracy.

Finally, I want to highlight the important role played by women in the Farc delegation. Although they did not serve as negotiators at the principal table—in contrast with the government, who did have women as plenipotentiaries—the Farc's female delegates took part in logistic activities, in the press and communications generally, and also in the subcommission on gender.

Two women were of special importance: Victoria Sandino, a true Farc warrior, who worked to protect the top guerrilla leaders and represented the Farc in the subcommission; and Sandra Ramírez, who had accompanied the guerrilla delegates in the exploratory phase. Other women who were active in the process were Camila Cienfuegos, Pablo Catatumbo's companion, and the young Dutch guerrilla fighter Tanja Nijmeijer, who had been seduced by a romantic idea of the revolution and joined the Farc in 2002, and ended up becoming a person the commanders greatly trusted and even employed as interpreter for international communications.

It is interesting to note that, in accordance with the peace agreement's commitments, ten members of the Farc, now disarmed and constituted as a political party, may occupy seats in Congress that were guaranteed for a four-year period from July 20, 2018—and this in spite of not having won the required number of votes in the March 2018 parliamentary elections. Several of those who were in Havana are now senators and representatives in Congress, although this does not exempt them from submitting to the Special Jurisdiction for Peace, which they have agreed to do.

Thus, Pablo Catatumbo is now Senator Pablo Catatumbo Torres; Victoria Sandino is Senator Victoria Sandino Simanca; Carlos Antonio Lozada is Senator Julián Gallo; Sandra Ramírez is Senator Criselda Lobo; Marcos Calarcá is Representative Luis Alberto Albán; Olmedo Ruiz is Representative Omar de Jesús Restrepo; Jairo Quintero is Representative Jairo Reinaldo Cala, and Sergio Marín is Representative Carlos Carreño.*

The Farc exchanged weapons for the ballot box, and bullets for democracy. That is the victory of reason over violence, which is the essential aim of any peace process.

* Iván Márquez's seat in the Senate has not been occupied, since he did not want to take possession due to discrepancies regarding the implementation of the Peace Agreement, and is now in hiding. Jesús Santrich's seat in the Chamber of Representatives is also empty since he also went into hiding in July 2019.

CHAPTER 21

"Nothing Is Agreed until Everything Is Agreed"

THE PUBLIC PHASE BEGINS

1. Gathered together in Oslo, Norway, spokespersons for the Government of Colombia and for the Revolutionary Armed Forces of Colombia–People's Army, Farc-EP, agree on the public inauguration of the Table of Conversations charged with developing the General Agreement for the Termination of the Conflict and the Construction of a Stable and Durable Peace. Thus, Phase 2 is formally initiated.
2. Comprehensive Agrarian Development is the first subject on the agenda agreed upon, and will be discussed as of 15 November in Havana, Cuba.
3. The parties will designate their spokespersons who will meet on 5 November in Havana to continue the necessary preparatory tasks.
4. We thank the guarantor countries, Norway and Cuba, for their hospitality in this process, and the accompanying countries, Venezuela and Chile, for their support.

On October 18, 2012, a first joint communiqué on the table for conversations containing the above four points was published in the Norwegian capital. Thus, we began the fourth formal attempt in the history of Colombia to find a dialogued and peaceful solution to the long and anachronistic armed conflict with the Farc guerrillas. The first had been in 1982, during the administration of Belisario Betancur, and had its headquarters in the municipality of La Uribe in the department of Meta; the second occurred between 1991 and 1992 in Caracas and Tlaxcala, Mexico, between the government of César Gaviria and the so-called Simón Bolívar Guerrilla Coordinating Board, which embraced the Farc, the ELN, and a remnant of the EPL; and the third was the

Caguán process, under the government of Andrés Pastrana, between 1999 and 2002, which took place in the demilitarized zone that extended over five municipalities: one in the department of Caquetá and four in Meta, covering a total area equivalent to the size of Switzerland. After half a century of armed conflict, we were fully aware that we had before us the most evident opportunity—and perhaps the last—to put an end to this absurd war between sons of the same nation. An opportunity we could not allow to slip through our hands.

Several factors led us to believe that this was going to be the definitive attempt. In the first place, we had successfully carried out the exploratory phase over six months in Havana, and had done so in secret and respecting absolute confidentiality. That phase had ended with a concrete, realistic, and limited agenda, in contrast with the maximalist agenda of the Caguán process. And it was an agenda that for the first time defined, with total clarity, the aim of the process: the end of the armed conflict and the leaving off of weapons by members of the Farc.

In the second place, the process was to be carried out in Cuba with no kind of demilitarization whatsoever in Colombia, and in the atmosphere of isolation, security, and calm that the island country provided. A process of such long and complex discussions would have been practically impossible to conduct in Colombia under pressure from all sectors of Colombian society and under the glare of the media's spotlight. Being in Havana allowed for sufficiently wide coverage and participation on the part of Colombia's civilian population, but without the exaggeration of news broadcasts and the publication of daily bulletins, as would have happened if the talks had been held in Colombia.

Discussing a peace agreement is like an artist painting a picture. If you look at it while it's still in the process of being created, all you see are splashes of paint, vague lines, unconnected fragments. The painting should not be shown until it's finished, when all its apparently crude and haphazard brush marks have been brought together harmoniously in the finished work.

In the third place, we were hopeful because of the devastating blows that the public force had inflicted on the Farc, especially in the six years prior to the official beginning of conversations. This had shifted the correlation of force in favor of the state and had led the guerrilla commanders to understand that they would never come to power by force of arms, and that for them it would be much more beneficial to negotiate peace than to continue with a war that, sooner or later, would lead to their extinction. To put an end finally to the conflict by force of arms would take the state's armed forces another decade, or perhaps two decades, and would cost thousands more lives and victims, something that nobody with even a minimal sense of humanity would desire.

And in the fourth place, we had restored relations with our neighbors, especially with the governments of Venezuela and Ecuador, and that enabled us to count on the regional support necessary to successfully carry forward this kind of process. In today's world, an asymmetrical war such as Colombia's cannot be brought to an end unless it can rely on wide regional backing.

TWO CONTRARY VIEWPOINTS

During the opening ceremony to inaugurate the table of conversations in Oslo's cold Nordic climate, the speeches made by the two heads of the respective delegations—Humberto de la Calle for the government, and Iván Márquez for the Farc—could hardly have presented a more glaring contrast. De la Calle gave a moderate, positive address in which he celebrated the occasion as a moment of hope. Márquez, by contrast, gave a speech that recalled what had occurred thirteen years earlier, when Joaquín Gómez read the address prepared by the Farc high commander Manuel Marulanda, who, in the inauguration ceremony at Caguán, had left his seat vacant. On the present occasion, Márquez recalled the Farc's repeated past claims, insisted on ideological confrontation, and justified the armed struggle. Many people found this disconcerting. His words didn't sound like the most appropriate way to begin a peace process.

I quote two passages from de la Calle's address that express the spirit of the conversations that were about to begin:

> One characteristic of this process is its confidentiality. We consider confidentiality essential. What do we mean by confidentiality? We refer concretely to what occurs at the negotiating table. We don't intend to prevent the Farc-EP from expressing their ideas. But if the content of the conversations should leak out, this would seriously affect the process.
>
> It is also essential that the proposals be opportune. From the government's politico-democratic viewpoint, public opinion is an important component. Today public opinion supports the process. But we are in a volatile situation. We know that, if at the end of Phase 2 we come to an agreement,

if there are evident signs that the conversations are on the road to success, certain sectors that are reticent or opposed to the process may change their minds and adopt a more favorable attitude.

However, in accordance with the rhythm of the negotiations, everything should happen at its appropriate moment. This is important too for the Farc-EP. It guarantees that we can apply our stated principle: "Nothing is agreed until everything is agreed."

But carrying on our conversations with discretion does not mean that we are hiding them from the public. On the contrary, there will be participation in accordance with the requirements of the negotiating table, as we have agreed. We have contemplated introducing a series of mechanisms to guarantee that the citizens can contribute with their proposals. And we have in mind mechanisms of final ratification of the agreements so that they do not appear as decisions made by the parties in isolation.

Here the head of the government's negotiating team had made reference to a very important principle that was central to the negotiation: "Nothing is agreed until everything is agreed." I had learned this rule, which is known as the "single undertaking principle," from my time as minister for foreign trade, where it was applied to the General Agreement on Tariffs and Trade, and which is still applied at the World Trade Organization that replaced it. So I recommended it to our negotiators.

What did this principle imply in the concrete case of the peace talks? It meant that the talks had only one goal; namely, the end of the conflict with the Farc, and that until a final agreement had been reached concerning the points on the agenda that led to that end—and that included disarmament and demobilization—nothing that had been discussed and approved would be considered definitive. The agreement had to be seen as a whole, and would not be considered as such until it included the totality of all matters debated, and approved with the consensus of both parties.

In accordance with this principle, each time a consensus was reached on any point on the agenda, it was considered to be a draft, and would become definitive only once it had been consolidated in the final agreement that would encompass all previous agreements.

De la Calle said something else that expressed a principle of realism we kept clearly in mind from the start of negotiations: the ending of the conflict with the Farc is a step toward peace in Colombia, but it is not peace itself. This is how he put it:

> The government wants to go over the points in the agenda that should guide us in our conversations. This agenda is a good tool for coming to the end of Phase Two. That day, the conflict will be over, arms will have been laid down, and what will begin will be the phase of simultaneous fulfillment of the obligations. . . . Is this peace? No, not yet. We are aware of that. The end of the conflict is the prelude to peace. To achieve peace, we have to undertake a complete transformation of society. We are ready to look for mechanisms that will guarantee what is contained in those aspirations.

Iván Márquez's speech, which was particularly long, was more like a revolutionary harangue than the presentation of a process of dialogue. He referred extensively to the subject of land—which has been central to the Farc's struggle—and criticized the "outrageously disproportionate earnings of a handful of capitalists" and the "soil-destroying practices of the big landowners." He attacked the mining multinationals who practice a kind of mining that, according to him, is "the devil of socio-environmental destruction." His speech also was intended to broaden the limits of the agenda that had been defined in the general agreement the delegates had reached at the end of August. "Peace does not mean silencing the guns but embraces the transformation of the state and a change in political, economic and military forms. Yes, peace is not simply demobilization." Márquez defiantly insisted on the will and ability of the guerrillas to keep fighting:

> Armed insurgency motivated by a just struggle cannot be defeated by bombs or technology or airplanes, no matter what fancy and varied names they might have. Mobile guerrilla warfare is an invincible tactic. Those who, drunk on triumphalism, talk of the end of the guerrillas, points of inflection and suchlike strategies, and believe our readiness to dialogue is an inexistent manifestation of weakness, are making a mistake . . . we feel in our hearts a sentiment of peace founded on the conviction that victory will always depend on the will and the mobilization of our people. This is a message of decision; as Alfonso Cano said not long ago, "Here in the Farc-EP, no one is unnerved. We are full of morale, the morale for combat."

In the midst of these contrary viewpoints, the dialogues began. In November, they were transferred to Havana, where they continued up to the end in the second half of 2016. What was absolutely clear—to the negotiators, to the government and to Colombian society—was that what was in store for us was not going to be easy, for we were facing an opponent who was ideological, dogmatic, and intransigent. In my address on September 4, 2012, though I had said that the conversations during the public phase would be over in a matter of months, not years, they did last, in fact, for four years. I had to pay dearly for saying that. As the process went on, the opposition and the media never ceased to remind me that I had calculated that the talks would not go on for more than a year. From this, I learned a lesson: in a process where you're not in control of all the factors, you should not place fatal time limits, because they engender expectations that, when not accomplished, will be turned against you.

Four years is not so long if you compare it with other processes around the world. It isn't too long if you bear in mind that you are putting an end to a conflict that had been going on for half a century. However, it did turn out to be too long for an expectant public opinion that was voluble and impatient, and demanded a quick solution.

Our era is one not only of asymmetric wars but also of asymmetric peace processes, as ours was. This presented me with the dilemma faced by anyone who exercises authority within a democracy and submits to democratic controls and expectations. There were political timetables I had to respect, a vociferous public calling for results, an implacable opposition, and opinion polls putting pressure on me day after day. By contrast, the guerrillas had none of these problems to worry about.

The wearying effect of a process that was taking so long was a factor that undermined people's confidence and was used astutely by our opponents. But making peace takes time, and you cannot hurry or force things. We were not going to agree to anything unreasonable just to get a quick result. We acted on that premise, fully aware that our aim was not to get an agreement at any price but to reach the best possible agreement for the future of Colombia.

A COMPLEX PROCESS

What was ahead of us was a process that was going to last for four years. This public phase was taken up with debates of enormous complexity, long and profound discussions, and the participation of all classes of the country's social sectors. Along the way, we met with many obstacles and upsets that we had to overcome, all of which tried the negotiators' patience and that of the public also.

I do not intend to provide here a chronological and detailed account of all the discussions that led the final agreement. To do so would be beyond the scope of this book. The final agreement was a document of over three hundred pages, itemizing the agreements reached in Havana on the five thematic points: comprehensive agrarian development, political participation, the end of the conflict, the problem of illegal drugs, and the problem of the victims, plus a final point concerning the implementation, verification, and countersigning of the agreement.

The negotiators' task was monumental. Seen in retrospect, one can understand why it took so much time to finally bring the process to an end. It was carried on in an atmosphere in which the negotiators maintained the respect and cordiality that ought to prevail always between adversaries who seek to end a conflict. This does not mean, however, that tensions and misunderstandings were avoided altogether. But despite these difficult moments, the negotiators kept on building a peace agreement, gradually, step by step, making known the drafts of partial agreements as each of them was reached, but adhering to the oft-repeated principle that nothing had been agreed upon until everything was agreed upon.

In all, fifty-one cycles of conversations took place, each of which lasted, on average, eleven days. They were held in the Havana Convention Center, and in each cycle the negotiators moved forward. First, they spent three days discussing and writing up the points. Then each group devoted another three days to analyzing the points among themselves, and then they would go back to three more days of debate. And so they progressed in a continuous round, working without taking a break even on Sundays or public holidays.

As promised, the process also allowed for participation on the part of civil society. Forums were held in Colombia, organized by the National University and the United Nations, where citizens and their organizations expounded their ideas and made suggestions to the negotiating table, which were then ordered and compiled by the organizers who dispatched them to Havana. Five national forums were convened, one for each point on the agenda, plus four regional forums in which the agenda's points were dealt with from the perspective of the country's diversity. In addition, as each point was being discussed, five delegations of victims traveled to Cuba to contribute their viewpoints and make their claims. To all of this must be added the contribution of ordinary citizens who expressed themselves through the negotiating table's website. More than 8,600 ideas and suggestions reached Havana via the internet.

In the course of the four years that the public phase lasted, the negotiators published ninety-four bulletins, three joint progress reports, and thirty-three joint minutes, all signed by representatives of both parties, not to mention other unilateral communiqués by the government and by the Farc in which each party expounded its point of view and, occasionally, differences and clarifications. Delegations were received from national and international groups, including unions, experts, and advisers, all of which enriched the debates.*

As president and the person ultimately responsible for the result of this attempt at peace, I followed step by step what was happening in Havana in the understanding that this was the principal objective not only of my government but also of Colombia. I held periodic meetings with the peace commissioner and the head of negotiations, as well as with national and international advisers, and with their help defined all the avenues to be explored in each discussion.

I had to make a lot of difficult decisions, and some risky ones, but I never ceased to believe that our goal was attainable. When others tended to doubt, I reminded them of something I had learned at the naval academy and that has guided me in all my life's undertakings. It's a lesson based on a sentence of Seneca's, the Latin philosopher: "Ignoranti quem portum petat, nullus suus ventus est," which can be roughly translated as, "If you don't know exactly where your port of destination is, there'll be no favorable breeze to help you." I have reformulated Seneca's maxim and use it always as my compass, expressed as follows: "He who knows exactly where his destination lies will find that even the most unfavorable winds will help him get there." And that is exactly what happened in the peace process.

We met with all kinds of obstacles. It was not easy to negotiate with guerrillas whose minds were fixed on their convictions, and these in turn colored by their ideology. In addition, we were submitted to fiercely persistent and obstinate opposition by sectors on the right under the leadership of ex-president Uribe. But in spite of all the tempests—or perhaps also thanks to them—we arrived safely at our destination.

* The Office of the High Commissioner for Peace of the Presidency of the Republic published in July 2018 the *Biblioteca del Proceso de Paz con las Farc-EP* in eleven volumes, where one can consult the final agreement and all the acts, communiqués, declarations, discourses, norms, and other documents that relate what was discussed and achieved from the secret phase down to the countersigning, verification, and implementation of the agreement.

CHAPTER 22

International Advisers

ASSIMILATING EXPERIENCES FROM AROUND THE WORLD

Just as we had studied the peace processes that had been attempted previously in Colombia—and not only those with the Farc, but those processes that had led to the demobilization of the M-19 and EPL guerrilla groups, and other minor ones—with a view to discovering their virtues and their defects in order to avoid repeating their mistakes, so too did we examine a broader spectrum of the peace processes that had been carried out in different parts of the world.

From the secret phase of our negotiations and up to the very last day, I had the good fortune to be accompanied by personal advisers. These were international experts whose experiences enabled them to look at things from a new angle and give us ideas that often helped refresh the process and attempt solutions, or open doors, that had not occurred to us. They advised me directly, and I often got them to meet with the negotiating team so they could see how the process was going and give us their opinions. Generously and with enthusiasm, they were constantly traveling from their home countries to Colombia. They even came at times they could have been on vacation, such as Christmas or New Year, and spent long hours working with me and the negotiators, sometimes at Casa de Nariño, others at Hato Grande on the outskirts of Bogotá, or at the presidential guesthouse in Cartagena. Thanks to them, the Colombian process was able to assimilate lessons from other efforts for peace around the world, such as those of Northern Ireland, or the attempts to solve the Arab-Israeli conflict, or the wars in Central America, especially in El Salvador.

THE EXAMPLE OF NORTHERN IRELAND

During the 1970s, when I was studying and working in London, the conflict in Northern Ireland was at its height. I even had a personal experience of IRA terrorism. It was October 9, 1975, and I was strolling along Piccadilly with my boss Arturo Gómez Jaramillo, manager of the Colombian Coffee Growers Federation and a second father to me. It was around nine o'clock in the evening when a bomb went off on the spot we had just left. The deafening explosion killed a twenty-three-year-old man and wounded at least twenty passersby. Gómez Jaramillo and I threw ourselves on the ground. By a matter of minutes, we had been saved from being among the victims. This made us realize, sadly, that not even London, the capital city of civility, was exempt from the senseless violence of extremists.

Northern Ireland's conflict between Catholic Republicans, fighting to break their ties to the United Kingdom and become part of the Irish Republic, and Protestant Unionists, who defended Ulster's right to retain its status as a British province, was a war they had been waging not for years, or even decades, but for centuries. Happily, in 1998, under the Labour government of Prime Minister Tony Blair, a peace treaty—the famous Good Friday Agreement—put an end to this historic confrontation. This achievement was given full recognition when the Nobel Peace Prize was awarded jointly to David Trimble, leader of the Unionist Party, and John Hume, leader of its counterpart, the Social Democratic and Labour Party.

Leaving aside the special features of each particular confrontation—the religious factor, for example, in the Irish case—there is much to be learned from the way the conflict was resolved in Northern Ireland, where, as in Colombia, children of the same nation were pitted against one another. This conflict resolution, in turn, had drawn from lessons left by the peace process in South Africa that put an end to apartheid in 1993, a process that also was acknowledged, that same year, when the Nobel Peace Prize was awarded to both South Africa's president, Frederik de Klerk, and the emblematic leader of resistance to that infamous and discriminatory regime, Nelson Mandela. De Klerk visited Colombia in 2016. And Lord Trimble came to our country also, early in 2017, to attend the World Summit of Nobel Peace Laureates in Bogotá. Both leaders shared with us their opinions and experiences, as well as giving our process their unqualified support.

It's worth mentioning that the agreements that resulted from both these processes—South Africa's and Northern Ireland's—were ratified by their citizens in a referendum. Given the features that the Irish process and the Colombian one had in common—the overcoming of a long war between citizens of the same country, the need to build a culture of reconciliation, and the sealing of the agreement by means of a popular vote—it was very valuable for me to have among the group of international advisers two British experts: Jonathan Powell and Dudley Ankerson.

From 1997 to 2007 Powell had been head of the cabinet under Prime Minister Blair, whose friendship and support I greatly value. Powell also headed the British government's negotiating team in the discussions that led to the Good Friday Agreement. As a result of this experience he published a book titled *Great Hatred, Little Room: Making Peace in Northern Ireland*, in which, among other things, he tells how Blair, following advice from Bill Clinton, was ready and willing, at a certain moment, to be the first leader of a Western power to sit down with terrorists. As it turned out, such a meeting never took place, but Blair always believed in the value of dialogue and arguments to convince the leaders of the IRA that they would be well advised to disarm and seek a peace agreement.*

Since he left British government, Powell has become a recognized consultant—one of the best, I would say—on armed conflicts around the world, to the point that, in 2014, he was appointed by Prime Minister David Cameron as special envoy to promote dialogue among diverse factions confronting one another in Libya.

Powell's experience, knowledge, and sense of reality were complemented by the academic ability and well-informed opinions of his compatriot Dudley Ankerson, PhD in history from the University of Cambridge and erstwhile diplomat in Argentina, Mexico, and Spain. Having also worked in British intelligence, Ankerson had a particular way of looking at things. He was especially knowledgeable on the Mexican Revolution and an expert on Latin American international relations. As a member of our advisory group, his ever discreet and sensible contributions provided discussions with an added value, thanks to his familiarity with our historical and regional context.

FROM CAMP DAVID TO THE COLOMBIAN PROCESS

For several years now, I have had the honor of enjoying the friendship and advice of Shlomo Ben-Ami, who holds a PhD in history from the University

* Powell is also author of other very good books such as *Talking to Terrorists: How to End Armed Conflicts* and *The New Machiavelli: How to Wield Power in the Modern World.*

of Oxford and was once Israel's ambassador to Spain, as well as the minister of public security, and of foreign affairs under the government of Prime Minister Ehud Barak from 1999 to 2001. In this latter capacity, he was one of the architects of the Camp David summit meeting in the year 2000 between Barak and the Palestinian leader Yasser Arafat that was promoted by President Bill Clinton and established parameters for negotiations aimed at solving the Arab-Israeli conflict. That same year, Ben-Ami also directed secret conversations with the Palestinian leader Abu Alaa in Stockholm. For more than a decade, he has been working as vice-president of the Toledo International Center for Peace, a foundation devoted to supporting and promoting peace processes that seek to prevent or solve conflicts around the world, and of whose advisory body I am a member.

In 2003, when I was president of the Good Government Foundation, we organized with Ben-Ami a seminar in which we studied the differences and similarities that existed between the conflicts in Colombia, Central America, and Israel-Palestine. To this event, we had invited Malcolm Deas, an English historian and expert in Colombia, and the Spanish general Luis Alejandre, who had worked in peace processes in Central America and made interesting comparisons between our conflict and the war ETA (Basque Homeland and Liberty) was waging in the Basque region of Spain.

I recall that, in July 2005, although I was not yet part of his cabinet, President Uribe invited me to accompany him on an official visit to Madrid and London. That same month, Uribe was about to pass the Law of Justice and Peace in which he defined the scope of his peace process with the paramilitaries, conceding them benefits such as alternative prison sentences of between five and eight years in exchange for confessions of their crimes and contributions to indemnifying their victims. In Colombia and elsewhere, this was criticized for its laxity toward criminals who had perpetrated the most atrocious massacres. In view of these criticisms, I invited the president to address members of the Toledo International Center for Peace under the auspices of Ben-Ami, to clarify doubts and obtain the support of an organization that enjoyed international prestige in matters of peace. President Uribe's visit to the center brought excellent results and strengthened the Israeli ex-minister's ties with the complex situation we were facing in Colombia.

From Madrid we flew to London where, on July 14, I accompanied the president on his visit to Prime Minister Blair. Exactly a week earlier, on July 7, London had been hit by four terrorist attacks carried out by Al-Qaeda: three explosions in the Underground and one in a bus, leaving fifty-six people dead and seven hundred wounded. In the aftermath of such a horrific event that had shaken the English and appalled the rest of the world, we presumed the British prime minister would cancel our meeting. But to our surprise, like the good Englishman he is, Blair received us at the appointed time in his office at No. 10 Downing Street. When we mentioned our fear that he would not be able to keep the appointment, he said: "That's what the terrorists want. That we alter our agendas because of them. And that's what we're not going to do. The best response to terrorism is normality." It was an example of dignity and fortitude in adversity that I would not forget, and that was typical of how the English have so often reacted. I have always admired their stoicism.

Ben-Ami contributed to the Colombian process the vision of a man who has given much thought to armed conflicts and peace processes in countries around the world, and applies to them a privileged intelligence, a serious criterion and great equanimity, qualities I have always admired. In addition, he has magnificent Spanish. Thanks to all of this, he provided me with great advice, and continues to do so.

THE LUCIDITY OF AN EX-GUERRILLA FIGHTER

An immensely important consultant was Joaquín Villalobos from El Salvador, who combines two special qualities: not only does he know a great deal about armed conflict and is an expert analyst, he himself had been engaged in one of Latin America's most complex and violent wars. As founding member and leader of the Farabundo Martí National Liberation Front (FMLN), a guerrilla group that took up arms against the government of El Salvador in 1980, Villalobos fought against the state's armed forces until 1992, when peace agreements were signed at Chapultepec, Mexico, that brought the conflict to an end. In fact, Villalobos was the guerrillas' delegate in the negotiations that led to this agreement.

After signing the peace agreement, the FMLN became a legal political party and two of its members, Mauricio Funes and Salvador Sánchez, have been president of the country. For a few years, Villalobos played an active role in politics, but finally broke with his party, went to study at Oxford, and has resided in England since 1995. From that time onward, he has participated as analyst and consultant in peace processes in different parts of the world, including Sri Lanka, the Philippines, Bosnia, and Northern Ireland. His first-hand experience in guerrilla fighting and in peace negotiations has resulted in his now being rightly considered an expert on the subject.

I met him during my time as minister of defense. In fact, he advised us a couple of times on the best way to combat the Farc, showing us how they operate and applying his inside knowledge of guerrilla warfare. Later, as president, I met him again in November 2010 at the Inter American Press Association's assembly in Mérida, Mexico—the one where I made a lighthearted reply to a journalist, referring to Hugo Chávez as "my new best friend," a joke I had to pay for. On that occasion, accompanied by my brother Enrique, we had a talk with Villalobos and invited him to help us in our efforts for peace in Colombia, efforts that were as yet at a very early stage. He accepted enthusiastically, and his advice, always lucid and reasonable, was of great help to me personally, and an important contribution to the process.

THE EXPERT IN NEGOTIATION

A fifth international consultant, the American professor William Ury, came to us through Frank Pearl, who had known him at Harvard. Ury was a co-founder of the Harvard Negotiation Program and had worked with my friend and much-admired teacher Roger Fisher, a world authority on negotiation. A book they had jointly authored, *Getting to Yes: Negotiating Agreement without Giving In*, is considered a classic on the subject.

As was to be expected, Ury brought us his technical and practical knowledge on the theory of negotiation, and his support and advice were advantageous not only to me but to all the members of our negotiating team, who put his teachings into practice in Havana. His mental clarity and his creativity in finding solutions to an impasse were particularly useful.

Thus were we able to set up a formidable team of international consultants—what's called a "dream team"—who supported me and provided me with illuminating advice at moments when I had to make some of the most difficult decisions. And the fact of having international advisers also enabled us to incorporate the experiences of other processes in different parts of the world, from whose triumphs—and failures, too—we had a lot to learn.

CHAPTER 23

The Message of Francis

"YOU ARE THE PERSON I HAVE HAD MOST IN MY PRAYERS"

Many international personalities—virtually all the heads of state and of governments whom I met during my eight years as president—expressed their support for the peace process and their willingness to help in whatever way was required. It was curious for me to contrast the way the process met with such popularity and support overseas with the attitude of many people in domestic politics who did their best to torpedo it, as if seeking peace through dialogue was somehow to betray the country. This paradox has been present in a lot of peace processes.

Among the many personalities for whom I nurture an immense gratitude there is one leader, more spiritual than earthly, whose support never ceased to move me, and whose help was of enormous importance for the country: I refer to Pope Francis, the Catholic Church's first *summo pontifice* to be born in Latin America.

The first time I saw him was at a particularly emotional event in the Vatican: the canonization of Mother Laura, Colombia's first saint, on May 12, 2013, before crowds gathered for the occasion in Saint Peter's Square. In the course of this solemn ceremony, the moment came for me to greet the pope, who shook my hand and told me he was praying for peace in Colombia. The next day, in a private audience, we spoke at greater length on the search for peace, and he said something to me I have engraved in my memory: "Only the courageous insist on goals of that kind that can be very costly, but they are the ones that are worthwhile."

In the words of Pope Francis, what we were doing with the guerrillas and with leaders in the region—he cited the example of my approach to President Chávez—are to be seen in the context of a "spirit of encounter" that implies accepting and respecting the differences that exist among human beings, but being prepared to work harmoniously on common concerns. "This is what we very much need in Latin America to make reality the dream of San Martín and Bolívar: the one great fatherland of Latin America," concluded the Holy Father.

Pope Francis was a constant voice of encouragement and support for the peace process in Colombia. And every time an occasion presented itself, in his different public pronouncements, he blessed the efforts our country was making to attain peace. Every time we met, he encouraged me to continue and not give up in the search for peace. And through my ambassadors to the Holy See and the Apostolic Nuncio, he sent me messages to strengthen my resolve: "Persevere, keep at the task, don't slacken off."

I next saw the pope in a private audience at the Vatican on June 15, 2015. That day he greeted me with the words: "You are the person I have had most in my prayers in recent times. I have prayed a great deal, a very great deal, for you, and for the peace process."

"I must be in serious trouble, Your Holiness, if you have to pray so much for me," I replied, jokingly of course, but sincerely moved. "And that is precisely what I've come for, your help and your enlightenment."

That day he reiterated his willingness and that of the Catholic Church to help in any way necessary. "Whatever I can do personally, or the church, you can rely on us. We support you. And if you need us to play a part, we are ready to do so, to help you."

About three months later, on September 20, 2015, in his historic visit to Cuba, and of all places in the Plaza de la Revolución, the pope made one of his most forceful pronouncements:

> At this moment, I feel it my duty to send my thoughts to the beloved land of Colombia, aware as I am of the crucial importance of the present moment when, with renewed energy and inspired by hope, our children are seeking to build a society at peace. May the blood shed by thousands of innocent victims over so many decades of armed conflict, united to that of Our Lord Jesus Christ on the cross, sustain all the efforts that are being made, including on this beautiful island, to achieve a definitive reconciliation. Thus the long night of pain and violence, with the will of all Colombians, may be transformed into an endless day of concord, justice, fraternity, and love with respect for the institutions and for national and international law, and a lasting peace. I beg you; we do not have the right to permit yet another failure on the road to peace and reconciliation.

His words were heard not only in Cuba but in every corner of Colombia. On September 23, the day after the pope left the island, I flew to Havana for my first personal meeting with Timochenko, the leader of the Farc, and we signed the long-awaited agreement on the foundations of the system of transitional justice that would be applied in response to the victims.

The pope's attitude of permanent support for the process earned him the fierce criticism of many on the extreme right, who branded him a communist Jesuit. Sadly, more than one among the Colombian bishops, those most conservative, also opposed the process in an underhand manner. And even openly, during the campaign for the plebiscite.

A VERY PECULIAR MEETING

My third private audience with Pope Francis was on December 16, 2016. I had just received the Nobel Peace Prize in Oslo on December 10, and had been engaged in official activities in Stockholm, Brussels, and Madrid. The last stage of this journey took me to Italy, where I was scheduled to greet His Holiness, as well as meet with President Sergio Mattarella and the recently designated Prime Minister Paolo Gentiloni. Another visit planned was to Assisi, the land of Saint Francis, where the Franciscan community was going to award me the Lantern of Peace, a recognition considered to be the Catholic version of the Nobel Prize.

It was our ambassador at the Vatican, Guillermo León Escobar—who died in December 2017, and was probably the Colombian with the best connections to the Roman Curia and a close friend of popes and cardinals—who told me of the paradoxical manner in which this award was decided.

César Mauricio Velásquez, a member of Opus Dei who had been press secretary of President Uribe and later his representative at the Holy See, recommended to his former boss the following very creative strategy aimed at delegitimizing the peace process: he suggested that the ex-president visit the friars of the Convent of Saint Francis—considered to be the custodians of peace, since they were the guardians of the tomb of the saint who is the patron of peace—and explain to them his objections and criticisms of the process in Havana. If Uribe managed to get these friars to make a pronouncement against the process, it would be a great blow to its credibility among millions of Catholics in Colombia. To carry out this plan, Uribe availed himself of a visit to Italy in July 2016—during which, every time he got behind a microphone, he accused my government of handing the country over to the Farc. He went with his adviser Velásquez to the convent in Assisi, where they spoke at length with the Franciscan friars.

The friars were alarmed by the diatribe Uribe launched against the peace process. So, to get a more balanced opinion, they called up Ambassador Escobar, inviting him to visit them in Assisi and explain the process from the government's point of view. After listening to his account, and with both positions on the table, these religious men deliberated and then made their decision: to award me the Lantern of Peace.

In Madrid on December 14, during a meeting at the Hotel Ritz with the Spanish prime minister, Mariano Rajoy, and Spanish businessmen, the president of Spain's telephone company, César Alierta, came up to me. It seemed Alierta moved in papal circles, for he told me the Vatican had asked him to inquire if I had any objection to Uribe joining me at the audience that I had scheduled with the pope two days later. The request seemed odd, to say the least, but on the other hand I couldn't say no to a petition from the Vatican, and maybe it could be an opportunity to smooth things over with Uribe and relieve the atmosphere of polarization that was so negatively affecting Colombia. So I said I had no objection, and accepted that the ex-president should be included.

Later I learned that this was an initiative of Fernando Carrillo, who had been elected the attorney general, though he had not yet taken possession. He had been minister of the interior and ambassador in Spain during my government. Through contacts in the Spanish Curia, especially with Monsignor Silverio Nieto, Carrillo had managed to get his idea into the Vatican, where it was approved in the belief that I had been notified of the plan. The truth is I learned of it less than forty-eight hours before the meeting was scheduled to take place.

With Colombia's prosecutor general, Néstor Humberto Martínez, acting as intermediary, the Colombian banker and business magnate Luis Carlos Sarmiento facilitated his private jet to fly Uribe, in haste, from Colombia to Rome.

At ten o'clock on Friday, December 16, I had the audience with Pope Francis, who congratulated me on the Nobel Prize I had just received and questioned me about the challenges that awaited us with the implementation of the agreement. He also said that he thought I had been very generous in accepting that the former president be included in the visit. Uribe had not yet arrived, so the pope concluded the audience and asked me to wait in an adjoining room for my predecessor, now leader of the opposition.

A little while later, I was invited to go back into the papal office. Uribe was already there and our mutual greeting was cordial enough. Then we sat down beside one another opposite the pope, who was sitting behind his desk. He expressed his pleasure that we were there and said he was ready to offer his help so that peace could become a reality in our country. He then invited Uribe to say a few words, and the former president began a thorough and detailed exposition on his disagreements and criticisms of the peace accord we had reached in Havana and had then modified to include the great majority of his observations and suggestions. But his attitude had not changed one jot; he came out with the same arguments he had been repeating in Colombia over and over again for months.

At a certain moment the pope looked at me with an expression of bewilderment, as if to say, *This isn't working*, and abruptly interrupted Uribe's discourse to say that he thanked us very much for coming to see him and that the doors of the Vatican, and of the church, would always be open to support Colombia. With great prudence and diplomacy, he brought the meeting to an end and took his leave of us.

On our way out, when we reached the door, Uribe went down on his knees before the pope and asked him to bless rosary beads and a medal he held out to him. It occurred to me that I should also kneel, so as not to appear arrogant. But I thought better of it. Once we were outside, Uribe said to me: "President, yield, yield a little." Really, I had no idea what he was referring to. After all, the final agreement had not only been signed but countersigned by an overwhelming number of votes in Congress. All that remained was to implement it in the best possible way, a task in which I had always invited the opposition to take part.

Uribe had organized for journalists to interview him when the visit was over, and he stated to the press that he had spoken clearly to the pope of his convictions but that President Santos had refused to move from his position. But that was not the question. We were not trying to convert the pope into an arbitrator on our divergent opinions regarding the peace agreement. Our intention was to seek an approach for the future that might diminish the polarization that was causing so much harm in Colombia. Sadly, this singular encounter, which could have been immensely useful, ended in failure.

That same day I had a meeting with Cardinal Pietro Parolin, the Vatican's secretary of state, and Cardinal Paul Richard Gallagher, secretary for relations with states, in which our minister of foreign affairs, María Ángela Holguín, also took part, along with our representative at the Holy See, Ambassador Escobar. Escobar was indignant at the way the meeting had been improvised, and at how meaningless the idea had been in the first place. Parolin said that they at the Vatican had been deceived because they understood I had been told of the proposed meeting from the start. When he found that this was not the case, he offered his apologies.

AN UNFORGETTABLE VISIT

For five days, from September 6 to 10, 2017, my dream, and that of all Colombians, finally came true: Pope Francis paid us a visit. I had invited him a few days after his election in March 2013, and had reiterated the invitation on many occasions. My insistence was at last rewarded.

The pope was very generous with us. He made the gesture of coming to Colombia and nowhere else on his trip, and he included on his tour visits to four of our cities: Bogotá, Villavicencio, Medellín, and Cartagena. His attitude, his simplicity, and his message of reconciliation won the hearts of everyone in Colombia, believers and nonbelievers alike. He met with the young, embraced and listened to the victims of the conflict, and presided at ceremonies that brought together millions of people. The leitmotif of his visit, "Let's take the first step," invited us to move forward, following on the agreement, toward an even more important and ambitious goal: reconciliation between all Colombians.

In one of our conversations during his visit, he said to me: "You have suffered divisions in your country on the subject of peace, and I too have had to deal with them in the bosom of the church."

The pope was surprised by the attitude of certain hierarchs of the Colombian church who echoed criticisms of the peace process and refused to comply with his instruction to support peace and reconciliation. Maybe it was because these bishops believed the lies that were propagated to denigrate the process, such as the supposed inclusion of a gender ideology—understood as the definition of gender not as a biological fact but as a social and cultural construction—in the agreement.

Perhaps that's why, on September 7, in a salon at the Cardinal's Palace in

Bogotá, he made this statement to all the bishops of Colombia in a tone of reproach:

> Colombia needs the vision proper to you as bishops to sustain the country in its courage on taking the first step toward definitive peace and reconciliation and the abdication of violence as a method. . . . You see with your own eyes and know better than anyone how this country's visage has been deformed; you are custodians of the fundamental pieces that make it a whole, notwithstanding its lacerations. Precisely for that reason, Colombia needs you to recognize its true face, full of hope despite its imperfections, to forgive reciprocally despite the wounds not yet completely healed, to believe that a new path can be found even when inertia pushes you to commit the same mistakes, to have the courage to overcome whatever can make it miserable despite its treasures.

An interesting incident during the papal visit was the deeply felt letter sent to Pope Francis on that same day, September 7, by Timochenko, and signed with his real name, Rodrigo Londoño, although he did add, in parentheses, one of his aliases: Timoleón Jiménez. It expressed sentiments that may seem surprisingly pious when you remember it came from the commander of a guerrilla of Marxist-Leninist origins, something that can only be understood by taking into account the context and the peculiarities of our culture, and of our conflict. Timochenko wrote to the pope as follows:

> I direct an organization that has given up arms and is reincorporated into society after more than half a century of war. We have forsaken any manifestation of hate or violence, we are inspired by the purpose of forgiving those who were our enemies and have caused our people so much harm, and we make an act of contrition that is indispensable if we wish to admit our errors and beg the pardon of all the men and women who, in whatever way, have been victims of our action.

To this, he added a petition:

> I don't know whether it would be truly proper to implore you, given the magnificent power of your prayers, to raise your voice and invite all Colombians to pray that the enormous effort involved in setting up the Table

> of Conversations, of debating at that table for years, of overcoming stubborn resistance to any agreement, and of finally putting an end to the conflict and building a stable and enduring peace, may not be frustrated. That is what we are praying for.

I pray for that, too. I do so every day.

At the end of his visit, after five days of intense activity that left him with a bruise on one eye due to a small accident that occurred as he was driving through the streets of Cartagena in his "popemobile," Pope Francis was tired but happy. I heard that he confided to a monsignor close to him that the visit to Colombia was the best of his whole pontificate.

As he was bidding us farewell in Cartagena, his last stop on the tour, I took the little badge with the dove of peace I had been wearing on my lapel since the process began as a symbol and reminder of our commitment, and gave it to the pope with these words: "Holy Father, I want you to have this dove that I have had with me all these years, as a remembrance of our gratitude. And I want you to have it because, fortunately, peace can now fly alone."

Since then, I no longer wear that beautiful symbol that had accompanied me for so long.

Pope Francis flew from Cartagena to Rome and left us all with a smile in our hearts. His visit was the most illustrious and charismatic we have had in a very long time, and his words sowed seeds of reconciliation and hope in our country. With his simplicity, his way with people, his human warmth, his clarity, he has been, and continues to be, the best friend the peace of Colombia could ever have.

CHAPTER 24

The Backing of the United States

THE UNCONDITIONAL SUPPORT OF THE OBAMA GOVERNMENT

Nobody can deny the strategic importance of the United States in the world in general, and even more so in our region. The United States has been the country with which we have jointly waged a relentless war on drug trafficking and terrorism. And with the United States we share the ideal of democracy; our liberators were inspired in theirs. They are also our principal economic partners, and they contributed, discreetly and generously, in our search for peace in Colombia.

My first meeting with President Barack Obama, as I have already mentioned, was in New York in September 2010, the day after our armed forces brought down Mono Jojoy, the Farc's military chief. That was in wartime, when a negotiated solution seemed far off.

The next time we met, things had changed for the better. It was in April 2012, when our country was the seat of the sixth Summit of the Americas, which brings together leaders from all over the continent. After the summit meeting had concluded, President Obama stayed on for a few hours and we had a bilateral meeting at the presidential guesthouse in Cartagena. Sitting there together and chatting informally, I told the president about the approaches we had made to the Farc and the secret conversations we had been carrying on with them in Havana over the previous two months in an attempt to define an agenda for negotiations.

His reaction was very positive. He said this was great news and would mean great progress for the whole continent, and that we could rely on his and his country's unconditional support in whatever way might be required. When I told him the conversations were being held in Cuba, he seemed especially interested and told me he also hoped that his country's relations with the island would develop toward a more open treatment. We agreed that

Cuba's support for peace in Colombia could contribute to better relations in general.

And so it was. Very discreetly, we played a part in helping those two sworn enemies, the United States and Cuba, to come closer. And the fact that our conversations were going on in Havana was a fortunate coincidence that helped those approaches to prosper. I personally spoke about that matter with President Obama and President Castro, as well as with former president Clinton and the Democratic senator Patrick Leahy, the oldest member of the US Senate and a man who exerted great influence on his country's international relations. My intention was to facilitate these approaches. We kept working on this with the greatest confidentiality, to the point that Barranquilla, Colombia's largest city on the Caribbean coast, was considered a possible venue for secret contacts between the United States and Cuba, contacts that were eventually made in Canada.

These discreet arrangements were consistent with what I, as host, had proposed to the Summit of the Americas in Cartagena, where I advocated the entry of Cuba to that multilateral event. These were my words:

> Isolation, the embargo, indifference, looking the other way—these attitudes have all shown how useless they are. In today's world, such treatment is unjustifiable. It implies an anachronism that keeps us anchored in the era of the Cold War that was overcome decades ago.
>
> Just as it would be unacceptable to organize another meeting of the hemisphere with Haiti on its knees, so would it be to do so and exclude Cuba.
>
> We cannot be indifferent to the process of change taking place inside Cuba, one that is more and more widely recognized and ought to continue. The time has come to overcome the paralysis caused by ideological stubbornness and seek minimal points of consensus so that the process of change comes to fruition for the good of the Cuban people.

Fortunately, my proposal was well received, and at the following summit, held in Panama in 2015, Cuba was present for the first time, represented by President Raúl Castro. I have always been convinced that differences are ironed out through dialogue. And to dialogue, you have to include, not exclude.

When President Obama announced on December 17, 2014, that the United States was reestablishing diplomatic relations with Cuba, I was happy as I reflected on what this meant for the hemisphere and for the world in general, and on the grain of sand that we had contributed for that to happen. The day that Obama—in the course of his historic visit to Havana in March 2016—went with his family to see the baseball game between the Tampa Bay Rays and the official Cuban team, the delegates from both the Colombian government and the Farc were there in the stadium among thousands of other emotional spectators, They were witnessing the end of one of the last symbols of the Cold War in the Western Hemisphere. All that remained was to end the armed conflict in Colombia. And a few months later we managed to do just that.

AN EXCEPTIONAL ENVOY

Apart from the governments of Cuba, Norway, and Venezuela—which, for obvious reasons, were aware of what was going on during the secret phase—President Obama was the first head of state with whom I shared news of the progress we were making in our efforts to achieve a peace process with the Farc. From then on, Obama was constantly attentive to how dialogues were proceeding and reiterated his support every time we met or spoke on the telephone. His vice-president, Joe Biden, and the United States secretary of state John Kerry, in particular, as well as Kevin Whitaker, the US ambassador in Colombia, were our permanent allies. I am particularly honored to have Kerry's foreword at the beginning of this book.

It was precisely Secretary Kerry who proposed that the United States designate a special envoy to accompany the peace process, and he suggested Bernie Aronson, whom I knew and who had very good relations with Colombia. He had been secretary of state for Latin American affairs from 1989 to 1993 under the governments of George Bush and Bill Clinton and knew the region well. Also, he had played an outstanding role as US delegate in the conversations that led to peace in El Salvador.

I gladly accepted the idea, and so it was that Bernie Aronson became his country's special envoy at the peace process as of February 2015. As such, he played an ever positive and realistic role and was able to communicate well with negotiators on both sides. He was continually in touch with Vice President Biden and Secretary Kerry, keeping them abreast of progress, and also of the problems. He was extremely active, traveling between Bogotá, Washington, and Havana, building consensus and proposing solutions. He kept members of the United States Congress informed in order to maintain a bipartisan consensus on support for the process, and even met with Uribe a couple of times to explain to him the positive nature of the process. To the same end, he visited President Maduro of Venezuela. He proved to be a true diplomat and man of action who put himself on the line for peace in Colombia.

THE CASE OF SIMÓN TRINIDAD

One particular concern, constantly on the minds of the Farc negotiators with respect to the United States, was the subject of inevitable questioning by journalists whenever they interviewed US officials. It was the question of Simón Trinidad, a Farc guerrilla commander who had played an important role as negotiator in the Caguán peace talks and was captured in Ecuador in 2004, deported to Colombia, and then extradited to the United States, where he was sentenced to sixty years in prison for having kidnapped three US citizens. Since then, he has been locked up in a high-security penitentiary in Colorado.

For the Farc, Trinidad's freedom became a question of honor. They even named him plenipotentiary at the negotiating table, and at the inauguration ceremony in Oslo they kept a seat vacant with his name on it. To emphasize his absence, a dummy with a full-length photo of him formed a backdrop to many of the Farc negotiators' pronouncements in Havana. But there was little we could do about it. Trinidad had been tried and sentenced by a US court, and any decision on his future was a matter for the US authorities and the US Justice Department.

It was conceivable that once the process was over, a final agreement signed and the Farc's weapons handed over to UN officials, there might have been some chance of his being freed. But in the meantime there was a change of government in the United States, and if his liberation was doubtful under the Obama administration, it became virtually impossible under Donald Trump's. All that we were able to achieve was to slightly improve his prison conditions, since up to then he was being held in solitary confinement.

Simón Trinidad, whose real name is Ricardo Palma, was a guerrilla fighter whose background was unusual in that he came from a well-off family in Valledupar. I knew him in the late sixties at the naval academy, where he was a recruit when I was already a second-grade cadet. I remember him as a likable lad though a bit crazy, whom I had to discipline more than once for rebellious behavior. After doing military service, he studied economy and took postgraduate courses in the United States. He rose to the status of bank manager in his native city, but disenchantment and anger at the continuous murders of members of the Patriotic Union, the party that was founded as a consequence of the Betancur peace process and to which he belonged, led him to give up everything, including his wife and children, and join the guerrillas.

If he had been in Colombia, he could have presented his case before the special justice for peace and have received benefits in exchange for telling the truth and helping to indemnify the victims. But his fate—at least for now—is to be shut up in a faraway prison cell.

PRESIDENT TRUMP AND PEACE IN COLOMBIA

It's no secret that President Trump adopted policies on the fight against terrorism, cooperation against drug trafficking, and the subject of migrants, among others, that were much harsher and more radical than those of his predecessor. Nevertheless, I can say that, as far as Colombia is concerned, he essentially supported, during the first half of his term, the peace process, although by the time he came to power the peace talks had come to an end, and we had begun the process of implementation.

My first conversation with President Trump was on November 11, 2016, when I phoned to congratulate him on his election as the forty-fifth president of the United States. It was a brief and friendly chat in which Trump said he liked Colombia a lot for two reasons in particular. "First, for your beautiful women . . . " It should be remembered that Trump owned the franchise of the Miss Universe contest for twenty years, and that Colombia has won the beauty pageant twice and has been six times runner-up. "And second," he went on, "because you have very good labor skills and some exceptional products. I can say that because I've spent millions of dollars on Colombian products, especially in steel."

This allusion astonished me. At first, I couldn't identify who was supplying the Trump organization, but later I was told it was Tecnoglass, a Barranquilla enterprise that was selling steel window frames for his hotels and other buildings. Paradoxically, it would be the same President Trump who, in 2018, imposed tariffs on steel and aluminum products entering the United States, not just from Colombia but from most of the world.

On May 18, 2017, I visited the White House and had an interview with

President Trump in which we talked about the usual matters of interest to our bilateral relationship: trade, the fight against drug trafficking, and finally Venezuela, whose democratic and human rights crisis was a matter of concern for us both. I also brought the president up to date on our progress in implementing the peace agreement with the Farc that we had signed in November of the previous year.

Our joint press conference, held after the private meeting, was one of the best attended in a long time at the White House. But not exactly on account of my visit. The reason for the exceptional crowd was that the day before, the deputy US attorney general Rod Rosenstein—the man who, according to the *New York Times*, had suggested recording conversations with Trump to get him removed from the presidency on the grounds that he was not capable of performing the duties of the office—had appointed a special counsel to investigate Russia's supposed interference in the campaign that got Trump elected. And he had appointed not just any attorney, but the former director of the FBI, Robert Mueller. That very morning Trump had tweeted: "This is the single greatest witch hunt of a politician in American history!"

Joe Scarborough, political commentator and anchorman for the television program *Morning Joe* on MSNBC, said later that he had felt very confused "watching Donald Trump sounding far less articulate than the president of Colombia, who actually seems to speak our language much better than Donald Trump even when he's not speaking our language."

Naturally, the first question a journalist asked President Trump was on the naming of Mueller as special counsel for the US Department of Justice. When the press conference was over, Ricardo Ávila, the director of *Portafolio*, a Colombian publication specializing in economics, asked the US president what his position was on the peace process, to which nobody had referred up to that moment. The president's reply was encouraging:

> Well, it's been a long process and it's a great thing to watch in the sense that the president did a fantastic job. That's not easy after so many years of war. So I am very, very proud to get to know you, and I really congratulate you. There's nothing tougher than peace, and we want to make peace all over the world. And you are really a great example of somebody that started it. I mean Farc is . . . that was a long, long situation, as you know very well, coming from the country. But I think the president has done a magnificent job. Not easy. But he's done a magnificent job.

CONVERSATIONS ON THE PROBLEM OF DRUGS

On September 1, 2017, I phoned President Trump from Bogotá to express Colombia's solidarity with the American people after the tragedy caused by Hurricane Harvey in the states of Texas and Louisiana. A week earlier, the US Drug Enforcement Agency had published a report on the increase in illegal crops in Colombia, and Trump said to me: "I'm really worried about the drugs." I reminded him that in our meeting at the White House I had explained the plan we were executing to forcefully eradicate fifty thousand hectares of coca plantations and a similar quantity by agreement with families who made a living from coca leaf crops to engage in a program of voluntary substitution. And I told him that this program was being carried out.

Our conversation was frank, direct, and cordial, and in no way was President Trump's attitude aggressive or chiding. Curiously, however, in early January 2018, the *Washington Post* published an article that purported to reveal inside information on my conversation with the US president. The report said that President Trump had given me a hard time and had complained that I was more concerned with the guerrillas than with the United States. It was a distorted version of our conversation, and there is no doubt it was maliciously intended. I don't know who the source was behind this supposed leak, but someone in the White House wanted to muddy things up.

Still, one thing was certain: Trump was not happy with the increase in illegal crops. Two weeks after our conversation, on September 13, 2017, an official US government memorandum signed by the president stated that "the United States was seriously considering designating Colombia as a country that had failed demonstrably to adhere to its obligations under international counternarcotics agreements due to the extraordinary growth of coca cultivation and cocaine production over the past 3 years, including record cultivation during the last 12 months." This implied a threat to decertify us as a partner in global counternarcotics efforts, which was not justified given the ongoing efforts we make in Colombia to combat the drug trade, while the consumption that stimulates it continues to grow in the United States, and in the rest of the world.

In the midst of this tension, I flew to New York to attend the annual assembly of the United Nations, and Trump invited me, along with other Latin American heads of government—Michel Temer, president of Brazil; Juan Carlos Varela, president of Panama; and Gabriela Michetti, vice-president of Argentina—to a dinner on the night of September 18 at New York's Palace Hotel to discuss what action could be taken as regards the complex situation in Venezuela, where, as the US president said, people were dying of hunger while the country was collapsing under the Maduro regime. On the US side, the highest echelons were present: Vice-President Mike Pence; Secretary of State Rex Tillerson; Chief of Staff John Kelly (by the way, a good friend to Colombia); General H. R. McMaster, the national security adviser; Juan Cruz, who had directed CIA activities in Colombia and was now director for Latin America of the National Security Council under orders from McMaster, and the US ambassador to the United Nations, Nikki Haley.

The meeting's purpose was to see in what way the countries in the region could cooperate to restore democracy in Venezuela. A month before, Trump had spoken of the possibility of using force if necessary. I repeated what I had said to Vice-President Pence when he visited us a few weeks earlier in Cartagena: Colombia does not agree with any kind of military intervention, and no Latin American country would support anything of the kind. And I added: "Venezuela is like a plane that is going to come down: we could help it to land gently or we could let it crash. I think we all want it to land gently. That's why all of us who are interested have to come to an agreement, not only the American countries but also important actors like China and Russia, over which we have very little influence, but you, President Trump, can certainly have."

I continued as follows: "We in Latin America, and I say this quite frankly, as one ought to speak among friends, we have a problem in dealing with the subject of Venezuela, and that is we don't know who we should talk to in the US government. That is why it would be ideal if you would designate a point person, and that would greatly facilitate our coordination."

Trump glanced around the room, taking in the officials who were accompanying him, all of whom were nodding their heads in agreement, and in a matter of seconds decided that the person to take the lead on the subject would be Cruz. We were slightly surprised, since normally one would have expected it to be someone from the State Department. However, it was evident that the US president saw the question of Venezuela more as a matter of security than of diplomacy.

After this meeting, I talked to Kelly, who admitted that the president's communiqué on the possible decertification of Colombia was unfortunate and said it had been the product of advisers who were filling the president's head with those ideas. A few days later, on October 24, I received a letter from Trump in which he recognized Colombia's fight against the traffickers. His message was couched in terms very different from those he had used in the communiqué of a month earlier:

> On September 13, I signed a Presidential Determination in which I noted concerns about the extraordinary expansion of coca cultivation and cocaine production in Colombia and the potential consequences of failing to curb those activities in the near future. I noted these concerns because I promised the people of the United States that we will prevent drugs from pouring across our borders, and I need your help to decrease the production and trafficking of drugs in Colombia. The United States stands ready to support you in your counternarcotics efforts. At the same time, I am working diligently to combat drug use here in the United States.
>
> Colombia is one of our best strategic partners and allies in the region. We commend the efforts that you have taken to confront transnational crime. The support and cooperation of the Colombian government—from military to law enforcement to development—is incredible and something we try to replicate with other countries.
>
> I am confident that your efforts will improve the problems of coca cultivation and cocaine production in Colombia. We will work together on this important issue, and I know that we will strengthen our already strong bilateral relationship.
>
> I enjoyed seeing you in New York during the United Nations General Assembly, and I look forward to continuing our conversation about the issues confronting our countries. Send my best to the beautiful people of Colombia.

JOE BIDEN: A RETURN TO COHERENCE

Many of President Trump's attitudes, not to mention public statements he made during the time I was president of Colombia, were ones he himself radically altered over the last two years of his administration. This is perhaps not surprising, given the extremely volatile and capricious nature of his personality. Even though he had congratulated us and expressed his praise for our peace process at a White House press conference, later, in his reelection campaign, that very process was to bear the brunt of his fiercest criticism.

In May 2017, Trump pointed to Colombia as an example for a world in search of peace. Yet, three years later, in his campaign speeches in Florida, he attacked Obama, Biden, and me for having negotiated "the terrible Obama-Biden-Santos deal with Colombian drug cartels." Thus, in accordance with his very personal style of misrepresenting things, he claimed that putting an end to our prolonged armed conflict with the Farc was tantamount to making some sort of shady deal with drug traffickers—a deal in which he included both his predecessor in the White House and former Vice President Biden, Trump's rival in the 2020 presidential election, as if they had been cosigners of the peace agreement. These false statements were designed to confuse electors and win the votes of Colombian residents in Florida, many of whom follow guidelines dictated by Uribe and his political party, the Democratic Center.

Despite Trump's efforts, however, following the November 3, 2020 election, the immense majority of US citizens—with more than eighty-one million votes, including the mail-in ballots that played a decisive role as they were counted in the weeks after—decided to return to the path of coherence and respect for the rule of law, multilateralism, and diplomatic procedures. They chose Joe Biden as their president—a refreshing decision not only for the United States but for Colombia also, and for the international community as a whole.

From his time as senator, Biden has shown himself to be a staunch friend of Colombia, keeping himself well informed of our problems and fomenting a bipartisan policy of support for our joint fight against the drug trade and our common search for peace. In the year 2000, he visited our country on two occasions at a time when he was one of the US Senate's promoters of Plan Colombia. Then, as vice-president, he supported the ratification of the free trade agreement between our two countries, as well as Colombia's entry into the Organization for Economic Cooperation and Development. In addition, he was our unfailing ally as we held peace talks with the Farc, a subject we discussed frequently, especially during his visits to Colombia in 2013, 2014, and 2016. President Obama appointed him as the US government's communication channel with Bernie Aronson, the United States' special envoy to the process in Havana. In November 2016, in acknowledgement of Biden's work for our country, at a ceremony in the Colombian embassy in Washington, I awarded him Colombia's most prestigious recognition; namely, the Order of Boyacá, created in 1819 to honor the Liberator Simón Bolívar and his armies after their victory in the Battle of Boyacá.

I had the pleasure of meeting Biden again at Lincoln Center in New York on December 6, 2018, when Conservation International distinguished us both with the Global Visionary Award in view of our support for the preservation of the environment. I am convinced that President Biden—whom I am proud to consider a friend—is a brilliant, decent, and honorable man who will guide the United States toward a future of progress and stability. His leadership will be marked by a strong dose of humanism and empathy, traits that are so important in world leaders.

His arrival to the presidency of the world's most powerful nation opens a window of hope for the planet, and represents, for Colombia, the return of a reliable ally who understands our country's problems and those of Latin America in general, and who believes in the power of dialogue to resolve differences, and in a comprehensive strategy to fight the drug trade—a strategy that favors the voluntary substitution of legal for illegal crops over the criminal prosecution of peasant farmers and drug addicts. Joe Biden understands how important peace is for Colombia. He followed closely our negotiations with the Farc guerrillas and, as president, will certainly give his full backing to the support and vigilance required on the part of the international community to ensure that the peace agreement is implemented.

In his campaign, Biden claimed that US citizens should choose hope over fear. They did, and this election has brought a ray of light and a breath of fresh air to the entire world.

CHAPTER 25

The World Bets on Peace in Colombia

A NEGOTIATION BETWEEN COLOMBIANS

A fundamental factor in the success of the peace process that we undertook was the cooperation and unwavering support of the international community. From multilateral organizations to heads of state and personalities from around the world, all expressed their backing of the peace talks in Havana. The fact that they offered their support for our process in Colombia—the only country in the Western Hemisphere in which an armed conflict was still going on—was a fundamental piece for peace in the region, and in the world. This support was expressed in multiple declarations of solidarity but also, whenever necessary, in concrete actions to stimulate and validate the process in Havana.

One must insist, however, that our process—even though, for the sake of convenience, it was taking place in another country—was a Colombian process, designed and agreed upon among Colombians and achieved by Colombians. By contrast with some other experiences in the world, we did not rely on any international mediator or intermediary. This we decided on from the start. Discussions on each point went on directly between the government and the Farc, and the negotiators themselves wrote up the agreements as they were being reached.

Norway contributed its ample experience and generous availability to resources in matters of conflict resolution. And Cuba, the other guarantor country, was a splendid host. Representatives of both these countries were constantly present at the negotiating table, but they did not intervene. They sometimes made suggestions aside from the table, but only when it was warranted because of certain situations of crisis or stagnation.

As for Chile and Venezuela, the accompanying countries, their role was mainly to act as witnesses and to validate proceedings. They visited the table in Havana to observe progress and see how the negotiation was coming along, and they helped us explain and convey news of what was taking place to countries in the region.

From the beginning, we made it clear that the international community would participate only to the extent that it became necessary, for we knew that what was essential was to devote time and effort to the negotiation between the parties. The most recent example was the Caguán process, where a group of countries friendly to the process was created, consisting of twenty-six different nations, coordinated by a smaller group known as the International Facilitating Commission, which encompassed ten of those countries. They held ongoing meetings with their respective ambassadors, inviting them to Caguán to bring them up to date on what was happening. All of this consumed precious time that would have been better spent working to reach an agreement.

In our case, thanks to the six months in which the delegates worked discreetly during the exploratory phase, a working method and an atmosphere of mutual respect was established, and this made it possible for the process to go ahead without any mediation or international intervention.

There came a moment, of course, when we were at the stage of implementing and verifying the agreement, especially on questions of disarmament and demobilization, when the participation of the United Nations was necessary and extremely useful, as we shall see.

I especially want to mention the permanent and effective collaboration offered by the International Red Cross and its delegation in Colombia, presided over first by Jordi Raich and later Christopher Harnisch. The Red Cross gave their support on every occasion—and they were many—when the guerrilla's negotiators had to be transported from inhospitable locations in Colombia and flown to Havana, and then from Havana back to Colombia. All of this to enable the guerrilla leaders to inform their troops in the jungle about progress in the negotiations.

Thanks to the careful planning of that first complicated transfer of Mauricio Jaramillo, alias The Doctor, and Sandra Ramírez from the Guaviare jungle to Caracas and then to Havana to begin the exploratory phase in February 2012, a precedent was established on the question of transport that was going to be applied dozens of times, and entailed the use of helicopters and airplanes bearing the highly respected insignia of the Red Cross.

EUROPE'S SOLIDARITY

Europe, the cradle of Western civilization with its long history and centuries-old traditions, has also been the scenario of the greatest tragedies of the twentieth century. That is why the constitution and the evolution of the European Union—an admirable initiative designed to overcome differences and cultivate an atmosphere of peace and cooperation—was the object of recognition by the Norwegian Committee that, in 2012, awarded the Nobel Peace Prize to that exemplary organization. It is worrying to see how that union is falling apart, like so much else to do with world order, and on so many fronts.

Europe's governments, its heads of state, with the majority of whom I had meetings, were especially supportive and enthusiastic on our country's peace process. At the center of the European Union, under the leadership of its representative for foreign affairs and security, Federica Mogherini, this support was translated into concrete actions such as the designation of a special envoy to the process and the creation of a trustee fund with an initial capital of 95 million euros to help finance the postconflict stage.

Mogherini, at the time Italy's minister of foreign affairs, had attended my inauguration on August 7, 2010, and as from that moment we have enjoyed an excellent personal relationship that she has enriched with two qualities I admire: intelligence and warmth. Just as the United States had appointed Bernie Aronson as special envoy to the process, in October 2015 Mogherini also designated a special envoy from the European Union in the person of Eamon Gilmore, an experienced Irish politician who had been, from 2011 to 2014, the Republic of Ireland's minister for foreign affairs and trade, as well as its deputy prime minister (Tánaiste). He had also taken part in the negotiation and implementation of Northern Ireland's peace process, an experience that was particularly valuable for us.

As Mogherini said, his designation was "a signal to the Colombians that the European Union is standing by their efforts to put an end to one of the oldest and most murderous conflicts in the world." This envoy's presence was particularly helpful, for Gilmore facilitated the coordination of all Europe's activities in favor of peace, motivating people and organizations to support the process. And even when the negotiations were over, he continued to collaborate with us during the implementation stage, visiting Colombia's different zones to identify areas of cooperation.*

* Eamon Gilmore has served as European Union Special Representative for Human Rights since February 2019.

* * *

Spain was a fundamental ally, beginning with the kings Juan Carlos and Felipe and the prime minister at the time, Mariano Rajoy. They supported us in every possible way, even in matters that were not strictly related to the peace process but opened up new opportunities for the Colombians.

I remember that on August 10, 2013, my birthday, while I was visiting Turbaco, a small town on Colombia's Caribbean coast, I got a call from Prime Minister Rajoy to tell me that Spain was going to propose to the twenty-six European countries that made up what was called the Schengen Zone that they exempt Colombian citizens from the tourist visa they had required up until that time. I told him that this news was the best birthday present I could have received. And his promise became a reality in December 2015.

With King Juan Carlos and Queen Sofía, my wife María Clemencia and I had a special relationship, as also with King Felipe and Queen Letizia, who have been very close to Colombia. It was very emotional for me that the first official act King Juan Carlos attended overseas after he had abdicated in favor of his son was my inauguration on August 7, 2014, as president for a second term. In the company of the other heads of state who were present, we paid the king a well-earned homage.

On a state visit to Madrid, Queen Letizia told me how impressed she was and how much she admired the progressive attitude of my government, especially for the fact that I had in my cabinet two women ministers—very capable ministers they were, too—who were living as a couple in a love relationship. My private secretary was also gay, as was his assistant, though they were not a couple. For me, this was irrelevant; I had appointed them for their professional expertise without even thinking of the implications their private lives might have. However, I understand that this is something unusual and shows a liberal attitude on the question of sexual diversity. Canada's prime minister Justin Trudeau also once commented that he appreciated the value of my decision on this matter. Naturally, liberal attitudes like these come with a price; I underwent criticism from the Catholic Church and from quite a few conservatives.

Another Spanish personality for whom I feel special gratitude and affection, for the way he identifies with Colombia's problems and for his commitment to our search for peace, is former prime minister Felipe González, to whom I had the pleasure of conferring Colombian citizenship in 2014. Few people are more deserving of it than González, who has spared no effort to accompany all our country's concerns, supporting positive initiatives and giving good advice when asked to do so by more than one Colombian president. I feel honored to have him as a friend.

* * *

With Portugal, Colombia's relations had always been cordial but rather distant. It was as if that nation of fado singers, poets, and navigators were hiding behind a transparent veil to which we would draw near but never cross. During my government, however, all that changed. This was due to the outstanding labors of the journalist Germán Santamaría, an old friend who had often worked with me before and whom I named ambassador in Lisbon. Thanks to him and to our foreign affairs minister, María Ángela Holguín, we achieved a level of trade, cooperation, investment, and tourism between our two countries such as Colombia had never known before.

I traveled twice to Portugal on state visits, and on several occasions received reciprocal visits to Colombia from the Portuguese president and his prime minister. The first to lend us his support was President Aníbal Cavaco Silva, who made interesting comparisons between the Colombian conflict and the long-drawn-out civil war in the former Portuguese colony Angola, a conflict that ended in a peace agreement in 2002. Others who helped us with enthusiasm were Prime Minister Pedro Passos Coelho and, after him, President Marcelo Rebelo de Sousa and Prime Minister António Costa. Paulo Portas, first minister of state and foreign affairs of Portugal and later deputy prime minister, also played a special role. His article "Only Hawks Make Peace," published in *El Tiempo* in May 2015, is one of the best dissections of the Colombian process. Nothing less could be expected of a country that put an end to a long dictatorship without firing a single shot. In Portugal's 1974 revolution to topple the dictator António de Oliveira Salazar, carnations took the place of bullets.

There's a bit of family history that makes me feel special affection for Portugal. In the early 1960s, my grandfather Enrique Santos Montejo, whose nom de plume was Caliban, was appointed ambassador to Portugal, a post he was very glad to accept since he was very fond of that country. However, on arriving in Lisbon, he was faced with the harsh reality of a system of government that was everything a liberal philosopher like himself abhorred. As a journalist, he had been subjected to censorship under Colombia's only dictatorship in the twentieth century, and he felt Portugal was going through what his own country had suffered a decade before.

As ambassador, he was able to offer political asylum to two of Salazar's opponents, which naturally did not win applause from the host government. In fact, because of his libertarian conduct, he was forced to resign before he had served even two months in the embassy. But he preferred that to living with a regime that had no regard for freedom, something he considered the most precious value of all. And in that I, his grandson, think as he did.

* * *

You don't ever forget a young love, and I will never forget my love for England. That was the country that welcomed me in the vibrant seventies, and where I lived unforgettable moments in the course of the ten years I studied and worked there and became inculcated with everything English: the country's history and philosophy, its people's stoicism and the way they look at life, and at politics.

I have already spoken of my friendship with the British ex-prime minister Tony Blair and of how, from the time he was in government, we together defended the thesis of the Third Way. As president, I had the opportunity of getting to know Queen Elizabeth II and Prince Philip better, as well as Prince Charles and his wife Camilla Parker-Bowles, and the two prime ministers David Cameron and Theresa May, all of whom, in every visit, encouraged me to persevere in the search for peace in Colombia and supported the process without hesitation.

England's strict protocol allows for no more than two state visits in a single year, and these are hosted by the queen. In 2016, King Felipe of Spain had to cancel his visit, so they received only mine that year. It was an unforgettable event, the first of its kind ever attended by a Colombian president. At the gala banquet in Buckingham Palace on November 1, Queen Elizabeth made a courteous gesture toward me that showed her human quality and her eye for detail. Apparently, she had been informed that as a student at the naval academy, I had played the bagpipes in the martial band. So in the middle of the dinner, she turned to me and said: "I know you used to play the bagpipes, so we have a surprise for you." At this, there appeared a dozen or so pipers dressed in their traditional Scottish kilts who marched around the table playing unmistakable highland airs. It was a lovely gesture, and I was sincerely moved by it.

My state visit took place less than a month after we lost by a minimal margin the plebiscite to seal the peace agreement. This is no doubt what inspired Queen Elizabeth to pay me the following generous compliment in her toast: "Although you have faced recent setbacks, to have come to the cusp of a historic peace agreement, against the expectations of many, is a testament to your courage and perseverance, and that of the Colombian people." And she quoted Laura Restrepo, a great Colombian writer: "War or indifference, it's hard to know which is the hardest to fight."

Prince Charles and Camilla had visited us in Colombia in October 2014 when we were engaged in the peace process. I took the prince to visit the Chiribiquete Park, an exceptional natural reserve and a place where indigenous cultures flourish. It's a region of breathtaking vistas in the depth of Colombia's Amazon, where you can see ancient Indian painted designs preserved for centuries on gigantic rocks. The prince, who has long worked as a defender of the environment, was amazed by the magnificence of Colombia's natural beauty, something we have been rediscovering thanks to the progress we have made toward peace. And his appreciation was not misplaced; in July 2018, the Chiribiquete park—with its 4.3 million hectares, an area greater than Switzerland and declared a protected zone—was included on UNESCO's list of World Heritage Sites, for its value as both a natural and a cultural reserve.

At the dinner I hosted at Casa de Nariño in honor of the royal couple, we provided two cultural performances: first a presentation by the Colombian dancer Fernando Montaño, soloist at London's Royal Ballet; and then a dance from Colombia's folk tradition, the Sanjuanero, typical of the department of Huila and one I especially like for its rhythm and joyful spirit. For Prince Charles, it was a revelation. Two years later, it would be my turn to be regaled with a musical interlude; namely, with the Scottish bagpipes at Buckingham Palace.

It is noteworthy that Prince Charles and Camilla expressed a desire to meet victims of the Colombian conflict. They attended a very emotional event at the National Center of Historical Memory in Bogotá, where they listened to the heartrending stories of many Colombians who had been affected by the war and learned of how we were beginning to make reparation to these victims and guarantee their rights.

With Prime Minister Cameron we also had an excellent relationship—so much so that he invited me to copreside with him over the first Anti-corruption Summit in London in May 2016. This was in recognition of the measures we had taken to combat this scourge, which is a veritable cancer attacking societies around the world. At that time, neither Cameron nor anyone else imagined that the following month, in the referendum he called to decide whether or not the United Kingdom would remain in the European Union,

Brexit was going to win by a narrow margin, a defeat that led him to resign as prime minister. I phoned him a few days later to express my solidarity, little imagining that a similar situation—influenced by fake news, distortions, and half truths—was going to occur in Colombia in October with the plebiscite to obtain popular approval for the peace agreement.

There's a popular saying: "If you see your neighbor's beard on fire, water your own." If only we had learned the lessons left by the disconcerting result of the Brexit referendum, we might have made a better effort at countering the campaign of lies that preceded the plebiscite. In the end, however, it was all for the good—as I will explain shortly.

* * *

In the case of France, President François Hollande made a very special gesture during his visit to Colombia in January 2017. He expressed his wish to visit the rural zones where the Farc members had gathered to prepare for their disarmament and incorporation into civil society. Together we visited one of these transitory camps in the municipality of Caldono in the department of Cauca, one of the most affected by violence.

It was anything but a mere protocol visit. France and the other member countries of the United Nations Security Council had unanimously approved the creation of a special UN mission to verify and monitor the bilateral ceasefire, as well as the demobilization and disarmament of the Farc. And President Hollande wanted to see for himself how this process was being carried out. It was the day's big news: the only war in the world that was coming to an end, and everyone wanted to be present to see it happen. In Caldono, the French president met officers from various countries who made up the UN international mission, wearing their distinctive blue jackets, as well as delegates both from the government and the guerrillas in khaki uniforms. All were living together in the same tent and working together to prepare the campsite for the guerrilla combatants who would arrive in a few days. Representing the Farc were Pablo Catatumbo and Marcos Calarcá, who was in charge of verifying the ceasefire and the leaving off of weapons. We were accompanied by Jean Arnault, the French diplomat who was directing the UN special mission, designated by the UN secretary-general.

President Hollande and all of us present were very moved by what was occurring. "Who would have imagined the president of Colombia and the president of France here in this camp for the disarming with the Farc representatives!" exclaimed President Hollande after his visit to the base camp.

"And to see them all in the same place, wearing the same uniforms and eating together in the same canteen."

During this visit, in Bogotá's Teatro Colón—where we had signed the final agreement two months earlier—the French president and I inaugurated the Colombia-France cultural year, a marvelous event that brought to our country representatives of France's art and culture, and took our artists and intellectuals to France.

In July 2017, after François Hollande had left the presidency in the hands of Emmanuel Macron, I visited France to inaugurate the semester in which the Colombians would "take" France, culturally speaking, and also to receive a doctorate *honoris causa* from Paris-Sorbonne University. I remember with special admiration the address given during that academic ceremony by France's minister of education, Jean-Michel Blanquer, a man very well informed about Colombia. The following is an extract from his speech:

> In the midst of the most adverse circumstances, criticized by many of your own followers, in the face of skepticism and disillusionment, [you] wagered in favor of words instead of arms, of intelligence instead of woeful passions. You have reminded us that trust is better than battalions armed to the teeth; you have managed to awaken national interest and make allies for democracy out of those who for many years were outlaws. And you were capable of exchanging arms for votes.

Mine was the first official visit of a foreign head of state received by President Macron, and that meant it was something singular, and flavored our relationship with a tone of spontaneity and intimacy. At the official banquet offered us at the Élysée Palace, opera music was mixed with Latin salsa interpreted by Yuri Buenaventura, a musician from Colombia's Pacific coast who has had a successful career in France. A new Colombia, a nation on its way to peace, is what one felt expressed in its art and joyful spirit in Paris.

We received encouragement in France not only from its presidents. Prime Minister Manuel Valls and the former prime minister and then minister of foreign affairs Jean-Marc Ayrault also visited Colombia to show their support.

* * *

Germany was no less helpful. We received constant support from Chancellor Angela Merkel and two presidents: Joachim Gauck, who in his youth had fought against the totalitarian regime of the German Democratic Republic and later worked to let victims discover the truth hidden in secret police files, an experience he shared with us in Colombia; and Frank-Walter Steinmeier, a great friend of our country, first as minister for foreign affairs and later as president.

In July 2016, the German parliament (the Bundestag) approved a motion of support for Colombia's peace process, and in April 2015 Germany's Ministry of Foreign Affairs had created the office of special commissioner for Colombia's peace process, designating for the role Tom Koenigs, a former deputy and a human rights expert.

On May 12, 2018, a very symbolic act occurred at the friary in Assisi, in Italy, where I handed the Lantern of Peace, the major recognition by the Franciscan Order, to Chancellor Merkel. I had received this award in December 2016, and the friars who guard the tomb of Saint Francis, the patron of peace, asked me to hand it this time to a person who, without a doubt, has been one of the most powerful women in Europe and at the same time one of the most supportive of emigrating populations in these early years of the twenty-first century.

I paid homage to her in a few words, and Chancellor Merkel—who described peace as "the most noble and universal obligation of politics"—replied also with a few words that touched my heart: "Your presidency and your mandate will become part of Colombia's history as a point of inflection because of your achieving peace and opening up the country to reconciliation."

* * *

I cannot conclude this inevitably incomplete account of the European continent's solidarity without mentioning two Scandinavian countries that assiduously supported the search for peace in Colombia, even before we had begun the process that led to the end of the armed conflict with the Farc: I refer to Norway and Sweden.

Norway, as I have already said, was a guarantor country at the negotiating table and placed at our service all of that country's experience in conflict resolution around the world. Norway's representative at the table, Dag Nylander, was involved in the process right from the start. Norway is a promoter of peace par excellence, and not for nothing was the nation that Alfred Nobel designated as responsible for awarding the maximum recognition of peace worldwide.

Prime Minister Jens Stoltenberg and, from the year 2013, Prime Minister Erna Solberg played a fundamental role in guaranteeing Norway's participation in the Havana dialogues. Their cooperation also embraced other areas, such as the clearing of zones planted with antipersonnel mines, and protection of the environment. It was a pleasure for me, in April 2018, to accompany Prime Minister Solberg to Leticia, a city in the middle of Colombia's Amazon jungle on the border with Peru and Brazil, to ratify the commitment of cooperation with our country in environmental issues until the year 2025. Minister of foreign affairs Børge Brende also was unfailingly attentive to the process, playing a fundamental role and accompanying us at several important moments. Today he is president of the World Economic Forum, where we again find great support.

The remembrance and gratitude I want to express to King Harald V and Queen Sonja, and to Prince Haakon and his wife Mette-Marit, are due, of course, to those memorable days in December 2016 when I was in Oslo to receive the Nobel Peace Prize. Their friendliness, their warmth, and their hospitality made that event even more unforgettable.

And then there is Sweden, ever ready to help us from the very beginning of the peace talks. That was why, when I dispatched Henry Acosta with my first message as president to the Farc, my proposal to the guerrillas was that we should hold our preparatory and exploratory meetings either in Sweden or Brazil, which their respective governments had already accepted. As it turned out, the meetings were held in Venezuela and Cuba, but we never ceased to appreciate Sweden's generous offer.

Sweden's role was fundamental at the start of the process. In fact, Sweden was the country that financed Acosta's activities, which were crucial in renewing contacts with the Farc. Two exceptional women, Lena Nordström and Marie Andersson de Frutos, Sweden's ambassadors to Colombia between the years 2005 and 2017, were discreet and efficacious allies in the search for a negotiated solution.

Princess Victoria, heir to the Swedish throne, visited Colombia in 2015, and I made an indispensable stopover in Stockholm—Nobel's hometown—after having received the Nobel Prize in Oslo, to salute and thank the royal couple, King Carl XVI Gustaf and Queen Silvia, and Prime Minister Stefan Löfven, for their steadfast cooperation with peace for Colombia.

THE EMBRACE OF THE REGION

If Europe and other continents—many countries in Asia, Africa, and Oceania—offered their solidarity, our own region, Latin America, was no less enthusiastic about the possibility of peace in Colombia. And that is natural, because peace in our country is a matter of regional security, since our conflict was causing adverse collateral effects in our neighboring countries and, in addition, was facilitating the production and trafficking of illegal drugs in the territories where the Farc exerted a degree of control.

To Cuba, our host country, I am extremely grateful. Most generously, and without making a fuss or expecting any kind of recompense, President Raúl Castro placed at the service of Colombia's peace process all the logistic support that was required, and was ever attentive to the way the process was developing. His representative at the table, Rodolfo Benítez, was a magnificent guarantor, a patient listener, and a conciliator when there were difficulties to be overcome. The dialogues—which included those of the secret exploratory phase—were carried on in Havana between February 2012 and the end of 2016, five years in all, and I am certain I could not have made a better choice of country.

When my government ended, in August 2018, another process was going forward, also in Havana: peace talks with the ELN, the last guerrilla group that still existed in Colombia. This process was taking advantage of the experience and hospitality Cuba has always offered us. In September, President Iván Duque withdrew the government's delegation and declared that dialogues would not continue until the ELN had liberated all their kidnap victims and ceased to carry out terrorist actions. Unfortunately the ELN did not understand the historical moment, and not only persist in kidnappings and attacks on oil pipelines and the petrol infrastructure in general, but on January 17, 2019, exploded a car bomb inside the police academy in Bogotá, killing twenty-two and wounding dozens more, all young cadets training to be police officers. With this abhorrent act, the ELN practically signed their own death sentence. In any case, the government broke off peace talks. I can only hope that, in a not too distant future, this guerrilla group will reflect and undergo a change of attitude and that a solution will be found that may finally bring total peace to Colombia.

The peace process with the Farc had a multiplying effect as regards Colombia's relations with other countries in the region. It opened the doors and the hearts of many government leaders who, in other circumstances, might have been indifferent. Thus was I able to establish good relationships, and even excellent friendships, not only with presidents whose ideological position was similar to mine—such as Sebastián Piñera in Chile and Enrique Peña Nieto in Mexico—but also with others who politically are poles apart, men like Evo Morales in Bolivia, and José Mujica in Uruguay. The latter became one of our principal defenders and also worked with Felipe González in the verification and implementation of our peace process.

The case of Venezuela is particularly relevant. No greater contrast could exist between presidents Hugo Chávez and Nicolás Maduro and myself, both temperamentally and ideologically. Nonetheless, we managed to have a harmonious relationship, thanks to which Venezuela played a special role in our peace process. Not only did it host and facilitate the preparatory phase, but those meetings made negotiation possible. It's a shame that the President Maduro's dictatorial attitudes, since he convoked a spurious constituent assembly in May 2017, have utterly ruined that relationship.

I could give many more examples of support from countries in the region. Not only am I a friend of Piñera; I had excellent relations also with Michelle Bachelet, a more left-wing president, and both decidedly supported Chile's decision to be present in Havana as an accompanying country. We were able to rely on the solidarity of Luiz Inácio Lula da Silva and Dilma Rousseff in Brazil, but also on that of their successor Michel Temer, whose political tendency is so different from theirs. Likewise in Argentina: both Cristina Fernández de Kirchner, of the left, and Mauricio Macri, of the right, supported the process. And so it was, too, in Peru with presidents Alan García, Ollanta Humala, and Pedro Pablo Kuczynski.

I am especially grateful to Alan García because of an incident that has to do with the guerrillas and my personal safety. García, pursued by the regime of Alberto Fujimori, sought asylum in Colombia between the years 1992 and 2000, where he made many friendships and established a lot of contacts. One of them was Iván Duque Escobar, a politician from Antioquia who had been both minister for mines and national civil registrar, a friend of my family, and mine also. Who would have imagined that his son, Iván Duque Márquez, would be my successor as president of the republic?

Somehow or other, García found out that the Farc planned to kidnap me near Anapoima, two hours from Bogotá, where I own a rural property for recreational purposes. The guerrillas were on my trail—I had been minister of foreign trade and appeared likely to become the Liberal Party's precandidate for the presidency—and they had detected that I was in the habit of riding a bicycle along a country road from the area known as San Antonio to the Anapoima township. At the time, I was not a friend of García's, but he sent me word via Duque Escobar to say I ought to cease those solitary bicycle rides. I took his advice, and later intelligence information was able to verify that the reason for his precaution not only was based on a real threat but had come just in time. García and Duque had saved me from the tragedy of being kidnapped.

When we were both presidents of our respective countries, García and I were the principal promoters of the Pacific Alliance, a group of regional integration founded by Colombia and Peru with Chile and Mexico, and which has become the most successful example of integration in Latin America. I have to give credit for this idea of integration on the part of the four Latin American countries with coastlines along the planet's largest ocean to an English lord, Tristan Garel-Jones. I met him in 1992 when he visited Colombia as the United Kingdom's foreign affairs minister for Europe and Latin America accompanying Prime Minister John Major—the first visit to Latin America by a British head of government. At the time, I was minister of foreign trade. Lord Garel-Jones gave me the idea later in a conversation we had in London. And finally it became a reality with President García—the most enthusiastic member of the group—along with presidents Piñera of Chile and Felipe Calderón of Mexico.*

* * *

Perhaps the best summing up of the broad range of regional and world support we had received was seen on September 27, 2016, when the peace agreement with the Farc was signed in Cartagena in the presence of representatives from every corner of the planet. There on the platform, witnessing this historic moment, were the United Nations secretary-general Ban Ki-moon; the president of the UN General Assembly, the president of the Security Council, and the UN high commissioner for human rights; the secretary-general of the Organization of American States, Luis Almagro; the high representative of the European Union, Federica Mogherini; the emeritus king Juan Carlos of Spain, and the presidents of Argentina, Bolivia, Costa Rica, Cuba, Chile, the Dominican Republic, Ecuador, El Salvador, Guatemala, Honduras, Mexico, Panama, Paraguay, Peru, and Venezuela.

Others who came for the signing of the agreement were the presidents of the World Bank, Jim Yong Kim, and of the International Monetary Fund, Christine Lagarde, and of the Inter-American Development Bank, Luis

---

* Alan García took his own life on April 17, 2019, when he was on the point of being arrested at his home for presumed acts of corruption. In a suicide note, he proclaimed his innocence and said that he preferred death to humiliating torture.

Alberto Moreno; the Ibero-American secretary-general Rebeca Grynspan; the executive secretary of the United Nations Economic Commission for Latin America and the Caribbean, Alicia Bárcenas; and the president of the CAF–Development Bank of Latin America, Enrique García. Also present was the US secretary of state, John Kerry; the secretary of state of the Vatican, Cardinal Pietro Parolin, and the foreign affairs ministers of Norway and Sweden, among many other dignitaries and personalities from many parts of the world.

It was a jubilant embrace of peace in Colombia. And it was the embrace of all Latin America, celebrating the promise of a continent converted at last into a continent without war, a peace zone, as the Community of Latin American and Caribbean States declared at its summit meeting in Havana in early 2014.

What has been the significance of all these expressions of support? Universal solidarity—not only that of the United States, Europe, and Latin America but of the entire international community—with a peace process that has been the only one in recent times with a real possibility of success.

This was how the UN secretary-general, António Guterres, put it at the General Assembly in September 2017, echoing the words of his predecessor Ban Ki-moon: "Colombia is the only good news that has come to us at the United Nations."

LESSON 5

The Importance of International Support

In the interdependent world of today, no country is alone, nor can any country presume to achieve great objectives like peace unless it is accompanied in the process. Only broad international support, above all regional support, can facilitate and guarantee the achievement of a peace agreement and then guarantee its complex implementation. Informing the international community, therefore, and inviting the community's participation and help whenever necessary, were essential steps we had to take to ensure the success of Colombia's peace process.

Those processes that have ended in agreements—as in South Africa, Northern Ireland, Central America, Indonesia, Sierra Leone, and Angola, to mention just a few—had as a common denominator the positive intervention of international organizations or of countries in their respective regions helping to further the peace talks as mediators, verifiers, guarantors, or witnesses. A model case is the one known as Esquipulas, built on the basis of the Contadora Group in which Colombia, Mexico, Panama, and Venezuela worked together between the years 1983 and 1985 to promote peace in Central America. And then, in Esquipulas, Guatemala, between the years 1985 and 1987, the presidents of five Central American countries—backed by other friendly nations who gave their support to the process—labored to produce a road map for peace in the region. In 1987, the Nobel Peace Prize was awarded to the president of Costa Rica, Óscar Arias, in recognition of the concept of regional coverage and the importance of friendly countries.

Asymmetrical wars like the one we had in Colombia between the state and guerrillas, who resorted to irregular and frankly terrorist methods such as attacks on the civilian population, the blowing up of energy pylons and oil pipelines, the use of antipersonnel mines and nonconventional weapons, and who financed their activities by committing crimes that included kidnapping, extortion, and drug trafficking—wars like this will never be brought to an end without the support of the region. A peace process requires, above all, the support of those neighboring countries that are affected by these criminal activities and that the guerrillas often use as territories where they take refuge.

To me, this was self-evident. And that is why the first step I took, even before sending the Farc a first proposal to dialogue, was to normalize relations with the government of Venezuela, and later with that of Ecuador, countries with which Colombia shared borders amounting to a total of 2,800 kilometers, borders that were particularly porous and unprotected. I realized that if these two countries did not adopt an attitude favorable to the process, it would be practically impossible for it to prosper.

The fact that the process was supported by two nations with whose regimes the Farc felt natural affinity—Venezuela as an accompanying country, along with Cuba as generous host and guarantor—helped mitigate certain understandable misgivings on the part of the guerrillas when the time came to dialogue with representatives of the Colombian government. Colombia, likewise, felt more at ease knowing it was accompanied by Chile as a counterweight in the ideological balance, and by Norway as guarantor with that country's ample experience in the resolution of international conflicts.

Our process had no need of mediators but made good use of the categories of guarantors and accompanying countries. In addition, we received very positive signals from the United States, the European Union, and Germany when they assigned us special envoys whose function was to facilitate and articulate initiatives on the part of those countries and with others in their region. And then, of course, there were expressions of solidarity, and often concrete contributions, by countries around the world, and by various multilateral organisms.

The International Red Cross, on countless occasions, made possible the complex business of transporting the guerrilla negotiators from Colombia to Cuba and back again. And the United Nations, toward the end of the process, played an outstanding role when the UN Security Council gave its approval to a special political mission comprising officers from several countries that established a three-way mechanism that included the United Nations, the Colombian government, and the Farc to oversee the verification, monitoring, and bilateral ceasefire, as well as the Farc's demobilization and disarmament. I held personal conversations with the presidents of the five permanent member countries of the Security Council, including Vladimir Putin and Xi Jinping, and all of them were most generous and enthusiastic. And the Security Council's role did not stop there; once the Farc was disarmed, the council gave its approval for the members of the special mission to continue accompanying us in issues such as the political, social, and economic reincorporation of the ex-combatants, as well as taking measures to ensure their personal and collective safety. This commitment was extended to encompass programs of protection and security for communities and organizations in the territories. It is worth noting that the six resolutions by the UN Security

Council in support of our peace process received unanimous approval, something that rarely occurs, and never for a number of different items. However, when you come to think of it, that is why the United Nations was created: to promote world peace.

In all these ways, therefore, the international community accompanied the Colombian process, supporting it without in any way interfering. And then, at the end of the conflict, the international community applauded the signing of the agreement and sealed with its approval the Farc's compliance with what had been agreed upon; namely, the leaving off of their weapons.

As president, I led the effort to obtain the maximum international support, and in that task, during the eight years of my government, I had the best of collaborators in Minister Holguín, a professional and a first-class diplomat who won respect and admiration in whatever scenario she worked and, when I requested her to do so, did not hesitate to employ her ability as a negotiator in giving the final touches to the agreement in Havana. There was a moment when she was tempted to postulate her candidacy for UN secretary-general, but she decided against it. In compensation, she was offered the presidency of the General Assembly, but again she declined.

CHAPTER 26

“We Mustn’t Give Up Halfway”

COMMITMENT TO THE RURAL COMMUNITY

On May 26, 2013, more than half a year after the peace talks had officially begun, the table in Havana produced its first significant result: a pre-agreement—not a final one, because of our principle: “nothing is agreed until everything is agreed”—on the first point of the agenda, agrarian development. The document was called “Toward a New Colombian Countryside: Comprehensive Rural Reform.”

This was an important advance that filled us with hope. Its significance was twofold: on the one hand, it was the first time in Colombia’s history that the government and the Farc had reached an agreement on a substantial issue—something they attempted at Caguán but that, after three years of discussions, they still had not been able to achieve. And on the other hand, the pre-agreement was about nothing less than land and rural development, the very issues that were at the heart of Farc’s grievance and the principal reasons for its half century of war against the state.

We, as the government, saw what had been agreed on this matter as an opportunity rather than a transaction. Colombia had for decades turned its back on the countryside—on farmers and rural workers in general—and had postponed indefinitely its obligation to solve the land problem and provide investment that was indispensable for improving our agrarian sector’s productivity and ability to compete. The table in Havana was the government’s best possible excuse for committing the state to give priority to the rural area and institute reforms that we should have carried out long ago.

For example, we agreed to create a land fund, chiefly comprising properties that had been acquired illegally. This was meant to provide agricultural workers who either were dispossessed or owned insufficient land with viable properties where they could work on farms they actually owned. And we agreed on a far-reaching program to legalize the titles of hundreds of thousands of agricultural workers who hitherto had been unable to document formal ownership of their properties.

In addition, we agreed to create a new agrarian jurisdiction to ensure the protection of the property rights of all those living in rural areas. And very important, too, was the setting up of special development programs in the territories that had been hardest hit by the conflict, and those with the greatest number of illegal crops.

If you wanted to look for one aspect more than any other that, in practice, illustrated the benefits of the peace process, you would find it in a recovery of the quality of life and general welfare in Colombia's more remote and isolated regions that for too long had been abandoned and submitted to violence. Our purpose was to bring the presence of the Colombian state and its social services, plus public and private investment, to the outlying regions. To do so, in 2017, in compliance with the agreement, we created sixteen development programs (Programas de Desarrollo con Enfoque Territorial, PDET), all focused on territories. These programs would be agreed on and executed by the communities themselves. By the end of 2018 more than 235,000 Colombians had taken part in drawing up these plans, which began to be executed in 2019 and will transform the most forgotten regions of our country.

The above is the concrete manifestation of what Sergio Jaramillo has called "territorial peace": the development and pacification of those territories that had been hardest hit by violence, a process implemented by means of citizens and communities working together with the authorities at every level. To the extent that all of this is put into practice, we can guarantee the nonrepetition of the injustice and inequity that have been the breeding ground of our conflicts. In other words, we are guaranteeing the nonrepetition of violence.

As was to be expected, we had hardly signed that pre-agreement on the first point of the agenda when all kinds of caricatures began to circulate to discredit it: that we were going to expropriate the properties of the landowners, that the land fund was designed for the benefit of the guerrillas and not the small farmers, that we were instituting an improvised and haphazard land reform. None of this was true, of course, and we did our best to explain things. What we had agreed on in Havana had as its essential purpose something no one could question: to devote the state's best efforts to the countryside, the scenario of Colombia's greatest poverty and inequality.

Álvaro Uribe, one of Colombia's major landowners with vast properties in the department of Córdoba, had defended the privileges of the large hacienda owners, which explains why he objected to the agreement—for the same reason he had opposed the Law of Victims and Restitution of Land, despite the fact that this law did not affect legitimate property owners who had acquired their land in good faith. Uribe never imagined that peace would imply a structural change in Colombia's rural areas. That is why he denied that there was an internal conflict, because if the conflict did not exist there would be no need to go to its root causes in order to solve it.

THE FIRST CRISIS

On August 22, 2013, aware as I was that time was going by and that it was important to start preparing the way for a future popular ratification of the agreements, which is something I had promised, my government, with the support of the parties of National Unity, presented to Congress a project to establish a statutory law to facilitate this. The aim of the project was to allow a referendum on the final agreement to be held on the same day as the country's normal elections, since this was prohibited under existing legislation.

My motive was perfectly clear: to have a mechanism approved that would enable us to vote on the agreements if possible on the same day as either the legislative or presidential elections scheduled for the following year—that is, March 9 and May 25, 2014, respectively. This would ensure that the greatest number of citizens would be likely to participate.

The fact of presenting this project put pressure on the negotiators to produce results more speedily, and it was also meant to facilitate a way of countersigning the agreements with a referendum or plebiscite. This was intended to counteract the Farc's insistence that the final agreement should be submitted to a constituent assembly. And so the initiative—whose aim was to open a door, not necessarily to pass through it—met with fierce opposition from the guerrilla delegation.

As a result, on August 23, the Farc decided "to take a break from discussions at the negotiating table and concentrate exclusively on an analysis of the scope of the government's proposal." To this, I replied with a concise but firm declaration:

> In this process, the one who decrees the pauses and places conditions is not the Farc. I have made the decision, therefore, to request the government's negotiators to come here immediately to assess the scope of this communiqué and that of the Farc's behavior with regard to the initiatives that have

no other intention than that of attempting to hasten the solution of the conflict. And this analysis we will make here. We will resume conversations when we consider it appropriate.

The next day I held a meeting in Bogotá with the head of our negotiating team Humberto de la Calle and other delegates, but by this time the Farc had let it be known that they were ready to renew conversations on the following Monday. Thus, this small crisis was overcome.

Timochenko, of course, did not let the occasion go to waste and produced a communiqué in which he criticized the law project we had presented, and added: "It is obvious that the government is putting pressure on us to reach an agreement before the end of the year. But the government's positions at the table are unmovable in that they do not deal with any aspect at all that concerns the established order."

On the first point, he was right; I wanted to produce an agreement if possible that very year, so as not to wear out people's patience. I also refused to negotiate the country's political and economic order, since that was not the purpose of the peace talks. They were my red lines. I had established them from the start, and the government's delegates made sure they were respected.

BULLETS FOR VOTES

Negotiations went on at a good pace, constantly nourished by proposals made by ordinary citizens in national and regional forums, or via the internet, as well as by contributions from experts. That explains how, on November 6, 2013, we were able to announce a second pre-agreement, this time on the issue of political participation.

This was another crucial issue. Every peace process aims at two things: to end the war and to offer a political option to those who lay down arms. That's why it was so important that we recognize the existence of an armed conflict. If it had not been admitted, if the Farc had been considered merely a terrorist threat, negotiations could never have led to participation in politics by the demobilized guerrillas. Only by accepting that there was, in fact, an armed conflict could it be understood that the guerrillas would disarm in exchange for their entry to the arena of legitimate democratic politics.

Exchanging bullets for votes, exchanging weapons for debate—that was what the peace effort was all about. The Farc had come into being in the midst of a political experiment known as the National Front that introduced a system by means of which Colombia's two traditional political parties, the Liberal and the Conservative, took turns at governing the fortunes of the nation over a period of sixteen years. The National Front was a success in that it put an end to partisan violence, but it had a negative effect: it excluded all other political forces from coming to power. That was the reason, at least in part, why certain left-wing political activists, imbued with Marxist-Leninist or Maoist doctrines, on seeing that the door was closed against their entrance to politics, took up arms against the state. Later, in the 1980s, when the government of Belisario Betancur began peace talks with the insurgents and a new party, the Patriotic Union, was created, there was, at last, a hope that the opposition could take part in democratic politics. But that hope was cruelly obliterated by the systematic assassination of the new party's members by obscure right-wing forces in cahoots with drug traffickers.

The challenge we faced was to achieve an agreement on political participation that would enable the ex-guerrilla fighters to play an active role in democratic politics. But we needed, also, to guarantee their physical safety and their legal rights. None of this, of course, would exonerate them from rendering an account of their actions to the justice system and to the victims in the manner that would be considered most appropriate in the final agreement.

In fact, we went even further. Since it was not a matter of simply ending the conflict but of eliminating the conditions that might be propitious for a conflict in the future, we agreed on measures to broaden democracy, to make elections more transparent, and to guarantee the political participation not only of the demobilized guerrillas but of political activists in all of the country's regions who, because of continual violence, had lived for decades without enjoying any representation among the decision makers who exercise power.

You well might ask what it was we agreed to. Well, among other things, we agreed to set in motion a comprehensive system of security for the exercising of political rights that would protect ex-members of the Farc once they had laid down arms, and would enable them to enter the political debate without running risks. This did happen, in fact, and it was very moving to see former guerrilla fighters protected by members of the armed forces against whom, not long before, they had been fighting. The ex-guerrillas also had as bodyguards some of their own men who were trained to form part of the security system to protect political leaders.

Sadly, since the signing of the peace agreement, many social and community leaders have been assassinated, as well as representatives of the victims or community leaders defending people's rights to properties. A growing number of demobilized ex-guerrilla combatants have also been murdered. Many factors and many individual killers have been responsible for these crimes: criminal bands that are locked in a war over control of illegal crops and illegal mining, illegitimate possessors of land that they refuse to restore to the rightful owners, right-wing extremists who fire at any symbol of reconciliation. Before leaving the presidency, I took measures to prevent and react against these crimes. We established a special commission over which I presided with the participation of international organs and human rights nongovernmental organizations to investigate this phenomenon. We also signed a declaration with the participation of representatives of all the political sectors, including my successor, Iván Duque—Uribe refused to sign—to strongly condemn violence against social leaders, which is violence against the peace.

It was also agreed that we should establish a statute for the opposition that would guarantee and protect opposition leaders, a fundamental right in any democracy. In this matter, we had been in debt for over twenty-five years, because such a statute had been contemplated in the 1991 Constitution but had never been established. I am glad to say that, a few weeks before ending my government, I managed to fulfill this commitment and left the statute in operation. It is one of the best guarantees for those who exercise the opposition in Colombia.

In addition to the above, we agreed to create transitory circumscriptions for the Chamber of Representatives in Congress so that territories that had most suffered violence and had therefore been excluded from taking part in politics would have two periods of representation in the legislative body. These circumscriptions did not manage to get approved by Congress, due to criticisms on the part of those who argued that they were seats for the Farc, when in fact they were seats in parliament for the victims. The task of implementing the project was left to the new Congress that took possession in July 2018. Unfortunately, on ending the first half of the legislative period in December, the project was rejected by the opposition led by Uribe. Its defeat was due also to a lack of interest on the part of other parties, and of the government itself. The project will have to be presented to Congress again, because we must not fail to fulfill our promises to the victims.

There's something else, and although it is not part of this same point on the agenda, it concerns an issue that arose when the conflict had ended, and which I mention here because it is central to the Farc's participation in politics as a way for the ex-combatants to play their part in democracy—disarmed, now, and converted into a political party. I refer to the fact that their representation in Congress was guaranteed for two constitutional periods beginning on July 20, 2018; in other words, for the periods 2018–2022 and 2022–2026. The political party that emerges from the demobilized Farc can participate in elections the same as any other political movement, and can elect senators and representatives. However, if they do not get the necessary number of votes, they will nevertheless have two periods guaranteed to them, and can count on at least five senators and five representatives.

And this was applied, despite the alarmist predictions of many who argued that the party of the former Farc—which continued to be identified with the same four initials, but these now stood for Common Alternative Revolutionary Force—would win a great number of votes because of their presumed ability to exert coercion on many people in zones where they had once had influence, or because of the immense sums of money with which they could buy votes. As it happened, in the March 2018 parliamentary elections they won little more than eighty-five thousand votes, between the Senate and the Chamber of Representatives; and this was not enough for them to elect a single member of Congress. In any case, the agreement was honored as a minimal guarantee of representation. And so, on July 20, 2018, eight congressmen and women from the Farc's party took possession of their seats in parliament. Two seats are waiting to be occupied. This is an important concession, but not a decisive one if you bear in mind that the Colombian Congress consists in all of 280 members.

In the parliamentary and presidential elections, it was a moving experience to see Farc ex-commanders who had never voted in their lives now exercising their franchise like any ordinary citizen. And to see their candidates for Congress running campaigns and addressing the public, their only weapon being the power of the spoken word, even though they were booed and heckled at times by people who couldn't bear to see them taking part in politics. For myself, I will always prefer to see a Colombian giving a speech aimed at winning votes rather than firing a gun aimed at killing his adversary. It was for that—precisely for that—that we had a peace process.

A DECISION AGAINST THE GRAIN

The process was moving forward. We now had pre-agreements on two of the main items on the agenda. But things were not going at the pace I had imagined, and I was worried that my period of government would end without our having ensured success. Meanwhile, the opposition fired all its guns, day after day, through the media and social networks, with tweets, memes, disinformation, and lies, to torpedo the process. They had virtually half the population doubtful about its advantages. Doubting the advantage of ending the war!

In these circumstances, the moment was coming when I had to decide whether or not I would run for reelection, taking advantage of the "little article" that my predecessor had introduced into the constitution to have himself elected again. He had left me that possibility. It is my conviction that this leads to creating caudillos and the cult of personality and that it is a threat to the due balance of power within the state. I have always believed that democracies should function according to the rules of their institutions, and not through caudillos. Aside from that, I was not interested personally in taking on another period in government. To govern is an immense privilege, but it is also a heavy burden and implies enormous sacrifices, both personal and family. I was certainly not a person obsessed with clinging to the ephemeral power of the presidency.

So I can say in all sincerity: I would have preferred not to have to have been reelected, but rather to have stood by and watched a new president carry to its conclusion that most important project for the future of Colombia; namely, the ending of half a century of conflict with the Farc, a conflict that had caused such pain and backwardness and had been disastrous for our country's progress.

However, the circumstances were not propitious. In October 2013, the Democratic Center, a political party formed under the leadership of Uribe, named its presidential candidate for the period 2014–2018. The man who was going to run for president was Oscar Iván Zuluaga, who had been Uribe's finance minister and who promised that the first thing he would do on getting into the Casa de Nariño would be suspend the peace process. Opinion polls showed that he had the support of a considerable percentage of the population, and I understood, with a mixture of realism and resignation, that it was my duty to keep on flying the banner of peace for another term until the process was concluded and a final agreement signed to end the conflict. There was no way I could abandon ship.

And therefore, on November 20, 2013, before the legal term for announcing my candidacy had expired, I addressed the Colombian people in a speech that began as follows:

> Today, I wish to announce that next Monday, November 25, in conformity with correct legal procedures, I will file a document with the Civil Registrar in which I will formally state my interest in running for the presidency for the period 2014–2018.
>
> I do this because I am convinced that we have moved forward enough for us to see that it is possible to attain a future of prosperity and peace that all Colombians deserve. I do this because when you see light at the end of the tunnel, you don't turn back. And we're not going to do that! We mustn't give up halfway. We have to finish the job that all of us have undertaken.

And I concluded with the following:

> I had hoped negotiations would have moved faster and that we would have achieved a final agreement in less than a year. But this has not happened. Things have taken longer. But one thing is certain: progress has been made in the talks and we have moved forward in very important ways.
>
> For the first time, we have reached agreement on fundamental issues such as rural development and political participation. The guerrillas have not only accepted to discuss demobilization, integration into society, and the laying down of arms but also they have accepted to abide by the rules of democracy.
>
> My duty as leader, my obligation as a Colombian, is not to permit that what we have gained in our efforts for peace be thrown away, gains we have achieved—and I will never cease to repeat this—thanks to the valor of our armed forces and the support of my compatriots.
>
> Peace is the supreme good of any nation. Peace should be above personal grudges and petty political wrangling. We should unite instead of dividing. That is why I will invite all sectors who support peace—including some who do not agree with me—to work together to defend what we have already achieved and to bring this process to a safe harbor.

CHAPTER 27

The Problem of Drugs

THE WAR THE WORLD IS LOSING

To our shame, just about everyone in the world associates the name Colombia with cocaine and sinister characters like Pablo Escobar, who have become popular antiheroes in films and successful television series. But this is not Colombia's fault. Rather, we are a victim of the fact that millions of people all over the planet are addicted to narcotics. Some of our best men and women—military and police, judges, journalists, politicians, presidential candidates—have lost their lives in the war against drugs, but we have not lost heart. On the contrary, we have devoted our country's human and logistics resources, with the support of the United States, to the fight against the production of cocaine and the drug trade. However, profits from that trade are so enormous that, even when you dismantle a cartel or capture a capo, new traffickers spring up and continue to reap the benefits of that illegal easy money.

Every demand creates its supply. That's one of the economy's elementary rules. And you see it in the case of drugs. So long as there is such a huge demand for cocaine and governments insist on maintaining the trade's illegal status, there will always be criminal organizations in Colombia and elsewhere ready to produce the product and sell it. When we in Colombia managed to wipe out the big cartels, the drug trade became a serious problem in Mexico. No sooner had we put an end to flights loaded with drugs from Colombia than the traffickers began using airstrips in Venezuela. There will be no end to this problem until we face up to its root cause, which is the massive consumption of alkaloids.

In 1961, the United Nations established the Single Convention on Narcotic Drugs. Ten years later, in 1971, US president Richard Nixon declared war on drugs. Half a century has gone by since then, and you have to admit that we have not won that war, nor do we look like winning it, despite all it has cost in terms of both money and human lives. It's like pedaling on a stationary bicycle. You look to your right, and you look to your left, and you see no change in the landscape; no matter how hard you try, you don't move forward.

Progress has been made by the use of all kinds of mechanisms—fumigating crops, aerial and maritime interdiction, extradition, police, and military pursuit. None of this, however, has been enough to control the drug trade, which is extremely versatile and adapts quickly to changing circumstances. Now, if there is one country in the world that, after making great sacrifices, has the moral authority to propose a change of strategy on drug control, that country is Colombia.

So, in April 2012, at the Summit of the Americas in Cartagena, which brought together thirty heads of state in the region, including President Barack Obama, I proposed that we take an objective, unbiased, and critical look at our efforts to combat the drug trade. On this occasion, we authorized the Organization of American States to undertake a study and an assessment of how this problem was being tackled in the Western Hemisphere. This included an analysis of possible scenarios following the methodology of Adam Kahane, the same Canadian expert in conflict resolution I had brought to Colombia in 1996 to help us design ways that might lead to peace.

I also proposed that a special session of the United Nations General Assembly be devoted specifically to the drug problem worldwide and that new possible solutions should be explored. The session was held finally in New York in April 2016 and came up with the following simple and sensible diagnosis of the situation: since we have been applying the same treatment, basically one of repression, for so long without having solved the problem, the time had come to rethink the treatment.

Some progress was made in the course of this special session. It was accepted that directives on how to handle the drug problem should be flexible and adapted to the particular circumstances of each country. Agreement was reached, also, on the need to guarantee access to legally controlled substances for scientific and medical use, and that measures should be adopted to reduce the risks and harm caused by consumption. However, much was still wanting. It had not yet been clearly stated that the drug issue should be confronted with respect for human rights, and that drug consumption should not be treated simply as a criminal activity but as a question of public health.

Above all, you have to be consistent. How do you explain to a Colombian peasant that he should go to prison for planting marijuana when any US citizen in Colorado or Washington is legally free to smoke grass, or even to produce and sell it? My proposal, as president of Colombia, was clear and insistent: our war on drugs should be attacking the strongest links in the chain; in other words, the big-time traffickers, the suppliers of chemicals used in the production of cocaine and the organizations that facilitate money laundering. We have to hit the mafias where it really hurts, pursing their ill-gotten gains and exorbitant profit margins, which are the real cause of such violence and corruption.

The time has come to accept, realistically, that so long as there is a demand for drugs, there'll be plenty on offer, and that consumption is not likely to cease. We have to accept, too, that just as we don't have a world free from alcohol or tobacco, neither are we going to have a world without drugs. But we can minimize the effects of a costly war that has not done what it set out to do. And this will not happen until the international community—and not just one country, because Colombia cannot do it alone—decides to modify its failed strategy and take an unbiased look at the problem. For example, we should study the experiences of regulated markets in countries like Uruguay, Portugal, and Canada to analyze their achievements, and their disadvantages too.

I don't have a magical recipe. Nobody has. But there is one thing I'm certain about, and have expressed often and in different world scenarios: we have to change our strategy, because we have been applying it for half a century and it doesn't work.

THE FARC'S INVOLVEMENT IN THE DRUG TRADE

In 2012, in Havana, in the exploratory phase, when we spent six months in discussions to define the points on the agenda, I insisted that my delegates include the problem of illegal drugs. I did this for the simple reason that the Farc, from the 1980s onward, had been participating in the drug trade; at first, they simply charged protection money to the growers, but later several guerrilla fronts became involved in the production, transportation, and exportation of cocaine, a lucrative business they used to finance their activities. There was no way we could ignore the fact that a relationship existed between the conflict and the trade in narcotics.

If it weren't for the drug trade, it is quite possible that the Farc would have been defeated long ago. Money from narcotics gave them a respite and largely explained how they had survived, buying arms and ammunition to continue their war. The Farc's involvement was undeniable, although their commanders insisted they had only charged a so-called tax on the product, a kind of toll on every kilogram of coca that left the areas the guerrillas controlled. I was insistent that the issue should be included in the agenda, and my delegates made sure it was; point number four was titled "Solution to the problem of illegal drugs."

In Havana, on May 16, 2014, after months of debate, and having listened to the concepts of experts and proposals from citizens and organizations, the negotiators reached another partial agreement, this time on the subject of drugs.

The first thing agreed upon was a program for the eradication and substitution of illegal crops, where not only would the coca plants be eradicated but work would be carried out with the communities to solve the problem. The aim was to draw up plans for voluntary substitution that would guarantee a stable income to growers who gave up planting illegal crops. The government reserved the right to fumigate if circumstances did not allow for manual eradication.

Another very important agreement was reached on demining land to ensure that rural workers would not fall into the trap of antipersonnel mines or be exposed to such a risk. The Farc committed to provide information on where mines were located. And in fact, even while the process was going on, a couple of pilot demining programs were put in practice in some country areas where soldiers from the army's local battalion worked alongside the guerrillas, the latter indicating where the mines had been planted.

When my government ended, on August 7, 2018, we had already made great progress in demining Colombia, which had occupied second place after Afghanistan among countries with the greatest numbers of victims of antipersonnel landmines. Now it was tenth on this shameful list. In 2006, 1,200 people had been victims; in 2017, this number was reduced to 57. And work went on; from 673 municipalities where mines had been planted, in 2018 we could declare 264 municipalities to be free of the suspicion of mines. The process continues with active international cooperation led by the United States and Norway and the participation of another twenty countries that formed the Global Demining Initiative for Colombia. To detect and deactivate mines is much more than a humanitarian obligation; it means recovering land and restores hope to Colombia's rural population.

And there's another important aspect, perhaps the most fundamental one: the Farc committed to contribute effectively—in different ways and by means of practical actions—to a definitive solution to the problem of illegal drugs and to put an end to their organization's involvement in the trade. The Farc negotiators never accepted that they had been traffickers, much less that they were "the world's largest drug cartel," as the US Drug Enforcement Agency and other US authorities had called them. However, they did admit to having links with the trade and were committed to breaking them.

This was a historic turnabout. The organization that had protected illegal crops and drug traffickers had now become an ally in the fight against this activity, supporting plans for voluntary eradication and crop substitution.

THE INCREASE IN ILLEGAL CROPS

In March 2015, the chemical weed killer glyphosate that we were using in Colombia to spray illegal crops was included on the World Health Organization's list of potential causes of cancer and a threat to human health. Based on these studies, our Constitutional Court ordered that the use of this substance be suspended as a precautionary measure since, once there was scientific evidence of a possible health hazard, of uttermost importance was the protection of our citizens' health.

As a result, that same year, 2015, the government suspended spraying with glyphosate. The opposition argues, of course, that we had made this decision at the negotiating table in Havana as a concession to the Farc. Completely false. Our decision was taken in light of the WHO studies and the decision of the Constitutional Court. And of something else: spraying illegal crops with glyphosate was extremely costly and totally ineffective.

Between the years 2000 and 2015, 1.8 million hectares of coca crops were sprayed with glyphosate and another 400,000 hectares were eradicated manually. Nonetheless, by the year 2012, the number of hectares planted with coca fell from 160,000 to 48,000, the lowest measurement we have had. It is clear that such meager results do not justify our effort. And that is due to two factors: the immediate replanting of crops and the proliferation of devices to prevent the weed killer from affecting the plants—including artisanal techniques such as the use of molasses to protect the coca leaves.

In 2015, when we suspended the spraying, illegal crops were already on the increase. A rise in the value of the dollar against the Colombian peso made this activity even more profitable and encouraged farmers to plant more crops. It must be admitted, too, that the partial agreement on this point with the Farc in Havana had a negative collateral effect; many coca leaf growers, realizing that they would not be treated as criminals but on the contrary would be included in programs for the eradication of crops and would receive benefits and support from the government, set about planting more coca than ever.

By 2017, illegal crops in Colombia increased to a record 180,000 hectares, according to estimates by the United Nations, or 209,000 hectares by United States estimates. This situation naturally alarmed the US authorities, beginning with President Trump, and the Colombian authorities also. For me, these results, although understandable for the reasons given here, were nonetheless frustrating. But it was only a temporary setback. Now that the Farc are no longer in the territories where they had been protecting hundreds of thousands of hectares and serving as intermediaries between the growers and the traffickers, the state's armed forces have access to areas where they had not ventured before, and it is to be hoped that the tendency will again be toward a decrease in the number of plantations.

The solution to the problem is structural and does not depend on whether we use aerial spraying or eradicate manually, even if we use low-flying drones to do the spraying. Rather, it depends on offering the farmers genuine opportunities to better their lot by sowing legal crops. And this could only be done after we had ended the armed conflict with the Farc. That was the only viable way out. In 2018, on leaving government, I had set in motion actions to eradicate 110,000 hectares of coca—70,000 by force, and 40,000 by agreements on voluntary substitution. And it is to be hoped that the situation will develop favorably.

It should be admitted, however, that it will not be easy for Colombia to cease to be the world's prime exporter of cocaine so long as the world refuses to effectively confront the problem of drug consumption. And so long as the immense fortunes produced by the drug trade continue to circulate unhindered in the international financial system, the war on drugs will keep on repeating its same failed strategy. In other words, we will continue to pedal without moving forward, mounted on a stationary bicycle.

CHAPTER 28

The Peace Elections

THE FIRST ROUND

The 2014 election campaign was longer and even more difficult than the one four years earlier when I was first elected. A president in office who is running for reelection has to work overtime. On the one hand, he must continue to fulfill his duties of government as if he were not a candidate, and at the same time, he has to travel around the country and take part in debates and demonstrations to explain his proposals and policies.

The economy was in good shape, unemployment and poverty were decreasing, the numbers of homicides and kidnappings were also notably reduced, the armed forces continued to hit the guerrillas hard—since we were negotiating while the conflict went on—and we had made significant progress on social issues such as free education for children at all levels in public schools as well as setting in motion a program of free homes for the country's poorest families. I had all of this in my favor as candidate for reelection. Nonetheless, the campaign was not based on the economy or employment or the war on poverty, nor even on our advances in matters of security. The campaign was based, almost exclusively, on the peace process.

While I was expounding the advantages of the peace we were negotiating, my main opponent, Oscar Iván Zuluaga, of the Democratic Center Party, was doing everything in his power to discredit the process. And not only Zuluaga but his political boss also, former president Uribe. They and all their followers were proclaiming to the four corners of the world that the process was tantamount to a surrender to the Farc and that we were promising the guerrillas impunity. They insisted that we intended to cut back on benefits for the armed forces and were placing the country in danger of becoming a new Venezuela. They went so far as to invent a new term, "Castro-Chavism," implying that a peace agreement would have the effect of installing in Colombia a government with an ideology like that of Fidel Castro and Hugo Chávez, with the catastrophic social and political consequences everyone could see in Venezuela.

In my campaign for reelection, I chose as running mate for the post of vice-president Germán Vargas Lleras, who had been my minister of the interior and justice and also minister for housing. This time I was sponsored by my party, the Party of the U, as well as by the Liberal Party and the Vargas Lleras's party, Radical Change. Apart from my candidacy and that of Zuluaga, there were three other candidates: Marta Lucía Ramírez, who had been my vice-minister in the Ministry of Foreign Trade and represented the Conservative Party; Clara López, a militant leader on the left who supported the peace process and represented the party called Alternative Democratic Pole; and Enrique Peñalosa, former mayor of Bogotá, for the Green Alliance Party, whose candidacy was based especially on promoting civic values.

A few weeks before the first round, it was revealed that Zuluaga was waging a dirty war on the peace process and on my candidacy. A video was discovered showing Zuluaga and the director of his campaign, Luis Alfonso Hoyos, holed up in some obscure cubicle with Andrés Fernando Sepúlveda, a professional hacker, who could be seen proudly showing the two men confidential information from military intelligence he had gotten access to, data on the guerrilla leaders negotiating in Havana. The video showed Sepúlveda explaining to the two men how this information was going to be used to discredit the peace process. Neither Zuluaga nor Hoyos seemed surprised by what the hacker was doing. On the contrary, they seemed to admire the fact that he had managed to get this illegal information, and they talked about how they could use it to undermine my campaign.

The video appeared in the media and led to the arrest of Sepúlveda and to Hoyos resigning from the direction of the Zuluaga campaign and fleeing the country. Zuluaga, against all the evidence, first tried to deny that he was the person who appeared in the video, and finally admitted he was there but had only dropped in to say hello but had no idea of what was going on and had certainly not approved of any illegal operation. Whatever one can say about his testimony, one thing was certain: the episode showed to what lengths the opposition was prepared to go to win the presidency.

With this scandal fresh in everyone's minds, the first round of the elections was held on May 25, 2014. Zuluaga came first, with 3,769,005 votes, equivalent to 29.5 percent, and I was second, with 3,310,794 votes, equivalent to 25.7 percent. The other three candidates won a significant number of votes: both

Marta Lucía Ramírez and Clara López came close to winning two million votes each, while Enrique Peñalosa won over a million.

THE SECOND ROUND

This first adverse result sounded a warning for the peace process, which was seen to be in danger due to the electoral advantage of the Democratic Center's candidate. Fortunately, in the course of the three weeks between the first round and the second, my candidacy gathered the support of many sectors of Colombia—especially from the Left—who supported the peace process even when they did not agree with other aspects of my proposals or of my government. So it was that people like López and the leader and survivor of the Patriotic Union, Aída Avella, announced they would be voting for me. So did Antanas Mockus, who had been my opponent four years earlier, and a lot of artists and intellectuals. I had the support, too, of a movement called Progresistas (Progressives) who were followers of Gustavo Petro, at the time the mayor of Bogotá. Ramírez decided to go with the Zuluaga campaign, although the majority of the Conservative Party's congressmen and women and the Conservative former president Belisario Betancur gave me their support. Peñalosa did not take sides but left his followers to decide for themselves.

In light of this new electoral panorama, my candidacy found itself strengthened by the spontaneous and multitudinous support of men and women on the left who, despite their criticisms of many aspects of my government, understood that peace was of fundamental importance, over and above any discrepancies they might have on other issues. Their support was absolutely crucial.

A week before the second round of elections, Zuluaga had an attack of laryngitis that caused him to suspend his activities, and he declined to take part in a programmed debate with me on television. Finally, on June 15, 2014, the Colombians had the last word, as expressed in the ballot boxes: 7,816,987—that is, 51 percent—voted for me; and 6,905,001 (45 percent) voted for Zuluaga. The peace process had been saved!

The result represented a historically singular swing in voting patterns; in 2010 I had been elected by votes from the right, and yet in 2014 I was elected by votes from the left. To these were added, of course, votes of the political center and of many other Colombians who had no affinity with any ideology but supported the process that we were carrying forward. Something similar—a change in the composition of the electorate—occurred with Charles de Gaulle in France and Ariel Sharon in Israel when they espoused peace movements.

Those 7.8 million citizens who had voted for me had, in reality, voted for peace. I hoped I would be equal to the challenge that represented.

CHAPTER 29

The Example of the Victims

"THIS STAGE WILL BE THE MOST DIFFICULT ONE"

In Havana, we had reached partial agreements on rural development, political participation, and the problem of illegal drugs. But the debates ahead of us were not going to be easy. We still had to discuss the point on the agenda devoted to victims, and that included guarantees with regard to the victims' right to know the truth, to see justice done, and to be assured of reparation and nonrepetition. Another point to be dealt with was the end of the conflict, which included the thorny question of laying down arms and the reincorporation of ex-combatants into civilian life.

Bearing this in mind, my address on August 7, 2014, at the inauguration of my second presidential term, included the following:

> I will use all the energy I have to comply with this mandate for peace. However, rather than celebrate what we have achieved, I remind you that we are entering the final phase of talks. And like all last efforts, this stage will be the most difficult one, and the most demanding. It is going to demand sacrifices from us all. And above all, it is going to require decisions. More than anything else, decisions about the victims.
>
> Can there be any family in Colombia that does not have a father or mother, a brother or sister, a cousin or a friend, who has not been a victim of this conflict? With the Law of Victims, we took an important step. But the crucial step is to put an end to the conflict, to guarantee that there will be no more victims and that the victims' rights will be respected in the best possible way.
>
> We must see a genuine willingness to tell the truth, to clarify what happened and explain why, as well as to participate in the process of reparation

and find a formula for justice that the victims and all Colombians will find acceptable.

Little did we know then that discussions on the victims were going to occupy us for a year and a half. They began on May 7, 2014, with a joint declaration by all delegates at the negotiating table on the principles that would serve as guidelines for debate on this issue. But discussions did not conclude until the end of 2015 and at times had the process teetering on the brink of an abyss, especially because of the difficulty in reaching an agreement on the question of justice.

"FORGIVENESS IS INFINITE"

Mao Tse Tung, before beginning his famous Long March in 1934, recalled an adage of Lao Tzu that I always like to bear in mind: "A journey of one thousand miles begins with the first step." That's how I understood the difficult path I had embarked on when, back in 1996, I organized that meeting at the Monserrat Abbey to seek creative solutions that might lead to peace in Colombia. Indeed even before that, in 1991, when I was in New York as minister for foreign trade and listened to a businessman telling me that there would be no real investment in Colombia so long as an armed conflict subsisted, I began to dream of peace. And that dream would become a reality only if we could find an adequate solution to the problem of the victims.

Over half a century, the armed conflict had produced more than eight million victims, and to recognize them, make reparation to them, and accompany them constituted a moral and historical debt that Colombian society had contracted. Paying it was going to take years, but we had to begin as soon as possible. We had to take the first step. And that first step, even before we had begun peace talks with the Farc, was the Law of Victims and Restitution of Land, to which I have already referred.

I kept constantly clear in my mind and heart that the goal of peace is twofold: on the one hand, to respond to the rights of the victims that the war has been responsible for, and on the other, to make sure there will be no more victims. And this conviction, which I transmitted to the government's negotiators, became the central axis of the process, an emphasis that made it unique in the world because the Colombian process was the first to place the victims at the center of the solution.

If we were seeking to end the conflict, it was to have no more victims. And if a form of justice was to be agreed upon, it would have to be a system of justice that was above all for them, and that would not be inspired by vengeance but by reparation.

At the very start of the process, I had a visit in Bogotá from Ronald Heifetz, founder of the Center for Public Leadership at Harvard's Kennedy School, where I had studied. And he gave me some sound advice: "Whenever you feel disheartened, tired, or pessimistic, talk to the victims. They, with their stories, their dramas, their courage, will give you the will and the strength to go on."

His words were always with me. And I put them into practice in the course of those years when, very often, there were dark clouds on the horizon and there seemed to be no way out, or when continuous criticisms began to make inroads on my resolve. To meet the victims, talk with them, listen to their tales of personal pain, but also to witness their courage and resilience, always helped me to persevere. If they were able to keep fighting, if they did not lose hope in the possibility of peace, if they were ready to forgive their tormentors, what right did I have to fall by the wayside?

What I discovered in all my conversations with the victims was something wonderful: while many people who had never been personally scarred by the conflict were insisting that the Farc be subjected to the most implacable justice, that the ex-guerrillas should be locked up in prison for years—something that is simply not viable in a peace process, since no subversive organization is going to sign an agreement to go to prison—the victims were telling me that, for them, more important than punishment for their persecutors was that they be told what had happened to their loved ones, many of whom had disappeared and whose mortal remains they had never been able to recover. Above all else, even more than reparations or justice, the victims wanted to be told the truth.

And there was something even more noteworthy: the victims expressed their solidarity with the peace process and did not place their personal pain ahead of the possibility of ending the conflict and thus ensuring that other Colombians would not endure what they had suffered. What a marvelous example they gave us, and continue to give us. For me, it has been an important lesson for my life.

I met with the victims on countless occasions and in many parts of the country, in events where the government was providing free homes or some other kind of state assistance, and each time I was given proof of their courage, generosity, and solidarity. I was deeply moved by everything they told me.

I especially remember one occasion when we were inaugurating the government's provision of free housing in Neiva, the capital of the department of Huila, and I handed the keys of a new apartment to a man who was missing a leg. José Plutarco Valencia was his name. "What happened to your leg?" I asked him, in presence of all those who were attending the act of inauguration.

"I lost it in the war, in the conflict. I'm a displaced person from Putumayo."

"Well, cheer up, Don José!" I said. "You now have a home of your own, where you can be with your children." José Plutarco looked at me with a sorrowful expression in his eyes and replied very faintly: "I lost them too, Mr. President. Both my sons were killed in the war."

On another occasion, a woman came up to me and said: "President, I need your help."

"How can I help you?" I asked.

"I am displaced from Urabá, and lost my husband. The guerrillas killed him. And the paramilitaries took three of my sons. One died, but I never found out what happened to the others. They were taken from me by force. Please help me to find them."

My eyes filled with tears. What can you say to someone who has survived such pain? The murderers might be guerrillas, paramilitaries, or even agents of the state, but the victim's suffering is the same. We had to put a stop to this torrent of violence. And we had to do so at once. The conflict had become an implacable and efficient factory producing victims.

My memory is full of these stories. One particularly painful case was that of the Turbay Cote family, some of whose members were political leaders in the department of Caquetá. Toward the end of the 1990s, the Farc exterminated almost the entire family. Constanza Turbay, who survived, lost her mother and two brothers, all three assassinated by the guerrillas. Her older brother Rodrigo, who was president of the Chamber of Representatives in Congress, was kidnapped and then murdered in 1997. Her younger brother Diego, who was president of the Chamber's peace commission, was shot along with his mother on the roadside in Caquetá on December 29, 2000.

Constanza took her courage in her hands and traveled to Havana with one of the five delegations of victims that went there to tell their stories and to give their point of view. She actually sat down beside members of that same guerrilla group that had destroyed her life. Iván Márquez, head of the Farc's negotiators, asked her forgiveness in the name of his organization and acknowledged the great error they had committed. And Fabián Ramírez, another guerrilla commander who had been in Caquetá when the family was murdered, told the truth—the very painful but necessary truth—about what had occurred. There in Havana, fifteen years after the tragic loss of her family, Constanza forgave the guerrillas. "Forgiveness is infinite," she said. And before she left Cuba, she made a statement in which she declared: "We the victims are exchanging our pain for the hope of peace."

HOMAGE TO THE VICTIMS IN OSLO

When I was asked who I would like to attend the ceremony in which I was awarded the Nobel Peace Prize in Oslo in December 2016, the first thing that came to my mind was that representatives of the victims should be invited. It was for them that we had made such an effort, and they had given us the moral support we needed to persevere. This recognition belonged to them more than anyone else.

And so it was that part of the official delegation that accompanied me consisted of victims of different actors in the conflict, among whom were the following: Pastora Mira, a courageous and generous woman whose father and husband had both lost their lives in partisan violence and whose two sons were murdered by paramilitaries, a story that brought Pope Francis to tears when he heard it during his visit to Villavicencio; Leyner Palacios, an extraordinary human being who survived the Bojayá massacre in Chocó; Liliana Pechené, a leader from the Misak community in Cauca, who represented the suffering of the indigenous people trapped in the middle of the conflict; Fabiola Perdomo, widow of one of the eleven deputies from the Valle del Cauca Assembly who had been kidnapped and murdered by the Farc in 2007; Ingrid Betancur and Clara Rojas, held captive for years by that same guerrilla organization; and the renowned writer Héctor Abad Faciolince, whose father, a medical doctor and human rights defender, was murdered by paramilitaries, a crime his son describes with a masterly pen in the most personal of his works, *El olvido que seremos* (published in the United States as *Oblivion*).

But they were not the only ones. When I looked around at the men and women who were on the flight with me to Oslo, several of them had been victims of the violence that has affected most of us Colombians in one way or another. There was my minister of the interior, Juan Fernando Cristo, whose father was killed by the ELN; the journalist María Jimena Duzán, whose sister was murdered by the paramilitaries, and the former senator Piedad Córdoba, who had been kidnapped by paramilitaries.

One of the most emotional moments during the Nobel Prize award ceremony was when I paused in my address and asked the victims of the Colombian conflict to stand up and receive the homage they deserved. And they did so, holding hands, and the expression on their faces reflected the sentiments of so many years of repressed anguish. All those present broke into a long and moving applause. There, in the solemn hall of the Norwegian capital—where people like Mikhail Gorbachev, Nelson Mandela, Yitzhak Rabin, Jimmy Carter, Barack Obama, and Malala Yousafzai had been paid homage—stood the representatives of eight million victims celebrating the end of a conflict that had robbed them of their loved ones or had stolen years from their lives and who, now that the war was over, once again could experience faith and hope.

There in Oslo, I recounted the story of Leyner Palacios, a joyful man and a proud representative of our Afro-Colombian ethnic group, who survived one of the war's most atrocious acts, one that occurred on May 2, 2002, in a tiny village called Bojayá, in the department of Chocó. That day, Farc guerrillas in combat with a group of paramilitaries fired a mortar that landed in the middle of the town's church where families had taken refuge. Some eighty people died, mostly children, and about one hundred were wounded. That day Leyner lost thirty-two members of his family, including his parents and three brothers. But he refused to give himself over to lamentations and a desire for revenge. He became a positive leader of his community and had the courage—because this requires courage—to pardon those who had committed this crime when they, members of the Farc, returned to Bojayá in June 2015 to beg forgiveness from the people whose town they had destroyed.

Forgiveness has a twofold liberating effect: it liberates the one who is forgiven, but the one who forgives is also liberated from the weight of rancor and the darkness of hate.

CHAPTER 30

The Rights of the Victims

"GREAT CALAMITIES ALWAYS CONTAIN A LESSON"

Perhaps what fundamentally enabled the government and the Farc to come to an agreement on the thorny question of the victims was the fact that the measures we took to guarantee the victims' rights would be applied without distinction to any of the perpetrators no matter what side they had been on in the conflict. In other words, we sought to indemnify and ensure that justice was done and reparation made for the rights of victims who had been harmed not by the Farc alone but also by paramilitaries, and by agents of the state who had betrayed their sacred oath and their uniform by committing war crimes.

In this way, we were not discriminating against anyone, and so were able to move forward toward the overall aim of the process, which was not limited to ending the conflict with the Farc but sought to do away with the conditions that might lead to a new conflict in the future.

Progress was soon made on the subjects of truth, reparation, and nonrepetition. But problems arose when we came to the issue of justice. Debates on that matter led negotiations to a veritable Gordian knot.

The Farc began with what we considered a useful proposal; namely, that a commission made up of academics be established to study the historical background to the conflict with the intention of helping the negotiators and the public in general to better understand the causes and the consequences of Colombia's armed conflict. And so it was that we created the Historical Commission on the Conflict and its Victims, made up of twelve recognized historians and experts in the social sciences, plus two compilers with extensive knowledge of the subject. The commission began its labors in August 2014. Its final report, consisting of twelve essays, each from a different angle in accordance with the emphasis and specialization of the particular author, was presented in January 2015. Since then, it has become a valuable document of study and consultation.

In the course of debate on the point concerning the victims, it was agreed also that, once a final agreement had been signed, a Commission for Truth, Coexistence, and Non-repetition should be set up, as well as a special unit with the mission of discovering what had happened to people who had been forcibly disappeared in the context of the armed conflict.

In many peace processes around the world, truth commissions have played a fundamental role when it came to reconciliation within societies that were divided. Such commissions have been created in places and contexts as diverse as South Africa, Guatemala, El Salvador, Sierra Leone, and Kenya. We studied the experience of each of these to learn lessons and not repeat mistakes that could be avoided. In addition, we carefully analyzed the joint report produced by the Kofi Annan Foundation and the International Center for Transitional Justice on truth commissions and peace processes.

What is the purpose of a truth commission? It is to allow the victims access to the truth about what happened in the conflict, to know why it happened and in what way it affected their loved ones. It is not the truth of just one group; it is the truth of society in general, and especially of all actors involved in the conflict. But the commission is not a judicial organ to collect statements or confessions that can be used in legal procedures. The truth is told in order to heal, to illuminate dark areas in the history of the conflict, to heal wounds and generate a liberating catharsis. Because nothing could be more certain than what is said in the Bible: "The truth will set you free."

On May 8, 2018, I had the satisfaction of swearing in the eleven members of the first truth commission in Colombia's history. It was composed of economists, lawyers, sociologists, philosophers, and physicians, who had been designated by an independent committee after an open call for proposals. At the head of the commission was an extraordinary man who has devoted his life to sowing the seeds of reconciliation in areas most affected by violence: the Jesuit priest Francisco de Roux, who for several years served as provincial father of the Jesuit community in Colombia.

The commission, which was to function for three years, would travel the length and breadth of Colombia in order to comply with its commitment, which was to furnish a report that would contribute to clarifying what had occurred in the course of the conflict, its impact and its consequences. This would provide information that would allow everyone to know who was responsible for what had happened and, as a result, be able to assess what the victims had a right to expect from society as a whole. Most important of all, the commission would make recommendations on the issues of coexistence and nonrepetition.

"Great calamities always contain lessons." These were the words of the writer Ernesto Sábato, president of Argentina's National Commission on Disappeared Persons, which produced an impressive document on the practice of forcibly disappearing people under the military dictatorship in Argentina. The document was titled "Never Again." And Sábato was right. If there is one thing worse than a calamity, it is not to learn the lesson it has left us. That is why a natural corollary of the process was the creation of the truth commission and an entity devoted to searching for people who had been disappeared.

The entity in question represented another contribution to truth. What it offered the victims was above all a respite from their anguish. Because there is nothing more distressing than not knowing what has happened to a loved one. It is estimated that in Colombia, over a relatively brief period of time, between forty-five and sixty thousand people were forcibly disappeared. The entity established to discover their whereabouts is similar to the truth commission in that its nature is extrajudicial and humanitarian. Its task is to determine the total universe of victims who had been disappeared and work with their families, and also with organizations that have experience in this type of search. Whenever possible, they will identify the remains of the victim and assist the families in giving them a final resting place. The entity began its work in the first half of 2018 under the direction of Luz Marina Monzón, an expert in criminology and criminal justice, and in human rights.

How much pain, how many tragedies, are hidden within a conflict that goes on for decades, as the Colombian conflict did? Institutions created as a result of the peace agreement, such as the historical commission, the truth commission, and the Unit for the Search for Disappeared Persons are gigantic steps forward, not only toward the truth but toward the healing of our society's afflicted soul.

THE GORDIAN KNOT OF JUSTICE

Although it proved relatively easy to make progress and reach an agreement as regards mechanisms that would contribute to truth, we soon saw that the most complex point on the agenda was the one concerned with justice. And this has usually been the case in peace processes everywhere. How could we solve the inevitable problem of finding a balance between justice and peace? On the one hand, society expects that those who have committed atrocious crimes or crimes against humanity should have to pay for them, and should normally do so behind bars. However, at the same time society is in urgent need of peace, a peace you cannot achieve at a negotiating table in exchange for sending the other side's negotiators to prison for the rest of their lives. No subversive group will sign a peace agreement to go to prison. Not in Colombia, nor anywhere else in the world.

In these exceptional circumstances in which a society is trying to find a way to end a war and create a situation where peace and coexistence can flourish, the concept of transitional justice has been adopted. It is a type of justice that does not permit society to take revenge on the criminals but devises alternative measures, mainly of a kind that makes amends to the victims. Only a system like this will allow for a successful transition from war to peace.

Our challenge, then, was to invent a system of transitional justice that would guarantee the most authentic kind of justice to be meted out without giving up the chance for peace. At the same time, we had to keep within the norms of Colombia's constitution and those of international treaties such as the Statute of Rome. This was no simple matter. It was almost like building a square triangle. But we had to find a way to do it.

As is customary, each side came to the table with a proposal that was at the opposite pole of the other's. While the government's negotiators were talking about a punishment that would entail a privation of freedom that could be reduced so long as the condemned person cooperated on the issue of truth and reparation, the Farc's negotiators took as their starting point the presumption that they would be granted total amnesty or a pardon for their crimes, as had occurred in other peace processes such as those carried out with the M-19 movement and the EPL at the end of the 1980s. But times had changed. Colombia, as signatory of the Statute of Rome, now acknowledged the jurisdiction of the International Criminal Court and was not entitled, for the sake of peace, to grant amnesties or indults for serious misdemeanors included in said treaty.

Little by little, we began to bring the two positions closer to one another, but months were going by and we were not reaching an agreement on this point. In fact, one got the impression that the process had gotten bogged down.

In August 2014, when we were in the middle of this debate, we had a visit from the German jurist Claus Kress, one of the creators of the International Criminal Court, who made the following remark in an interview:

> International criminal law does not provide a clear answer. That is why I believe Colombia is so important. Depending on how you solve this dilemma, a precedent will have been created, and you can be sure the rest of the world is looking on with great attention. My advice is that you use your faculty for making judgment but, at the same time, use your reason. That is to say, keep in mind people's idea of justice, but not forgetting that the prime concern is to put an end to a bloody conflict.

Meanwhile, the atmosphere at the negotiating table reached the point of exasperation and voices were being raised. Whenever dialogues came to a dead end, as they often did, the negotiators on both sides would go to the Norwegian embassy to carry on discussions. And Norway was always ready to serve as guarantor and facilitator in the best possible manner. In one of these discussions, sitting around the dining table, Joaquín Gómez of the Farc exclaimed: "If a solution is not found, we'll go back to war!"

Another Farc negotiator, Mauricio Jaramillo, alias The Doctor, pointed an accusing finger at the government's delegates and said: "If you don't cede on this point and the problem is not solved, all those who die in this war from now on will be on your heads."

This kind of behavior is inherent to negotiations. Even when discussions are conducted with respect for the other side, emotional crises can arise that sometimes lead to a shouting match.

THE COMMISSION OF JURISTS

While this difficult situation was being prolonged, I held frequent meetings with the negotiating team, especially with Sergio Jaramillo and Humberto de la Calle, urging them to come up with creative solutions that would include sanctions that were in accord with our international obligations. But it was hard to see light at the end of the tunnel. We seemed to have run up against a brick wall. We were all disheartened, and I even fell to thinking that failure to reach consensus on this point could mean the collapse of the whole enterprise.

At this juncture, US Special Envoy Bernard Aronson made the following recommendation: "If you've come to a standstill on this point, why not appoint an independent commission of experts to see if they can solve the problem? I mean new people who can take a fresh look at the issue, and have autonomy to come up with a solution."

I liked the idea, and so we proposed to the Farc to create a commission of jurists, three representing them and three for us, all freely selected without constraint of any kind, who might produce a recommendation on how to overcome the problem. They accepted, only adding that neither of the parties would have the right to veto a designation made by the other, perhaps having in mind the choice of Álvaro Leyva, who had been advising us and whom they would now invite to be their consultant. We had no problem with this. And so it was that in June 2015 this solution would unblock the stalemate in what had become the longest and most crucial debate in the whole process.

On our side, I appointed two former presidents of Colombia's Constitutional Court, both highly respected in juridical circles for the judicial decisions they had promulgated and for their progressive views on the defense of civil liberties guaranteed by our constitution; they were Manuel José Cepeda and Juan Carlos Henao. Cepeda had been consultant to Presidents Virgilio Barco and César Gaviria—forming part of what had been nicknamed "Gaviria's kindergarten" because its components were all quite young—and had taken part also in the constituent assembly that produced the 1991 Constitution. More recently, he had been my adviser in the presidency on particularly thorny questions for our country, such as the border dispute with Nicaragua that was being adjudicated in The Hague. Henao, for his part, held a doctorate in law from the Sorbonne, enjoyed great national and international prestige, and was of an outgoing temperament and very progressive. At the time, he was rector of the Externado University of Colombia.

The third member of the commission on the government's side was someone wisely recommended by the US special envoy Bernie Aronson: the American jurist Douglass Cassel, professor at the prestigious University of Notre Dame and a man with an international reputation in the field of human rights. My concern was to ensure that any agreement we might finally reach—after all, our intention was to respond to the victims' right to see justice done—would not contravene any existing protocol or treaty on human rights. In this, Professor Cassel's contribution was going to be decisive.

On their side, the Farc designated the Spanish politician and lawyer Enrique Santiago, a member of Spain's Communist Party, who had many years of experience in questions of human rights and international humanitarian law.

They also appointed Álvaro Leyva, a man who had already spent several decades attempting to bring together the guerrillas and the government for peace talks, and Diego Martínez, a lawyer devoted to the defense of human rights.

I began by calling a meeting at Casa de Nariño with Sergio Jaramillo, de la Calle, Cepeda, and Henao to clarify the mission we were entrusting to our jurists, and to give them my instructions. The first thing I said was that, being experts in legal matters, they could go ahead with complete autonomy, although I wanted them to be in constant communication with Jaramillo and de la Calle. I assured them, also, that they would have a direct line to my office and could call me whenever they felt they needed to make some comment or consult me on any difficulty. And so it was; we were frequently in contact and came together for meetings on an almost weekly basis.

There was one thing I told them they must not forget, and that was that we had drawn certain red lines they should not cross. I insisted that there would have to be a court of justice to investigate—and pronounce judgment on—the highest-ranking members of the Farc, who bore the most responsibility for their organization's activities, and that they should be sanctioned, preferably with prison sentences.

With these instructions, and in the company of Professor Cassel, our jurists flew to Havana, and there, on July 26 at the Norwegian embassy, had a first meeting with their counterparts.

That was the moment when a process of negotiation began between our jurists and those of the Farc, debating within the commission. In reality, though, it was not so much a negotiation as a truly collective creation in which representatives on both sides worked tirelessly, harmoniously, and in accordance with the strictest norms of international law and human rights, but also applying those norms creatively where necessary so as to adjust them to the reality of the Colombian conflict. The six members of the commission worked as a single team. They held several meetings in Havana, in the Norwegian embassy, and later in Bogotá in Henao's apartment, and as discussions proceeded, they kept their respective delegations informed of any progress that was being made. On one afternoon, I paid them a visit, and as the elevator was out of order, I had to climb five flights of stairs to get to the apartment. It was worthwhile, because I saw for myself the atmosphere of respect and camaraderie that reigned among the commission's members, who had such an important matter on their hands.

On September 19, after two months of virtually continuous work and one last sleepless night in Henao's apartment, the jurists produced the draft of what was to become the agreement on justice for peace. It was an agreement that, while fully respecting international treaties and Colombia's constitution, managed to find a solution to the most difficult dilemma of the whole process: how to achieve maximum justice without sacrificing peace.

CHAPTER 31

A Model of Justice for the World

THE BASES OF THE DISCUSSION

During their first two days in Havana, the jurists agreed on certain principles on which they would build Colombia's transitional justice system. They formulated these principles in a first working document on July 27, 2015.

From that moment, a series of issues were clarified as a starting point from which to move forward. For example:

- That the principal aim of any comprehensive system of truth, justice, reparation, and nonrepetition is the consolidation of peace and the guarantee of the victims' rights.
- That the principal juridical parameters of reference would be international legislation on questions of human rights and international humanitarian law.
- That although the state has the power to grant the broadest possible amnesty once hostilities have ceased, there are crimes that are not eligible for amnesty or pardon, such as crimes against humanity and others defined in the Statute of Rome.
- That the concession of amnesties, pardons, or another benefit does not exempt the person benefited from the obligation to contribute to the truth, and the extent of that contribution will serve as a measure to decide on the extent of possible benefits.
- That in cases where an amnesty or pardon is not granted, there will be sanctions for those responsible.
- That the mechanisms and procedures for members of the Farc, agents of the state, and other actors who have participated in the conflict may be different but must always be balanced and fair.

- That the imposition of any sanction within this system will not be an obstacle to participation in politics.

This last point, which has been criticized by some Colombians, was essential. Because the final aim of any negotiation with a subversive group is that the guerrillas lay down their arms in exchange for an entry into politics. That's why, no matter what sanctions they might be submitted to, the penalty has to be compatible with their playing a part in politics. The guerrilla delegation was not going to sign an agreement that would put them in prison or condemn them to ostracism within our democratic system.

A great step forward had been taken in those first two days. The objectives here elaborated gave us a glimpse of a possible solution to a problem that had caused negotiations to be bogged down for almost a year.

THE JUSTICE WE ACHIEVED

A few issues still had to be dealt with: for example, what sanctions would be imposed, how to include drug trafficking as a connected crime, and whether or not it could receive an amnesty or pardon, plus the question of extradition.

On this last point, extradition, it was agreed that no one would be extradited for crimes committed during the conflict or occasioned by it. Extradition could be applied, however, for any crime committed after the conflict had ended. That explains why Jesús Santrich, a negotiator and guerrilla commander, is required by American authorities to face charges of conspiring to export cocaine into the United States. They argue that he should be extradited because his offense was allegedly committed after November 24, 2016; that is, after the signing of the agreement that put an end to the conflict.

For the Farc, drug trafficking was a particularly thorny question. If you take into account that their organization obtained an enormous income from protecting illegal crops or from their active role in the drug trade over several decades, it would seem virtually impossible that any of its members could be amnestied. So what was finally decided on was to consider drug trafficking as an offense connected to the group's political offenses, and therefore eligible for amnesty. This was based on the presumption that the said illegal conduct was carried out to finance their rebellion and there was no question of personal enrichment, nor did their part in the trade include crimes against humanity, or any other kind of serious crime, including genocide. In that sense, therefore, if the group's part in the drug trade was a source of income destined exclusively to financing their rebellion, it could be considered an offense connected to political offenses, but only if it was carried out before the signing of the peace agreement. Any crime, including trafficking, committed after that moment would be dealt with by the normal system of justice and would lose the right to any kind of benefit that derived from the agreement.

But another thorny question was yet to be faced: what sanctions should be imposed for serious crimes that were not eligible for amnesty? At the beginning, the Farc refused to agree to any sanction that was not related to restoration, with no kind of restriction or privation of freedom. The government, on the other hand, proposed sanctions that included some prison sentences. In the end, we met halfway: for those who contributed to the truth there would be sanctions that effectively put limits on freedom. But these sanctions would not mean a loss of freedom altogether, although they could imply a prison sentence if the individual did not contribute to truth, or delayed in doing so.

It was agreed that this system be applied by a special peace court consisting of highly qualified magistrates chosen by organizations that enjoyed great credibility and experience in these matters, whose objective would be to investigate, judge, and sanction offenses committed during the conflict, not only by members of the Farc but also by military personnel, the police and other agents of the state, and even civilians who might have recourse to this jurisdiction.

The significance of this agreement deserves special mention. It was the first of its kind achieved within the parameters of the Statute of Rome. The Farc were accepting what no other guerrilla organization had accepted in a negotiation. And they did so because international criminal justice had imposed certain rules that could not be ignored, but above all, because the justice system agreed upon was designed to judge not only the Farc's members but all actors in the conflict.

THERE WAS NO IMPUNITY

The word *impunity* was constantly on the lips of Colombians in the course of these discussions. The process's opponents—led, as usual, by Uribe—never tired of repeating that what we had agreed on in Havana was a regime of impunity for the guerrillas and that this was an affront to the victims and to society in general. The nation's attorney general at the time, Alejandro Ordóñez, called the agreement "a bazaar of impunities."

In fact, however, we had not agreed to impunity of any kind. On this point the agreement was very clear: it excluded any possibility of amnesty or pardon for "crimes against humanity, genocide, serious war crimes—in other words, any breach of International Humanitarian Law committed systematically—the taking of hostages and any other serious privation of freedom, torture, extrajudicial executions, forced disappearance, violent carnal access (i.e., rape) and other forms of sexual violence, the capturing of minors, all in conformity with what is established in the Statute of Rome."

None of these crimes would be left unpunished. Serious crimes would be investigated, judged, and sentenced by the special jurisdiction for peace, but punishments would be meted out not in a spirit of revenge or retaliation but rather in a manner in harmony with a nation that seeks reconciliation and respect for the rights of the victims and the consolidation of peace. The following are the sanctions agreed on for the abovementioned offenses, so long as they were committed in the context of the conflict or occasioned by that conflict:

- Those who tell the whole truth—that is to say, who give a full and detailed account of the offenses they committed and the circumstances in which they took place, and provide sufficient information to attribute responsibilities and guarantee the satisfaction of the victims' rights—and admit their responsibility, will be sentenced to an effective restriction of their freedom of between five and eight years' duration, and must perform works to make reparation to the victims.

What is implied by the phrase "effective restriction of freedom"? It means that those sanctioned—duly monitored and supervised—will be confined within an area no greater than the transitory rural zones of normalization; in other words, the areas agreed upon as places where the Farc guerrillas are to assemble and be demobilized.

- Anyone who tells the truth and admits responsibility, but not from the start but only after some delay—so long as this occurs before the person received the sanction—will be sentenced to between five and eight years in prison.

- Those who refuse to tell the truth and admit their responsibility—and who are guilty of serious crimes—will be given prison sentences of from fifteen to twenty years.

The regime of punishments we established was a special one and was designed to achieve peace and give satisfaction to the victims. But, as can be seen, it certainly was not a regime of impunity.

KEEPING A PROMISE

From the very start of the peace talks, I constantly assured the military and the police that I was not going to allow that what had happened in previous processes should occur again this time; namely, that while the demobilized guerrillas received all kinds of benefits, some even rising to important posts in public life, agents of the state who had fought against them, often in defense of democracy, were tried in a court of justice for acts related to the conflict and ended up serving long prison sentences.

That was my commitment, and it was included in the agreement where it was made clear that the application of justice for peace would be differentiated, but always fair and simultaneous, bearing in mind, also, that soldiers and policemen act on the presumption that they are doing so lawfully since they are engaged in their mission of maintaining public order and protecting the population. If their actions run counter to this mission, such a deviation from power must be proven.

This was reassuring for members of the public forces. However, paradoxically, it did not find an echo in the intransigent opposition of the Right and among certain generals in retirement. Uribe insisted that we were treating the military as if they were the same as guerrillas, which was an affront to their military honor. In fact, quite the opposite was the case: we were guaranteeing them rights and benefits similar to the ones the demobilized guerrillas had access to, in order to avoid repeating cases of injustice that had occurred in the past.

Finally, in 2018, when the Special Justice for Peace (Justicia Especial para la Paz, JEP), began to function, certain military men who were under investigation in the normal courts of justice for acts related to the conflict, were the ones who began voluntarily to have recourse to transitional justice, realizing that this would be to their advantage. One of the first to do so was the retired general Mario Montoya, who had been commander of the army under the government of Uribe and had important achievements to his credit, including Operation Checkmate. General Montoya, under investigation for alleged involvement in the affair known as "false positives," although he has proclaimed his innocence, has calmly opted for submitting his case to the system of justice that was created thanks to the peace agreement, because he believes in its structure and procedures, and also in its officials. Many other military officers and policemen have had recourse to the JEP as a tribunal that not only dispenses justice but guarantees fair treatment with respect to the benefits the ex-guerrilla fighters can enjoy.

A MODEL FOR THE WORLD

Professor Kress was right when he said that the Colombian process was of great importance for the world: "Depending on how you solve this dilemma, a precedent will have been created, and you can be sure the rest of the world is looking on with great attention."

Undoubtedly, what the process achieved on the question of justice was something exceptional. It was the first time a government and an illegal armed group—in a peace agreement, and not as a result of later impositions—created a system for rendering accounts before a national tribunal for crimes that were regarded as international offenses, and other serious felonies, and submitting to its judgments.

Other tribunals have been created by the United Nations Security Council, such as the international criminal tribunal for the former Yugoslavia and Rwanda. But in our case, we managed to create a jurisdiction—not international, but national—by consensus of the parties in conflict.

One must acknowledge the excellent work carried out—and in record time—by the members of the commission of jurists, to which we should add the name of Yesid Reyes, a highly qualified lawyer. Reyes was minister of justice at the time that the negotiators in Havana were debating the point on the victims, and his contributions as an expert in criminology were immensely useful and pertinent. His services were fundamental, too, when it came to renegotiating the agreement with the Farc after the plebiscite. He has another special qualification: he himself was a victim of the conflict, and in the most horrible manner. His father, Alfonso Reyes Echandía, a dearly loved and immensely admired magistrate, was president of the Supreme Court of

Justice in November 1985 when M-19 guerrillas took the Palace of Justice by storm, sparking off a tragedy in which Reyes was killed, along with ten other members of that same high tribunal and dozens of civilians, soldiers, and guerrillas. The guerrilla attack and the response of the state, in which there were no doubt faults and excesses, was the greatest holocaust our justice system has ever suffered. Yet Reyes's son, Yesid, like so many other victims, has responded with serenity and has displayed a generosity of spirit manifested in his ability to forgive and carry on with his life.

The International Crisis Group, one of the most important institutions in the field of prevention and resolution of international armed conflicts—to which I now have the honor to belong as member of the board of directors—qualified our agreement on transitional justice as "a firm step forward, efficacious and intelligent . . . a balanced and sensible solution in face of the complex dilemmas a conflict presents."

The Toledo International Center for Peace hailed the agreement as "consistent with the principles of universal justice that responds to the legitimate clamor for peace without impunity" and can serve as a model "to unblock other peace processes."

I am certain that what we agreed upon on the question of justice is the greatest and most innovative contribution the Colombian peace process has made to world peace, because its principles and development can serve as a model for many conflicts as yet unresolved.

CHAPTER 32

The Point of No Return

A GENERAL IN HIS LABYRINTH

The peace process survived many crises and setbacks, some of them due to problems of public order that had nothing to do with the peace talks, and others—such as our delay in defining the subject of victims—due to the complexities of the negotiation.

A very serious crisis occurred on November 16, 2014, when General Rubén Darío Alzate, commander of the Titan Joint Task Force assigned to the department of Chocó—a force I had sent into action in January of that same year—and his assistant, Corporal Jorge Rodríguez, accompanied by a lawyer, Gloria Urrego, coordinator of special army projects in that department, were kidnapped by the Farc's Front No. 34. This guerrilla action was a violation of the guerrillas' promise not to continue kidnapping, and was caused, too, by the general's imprudence; without advising anyone, and without an escort of any kind, he was traveling on a launch down the Atrato River toward a tiny village to make contact with the community. Both he and the corporal were in civilian dress. The man who operated the launch that transported them to the village warned the general that he was in a red zone where the guerrillas were very active, but the general did not take heed of what the man told him. As a result, he gave the guerrillas an opportunity to capture the highest-ranking officer they had ever held in their power since the conflict began fifty years ago. To make matters worse, a week before then, the Farc had captured two soldiers in the department of Arauca, on the other side of the country.

On the day of the kidnapping, I made a public statement, making it clear that Farc had to assume full responsibility for the general's life and integrity, as well as that of the corporal, the lawyer, and the two soldiers. And I ordered our negotiators, who were in Bogotá getting ready to return to Havana to begin a new cycle of conversations, to call off their trip. It's true we were negotiating in the middle of the conflict, but there were certain minimal agreements that had to be respected, and the guerrillas were violating them.

On November 25 the two soldiers were set free, and on November 30—two weeks after he had been kidnapped—General Alzate, the corporal, and the lawyer were also liberated, thanks to the good offices of the guarantor countries and the International Red Cross. Pastor Alape, a member of the Farc's secretariat and of their delegation in Cuba, also traveled to the Chocó region to oversee the liberation of the captive general. We had lived through two weeks of anxiety, amid rumors spread by the media with everyone speculating on the possible intentions of an army general who had behaved so irresponsibly and whose recklessness had endangered the whole peace process. But I remained calm, despite being under immense pressure to break off negotiations. I knew it was a situation that could be resolved, and that it had been due to an error by the general rather than a return of the Farc to its kidnapping strategy. And so, as soon as the episode was over, I authorized our delegation to return to Havana.

Two days after his liberation, General Alzate gave a press conference, accompanied by his wife and two children, in which he announced that he was resigning from the army as an act of responsibility after the harm his capture had caused to the institution. "My desire to give service and my love for the people of Chocó led me to not apply the security procedures that I should have adopted to travel," he said. But this kind of error is one that an officer cannot afford to commit, least of all a man of such high rank.

"HOW MANY MORE CORPSES DO WE NEED?"

In the early months of 2015, the ferocity with which the Farc fought seemed to have abated. From December of the preceding year, the guerrillas had decreed a unilateral and indefinite ceasefire; they had also announced their decision not to recruit minors, and had reached an agreement to begin a pilot project of humanitarian demining. On March 10, in light of the evidence of goodwill on the part of the Farc, I decided to make a reciprocal gesture to continue diminishing the intensity of the conflict: I ordered the armed forces to suspend the bombing of Farc camps.

However, we were rudely shaken out of any false sense of complacency on April 14 by a lamentable act that caused general consternation. Around midnight, a guerrilla contingent attacked a group of soldiers who were sleeping in a sports stadium in a village in the municipality of Buenos Aires in the department of Cauca. Eleven men were killed—a sergeant, a corporal, and nine infantrymen—and another twenty were wounded. It was a total massacre.

In the face of such a brutal breaking of the Farc's promise of a ceasefire, I lifted the suspension of bombing and ordered the troops to combat the subversive group with greater intensity.

An investigation by the authorities revealed that a lack of discipline had led the military contingent to commit tactical errors: in contravention of superior orders, the soldiers had spent more than twenty-four hours in the same place, and, confident that the Farc would keep to their promise of a ceasefire, they had not taken the customary security measures.

I grieved for the deaths of those soldiers and felt, as did all Colombians, the sorrow their families were experiencing at that moment. At the same time, I realized that the military had been in error and the massacre could have been avoided. The Farc, for their part, claimed that their contingent had responded to a siege by the military. Nonetheless, they ratified their intention of maintaining a unilateral ceasefire.

On May 21, in a joint operation, the armed forces and the police struck the guerrilla structure a devastating blow and evened the score with the guerrilla group that had murdered the soldiers in Cauca a month before. Twenty-six guerrilla fighters were killed, and the Farc, as was to be expected, lifted the ceasefire and went back on the offensive.

This was war, the *lex talionis*, the law of retaliation, an eye for an eye and a tooth for a tooth. For centuries, this law has ruled humanity and has led to ever-increasing scenarios of violence. Our armed forces had done what they had to do, but as a human being, I felt we had to stop this bloodshed, and the sooner the better. In an address the day after the military attack on the Farc, I made the following statement:

> The majority of Colombians applaud this blow against the guerrillas, and we all acknowledge the work of our soldiers and policemen in accomplishing their mission. The guerrillas will now be thinking about how to retaliate. But it is precisely that spiral of violence, hate, revenge, and retaliation that has led us into fifty years of war. We have to stop it and transform it into a spiral of pardon and reconciliation.
>
> That is the great challenge facing all Colombians in our hearts. To put aside hate and rancor. Our goal, our purpose, has to be to end this war and end it as soon as possible. . . . I call on you, members of the Farc. The time

has come for negotiations to move faster. How many more corpses do we need before we understand that the time has come for peace?

FIRST MEETING WITH TIMOCHENKO

Once the bases for what was going to be a solution to the problem of justice had been established by the commission of jurists on September 19, 2015, and approved by the negotiating table in Havana—although this point had not yet been definitively committed to paper, a task that would not be concluded until the end of November—we were ready to let the country know of this great step forward. We needed to revive the Colombians' enthusiasm and hope, which had been diminishing as so many months went by without our having anything new to show.

We decided to announce this in Cuba, in my presence and in that of the Farc's top leader, on September 23. We would have liked the signing of the basis for the creation of the JEP to have taken place in the presence of Pope Francis, who had been in Cuba from September 20 to 22. However, the Vatican thought, quite rightly, that the pope could hardly endorse an agreement that was not yet complete to stop a war that was still going on.

I had a second reason for going to Havana. Officially, I would be there to give protocol status to the progress made on the issue of justice. But I had something else in mind that nobody yet knew about: I intended to put a time limit on the signing of a final agreement. I am very aware, and advisers have always told me, of the inconvenience of setting deadlines. At the start, I said that the talks would be over in a matter of months, not years, but after the first year had gone by, and then the second and the third, people were quick to remind me of my exaggerated optimism. Of course, any naming of a specific time lapse is susceptible to variation, especially if it depends on others, and in this case, on a guerrilla movement whose best ally in negotiations was precisely the time factor.

Nevertheless, now that we had overcome one of our major obstacles, that of the justice issue, I felt I ought to insist on a final date in order to create a sense of urgency among the delegates on both sides and make things move faster. After consulting with the government's delegates, we decided that another six months would be enough if they could hurry things along, and above all, if there really was a will to reach that final agreement.

I asked the government's team to advise Timochenko and his delegates of my proposal, but their reply—as I might have expected from a guerrilla who was in anything but a hurry—was in the negative. They were not prepared to place a time limit on the process. That being the case, on the night before the ceremony in Havana, with everything ready for the signing, I canceled the trip because no agreement had been reached on this point. I wasn't kidding. I was determined not to go. And the guerrillas got the message. They realized the importance for them of having the president of Colombia physically present for the first time in the process. So their negotiators got a move on, and finally, albeit with reluctance, the Farc delegation accepted the time limit. And I flew to Havana.

Why was I fixing a deadline? Basically, to oblige the negotiators to increase the pace. And it worked. We agreed that the final agreement for ending the conflict would be signed at the latest in six months—that is, on March 23, 2016—and the Farc would lay down their arms within sixty days of the signing of said agreement. As things turned out, they did not keep to the date and the agreement was not ready to be signed until five months later, in August 2016. Still, although the Farc would have been quite content to delay things for another year or two, having a chronometer going *tick-tock* over their heads forced them to negotiate without too much delay.

Now that the decision on a time limit had been made, I met with Timochenko on September 23 in a private room at the Havana Convention Center. A Colombian president had not met with a commander of the Farc since February 2001, when President Andrés Pastrana and the historic guerrilla leader Manuel Marulanda came together at Los Pozos in the demilitarized zone in an effort to resuscitate the already moribund Caguán peace process. Over fourteen years later, a similar meeting was being held, but this time in an atmosphere of reasonable optimism. Having successfully crossed the bridge of the justice problem, the process had reached a point of no return.

Our encounter was brief and cordial, but tense nonetheless. Timochenko was recovering from a bout of dengue, a tropical illness, and was not at his best. "Look, Timoleón," I said, "you and I have been fighting one another, but now we're in the same boat, rowing in the same direction. If we want to reach our goal, which is peace, we'll have to pull together. I want you to know that I'm committed to this. For me, it's not a game."

"Nor is it for me either," he said. But then he added: "Mr. President, I don't think it would be a good idea to fix a deadline for the final agreement. A lot of difficulties could arise." I was dumbfounded. They had told me we had an agreement on the deadline, and that's why I made the trip. Only later did I learn that the guerrilla negotiators hadn't told Timochenko. He had arrived in Havana at dawn that morning and thought the matter was still under discussion. "So why am I here? To waste my time?" I said, visibly annoyed. "It's already decided. If not, I wouldn't have come."

We called for the heads of the negotiating teams, Humberto de la Calle and Iván Márquez, and after a brief conversation in which I emphatically insisted on the deadline, the matter was cleared up: there would be a deadline, and it would be announced that same day, although Timochenko was still not too happy about it. "President," he said. "My concern is that if we don't keep to the deadline, everyone will blame us, while you have access to the media and can give your version of things."

"That's not going to happen," I assured him. "We're in the same boat, and we're not going to let it sink."

After I had made that promise, we went into the building's main hall, where the media and some special guests were waiting for us, and together we made a double announcement, which the country received in a spirit of hope: first, that we had agreed that the final accord should be signed in a lapse of six months and that sixty days later, the Farc would disarm; and second, that we had reached an agreement on the bases for what was to be the system of transitional justice.

During this act, Timochenko and I were sitting at the main table on either side of the Cuban president Raúl Castro. Once the event was over, and in the midst of applause from the delegations and special guests, I offered my hand to President Castro. At this, Timochenko stretched out his hand to me. Castro took it and joined our hands, placing his over ours to give, as it were, a seal of authority to what had just taken place.

I had been rather circumspect, not showing the emotion I was feeling. My advisers—and especially Martín, my son—had insisted I should not show affection to the leader of the Farc so as not to add further fuel to the arguments of the critics who had dubbed me "Castro-Chavist" and friend of the guerrillas. I now think that such guardedness was absurd and that we ought always see the human being there is in us all so we can connect with the one in front of us, even when he's our enemy.

Six days later, on September 29, before the Seventieth General Assembly of the United Nations in New York—during a session that, coincidentally, was presided over for the first time by a Colombian woman, our ambassador María Emma Mejía—I told the international community of the progress we were making in the only peace process in the world that appeared to have hope of success. And I concluded with these words: "In Colombia—in less than six months—bells will be ringing to announce the glad tidings of peace. We pray that all the clocks in the world be synchronized with ours at that same moment, a moment of peace! A great moment for humanity!"

MUCH MORE THAN JUSTICE: A COMPREHENSIVE SYSTEM

Finally, on December 14, 2015, after a year and a half of negotiations, we were able to let the Colombian people know that we had reached an agreement on point four of the agenda: the victims. The agreement included everything to do with the issue of justice for which, after a great deal of effort, we had found a concrete solution. What we had finally created was a complete system to satisfy the rights of the victims—the center and main objective of our peace process.

The system agreed upon was called the Comprehensive System of Truth, Justice, Reparation and Non-repetition, and included a body of institutions whose aim was to guarantee the rights of the victims and contribute to the country's reconciliation. These were the Special Justice for Peace; the Commission for Truth, Coexistence and Non-repetition; and the Special Unit for the Search for Disappeared Persons in the context of the armed conflict or because of it, all of which began to function in the first half of 2018.

LESSON 6

The Victims and Their Rights Should Be at the Center of the Solution

> The hour of the victims has arrived. We have taken a gigantic step. The process in Havana is not simply a conversation behind closed doors. It is above all, and before all else, a step on the road to giving satisfaction to the victims of massive violations of their rights. This is the only way we can achieve true peace. And it is, at the same time, what encourages us and gives us strength in the midst of discussions at times plagued with discrepancies. However, by the same token, it is the raison d'être and the moral imperative that drives us to exhaust all the possibilities of dialogue in order to close this horrendous circle of violence that the Colombians have been suffering for half a century.

With these words, the head of the government's negotiating team began his address on the point concerning victims on the negotiation's agenda. They sum up extremely well the spirit of the Colombian peace process and the agreement that was reached. We went very much further than a simple regulation of the factors required to end the conflict: justice, demobilization, reincorporation, disarmament, and political participation. Because we were not attempting merely to reach an agreement to end the war but to end the cycle of wars that Colombia had been suffering almost since the country's independence and, uninterruptedly, since the end of the 1940s.

To end this long and perverse cycle of violence, it is not enough to silence the guns—although that is an important first step. What has to be achieved is true reconciliation, and for this it is indispensable to heal the wounds. Wounds will remain, of course, to remind us of the pain and the tragedies people have endured. But we can advance toward the future without bearing the burden of the past. That is why we must concentrate on guaranteeing the rights of the victims that the violence engendered for decades—and we must do this without distinguishing between victims and perpetrators. That way, we can achieve relief for those who have suffered—a relief because of justice that has been imparted, reparation that has been received, pardon that was begged for, and, above all, truth that has been revealed. And we must guarantee that the cycle will not be repeated; that is to say, that there will be no more victims tomorrow.

Many nations have done this, and the process of healing has lasted for decades, sometimes for centuries. We wanted to begin even before the start of the peace process. And that is why we set in motion the Law of Victims and Restitution of Land. Then, during the process itself, we placed the victims at the center of the solution, which helped facilitate discussions. It was easier to reach a consensus when we placed the emphasis on satisfying the rights of the victims rather than focusing on society's retaliation in the abstract when faced with a perpetrator of violence. In the final analysis, it was a question of humanity.

The justice we agreed upon is, above all, a justice for the victims. We had to respond to the victims who suffered in the past but, at the same time, avoid potential victimization in the future. Fundamentally, that is what transitional justice is about. Truth, too, is above all for the victims. Likewise the efforts to ensure reparation and guarantee nonrepetition. That is why the victims' participation was so important. For other issues on the agenda, there was a national forum per subject matter, but when we came to the point on the victims, we held regional forums as well. Over three thousand victims took part. And five delegations representing the victims traveled to Havana to participate in the process. They were made up of victims of the guerrillas, the paramilitaries, or agents of the state, without distinction, each delegation made up of twelve people who expounded their viewpoint and told their stories directly to the negotiators around the table. In addition, some twenty-seven thousand contributions were made by filling out forms either physically or virtually. All of this was taken into account in the creation of the Comprehensive System of Truth, Justice, Reparation, and Non-repetition.

After the Colombian process, it is unlikely that any other process in the world will be carried out without having as its central theme the rights of the victims, because that is the most human focus and the one that best contributes to a negotiation that is both fair and prompt. When my government came to an end, already some nine hundred thousand victims had received reparation, and dispossessed rural workers had been given legal titles to farmland that, taken together, added up to more than three hundred thousand hectares.

As Professor Heifetz had predicted, the victims were the ones who gave the greatest impetus and vitality to the process, and will also be its principal beneficiaries, as is right. They gave me unforgettable lessons in generosity, solidarity, the ability to forgive, resilience, and grandeur of spirit. So this lesson is the most important of all: victims and their rights should be at the center of the solution.

CHAPTER 33

The End of the Conflict

GENERALS IN HAVANA

Debates on the last point on the agenda, the end of the conflict—with its components; namely, a bilateral ceasefire, demobilization, and disarmament—began in March 2015, concomitantly with the point on the victims. Initially, discussions were carried on by a technical subcommission working in parallel with the main negotiating table. This was important, and looking at things now in retrospect, we could have done the same with other points on the agenda, carrying on discussions simultaneously instead of in chronological order. This would have moved negotiations along in a more expedited manner. On the other hand, however, it is possible that the Farc would have had difficulty in providing a team of negotiators who could adequately handle this kind of plan. Fortunately, it worked for this final point, the end of the conflict.

Here we introduced a novelty that was fundamental and yet had never been tried in any former attempt at peace. Since we were going to discuss technical and operational matters about which civilians have little expertise, we decided to invite five generals and an admiral, all in active service, to take part in the debates. No one better than they, with their knowledge and experience, to guide us in the steps we should take to effectively bring the conflict to an end.

To head our delegation in the subcommission, I designated a general of the army, Javier Flórez, who at the time was chairman of the Joint Chiefs of Staff of the Military Forces. I knew him well and I was well informed on his operational ability and his qualities as a human being. He had commanded the joint task force that was created to combat and neutralize the Farc in the Eastern Plains and Orinoquia, the most important areas financially and logistically for the guerrillas. He had also taken part in operations that had brought down members of the guerrilla's Secretariat. In short, he was a troops' general, greatly admired by his men. He accepted, responsibly and with enthusiasm, my invitation to work in Havana to obtain the best possible conditions, from a military point of view, for making concrete decisions to end the conflict. He would be accompanied by generals Martín Fernando Nieto and Alfonso Rojas, also from the army; Oswaldo Rivera, from the air force; Álvaro Pico, from the police force; and from the navy, Orlando Romero, who is today a vice-admiral. All of these men had fought the guerrillas on the ground, yet were now ready to sit down with their adversaries to agree on a ceasefire and demobilization.

Those on the political right, ever critical of everything about our peace process, raised their voices to denounce this scandal. According to them, it was humiliating and undignified for high-ranking officials in active service to have to sit down at the same table with the guerrillas. It's treating the armed forces as equivalent to terrorists, tweeted Uribe. In fact, it was quite the opposite. It would have been undignified and humiliating if people who were neither army men nor police—lacking their experience and knowledge of war and of the terrain—were to be in charge of such delicate matters that would necessarily involve our soldiers and our police officers. The men who had directed the war would now help us to build the peace.

The guerrilla founder and leader, Manuel Marulanda, had said this years ago, and he was right: "Only when there are military personnel at the table will you have peace."

For the Farc, the subcommission comprised several guerrilla leaders coordinated by Carlos Antonio Lozada. They included veteran commanders such as Joaquín Gómez, Romaña and Fabián Ramírez, among others.

During the debates, nobody wore a uniform. At the start, as was to be expected, things were tense. After all, the men now face to face with only a table between them had spent decades trying to kill one another. After a while, however, an atmosphere of cordiality and respect prevailed. They even ended up swapping anecdotes and recalling events that took place during the conflict. General Rojas, for example, had been the officer in charge of the Rapid Display Force (Fudra) in August 2007 when he and his men attacked Lozada's guerrilla camp. Lozada had escaped, though badly wounded. In Havana, they talked of these battles and each man would tell the other his side of the story. Lozada said to Rojas, "You eviscerated me!" and to prove it, raised his shirt to show the scars on his belly.

I was defense minister at the time we carried out the operation against

Lozada. We had been pursuing him as head of the Farc's urban militias, and I was carefully following the development of the operation to eliminate him. He managed to get away, but we found his portable computer and that provided us with key information on the guerrillas' activities and strategies. We discovered that they had concrete plans to assassinate at least ten public figures, including President Uribe; his interior minister, Fernando Londoño; and me. They had also been tailing the banker Luis Carlos Sarmiento and former vice-president Humberto de la Calle. In my case, they had amassed data on my timetable, routes, activities, the neighborhood where I was living, and the vehicles I used. They even had information on my security scheme.

While recovering from his wounds, Lozada was cared for by a young woman from the guerrilla organization who went by the name of Milena, and they fell in love. Once the conflict was over, like a lot of other guerrilla couples, they had a daughter, Dalila, conceived, like the peace agreement, in Havana. I met Lozada in Cartagena in September 2016 at the signing of the agreement. I was shaking hands with the man who had tried to kill me and whom I, as defense minister, had been doing my best to eliminate. He told me his story and I found it very moving. He and I had been adversaries, but Dalila was a child of the peace. So I offered to guarantee that she could one day get into university, and I was able to do this courtesy of Global Education.

Our high-ranking military officers carried out their labors admirably, and also served as a bridge, helping members of the armed forces to understand the progress and development of the process. We had, too, important international support at the highest level: the French diplomat Jean Arnault, who had taken part in missions in Guatemala, Burundi, Afghanistan, Georgia, and Pakistan, came to us as delegate of the United Nations secretary-general to participate in the subcommission to end the conflict. Later, Ban Ki-moon would appoint him special representative and head of the United Nations mission in Colombia. As such, he played a fundamental role in implementing the peace accord, a work he accomplished right up until his mission was completed in December 2018.

In January 2016, the subcommission submitted its recommendations to the negotiating table, and on the basis of this document—the result of an agreement between men from both sides who were experts in matters of war—a complex mechanism was elaborated to facilitate a dignified and effective end to Colombia's—and the Western Hemisphere's—longest war.

THE ROLE OF THE UNITED NATIONS

The process was now in its final stages. We didn't manage to get everything agreed on schedule, by March 23, 2016, but having fixed a deadline did help to get negotiations moving faster. The main thing was that we were now on a path that would certainly lead us to the end of the conflict and, before that, to a bilateral and definitive ceasefire. At this stage, with all the points agreed upon, it didn't make sense to negotiate in the middle of war. Nobody wants to be the last person killed before a peace agreement is signed. The time had come to close down the victim factory.

As early as October 29, 2015, after a meeting with the minister of foreign affairs, María Ángela Holguín; the peace commissioner, Sergio Jaramillo; the head of our negotiating team, Humberto de la Calle; and the UN delegate Jean Arnault, we saw that the best way to hasten the process and come as quickly as possible to a bilateral and definitive ceasefire would be to request the UN Security Council for a mandate to create a special mission to verify and monitor such a ceasefire.

I immediately got in touch with the five governments that had a permanent seat on the council. I spoke personally with the British prime minister, David Cameron; the French president, François Hollande; and the US secretary of state, John Kerry; all enthusiastic friends of Colombia's peace process, and they assured me of their support. With China's president, Xi Jinping, I had a meeting on November 18 in Manila on occasion of the Asia-Pacific Economic Cooperation summit to which Colombia was the only nonmember invited. The following day I met with the Russian prime minister, Dmitri Medvedev. I had already had an opportunity to have a first contact with President Vladimir Putin on July 16, 2014, at the summit meeting of the BRICs countries in Brazil. The day after our meeting, Putin returned to Russia and his plane flew over the exact coordinates of the Malaysia Airlines jet on route from Amsterdam to Kuala Lumpur that was brought down by a missile fired from Ukrainian soil. Putin's plane had flown over that very spot just minutes before, and there was speculation about a possible attempt on his life. However, after four years of independent investigation into the attack, it was shown that the missile had been launched by the Russians. But to return to the issue of the Security Council, both Russia and China gave it their full support.

As a result, on January 25, 2016, the UN Security Council passed a resolution to create the special mission of verification and monitoring of the agreement with the Farc on a bilateral and definitive ceasefire, and on the laying down of arms. The resolution was passed with the unanimous vote of all fifteen members of the council, something that had rarely occurred.

Then, on September 13, 2016, another resolution was passed on the mission's size, mandate, and operational specifications. The following year, on July 10, 2017, a second mission was created to accompany the reincorporation of the ex-guerrillas into civilian life and to verify their safety and that of communities that had been victims of the armed conflict. On September 14 the same year, the size and mandate of the second mission were defined. Then, on September 13, 2018, this mandate was prolonged for a year more, and, finally, it was prolonged for another year on September 12, 2019. All six resolutions received the unanimous vote of the United Nations' top organ for security and world peace—something that had never happened before.

The role of the United Nations—with the unconditional support of Secretary-General Ban Ki-moon and later his successor, António Guterres—was crucial in the final stages of the process, and is still of vital importance for the implementation of the agreement. Above all, it affords us an indispensable element: the confidence that everything agreed on will be carried out under the vigilance and control of international experts.

THE LAST DAY OF THE WAR

On June 23, 2016, I went back to Havana and encountered a much more relaxed atmosphere than I had the year before. Not surprising, since we were going to make a decades-long dream come true. Although we had not yet reached the point of signing the final agreement—there were a few matters still to be defined and put on paper, we had come to a point where everything indicated we had almost reached our goal: a bilateral and definitive ceasefire, the end of hostilities, and a definitive chronogram for the laying down of arms once the final agreement was signed.

Very early that morning, I tweeted a message: "On my way to Havana to silence the guns forever." We flew out of Bogotá at seven a.m. in a plane bursting with good cheer. Most of my ministers were on board, as well as my brother Enrique, plus the president of the Senate and former president of Colombia César Gaviria. Other special guests were waiting for us in Havana: representatives of support from the international community, beginning with Ban, accompanied by the president of the General Assembly and the president of the Security Council. Five heads of state from the region were there to witness the event: the presidents of the accompanying countries, Michelle Bachelet of Chile and Nicolás Maduro of Venezuela; the president of Mexico, Enrique Peña Nieto; the president of the Dominican Republic and CELAC, Danilo Medina; and the president of El Salvador, Salvador Sánchez. The foreign affairs minister of Norway, Borge Brende, was among the guests, and also, of course, the special envoys of the United States and the European Union, Bernie Aronson and Eamon Gilmore. They had all come in response to the good news: that day, Colombia's war with the Farc would be over.

The following were our specific commitments:

- Above all else, to end definitively offensive actions between the armed forces and the Farc.
- Create a mechanism for monitoring and verifying. This would be composed of three groups: (1) a mission of unarmed observers from the United Nations; (2) the government—represented in the armed forces; and (3) the Farc. This mission would be charged with ensuring compliance with the ceasefire and the laying down of arms.
- Create rural zones and provisional camps for normalization—at the start, the Farc wanted more than eighty zones for the concentration of their members, but finally there were twenty zones and seven camps. In these zones, thousands of guerrilla combatants would gather during the ceasefire and would begin their preparation for reincorporating into civil society.
- A timeline for the laying down of arms and the final disposal of these arms by the United Nations, to be carried out in several stages and in a lapse of 180 days after the signing of the final agreement.

These were very significant and concrete aims. We could never have imagined, just six years before, that the Farc—after a complex process full of difficulties but also of goodwill—would now be signing a commitment to give up arms and, without them, enter civil society to take part in the procedures of democracy.

In the midst of applauses from all present, applause that was echoed in public squares around the country where the event was being watched on gigantic outdoor screens, de la Calle and Márquez, heads of the negotiating teams, signed the agreement on the bilateral and definitive ceasefire and the laying down of arms. At 12:42, under a midday sun, Timochenko and I also signed, and at that exact moment—more than fifty-two years after it had begun—the armed confrontation between the Farc and the Colombian state ended for good. Never again would anyone be killed because of that conflict. Those present could not hide their emotions. Many could not hold back their tears, mixed with expressions of happiness. Our host president, Raúl Castro, took the floor and addressed the assembled guests. "Peace will be a victory for the Colombians," he said, "but also for everyone in the Americas."

Next to speak was Ban, who reconfirmed the United Nations' commitment to helping "convert this extraordinary process of negotiation into an exemplary implementation of commitments to peace." Then Timochenko made a speech, concluding with words of exhortation: "Let this be the last day of war."

When he stepped down from the podium, I went up to him and gave him a "bullet pen." I got this idea from my education minister, Gina Parody: a pen made of bullet material, symbolizing the transition from war to words. It was inscribed with a sentence I quoted to the Farc commander: "Bullets wrote our past, education will write our future."

The ceremony ended with my address, in which I said the following:

> All my life, from that day, almost fifty years ago, when my mother handed me a rifle representing the arms of the republic—a ritual still practiced by anyone entering the naval academy—I have been an implacable enemy of the Farc. I doubt if there is any Colombian who has combated them with greater fervor and determination.
>
> Now that we have signed the peace, as head of state and as a Colombian, I will defend—with no less determination—their right to express themselves and to continue their political struggle by legal means, even though we may never agree. This is the essence of democracy, to which we are glad to give them welcome.

CHAPTER 34

"The Horrible Night Is Over"

"WE HAVE AGREED ON EVERYTHING"

On August 24, 2016, just two months after signing the bilateral and definitive ceasefire, the negotiators published the most anticipated of their joint communiqués to announce that they had "reached a final agreement, comprehensive and definitive, on the totality of all points on the agenda."

This long communiqué included the following paragraph: "After a confrontation that lasted for over half a century, the national government and the Farc-EP have agreed to put an end definitively to the internal armed conflict."

These few words sum up succinctly the realization of a dream that for decades we had been trying to make come true, that had been too long delayed, but that had, at last, become a reality.

In addition, each of the heads of the two negotiating teams wrote his own communiqué, reflecting on the process. Humberto de la Calle's text ended with a profound personal reflection:

> To have reached an agreement with the Farc-EP does not mean either of us has betrayed his convictions. My convictions and values remain intact, and I imagine those of the guerrillas also. The negotiating table was not an exercise in condescension nor an exchange of impunities, but it did signify, for me, that I have grown spiritually, that I now know Colombia better, and that what so many of my compatriots have suffered pains me more than ever before, but I have also learned a great deal about the Colombians' capacity to resist, their generosity and their joyfulness.

On the Farc's side, Iván Márquez wrote the following: "We can proclaim that the war with arms is over and now begins the debate with ideas. We confess that we have just concluded the most beautiful of all battles: that of laying the foundations for building peace and coexistence."

On the afternoon of August 23, the day before the public announcement, I was in my office in Casa de Nariño, waiting for news of the close of the negotiation stage. For me, this was the culmination not of six but of twenty years of work and initiatives, on different fronts and with diverse strategies, to achieve this result: peace with the country's largest and oldest guerrilla army, and peace for Colombia. I was twelve years old when the Farc came into existence, and have lived my life in the midst of armed conflict—first the partisan war between Liberals and Conservatives, then the guerrillas' fight against the state, added to the perverse activities of drug traffickers and paramilitaries. Many generations of Colombians, mine included, had not known a single day of peace. The end of this conflict was the start of a new era.

This process had taken a long time to get off the ground: a year and a half of messages, secret contacts, and preparatory meetings in Venezuela; half a year of confidential exploratory meetings in Havana to define the agenda; and four years of negotiations in peace talks around a table. An enormous effort, and a generous investment in time and work on the part of the negotiators, consultants, participants from the international community. Finally, we were seeing the fruit of our labors. We had insisted that "nothing is agreed until everything is agreed." And now, at last, after countless debates, we could say: "We have agreed on everything."

My private secretary, Enrique Riveira, came into my office and said: "The foreign affairs minister wants to speak to you from Havana." So it was that, even before I got calls from Jaramillo and de la Calle, María Ángela Holguín had given me the best news ever: negotiations with the Farc had been successfully concluded. Riveira and I embraced one another and then went across to his office that has a balcony where we could smoke a cigarette. It's a secret vice of mine, which I succumb to only on rare occasions, and this was the first cigarette I could enjoy without the shadow of war hanging over Colombia.

THE LAST GUERRILLA CONGRESS

Now, since I had promised the Colombians an opportunity to ratify the final text of the agreement with their vote, in my address to the Colombians on

August 24 to celebrate the end of negotiations, I announced a plebiscite to be held on October 2. I also announced that on August 25 the complete agreement would be published, as well as summaries in explanatory pamphlets, on websites, social networks, and the communications media in general, so that every Colombian would have a chance to read and study it and decide how he or she would vote in October.

The Farc, for their part, also had to validate the agreement with their people. To do so, their general staff called for the Tenth National Guerrilla Conference, to be held between September 17 and 23 on the plains of Yarí in the rural area of San Vicente de Caguán, the municipality in Caquetá that had been the epicenter of the previous peace process. It was the first time the Farc had come together for a national conference without having to do so clandestinely, but in full view of everyone, because this time their meeting was being held with the protection afforded by the bilateral ceasefire. In fact, it was covered exhaustively by the news media. And there, in Yarí, delegates from all the guerrilla fronts gave their approval to the agreement.

And something very important began to appear among ordinary members of the guerrilla army: there was a rebirth of joy and the right to have a family. Guerrilla couples who had submitted to the rigors of war and were continually on the march were uncertain about the future, and women were forbidden to get pregnant. But when it was known that a peace agreement had been reached and the ceasefire was declared, many couples who had long wanted to have children saw they could now make that dream come true. In the months that followed, you could see dozens of guerrilla women proudly showing off the swollen bellies that carried a new human being. It was the triumph of life over death.

"IN FURROWS OF PAIN, PEACE IS NOW BEING GERMINATED"

Meanwhile, the government prepared for the plebiscite, employing every possible means to explain the agreement so it would be understood by the population. At the same time, we made preparations for the official signing of the agreement, which we decided should be held in Cartagena, for a very special reason: Cartagena is the historic city where Saint Peter Claver carried out his humanitarian apostolate to the slaves, and he is the patron saint of human rights. It was a fitting site for our ceremony since the agreement was based on human rights and was centered on the victims.

It seemed to me a good idea to carry out the formal act of signing the agreement a few days before the plebiscite, thinking that the moment would be so emotional that the Colombians would be even more motivated to go the ballot boxes and ratify the peace we had signed. But this did not happen. On the contrary, it turned out to be counterproductive. Since the signing was accompanied by such a solemn act in the presence of representatives of the international community, to many Colombians who would have voted yes it looked as if the agreement was already a fact and so they did not bother to vote on the following Sunday. Our opponents, by contrast, took advantage of the event to campaign against the agreement and gained the limelight by criticizing us for having celebrated our victory ahead of time. Uribe made the trip to Cartagena on the day of the ceremony to lead a demonstration in favor of the no vote.

In the presidential guesthouse in Cartagena, I spent the day before the ceremony preparing my speech. It was an exceptional moment and I wanted to mark the occasion by opening my address with words from our national anthem that had been written by Rafael Núñez in the nineteenth century, and that all Colombians know by heart: "Oh, unfading glory! Oh, immortal jubilation! In furrows of pain, good is already germinating." And I added a new slant to those verses: "In furrows of pain, peace is now being germinated!"

On Monday, September 26, Cartagena had rarely looked so good. The beautiful port city was to be the site of an event Colombia had long been waiting for, and the historical center was bustling with visitors all dressed in white, getting ready to attend the official signing of the agreement. At midday, however, a torrential storm broke out and sent everyone running for cover. Fortunately, at three o'clock in the afternoon the sun was out again and people began to arrive for the ceremony, a celebration of hope, in the main square of Cartagena's convention center.

The act was full of symbolism and emotion. On the central platform there were heads of government and representatives of foreign countries, dignitaries from international organs, plus the negotiators from both sides. Timochenko and I greeted one another cordially, far removed now from the tensions that had marked our first encounter. We knew we were keeping an appointment with history. On the square below us, hundreds of people—many of them victims of the conflict—waved white handkerchiefs and cried out, "Yes, it's happened! Yes, it's happened!" Enthusiasm and joy could be seen everywhere.

One of the most impressive moments came when a chorus of women from Bojayá, the village that had been razed by guerrilla violence in May 2002, intoned the traditional song of praise—a typical Chocó mantra sung at funerals—with lyrics about peace and a plea that war never be waged again in Colombia. To conclude the event, a chorus of children stirred the public with their interpretation of the Ode to Joy from Beethoven's Ninth Symphony.

In the midst of a standing ovation, our hearts overflowing, Timochenko and I signed the agreement. We signed with the bullet pen that symbolized our country's transition from war to peace. After we had signed, I did something I would do later with Pope Francis: I took the little brooch with the figure of a dove that I had pinned to my shirt and handed it to the man who up to that day had been the last leader of the Farc. He smiled and pinned it to his own shirt.

This was followed by a speech from Timochenko during which something happened that the crowd had not expected. My younger son, Esteban, had done military service in the army and has a high regard for the armed forces. So it occurred to him that, at the moment homage was being paid to the sacrifice of Colombia's soldiers and policemen, he would organize for three Kfir planes from the air force to fly across Cartagena's sky in representation of the armed forces. I thought it was a good idea, and Esteban coordinated the display with General Carlos Eduardo Bueno, commander of the Colombian Air Force. But things didn't work out exactly as planned. The act went on for longer than we had foreseen, Timochenko made a very long speech, and the Kfir planes that had been flying around nearby awaiting their turn found they were running out of fuel. So they were ordered to fly at once over the official platform, which they did. It was already past six in the evening and Timochenko, still talking, was referring to a character from García Márquez when, in the middle of sentence about how "the love of Mauricio Babilonia for Meme could now last forever," the supersonic jets thundered over our heads with a frightening roar of engines that shook us like a tremendous explosion. Once we had more or less recovered our composure, people broke into applause, and Timochenko remarked with good humor: "Well . . . they came here to celebrate peace, not to drop bombs."

Aside from this humorous incident, Timochenko's speech contained a couple of memorable passages: one, when he began with a phrase that has become his group's slogan, "Our only weapon will be the word"; and two, when he said "In the name of the Farc-EP, I sincerely beg all the victims of the conflict to forgive us for all the pain we have caused them in this war."

The majority of the victims are prepared to forgive. But one can imagine how important it was for them to hear a plea for pardon from the one who had caused the harm. In that way, both sides are freed.

To conclude the ceremony, I stood up and made the most important speech of my life, addressing my remarks to the assembled public and to the whole country. I thanked the negotiators, the international community, the armed forces, and the victims. I acknowledged, too, the goodwill and the seriousness the Farc delegates had shown during the peace talks. And I added what follows: "Every peace agreement is imperfect because it is precisely that: an agreement, in which both sides have to make concessions. But we know that on this occasion we have reached the best agreement possible. I prefer an imperfect agreement that saves lives to a perfect war that continues to sow death and suffering in our country, among our families."

And as I had begun by quoting from our anthem, I ended by recalling one of its most notable phrases: "The horrible night is over!"

PART FIVE

Building Peace (2016–2018)

CHAPTER 35

The Plebiscite

A SUI GENERIS AGREEMENT

The agreement we achieved, with all its components, was analyzed and evaluated by specialized institutions in different parts of the world. One of the most important of these was the Kroc Institute for International Peace Studies at Notre Dame University, which categorized it as one of the most complete and innovative peace agreements in the history of such processes worldwide. A professor at this university, John Paul Lederach, said that "comparatively, the Colombian agreement offers one the most promising platforms for ensuring a sustainable peace."

What does the Colombian peace agreement have that makes it sui generis?

- It is an agreement centered on the victims: on acknowledging them and guaranteeing their right to justice, truth, reparation, and nonrepetition.
- It includes a model of transitional justice in which, for the first time, both parties in the conflict submit voluntarily to a tribunal that will investigate, make judgment on, and sanction the offenses committed in the course of the conflict or occasioned by it, which will be considered serious war crimes or crimes against humanity. It guarantees nonimpunity with respect to these offenses, and will sanction them with punishments that go from five to eight years of effective restriction of freedom and up to twenty years' imprisonment, depending on the perpetrator's contribution to truth. All of this in accordance with the parameters established by the Statute of Rome, international treaties on human rights and international humanitarian law, and Colombia's constitution and laws.

- In the words of Borja Paladini, the Kroc Institute's representative in Colombia, the Colombian agreement is one of the most innovative because "it is the one that contains the most instruments for protecting, guaranteeing and verifying. Also, because it develops, in the most detailed and comprehensive manner, the conflict's substantial issues—its root causes—as matters that require solutions: the land question, political participation, the quality of democracy, the fight against the drug trade and the substitution of illegal crops. And finally because it develops, as no other agreement had done, subsidiary issues such as women's rights, ethnic groups, the victims, and because the whole agreement is permeated by a focus on human rights."
- For the first time, high-ranking officers of the armed forces in retirement—an ex-commander of the military forces and a former director-general of the police force—acted as plenipotentiary negotiators, while other high-ranking officers, this time in active service, participated in analysis and discussion on the subjects of ceasefire and disarmament.
- Another innovative factor was the creation of a subcommission on gender that made sure women's voices and the gender perspective were included in the agreements.
- There were also meetings with ethnic communities—indigenous and Afro-Colombians—who were profoundly affected by the conflict. This led to incorporating a chapter on ethnicity into the final agreement.
- And something fundamental: The agreement went beyond merely silencing the guns; it ensured the recovery and comprehensive development of those rural areas most affected by the violence, what we called "territorial peace." For this, we agreed to put in motion sixteen development plans with a territorial focus, the PDET, discussed and constructed by the communities themselves, where priority would be given to the public works most urgently needed for the community to integrate into the economic and social dynamics of the rest of Colombia.

The abovementioned elements meant that the peace agreement signed by the Colombian government and the Farc was the first of a new generation of agreements around the world that would understand, thanks to our agreement, that an agreement on peace is designed not only to stop the war but to generate conditions that will prevent it being repeated.

"REFERENDUMS ARE IN THE HANDS OF THE DEVIL"

When it comes to analyzing past events, we're all sages. But decisions are made in the present, and so can be erroneous. From the start of the exploratory phase in Havana in February 2012, the Farc and the government coincided—and I constantly insisted—that, at the end of the process, there should be some form of popular consent to ratify the agreement. This would provide the peace agreement with greater legitimacy, especially as we were including issues that went beyond the guerrillas' demobilization and disarmament, such as land, the broadening of democracy, the problem of illegal drugs, and the comprehensive coverage we wanted to offer the victims.

Putting the question to the public seemed to make a lot of sense, and nobody thought for a moment that, after a tremendous effort of negotiation in which each side had to cede on one point or another, the citizens would reject an agreement that was going to put an end to half a century of war. The Farc were in favor of a constituent assembly, but that would only open a Pandora's box of multiple reforms that would go far beyond what had been agreed on. We in the government studied the possibility of a referendum, but decided it would not work in practice because the citizens would have to vote on each issue separately. Finally, we hit on the idea of a plebiscite, a proposal the guerrilla delegation finally accepted, but only after much debate back and forth. The plebiscite would consist of just one question to which the reply would be yes or no: "Do you support the final agreement to end the conflict and build a stable and enduring peace?"

We were proud of what we had achieved. In the words of de la Calle, it was "the best possible agreement." We knew we had made an enormous effort and confidently entrusted the result to the Colombians for their approval. But we forgot something that history should have taught us: that in referendums or plebiscites, people vote on anything but the question being asked. Very often, the vote is decided on such factors as emotions, a whim of the moment, the government's approval rating, and so forth.

In 1969, when the great French leader Charles de Gaulle called for a referendum to give greater autonomy to his country's regions, he lost and ended up resigning. Some attribute to him a phrase that has become famous: "Referendums are in the hands of the Devil." Because, when all is said and done, emotions are the deciding factor, rather than rational thinking. That was what happened in the United Kingdom in 2016 when Prime Minister Cameron, convinced he was going to win, called for a referendum to ask the

British whether or not they wished to continue in the European Union. To everyone's surprise, the majority voted for Brexit; that is, to leave the union.

They were encouraged to do so by a series of lies and exaggerations like the 350 million pounds sterling that Britain was supposedly sending every week to the Europeans, or that Turkey was about to become a member nation and would oblige England to receive millions of Turkish immigrants. On the day after the Brexit vote, the "Regrexit" movement began; millions of those who had voted to leave the union discovered they had been misled and began to fear the consequences of their decision. Cameron had to resign. In December of that same year, the Italian prime minister, Matteo Renzi, was also obliged to step down because of a lost referendum. These two European leaders had become close friends of mine and were enthusiastic supporters of our peace process.

I embarked, and embarked the country, on a plebiscite, convinced as I was that this would give added strength to our agreement and would help unite the Colombian people in their efforts to implement the agreement and begin to build peace. And besides, I was committed to submitting the agreement to popular approval. It was a promise I had to honor. I never tired of repeating, "The Colombians will have the last word." But I never imagined, or foresaw, that the opposition's lies and half truths would have such an effect, nor that a nation that had suffered so much because of a war would be capable of putting its end in jeopardy.

It was a mistake, as events were to prove. If I could turn back the clock, I would not play the popular-vote card. However, as the saying goes, "God writes straight with crooked lines." And the situation, which looked bad, ended up becoming a new opportunity.

"LIE, THEN LIE AGAIN, AND SOMETHING WILL STICK"

The adage "Lie, then lie again, and something will stick" is an ancient one. It was already in vogue, with different variations, in the time of Alexander the Great when his adviser Medius of Larissa said: "Sow calumny, bite with it, and when people have healed the wound, the scar will still be there." It has been attributed to Goebbels, Hitler's sinister propaganda minister, so much admired by Uribe's ideologue José Obdulio Gaviria, and it was popularized in Colombia by the Conservative leader Laureano Gómez in the incendiary debates in which he was a prominent figure in the first half of the twentieth century: "Slander, slander, something of the slander will stick."

It isn't easy to defend oneself from lies, or from half truths that are falsehood's best allies. It's even harder now in these times of the internet and social networks when the lies fly like the wind. And I have to admit that neither we in the government nor friends of the process were able to credit how much weight citizens would give to the lies being spread about, and how they would influence the way people voted in the plebiscite. We scarcely found time to refute one lie when ten new ones were in circulation. And so our opponents gained ground that we did not manage to recover with pedagogy.

In WhatsApp chain messages, our opponents published outlandish falsities that people innocently believed and sent on to their contacts.

They said, for example, that Senator Roy Barreras, a government plenipotentiary at the negotiating table in the closing months, had presented a project that needed only one last debate before it became law, and would reduce pensioners' monthly allowance in order to use their money to finance the guerrillas' reincorporation.

One of these links, named "Timo for President," made out that the agreement was a first step to guarantee Timochenko the presidency of Colombia, arguing that the Farc were going to win the elections because of the immense sums of money they had accumulated and because they would oblige people under threat to vote for their candidates. Thus would "Castro- Chavism" be imposed on Colombia.

Other links claimed that we were about to do away with, or at least reduce, the armed forces. They also said the agreement would put an end to private property, that it would eliminate subsidies for the poor and that millions of hectares of land were going to be expropriated from their owners and handed over to the guerrillas.

Perhaps the lie that did us the most damage—and spread like wildfire in the week before the plebiscite, not giving us time to react—was the one that accused us of signing an agreement that established gender ideology; that is, that a person's sexual identity is a social construct rather than a fact of nature. The attorney general, Alejandro Ordóñez, a radical Catholic whom President Duque later appointed ambassador to the Organization of American States, recorded and widely circulated a video saying that in the Havana agreements gender ideology appeared "with infinite intensity." To which he added, without so much as blushing: "The intention of the government and the Farc is to establish gender ideology as a constitutional norm. . . . They are using the peace process as an excuse to impose gender ideology. Bear this in mind on October 2. You will be deciding the future of Colombia. You will be deciding the future of your children. You will be deciding the future of the Colombian family."

Memes and posters appeared everywhere with this message: "NO to abortion. NO to those who attack the family. NO to gender ideology. That's why I say NO to the Havana agreements." The worst part was that people believed all this, beginning with the pastors of Protestant Christian churches, and many—a great many—Catholic priests who advised their parishioners to vote no if they wanted to avoid belittling the concept of marriage and the family, or violating the right to life of the yet unborn.

They were lies, total lies. Nothing of all this was in the agreement. It did implement a focus on gender—something very different from gender ideology—in order to make visible and give priority to women's rights, as women had been the conflict's principal victims. But the agreement did not touch on subjects like abortion, same-sex marriage, or a definition of the family.

This defamatory campaign had a profound effect on the electorate. So much so, that surveys carried out after the plebiscite showed the issue of gender ideology was the lie that most motivated people to vote no. In later meetings with Christian pastors and Catholic priests, several admitted to me they had been naïve because they had not read the agreement, while others simply said they had been hoodwinked.

A few days after the plebiscite, this whole fabric of deceit was revealed in an interview published in the daily newspaper *La República* in which the no campaign's manager, Senator Juan Carlos Vélez, ingenuously confessed what the opposition had done.

The interviewer's question was: "The yes campaign was based on hope for a new country. What was your message?" To this, Vélez replied: "Indignation. We wanted people to go to the ballot boxes really stirred up."

"So, what was your strategy?"

"We discovered the power of the social networks. For example, in a visit to Apartadó in Antioquia, a local councilor showed me a picture of Santos and Timochenko photographed together, and underneath was the phrase: *Why give money to the guerrillas when the country's economy is in such a bad state?* I published it on my Facebook and within days, I had 130,000 viewers who, in turn, had sent the message on to a total of 6 million people. . . . We had expert advice from strategists in Panama and Brazil who recommended we should not focus on the content of the agreements, but center our campaign message on indignation."

Such unabashed revelations on the part of the no campaign's manager left the Colombians dumbfounded. The upshot was that Senator Vélez realized he had said too much and resigned from the Democratic Center party. A few weeks later, in December, the Council of State drew attention to the notorious fact that the no campaign had employed lies "on a massive scale and systematically." But it was too late. The damage had been done.

I know I made a mistake—and I don't mind admitting it—when, anxious to promote a yes vote, I appealed to people's fear instead of their hope. On one occasion, in a public meeting with Felipe González during the World Economic Forum on Latin America held in Medellín, I said that if the agreement was not approved in the plebiscite, we would be going back to war. I went even further, and added: "Reliable sources have informed us that the guerrillas are prepared to go back to war, and to urban war, which is more devastating than rural war." This was true. Younger members of the Farc were saying so, as I learned from intelligence organs. But it made a bad impression on people who saw it as a kind of threat. It was a mistake I tried not to repeat. It was not necessary to generate alarm in order to motivate Colombians to support peace.

RESIGNING IS A POSSIBILITY

When I got up on October 2, 2016, the day of the plebiscite, I felt certain that, in spite of the campaign of lies, the Colombians were going to give their enthusiastic support to the peace agreement. That morning I did what I had done before the four elections in which I had taken part: I went with my family to the Church of the Miraculous Virgin, for whom my wife has special devotion, to commend ourselves to her protection. In the afternoon, I invited the principal promoters of the yes campaign, headed by César Gaviria. I also invited the negotiators, ministers, and other members of government to be with me in the presidential residence on the third floor of the Casa de Nariño, where we would receive the election results. After the results came out, I planned to go to Hotel Tequendama, where hundreds of sympathizers had assembled, to salute them and give an address. I had gone over that speech many times, since I wanted to project the country toward a future in which the nation would come together as one. Here are some phrases from the speech I never made:

> Today—yes, today!—the split between yes and no has come to an end. Every person's opinion is to be respected and there is no reason why our differences should lead to permanent animosity, nor leave wounds that cannot be healed. If among families, or in the workplace, or among groups of friends and social networks, a breach has occurred between those who hold views different from ours . . . the time has come to unite!

That Sunday, Colombia's climate went crazy. Hurricane Matthew reached category 5 and its fury was felt especially on the Caribbean coast, the region where I had great support and where opinion polls had shown a preponderance of people in favor of the yes vote. Fierce downpours of rain, tempestuous winds, and flooding prevented thousands of citizens from voting. And not only there. It rained continually over the whole country during the hours that people were going to the ballot boxes.

Our worry was whether we would manage to get enough votes—that is, 4,536,993 yes votes—to bring us over the threshold required for the result to be valid. We were concerned, also, of course, that the yes votes would be in the majority, although we tended to take this for granted. The governors of the Caribbean departments asked the National Electoral Council to extend voting hours in those municipalities especially affected by storms, but their request went unanswered. The central government could have authorized the extension, but we did not want to intervene in any way that might have cast doubts on the validity of the final vote. We knew the opposition had planned a campaign to denounce a supposed fraud, as they had done in previous elections, and we did not want to provide any kind of justification for protests and disqualifying statements that might have tainted the result. Nonetheless, there is no doubt that prolonging voting time in the Caribbean would have meant a victory for the yes vote.

At Casa de Nariño, everyone felt optimistic. While my guests were gathering in an adjoining room, I sat in the library with de la Calle, the head of our negotiating team, to watch the results as they came in. With the usual efficiency and speed, the registrar began to publish results at four o'clock, once the voting was over. By twenty past four, we got the first bulletins; with 15 percent of votes counted, yes votes were in the lead, but only by a narrow margin. De la Calle pointed out to me that it would be a good idea to include in my address a reference to the fact that although we had won, the voting had been extremely close. I agreed, and called for my speechwriter Juan Carlos Torres, with the intention of asking him to introduce this idea into what I had prepared. However, no sooner did Torres arrive with his notebook ready to jot down a few words than bulletins began to show a change in the tendency: the number of no votes was increasing faster than yes votes until finally, with 70 percent of votes counted, the nos were in front.

I was sitting behind my desk, de la Calle at my side and Torres in front of me, the three of us looking, incredulous, at the television screen. We could hear our guests talking in the other room. María Clemencia and our two sons and our daughter were out on the balcony that leads to the library, hugging one another and crying. In the library, we scarcely did more than mutter a few words in hushed voices. I kept repeating: "I didn't count on this. I never counted on this."

It took only a few minutes before the final result came through: 13 million Colombians had gone to the polls—well above the threshold—and of these, 50.2 percent voted no, and 49.8 percent had voted yes. There were just 53,908 votes of difference.

Over the years, I have developed a kind of armor plating that, in a crisis, shields me from giving way to my emotions. This saves me from becoming overly euphoric in moments of success but also prevents me from falling into the abyss of a defeat. I simply look at what has occurred and try to think of alternatives. This has given me the strength to face difficult situations, and did so now as I stared at that screen and saw the possible collapse of years of work for peace to which I had committed my government and my own political capital.

"I'll have to analyze all the options," I said. "All of them. One of which would be to resign."

"That's true," said Torres. "There's always the question of political responsibility."

"Well, de Gaulle did that in France. And Cameron in England," added de la Calle. This was followed by a long pause. Finally, de la Calle broke the silence. "We'll be sending them back to the jungle," he said, more out of dejection than conviction.

Another lengthy silence ensued, the minutes slowly draining away like our hopes for peace. Then Torres began to speak. "Mr. President, I know resigning is an option. But this isn't a landslide victory for the nos. They didn't beat us seventy-thirty or anything like it. In practice, this is the same as a draw. And you will have to continue to represent that half of the population that believes in peace and in the agreement."

I didn't reply. My family was still outside, not wanting to burst in, respecting what we were going through at that moment. Then the door opened and in walked Sergio Jaramillo. He sat down beside de la Calle. The two men who had spent years leading the process were sharing with me this unexpected negative result.

"What should we do, Sergio?" I asked.

"What you have always taught us at such moments, Mr. President: keep calm."

I began to recover my composure—in fact, we all began gradually to recover—and I started posing a few questions and looking for solutions. "We'll have to see how the Farc people are reacting," I said. "Where are they right now?"

"They're gathered together in Havana," said Jaramillo. "They're probably as surprised as we are."

"I could call them and see how they are," suggested de la Calle.

At this moment, the guests started to come in: the negotiators; the foreign affairs, interior, and defense ministers; Senator Barreras; María Clemencia and our children; and Enrique, all looking downcast and with expressions of disbelief on their faces.

Many of those present were affected emotionally, beginning with the members of my family. I knew that in these conditions, they would not be my best counselors. So I withdrew for a few minutes to reflect in silence. I needed to be alone. I took a deep breath and began to meditate. Then, having steadied my nerves, I began to ask myself what I should do. And one single response became clear to me: I had to persevere. The only responsible way forward was to persevere.

Having decided on that, I went back to the library, and we spent a few minutes tossing ideas back and forth. We were faced with what was virtually a draw. The country was split in two; half the people liked the agreement as it was, while the other half wanted us to introduce changes. But everyone wanted peace—at least that's what they were saying. So the solution was to be found in dialogue, as in any dialectic crossroads. We would call for a broad national dialogue to see if we could agree on what should be altered, what suggestions for change we might incorporate into the final agreement. We would have to convert this dilemma into an opportunity to unite the population.

General Jorge Enrique Mora, a man accustomed to facing difficulties and inspire morale in his troops, then said something that hit me: "Mr. President, you are a leader. What is needed at this point is that you speak and tell us what to do. But don't delay. In these matters, time is of the essence."

We didn't have a Plan B, I have to admit it. It never crossed our minds that we were going to lose, and that's why we didn't have words prepared for the occasion. I gave Torres instructions on what I wanted to say and gave him fifteen minutes to prepare a draft. He literally ran out of the room and made for his office on the first floor.

A quarter of an hour later, I went down to where he was working and found that he had almost completed a brief statement. I sat at his desk and read through it a couple of times, making adjustments here and there as I went along, fully aware that a single word could mean the survival or otherwise of the peace agreement.

Then I went upstairs to deliver my address. I spoke for just three minutes, doing my best to create an atmosphere of calm and confidence among all of my compatriots: those who had won a hairsbreadth victory with a no vote, the yes voters who had narrowly lost, and the great majority who had not voted at all. Standing beside me, unable to disguise their evident feelings of concern, were Jaramillo and de la Calle, along with the rest of the negotiators—Minister Holguín, Generals Naranjo and Mora, Frank Pearl, Gonzalo Restrepo, and Senator Barreras, as well as the interior minister, Juan Fernando Cristo.

Over and above anything else, I wanted to leave no doubt that I accepted the result of the plebiscite and the victory of the nos. I announced that on the following day I was going to bring together all political forces, beginning with those who had voted no, to listen to their ideas and decide on the best way to go forward. I also said that the next day our chief negotiators, Jaramillo and de la Calle, would travel to Havana to inform the Farc negotiators of the result of our political dialogue. I assured the Colombians that the bilateral ceasefire was to be maintained, and I added something that has been a maxim guiding me all my life and that I was putting into practice more than ever at this time: "I have always believed in the wise Chinese saying: Look for opportunities in every situation. And here we have an opportunity that has been presented to us with the new political reality made manifest in the plebiscite."

I concluded with the following: "I will not give up. I will continue to seek peace until the last minute of my presidency, because that is the way that enables us to leave our children with a better country."

CHAPTER 36

From Hell to Heaven in Five Days

THE GREAT NATIONAL DIALOGUE

We didn't have time to sit and lick our wounds. We had to act, and quickly. As we had announced, Jaramillo and de la Calle flew to Havana on October 3 to meet with the Farc negotiators, who reacted very sensibly to the situation. The spokespersons for the no campaign had said they did not want to scrap the peace agreement, but modify it. So that was the route open to us. The truth of the matter is that the nos were as astonished at the result as we were. The representatives of the guerrillas, for their part, were realistic and accepted reopening negotiations to consider the possibility of making a few changes.

Meanwhile, in Colombia, I set out on a marathon of meetings with representatives of civil society and politicians from all parties and movements. Many reassured me of their support, while with others we cleared up doubts and misunderstandings—as, for example, on the alleged gender ideology question. In the case of a third group, we listened to their concerns and promised they would be taken into account in Havana. We couldn't guarantee they would all be included in discussions, but we would do our best.

On October 5, I had two important meetings at Casa de Nariño. The first was with former president Andrés Pastrana and his erstwhile commissioner for peace, Camilo Gómez. To my surprise—and that of many others—Pastrana, who had carried out an ambitious peace process with the Farc, clearing a demilitarized zone the size of Switzerland as a space for dialogue and including on the negotiation agenda every possible subject that concerned the state, had now become a bitter critic of our process in Havana.

Not even his closest friends could understand this. Pastrana's attitude had led him to join forces with the last person you could have imagined: his fellow former president Álvaro Uribe, with whom, years before, he had fallen out due to their marked differences of opinion on almost every issue.

"Mr. President," I said to him, "just as I have acknowledged the victory of the nos, I trust you will help us to move this dialogue forward to improve the agreement and salvage it. Your government's program was based on seeking peace. You, more than anyone, understand the difficulties involved in a negotiation, and now you have the opportunity to contribute to achieving the peace for which you fought so hard. You can be the one to save the peace, and in that I will ensure that you get top billing."

He seemed well disposed to my suggestion, and indicated he had delegated Gómez to explain his suggestions on how to modify the agreement and clarify certain points. For my part, I delegated the defense minister Luis Carlos Villegas and the negotiator and former peace commissioner Pearl, both friends of Pastrana. I have to say that absolutely all of the precise observations that Pastrana suggested were respected and included in the revised agreement. However, although at a certain moment he told me he was satisfied with the final result, in the end he remained obstinately opposed to it. Neither his friends nor I ever understood his attitude. "Arrogance, envy, and vanity," was the explanation I heard from someone who knows him well.

As soon as we had concluded the meeting with Pastrana, Uribe—the principal leader of the no campaign—arrived with Attorney General Ordóñez, Senator Iván Duque and ex-minister Marta Lucía Ramírez—later president and vice-president, respectively, of Colombia—Senator Paloma Valencia, former congressman Rubén Darío Molano, ex-ministers Oscar Iván Zuluaga and Carlos Holmes Trujillo—later foreign affairs minister and minister of defense—the Christian pastor César Castellanos, and the journalist Diana Sofía Giraldo, director of a foundation for victims.

Included in this delegation, to my amazement, was the retired general Héctor Fabio Velasco. This was a man who had been commander of the air force in Pastrana's government and during the first year of Uribe's, but who had been removed from active service under a cloud, having allegedly hidden and manipulated information on a massacre perpetrated in Santo Domingo, a small town in the department of Arauca, on December 13, 1998. These accusations, given credit by US investigators, referred to an incident in which Colombian Air Force planes dropped bombs on the village, causing the deaths of seventeen of its inhabitants, including six children. I could not understand why Velasco should be among the substantial group of personalities that accompanied the ex-president.

Not since the time, years before this, when he had decided to slander me, call me traitor, and convert himself into my most implacable opponent, had Uribe set foot in Casa de Nariño. After a formal handshake that was amicable enough, though cold, we conducted a meeting that lasted for about three hours. For the occasion I had chosen the Strategy Room and was accompanied by some of my ministers and several members of our negotiating team. I began by welcoming the visitors and placing the government at their disposal for a dialogue that would salvage the peace agreement. They exposed their points of dissent, which we listened to attentively. We then requested that they put their suggestions in writing so that we could analyze them and take them to Havana for discussions with the Farc delegation. Once again, I delegated Minister Villegas to take charge of these contacts, along with the foreign affairs minister and the head of our team of negotiators, de la Calle, who was traveling back and forth between Bogotá and Havana. In subsequent meetings with promoters of the no campaign, this commission was augmented with the presence of our interior minister, Juan Fernando Cristo, and the former minister of justice Yesid Reyes, plus other negotiators such as Senator Barreras and Generals Naranjo and Mora, among others.

I had the impression it was not going to be difficult to reach a new agreement that would incorporate the majority of the observations, most of which could be easily included; in fact, some were no more than clarifications. I felt sure that, with goodwill on all sides, we would soon solve the problem.

Meanwhile, something phenomenal happened. All around the country, people, especially the young, began to take to the streets. Day after day, they filled plazas and public parks in support of peace, carrying posters that read: "Peace Agreement, NOW!" And it wasn't only those who had voted yes, but many who had voted no but now felt they should rally behind the cry for peace. And there were others, too, who repented not having gone to the polls and, by their abstention, allowing the country to enter such a state of uncertainty. The Plaza de Bolívar, in the center of Bogotá, was the scene of multitudinous, totally spontaneous demonstrations. The plaza was filled with tents set up around the statue of the Liberator to create a "peace camp" that the protesters swore would not be lifted until white smoke billowed to show the agreement had been approved.

In a sense, this was a positive and unexpected consequence of our defeat in the plebiscite: the country united, clamoring for peace.

AN EARLY MORNING CALL

Both the year before, and then again in 2016, my name was among those nominated for the Nobel Peace Prize because of the efforts I was making to end the armed conflict with the Farc. Timochenko's name also appeared among the nominees, and Colombia's victims, too. To say I felt indifferent about this nomination would be untrue. Of course, I considered it an immense honor—as somebody once called it, the greatest honor a human being could receive. But it was not a priority of mine or something I had set my heart on. It was too much, far beyond my wildest dreams. So, sheltering behind the breastplate that protects me from emotional tempests, I had let myself be convinced the prize was not a viable proposition, that it just wouldn't happen.

In October, the day came when the Norwegian Nobel Committee usually announced the winner of the prize, but I was not following it with any special attention. On Thursday the sixth, I worked in my office until late at night, while at the same time keeping an eye on Colombia's football team in Asunción playing against Paraguay in an eliminatory match for the World Cup to be held in Russia. Happily, we won 1–0. By midnight, I was tired and fell fast asleep in my bedroom, alone, since María Clemencia, saddened by the result of the plebiscite, had gone off to spend a few days at our farm in Anapoima. Martín and María Antonia were in their respective apartments, and Esteban had gone back to the University of Virginia to resume his studies.

I was in the middle of a deep sleep when the phone rang. Somehow I managed to lift the receiver and heard, hazily, the voice of my son Martín sounding very emotional and telling me that Ingrid Betancourt had called him to say they had given me the Nobel Peace Prize. I was so sleepy that although I heard the words, it was as if they were part of a dream I was having. "OK," I said, "we'll talk tomorrow." I hung up and went back to sleep. Martín phoned me again, and this time, a bit more awake, I understood what he was saying and realized the enormity of the news he was giving me.

It's not easy to express what you feel. This is the planet's most important acknowledgment for work on humanity's most crucial issue, peace, and maybe that's why what I felt, more than euphoria, was a sense of humility and unworthiness, sensations that arise when you least expect them. I felt humbled by what was meant by the challenge of seeking peace and coexistence in a world plagued with conflicts, and to realize that this honor was placing me in the company of titans for peace—people like Martin Luther King, Nelson Mandela, Mother Teresa, the Dalai Lama—who had been awarded this prize in the past. This was a recognition that had been sought in vain by Churchill, Roosevelt, and Stalin, who, despite their differences, had saved the world from Nazism. It was a prize the committee had not managed to award even to Gandhi, the apostle of nonviolence.

Martín got in his car, picked up María Antonia, and drove to the Casa de Nariño, arriving at dawn to congratulate me and wrap me in their embraces. María Clemencia got back from the country in a hurry, and Esteban flew in from Virginia that same night. You could say that, in a matter of five days, we had gone from hell to heaven.

At four thirty a.m., before they had arrived, I got the official call from the president of the Norwegian Committee, Kaci Kullmann Five—who was to die soon after, in February 2017—announcing my designation. Almost at once, a journalist from the Nobel organization, Adam Smith, called me for an interview. I told him, in all sincerity, what I've always felt about this prize; that it was not just for me but for Colombia: "This is a prize for the victims and for the Colombians. It's a very important prize, and I accept it in the name of them all, people who have suffered fifty-two years of a war we are about to end."

A PAT ON THE BACK FOR PEACE IN COLOMBIA

The communiqué published by the Norwegian Committee on awarding me the prize made it clear that it was in homage to the Colombian people and to the victims' loved ones. The committee even referred to our defeat in the plebiscite, seeing it as a challenge and an opportunity.

> President Santos initiated the negotiations that culminated in the peace accord between the Colombian government and the FARC guerrillas, and he has consistently sought to move the peace process forward. Well knowing that the accord was controversial, he was instrumental in ensuring that Colombian voters were able to voice their opinion concerning the peace accord in a referendum. The outcome of the vote was not what President

> Santos wanted: a narrow majority of the over 13 million Colombians who cast their ballots said no to the accord. This result has created great uncertainty as to the future of Colombia. There is a real danger that the peace process will come to a halt and that civil war will flare up again. This makes it even more important that the parties, headed by President Santos and FARC guerrilla leader Rodrigo Londoño, continue to respect the ceasefire.
>
> The fact that a majority of the voters said no to the peace accord does not necessarily mean that the peace process is dead. The referendum was not a vote for or against peace. What the "No" side rejected was not the desire for peace, but a specific peace agreement. The Norwegian Nobel Committee emphasizes the importance of the fact that President Santos is now inviting all parties to participate in a broad-based national dialogue aimed at advancing the peace process. Even those who opposed the peace accord have welcomed such a dialogue.

What's certain is that the Nobel Prize arrived at just the right moment, like a gift from heaven, and made us feel as if the whole world was giving us a pat on the back and urging us to go ahead and bring the peace process to a successful conclusion. That's how the Colombians understood it as they continued to fill the public squares with banners that said: "Peace Agreement, NOW!"

CHAPTER 37

An Irrational Opposition

THE MEETING IN RIONEGRO

The honor I received from Norway did not tempt me to drop my guard. On the contrary, I continued to strive with greater effort than ever to save the peace. We had to keep on dialoguing with everyone to reach a consensus that would enable us to get a new agreement as soon as possible. As early as September, the guerrillas had been on the move, approaching the rural zones where it was planned that they would gather to begin the demobilization process. But everything had come to a sudden standstill, like in the game of statues that Colombian children play. The bilateral ceasefire was still being respected, but so long as no certain agreement was signed, the truce was very fragile and could be broken by the least act of provocation.

My meetings with the spokespersons of the no campaign were not restricted to those I held with Uribe and Pastrana. I spent long hours listening to the concerns and suggestions of every kind of representative of Colombian society: business associations, working men and women, and the churches. It was fundamental that we dilute the overwhelming influence of Uribe, who was the no voters' most visible leader, but not its only one. I had the impression that Uribe would not be satisfied with anything that might be proposed—that is to say, with anything less than throwing the whole peace agreement overboard. And I wasn't wrong.

The no-vote spokespersons finally presented their commentaries, summarized in sixty proposed modifications of the agreement, which our negotiators took to Havana to discuss with the Farc delegation. There followed long days of extensive debates, since there were some points on which the guerrillas would not budge. For example, in the original agreement it was accepted that some of the magistrates who made up the peace tribunal could be foreigners, but the no voters' representatives insisted they all be Colombians. After more than two weeks working day and night, the Farc accepted fifty-eight of the sixty modifications. That is 97 percent. Undoubtedly a great achievement. The only proposals they did not accept were those that defined what would be crucial aspects for the future: that the guerrilla commanders could not take part in politics and that their sanctions and conditions of reclusion should be more severe. On November 12, the delegations announced in Havana that they had arrived at a new agreement incorporating the immense majority of the observations and suggestions they had received.

That same day, before this announcement had been made public, I was attending an event at the Colombian Air Force base in Rionegro, Antioquia, half an hour's drive from Medellín. Via General Maldonado, chief of the presidency's military office, I let Uribe know of my intention to visit him at his home in Rionegro to inform him of our progress. He replied that he would prefer we met at the air force base, which is what we did. He arrived in the company of Juan Gómez Martínez, former governor of Antioquia and former mayor of Medellín, and Claudia Bustamante, an incendiary tweeter and passionate follower of Uribe. I was accompanied by the defense minister, Luis Carlos Villegas.

I was greatly surprised that the first subject the ex-president wanted to talk about was not the peace agreement but something quite different. He referred to his protégé, Andrés Felipe Arias, former minister of agriculture, whom, in July 2014, the Supreme Court of Justice had sentenced to seventeen years in prison for embezzlement by appropriation in favor of third parties and the celebration of contracts with disregard for the legal requisites, offenses committed in development of a government program known as Agro Ingreso Seguro (Agrarian Assured Income). At the time, Arias was living in Miami and the Colombian court had requested the US authorities to extradite him. Meanwhile, he remained at the disposal of the US Justice Department.

Uribe, of course, claimed that Arias was victim of a plot by my government to bring him back to Colombia in chains. But then, Uribe always plays the role of victim, and behind every charge brought against him or his inner circle he perceives, or pretends to perceive, an act of political persecution. However, the fact is we had never raised a finger against Arias or against any member of the opposition, despite the barbarities that Uribe constantly spouted overseas about me and my government. In the case of Arias, I had actually offered him the post of Colombian ambassador to Italy, but that was before he got into problems with the law. I also assigned his wife a bulletproof vehicle. And when he was arrested, I offered him the most comfortable quarters available at the military canton, as I did with all Uribe's ex-officials who received prison sentences.

"Mr. President," Uribe said, as soon as we met, "I'm concerned that your government continues to persecute Andrés Felipe Arias."

This riled me, but I remained calm. "President Uribe, my government persecutes nobody. And by nobody, I mean nobody! As you well know, in Colombia there is a division of powers. The Supreme Court is autonomous in making its decisions, and all the Ministry of Foreign Affairs does is to carry out the formal procedures required by law."

Uribe took the matter no further, but our meeting had gotten off to a bad start. Next, Uribe—who always prefers to talk rather than listen—proceeded to expound his usual list of criticisms of the agreement. In fact, he went beyond the usual, insisting that it had been a mistake to recognize the existence of an armed conflict. It was then I knew for sure that with him I was wasting my time. His willingness to accept the agreement, even with changes, was null. Because once you deny the existence of an armed conflict, you just cannot have a peace process.

I told the former president that after lengthy and intense sessions spent persuading the Farc delegates, not to mention several weeks devoted to hearing his objections and those of his followers, we were finalizing a new agreement that would include the great majority of his suggestions. Obviously, we could not include them all, since that would mean altering in a matter of weeks what we had achieved after years of discussion. But the progress we had made was fundamental.

"Mr. President," said Uribe, "what you're doing is notifying me, not consulting me." He asked me to leave the agreement open until the changes were submitted to a new discussion by the promoters of the no vote. That would be easier said than done. The ceasefire was getting shakier with each passing day. I was in permanent contact with our negotiators in Havana, and I knew we were walking on thin ice. The Farc had ceded a lot of ground, but if we were to further prolong discussions, we would be running the risk of the whole process breaking down. I told Uribe this, but he was not prepared to modify his position, not by one millimeter.

Having reached this point, he asked me to allow him a few minutes to prepare a communiqué he would read to the press once our meeting had concluded. He wrote down what he wanted to say and showed it to me. I told him I had no problem with it; it was, in fact, a faithful account of our talk. It simply said that Uribe had requested the new text of the agreement not be considered definitive but disseminated for consultation by the promoters of the no vote, and by the victims, so they could study it and make their comments and suggestions.

If I had accepted this, we would be on the road to perpetual negotiation. He had left me with no margin of maneuver. The people were calling for an agreement, and the guerrillas were in a limbo that couldn't go on much longer. There was no way we could get the Farc to make further concessions. They had reached their limit. And so had I.

THE URIBE FACTOR

In Colombia's recent history, there is no record of any government plagued with such implacable opposition as that which I had to put up with from my predecessor. I confess I was, and still am, amazed at his degree of pugnacity and ability to undermine with his criticisms. I ask myself, how did Uribe get like this? His animosity and permanent bickering was something I rarely commented on so as not to make matters worse, and also because I did not think of him as an enemy. Besides, any comment of mine might have contributed to the absurd and undesirable polarization the country was being submitted to.

I had been a minister in Uribe's cabinet, and am the first to acknowledge the progress made on many fronts during his administration—even as he does not acknowledge any made in mine. I always hoped to maintain a positive relationship with him during my government. This, unfortunately, was not to be the case.

I met Uribe in the 1980s, although we never became friends. My father, Enrique Santos Castillo—like Uribe, a "right-wing liberal"—liked him and saw to it that the family's newspaper, *El Tiempo*, supported him during his governorship of Antioquia from 1995 to 1997. But I was never close to him. It was José Roberto Arango, an Antioquian businessman and friend of my father's who became consultant to Uribe as president, who insisted I should get to know him.

Following on Pastrana´s government, in which I was finance minister, Uribe came to power, and although I was not what you might call "Uribist," I wasn't particularly critical of his administration. My columns in the press weighed up the good and the bad—or rather, the less fortunate—elements in what I think were balanced judgments. In any case, after the futile effort wasted on the Caguán process, I sympathized with Uribe's flagship policy of Democratic Security and his determination to treat the guerrillas with a firm hand because that was the only way we were likely to get them to talk peace seriously and realistically.

This attitude was one I shared with certain Liberal Party senators who were also attracted to Uribe's style of government: people like Oscar Iván Zuluaga, Luis Guillermo Vélez, and Aurelio Iragorri Hormaza. With them, among others, we founded the Party of the U, and our outstanding victory in the parliamentary elections was a determining factor for Uribe's reelection. It was then, in his second administration, that he offered me to accompany him as minister of defense, which Uribe considered his most important ministry, in charge, as it was, of executing his Democratic Security policy.

As minister, I always had a cordial relationship with him, both respectful and amicable. But I was never part of his Sanhedrin, his inner circle, that included his private secretary, Alicia Arango; the man I already mentioned, José Roberto Arango; his adviser, José Obdulio Gaviria; his press secretary, César Mauricio Velásquez, and his agricultural minister, Arias. Fabio Echeverri was another member of that circle, despite the fact that, some years earlier, he had suggested to President Belisario Betancur that he should force Uribe to resign as mayor of Medellín because of his possible connections to the drug trade. Betancur was concerned and requested the Antioquia governor, Álvaro Villegas, to relieve Uribe of his post. But Villegas refused, although in the end Uribe and Villegas both resigned.

The members of the Sanhedrin treated me with respect, as I did them. But they knew I wasn't used to blindly obeying orders, that I had a considerable track record of public service and, to put it bluntly, I was my own man.

One day, Gaviria called me on the direct line to the presidency—the so-called falcon line—and asked me, as if it were the most normal thing in the world, to tap the phone calls of Piedad Córdoba, a Liberal senator known to be close to Hugo Chávez. I roundly refused, and asked him never again to come to me with any such suggestion. Perhaps that was why they decided to use the Administrative Department of Security rather than military intelligence for their phone bugging, which would one day come to light and cause such scandal.

One thing they did know, and that was that I was devoted to my work but was not part of their group. Later Uribe supported my candidacy, but not because I was his favorite. His pupil and the apple of his eye was Arias. But

Arias had lost to Noemí Sanín in the Conservative inner-party election for nominee, and I was the most viable candidate left who was likely to continue the Democratic Security policy, Uribe's principal legacy.

Uribe is, by temperament, irritable in the extreme, as he is first to admit. But I have to say that, while working under him as minister, he never once raised his voice to me. With others, however, he was not always so self-controlled. I remember once, traveling in the presidential plane in the company of Alicia Arango, General Óscar Naranjo, and other government officials, someone from the press office passed him a mobile phone, insisting he give an interview to a journalist who was on the line. He reacted angrily to a question the interviewer put to him, presumably about his sons' business ventures, and flew into such a rage that he hung up in a fit of fury and flung the phone back at the pressman. The apparatus missed the mark and, after narrowly grazing General Naranjo's head, shattered into smithereens against the plane's window.

During my presidency, on the few occasions we met, he was most respectful. But it was quite another matter whenever he mentioned me in his speeches or interviews, and even worse when he inveighed against me and my government in his multiple daily tweets—a form of intense communication he has in common with Trump and other populist leaders.

I have often wondered—but never found out—what kind of a raffle it was in which I won Uribe's animosity, an ill feeling that has been so counterproductive for the country. Maybe it was because I sought peace through dialogue, something he himself had attempted in vain. Or perhaps it was because I gambled on normalizing relations with the Chávez regime in Venezuela. He saw Chávez as his enemy—as he had been mine, too. Nevertheless, Uribe also tried to patch up those relations, but without success. I know he objected to the fact that I included in my cabinet two very worthwhile men for whom he nurtured a deep dislike. But that was my prerogative as president. Perhaps the reason was that I had accepted the existence of an armed conflict, something he had always denied. But if I had not done so, there would have been no peace process.

The Uribe factor was like a weight hanging around my government's neck. Up to the very last minute, Uribe conspired against the peace agreement, which he considered equivalent to surrendering to terrorism. On July 20, 2018, when I addressed Congress for the last time and gave a balance of my eight years of government, Uribe, sitting in the place allotted to him in the

Senate, never once lifted his head to look at me, but spent the time compulsively firing off tweets to refute, sentence by sentence, everything I said. In less than an hour, he wrote and sent seventy tweets, beating his own record; during my speech the year before he had sent forty-two. It's an obsession of his, of this there's no doubt. And it's contagious; most of his followers suffer from it. This obsession blinds him and didn't let him see the light of peace that was appearing and increasing in our country.

Nonetheless, there's a positive aspect to this: it made me work harder . . . and better.

THE DUQUE I KNEW

Iván Duque Márquez, Colombia's new president, my successor since August 7, 2018, was elected thanks to the support of Uribe and the Democratic Center party. However, I feel—or want to feel—in my heart that he has not inherited his mentor's animosities and obsessions. At least, I hope not, because I trust in his good nature. And I have good reason, since he worked with me from the time he was a law student in his twenties at the Sergio Arboleda University.

I got good reports on Duque from two sources: Lulú Bernal of the Santa Fe Radio, a good friend of his mother and mine also, and Samuel Yohai, a businessman who was close to Duque's father, Iván Duque Escobar. So it was that he began working with me at the Good Government Foundation, along with other young men, including Juan Carlos Pinzón. They weren't earning much more than their bus fare, but they were enthusiastic lads, studious and disciplined. They became part of the youth that campaigned for my precandidacy for the Liberal Party. I told Duque he should follow his father's footsteps and get more involved with the Liberals. Iván Duque Escobar—the man who saved me from being kidnapped, as I said earlier—had been governor and minister as member of the party. His son took my advice.

When I became finance minister in the year 2000, I invited Duque to work with me as consultant, and I put him in charge of royalties, a very responsible post. As usual, he fulfilled his duties admirably. In 2001 there was an opening in Washington for adviser to the Colombian delegation at the Inter-American Development Bank, and I sent him on that mission, an appointment he was delighted to accept. He worked there until 2013, earning the respect of the bank's president, Luis Alberto Moreno, who placed him at the head of the entity's cultural activities.

In the second half of 2010, Duque began to assist Uribe on particular issues. These included a United Nations investigative panel to which Uribe had been assigned for the purpose of formulating a concept on an incident that had arisen between Israel and Turkey. The ex-president thought highly of Duque's ability and invited him to be one of the Democratic Center's candidates for the Senate for the period 2014–2018. Because of this, Duque returned to Colombia and entered Congress, where he showed himself to be a dedicated congressman, though very critical of my government, as was natural, since that was Uribe's policy, and Uribe was the head of the party for which he had been elected.

The Duque I knew and supported was the young Duque, imbued with Liberal ideas, studious, cheerful, and an inveterate reader. On August 7, 2018, I was succeeded in the presidency by a different Duque who had become a militant of the Right. Into his hands I entrusted our peace agreement, entering its implementation stage, with the Farc disarmed, demobilized, and converted into a political party. I hope, for the good of Colombia—as I said in my final address to Congress—that he, his government, and the new members of Congress will show vision and intelligence and take good care of the peace. Because what is at stake is not Juan Manuel Santos's peace, but the peace of Colombia.

CHAPTER 38

The Path to a New Colombia

THE NEW FINAL AGREEMENT

The new peace agreement, incorporating all the changes, was placed at the public's disposal on November 14, 2016, and we began a new pedagogical task to explain the changes. I have to admit—and I have always done so—that the agreement was improved after we had incorporated all the suggestions. Our having lost in the plebiscite was useful in a sense, because it put pressure on the Farc to cede a little more on certain issues about which they had been reticent. However, one never knows to what point one can exert pressure before the rubber band snaps.

The defeat at the polls on October 2 was converted into an opportunity, which we used to polish and improve many points. Some activists on the no side, several Evangelical pastors, the Catholic Church, young people in general, the victims, governors and mayors, and the international community, greeted the new agreement with hope, acknowledging its improvements. And that made us decide to go ahead. We could not continue to further delay its application just because of the obstinate opposition of Uribe and Pastrana, for whom no changes would ever be enough.

And therefore, on November 24, 2016, in Bogotá's Teatro Colón, we conducted the solemn act of signing the new final agreement, once again in the presence of the Farc delegates and those of the government, but without so much fanfare nor the presence of the international guests who had witnessed the event in Cartagena. The ceremony was a sober one, but no less emotional for that, especially since we had overcome one of the difficulties we had least expected and were signing an agreement that not long before had looked as if it were moribund.

I considered that the calling of a new vote would be extremely wearying for a country that was breathing easy with the signing of the new agreement. Also, legally I was not obliged to do so. And to be frank, I had learned a lesson and did not want to take a new risk. The Constitutional Court had given us a way out in the event that we should lose the plebiscite: if a new agreement were negotiated, we could have recourse to Congress for its approval, which is the usual route. And so that was what we did. After all, Congress is democracy's most representative body, and that was the procedure established under the constitution. Early in December, therefore, the agreement was approved in Congress by an immense majority. The combined votes of the Senate and the Chamber gave us 205 votes for, and 0 against. The Democratic Center refrained from voting.

And to complete the participation of the three branches of power, the magistrates of the Constitutional Court unanimously approved and countersigned the final text. Later, in October 2017, the same court also approved the legislative act by virtue of which the agreement was given juridical status. This meant that the following three presidential periods would be obliged to respect what was contained in the agreement. After all these steps had been taken, the new agreement that ended the conflict with the Farc was converted into a juridical reality that could not be modified.

Internationally, the final agreement was deposited with Switzerland's Federal Council in Berne, which holds the Geneva Conventions that are the cornerstone of international humanitarian law. And on March 24, 2017, the agreement was placed in the hands of António Guterres, the United Nations secretary-general, and of the Englishman Matthew Rycroft, at the time president of the UN Security Council. On receiving it, Guterres had this to say: "A peace agreement in the times we are living is something precious and of an enormous importance."

TORCHES IN OSLO

If it is impossible to describe your feelings when you receive the news that you've been awarded the Nobel Prize, it's even more difficult to describe how you feel when you are actually receiving it.

The ceremony was held in Oslo's City Hall on December 10. I was in Oslo from the ninth to the twelfth in the company of my family and the negotiators, some of the victims, several ministers, plus relatives and close friends.

I received nothing but appreciation and support from the Norwegian authorities—King Harald, Prime Minister Erna Solberg, the minister of foreign affairs Børge Brende, the members of the Norwegian Committee and parliament—and from the people around me.

In my acceptance speech, I spoke of the peace process, of our difficulties and our triumphs, of the lessons we had learned from other processes and those we were leaving for the rest of the world. I also paid homage to the victims, which was the most emotional moment of all. But I did not speak only of peace in Colombia. I also invited all humanity to discover and celebrate our diversity and at the same time, our oneness; we are all ONE—like that, in capital letters—and whatever happens to any human being happens to us all. My invitation was—and still is—to exchange fear, discrimination, and violence for love, tolerance, and compassion—an invitation the audience received with warm applause.

"The name of this one people is the world," I concluded. "And the name of this one race is humanity."

That night, to my surprise, at the banquet in my honor at the Grand Hotel, Olemic Thommessen, president of the Norwegian parliament, said in his toast that my words had been "The best speech they had ever heard in Oslo's City Hall." Not too bad, I thought, considering what giants had gone before me.

That same evening, before the banquet begins, there is a tradition according to which the prizewinner steps onto the hotel's central balcony and is greeted by a march of citizens bearing torches. The scene was unforgettable. Hundreds of people with flaming torches in the midst of a cold Nordic night proceeded along the city's most popular street, Karl Johans Gate, and came to a halt beneath my balcony to greet and be greeted by me. Among the crowd there were a lot of Colombian flags waving, and when I heard cries of "Viva Colombia!" my soul was filled with joy.

The next day I visited the Nobel Museum, where I was surprised to find a complete exhibition of photographs of the Colombian conflict and our transition to peace, including a large-scale portrait photo of me. This exhibition was open all year. And there was more to come. On the night of December 11, there was a concert in my honor at Oslo's Telenor Arena, a modern coliseum with seating for nine thousand people. There I made a short speech and we enjoyed a wonderful musical spectacle whose main performers were Sting and the Colombian pop singer Juanes.

This was Norway, and the world, celebrating with torches and music the peace accord we had signed in Colombia, and the peace we were beginning to build.

FARC'S MARCH TOWARD PEACE

Just as 2016 was the year we agreed to end the conflict, so was 2017 the year for making peace become a concrete reality. We Colombians watched in wonderment the television images of trucks, buses, and launches making their way along rough country tracks and wide-flowing rivers, transporting hundreds—no, thousands—of Farc combatants to the zones where they were to gather to disarm and demobilize. Country people greeted them along the way and applauded as they passed by on their journey toward peace.

Thirteen thousand men and women, between combatants and militias—that is, members of the Farc's urban support network—were engaged in a process of reintegration. Half of these were combatants, a quarter of them militias, and the rest were imprisoned in Colombia's jails.

Some guerrilla groups—especially those most involved in the drug trade—refused to demobilize and became dissidents, forfeiting their right to the benefits we had agreed on. It is estimated that the different rebel factions amount to about 1,300 in arms; that is, 10 percent of those that did demobilize. This percentage is really quite normal, even below the average number in any peace process. These dissidents are no longer considered guerrillas but bands of common criminals working for the drug traffickers, and are forcefully combated by Colombia's armed forces.

With the United Nations mission of verification and monitoring, there began the process of laying down arms in each of the rural zones, and these weapons were classified, inventoried, and stored in large containers. The process of the laying down of arms concluded on June 27, 2017, and we celebrated with a ceremony in the municipality of Mesetas, in the department of Meta, where once again I met with Timochenko. I had just gotten back from France, where I had a meeting with President Macron, so I began my speech with a quote from the great French writer Victor Hugo: "A day will come when there will be no more wars. A day will come when men will cease to take up arms against one another."

A year had gone by since we signed the ceasefire in Havana, and now we were ending the process of disarmament, leaving the weapons in the hands of the United Nations. What progress we had made! And how much Colombia was benefiting! A couple, both ex-guerrilla combatants, came on to the platform with a baby in their arms, and Timochenko lifted the baby up while I took its hand. It was hard to believe that not long before we had been killing one another, and we had been doing so for fifty years, when we have so much in common: we are all Colombians and, above all, human beings.

And we had another symbol of this event, similar to the bullet pen. A year before, a Colombian artist, Alex Sastoque, had given me two sculptures, which he had named *Cultivating Peace*. Taking as his base an AK-47 rifle, he had converted it into a shovel for digging in the soil. It suggested to me that, whenever I found the right moment, I should give one of the sculptures to the Farc commander. That day, at Mesetas, after the handing over of weapons, I gave Timochenko this rifle/shovel that illustrated, with the unique synthesis proper to art, the transition from war to honest and productive labors.

Seven weeks later, on August 15 in La Guajira, we held another act, this time to close and dispatch the last weapons container that left the rural zones and would remain in the hands of the United Nations. As was agreed, this institution melted down these weapons to be converted into three monuments to peace: one in Bogotá, to be executed by the Colombian artist Doris Salcedo; a second in New York, as acknowledgement to the United Nations; and a third in Havana, in gratitude to the city that had hosted the dialogues.*

That same day, when there was no longer a single weapon in the zones and the camps, they ceased to be called "normalization zones" and became known as "territorial areas for training and reincorporation" intended above all, to support the ex-guerrilla fighters and prepare them to become integrated into society.

In all, the United Nations mission collected 8,994 individual weapons—more than one for every combatant, something that had not occurred in any other process in the world—and 509 collective weapons for combat support; about 1.8 million rounds of ammunition for short-range weapons; more than 38 tons of explosives; 11,015 hand grenades; 3,528 antipersonnel mines, and 4,370 mortars. These arms, which had been hiding death and pain in their dark barrels, would now never be fired again.

* After melting thirty-seven tons of Farc weapons, Doris Salcedo delivered her installation called *Fragmentos* (Fragments), located in downtown Bogotá, in December 2018. It is a floor of sheets made from metal, hammered out by women who had been victims of sexual violence in the context of the war, on which visitors can tread, in a building that, for the next fifty-two years—the time that the confrontation lasted—will house exhibitions related to the armed conflict.

A RENEWED DEMOCRACY

Implementation is under way, and despite the difficulties, a lot of progress is being made. The implementation process is accompanied by the United Nations, the European Union, and several national and international bodies. For verification, we also count on the support of a commission of notable personalities, comprising my good friend and fighter for peace at my side for over twenty years Felipe González, and Uruguay's ex-president José "Pepe" Mujica, who knows better than anyone, from personal experience, what it costs to go from being a guerrilla to entering the democratic process, and the importance of reconciliation. From March 2017 to mid-2018, both men came to Colombia several times to verify implementation conditions, always encouraging the Colombians with their messages of hope.

The 2018 elections were the best proof of how things are changing in Colombia. There were parliamentary elections as well as two rounds of presidential elections, all notable for the atmosphere of security, transparency, and calm in which they were conducted, and with relatively high participation on the part of the citizens. For the first time in many years, in no region did we need to transfer voting booths from one place to another for security reasons.

The Farc—converted now into a political party, the Common Alternative Revolutionary Force—presented candidates for Congress and won more than eighty-five thousand votes between the Senate and the Chamber of Representatives. This was not enough to win them a seat in Congress, but they did have ten seats guaranteed them through the peace agreement—five in the Senate and five in the Chamber—over the next two periods. But the impressive part was seeing former guerrilla commanders, including Timochenko and Pablo Catatumbo, casting their vote like any normal citizen, for the first time in their lives.

On July 20, 2018, as I gave my inaugural address to launch new sessions of Colombia's Congress and, from where I stood on the elevated principal platform in the Elliptical Room, as it is called, looked down on this great hall packed to overflowing with the senators and representatives who would spend the following four years passing laws to guide the republic's fortunes, I could not help rejoicing at all our democracy had gained in strength and variety. The 2018 Congress was no longer what it had been a few decades before, when Liberals and Conservatives were the only ones with access to power and enjoyed exclusive shares in the state's bureaucracy. This new Congress consisted of a dozen different political parties of diverse tendencies, among them the party that bears the initials—but no longer the same message—as the extinct guerrilla army.

There they were, responding as their names were called, congressmen and women who not long before had been guerrilla commanders and were now seated just a few steps away from Uribe. He did not so much as acknowledge their presence, as he had not acknowledged mine. He kept his attention fixed on this mobile phone. But there was Senator Gustavo Petro, ex-member of the M-19 guerrilla movement, demobilized years before, and runner-up in the recent presidential elections, who obtained his seat in parliament thanks to the Opposition Statute that the peace agreement had led us to approve. There, too, were Senators Roy Barreras and Iván Cepeda, who had supported the peace talks so strongly, and Senator Antanas Mockus, my rival in the 2010 elections and later my staunch ally in the search for peace. And alongside them, an array of Democratic Center party members—with a president now in the Casa de Nariño—who insist on trying to modify an agreement that does not allow for any possible legal alteration.

This is the new Colombia, where differences can coexist. This is the new Colombia, diverse and full of nuances, that is beginning to understand what it means to have such potential, and without violence. This is the triumph of hope against fear. This is Life winning over Death. These are bullets that have been changed into words.

We had trodden a long and difficult road, but it had been worthwhile—for it was the long road to peace!

It Was Worthwhile

BUILDING PEACE IS LIKE BUILDING A CATHEDRAL

On August 6, 2018, the day before I ended my term of government, I gave a final televised address to my compatriots, in which I said the following: "I've always said that the peace was not mine but yours. Today I leave that peace in your care, like someone leaving a small child in the hands of its foster parents."

The possible peace, the necessary peace, the imperfect peace, the fragile peace we have achieved with the largest and most powerful guerrilla army in Colombia was not, nor could it be, the legacy of a government, but must be taken up, cared for, and defended by all Colombians.

Because peace cannot, and should not, have a particular political color. It is one of society's fundamental needs if that society is to progress and develop equitably. It is the most important inheritance we can leave our children and future generations.

A few years have gone by since I left office, and I have calmly and happily taken up my life as ex-president, in retirement from local political activity but always ready to contribute my grain of sand in the building of peace, in the fight against poverty and in the defense of the environment, not only in Colombia but worldwide. From my new watchtower, I serenely—but often worriedly—contemplate the way things are occurring in the postconflict stage, where we see difficulties and setbacks, but with progress being made, because the agreement we achieved and its effects were designed to endure in spite of all possible obstacles.

My successor, President Duque, is a member of a political party that, under the leadership of ex-president Uribe, torpedoed, criticized, and doggedly opposed the peace process. Nonetheless, the agreement's implementation has continued because it is reinforced constitutionally and because we made sure that the principal laws were approved to guarantee the reincorporation of the ex-guerrillas into civilian and political life and the efficient operation of the system of truth, justice, reparation, and nonrepetition in favor of the conflict's victims. We also created, put together, and ensured the financing of institutions that are necessary to put the agreement into effect, including among others the Special Justice for Peace, the Truth Commission, the Unit for the Search for the Disappeared, and the Agency for Territorial Renovation. In other words, the agreement has a life and a dynamic of its own that every democratic government is obliged to respect, and to make others respect.

What we signed, we signed in the name of the Colombian state, not that of the government, much less of a particular president. In addition, the Constitutional Court decreed that in the course of the next three governments—that of Duque and the two following—no reform or law could be passed that would in any way contravene what we had agreed upon.

The international community, for its part, in statements by the United Nations and the European Union, has made clear to President Duque that it is attentive to and ready to ensure the implementation of the agreement, one that they consider a model for the rest of the world. This affords an additional guarantee that it will be correctly applied.

Of course, it won't be easy. Just as making peace is harder than making war, building peace is harder than silencing the guns. Building peace is like building a cathedral. It has to be done brick by brick, pillar by pillar, stained-glass windows created one after the other, in a process that takes years or decades, but which reaches its conclusion in the erection of a marvelous and enduring structure.

What is still lacking are certain important laws that will ensure the agreement is carried out in its entirety. These include laws on the subject of land and, in general, the implementation of the chapter on comprehensive rural development. Also, Congress is still in debt to victims in those zones most affected by the conflict who await the creation of special, transitory circumscriptions that will guarantee them a seat in the Chamber of Representatives. I am hopeful that the government and congress members—many of whom are sincerely committed to peace—will honor their promise to the state with regard to these pending tasks.

The building of territorial peace necessarily requires programs of development with a territorial focus, the PDET, designed to transform those regions that were hardest hit by the conflict. As was planned, these programs were discussed and approved by the affected communities themselves in the course of the year 2018 with the intention of setting them in motion in 2019.

That was agreed upon, and it is one of the great innovations of this peace process. By the end of 2019, all sixteen PDETs had been subscribed to. With these road maps, which should be executed over the next ten to fifteen years, Colombia's most abandoned regions will be progressing unfailingly toward overcoming poverty and creating opportunities.

If there is one thing that fills me with hope it is seeing how the former Farc guerrillas have formed a political party, which bears their initials: *F-A-R-C*. Despite obvious problems and differences of opinion among themselves, this party, born out of the agreement, operates in conformity with the rules of democracy and contributes its point of view like any other political movement. This is what a negotiated peace is all about, and it is happening. It was significant, for example, to see how the leaders of the Farc political party condemned the atrocious terrorist attack by the ELN on a police academy on January 17, 2019.

In addition, on January 12, 2019, the government's high commissioner for the postconflict, Emilio Archila, in response to criticisms on the part of Iván Márquez, the former head of negotiations with the Farc, published a communiqué in which he underlined facts such as the following:

- 13,043 ex-combatants of the Farc received benefits from the peace agreement.
- In 2018, the government approved some twenty collective production projects evaluated at 15 billion pesos (equivalent to approximately US$5 million) that benefit 1,311 ex-members of the Farc-EP.
- Nine out of every ten ex-combatants receive a monthly subsidy for living expenses, 10,000 are covered by a pension scheme, and 98 percent have been enrolled in the health system.

There is still a lot to be done. The state's unwieldy bureaucracy moves slowly, certainly not at the rate one would desire. Nevertheless, it seems the agreement is being complied with, and all Colombians should be vigilant that it be put into effect completely. It is encouraging to see Duque's government defending its commitments. Let's hope this is more than just words.

PEACE WITH THE FARC IS NOT THE END OF VIOLENCE

Many feel disconcerted on observing that, in spite of the agreement reached with the Farc, violence continues to afflict some of the country's regions. We always knew this would be so, and we predicted it; the end of the conflict with the Farc was an indispensable step forward on the path to peace, but would not bring total peace. The oldest and most powerful guerrilla group in Latin America has stopped fighting and given up its arms, but foci of violence persist, caused by criminal organizations working for the drug traffickers plus a number of Farc deserters who refused to take part in the process and could no longer be considered guerrillas, but simple drug traffickers. As well as these, there is the much smaller and focalized guerrilla force, the ELN, which missed the opportunity to make peace and prefers to persist with their terrorist activities.

A matter for particular concern are the continuous murders of social and community leaders, largely carried out under orders from illegal occupants of land who refuse to give them back to the original owners whom they dispossessed. Another source of violence and murder is the drug trade cartels concerned over the substitution of crops that will leave them without their raw material. The government, the prosecutor general, and the armed forces should employ everything they have to put an end to this bloodletting and bring those responsible to justice.

In February 2017, I installed—and later brought together on several occasions—the National Commission of Guarantees and Security, an entity headed by the president of the republic that includes state bodies and demobilized Farc guerrillas along with international and human rights organizations. During its first five months of government, the new administration did not hold a meeting of this commission, despite the fact that social leaders and demobilized guerrillas continued to be murdered. Finally the government decided to bring the commission together in January 2019, but it has not employed, or set in motion, the tools we created by means of several decrees designed to combat this criminal activity; I refer to entities such as the High Level Comprehensive System of Security for the Exercise of Politics, which is also headed by the country's president. I trust that these omissions will be corrected and that the entities mentioned will serve to put a stop to the present painful situation. But that will not happen, of course, without personal leadership on the part of the president.

Behind all this violence over the past four decades, there lurks the obscure trade in illicit narcotics and the failed strategy of the so-called war on drugs. So long as this multinational business continues to guarantee the enormous profits it generates at present—and that largely because it is prohibited—there will be criminals involved in it, sowing death and corruption in their path. In

2018, thanks to the strategy we left in place—namely that of eradicating illicit crops—and also to our development plan, the armed forces manually eradicated 60,016 hectares and substituted legal crops. Then, in compliance with agreements made with coca-growing families, the plan embraced another 27,555 hectares, for a total of 87,571 hectares of coca crops eradicated—nearly half the illicit crops identified in 2017 by a United Nations monitoring system. Thus, in just one year, we got close to the goal we had agreed upon in early 2018 with the United States for a five-year period: the eradication of 50 percent of illicit crops.

Colombia continues to do battle against the drug trade—employing the stick-and-carrot technique—but this war will not end until the world commits to revising and changing its strategy to combat this criminal activity.

COLOMBIA IS NOT THE SAME

I am penning this updated epilogue for this book's English edition in January 2021, more than two years after concluding my term of office, and more than four years after we signed the peace agreement with the Farc. As I write, I contemplate the beloved country that I had the privilege to preside over for eight years, and looking back on what we did—in the midst of challenges and misunderstandings, with our blunders and our successes, our sorrows and our joys—I feel it was all worthwhile.

Colombia is not the same. It is certainly not the country it was at the end of this century's first decade. From a country condemned to a perpetual war, we have become a country where investments soar, poverty and inequality have been diminished as never before, tourism is flourishing, and hope is growing. We are a country that makes its presence felt, with dignity, in international scenarios.

Colombia is not the same. The number of foreign visitors beat all records in 2018, and is expected to keep growing once the COVID-19 pandemic ends. It is no simple coincidence that the *New York Times*, the *Guardian*, and *Forbes* magazine pointed to our new country as a place they recommended to visit in 2019. And it's not just foreigners. Thousands of Colombians abound on the highways and in the parks and nature reserves, now able to enjoy in peace a territory that for a long time they could not visit out of fear.

But most important of all: the lives that have been saved, the wounds avoided, the number of men and women who will no longer be maimed by war—a war that seemed endless. Half a century of conflict with the Farc has been relegated forever to the past.

Today, when I take my little grandchildren Celeste and Mariano in my arms, I see in them all of Colombia's children who now have the right to live in peace without being afraid. That's when I forget the hard moments, the difficult decisions, and the unjust criticisms, and think only of our duty to continue cementing and building a peace and a world that is tolerant and free from violence. I look into their innocent eyes and listen to their laughter, and am deeply moved and feel in my heart that all the effort, all those sleepless nights, had been meaningful.

It was worthwhile. Yes, without a doubt, it was all worthwhile.

Peace in Colombia

From the Impossible to the Possible
Nobel Lecture
Oslo, December 10, 2016

Your Majesties; Your Royal Highnesses; distinguished members of the Norwegian Nobel Committee; dear fellow citizens of Colombia; citizens of the world; ladies and gentlemen,

Six years ago, it was hard for us Colombians to imagine an end to a war that had lasted half a century. To the great majority of us, peace seemed an impossible dream—and for good reason. Very few of us—hardly anybody—could recall a memory of a country at peace.

Today, after six years of serious and often intense, difficult negotiations, I stand before you and the world and announce with deep humility and gratitude that the Colombian people, with assistance from our friends around the world, are turning the impossible into the possible.

A war that has brought so much suffering and despair to communities all across our beautiful land has finally come to an end.

Like life itself, peace is a process with many surprises. Just two months ago, people in Colombia and indeed in the whole world were shocked to learn that, in a plebiscite called to ratify the peace agreement with the FARC guerrillas, there were slightly more no votes than yes votes.

This outcome was completely unexpected.

A flame of hope had been lit in Cartagena a week earlier, when we signed the agreement in the presence of world leaders, and now that flame appeared to be suddenly snuffed out.

Many of us in Colombia recalled a passage from *One Hundred Years of Solitude*, the great masterpiece of our Nobel Prize laureate Gabriel García Márquez, which seemed to illustrate the moment we were living: "It was as if God had decided to put to the test every capacity for surprise and was keeping the inhabitants of Macondo in a permanent alteration between excitement and disappointment, doubt and revelation, to such an extreme that no one knew for certain where the limits of reality lay."

We felt that we ourselves were inhabitants of Macondo, a place that was not only magical but also contradictory.

As head of state, I sought to understand the significance of this unexpected setback and called at once for a broad national dialogue to seek unity and reconciliation. I was determined to turn this setback into a chance to develop the widest possible consensus for reaching a new agreement.

I devoted myself to listening to the concerns and recommendations of those who had voted no, of those who had voted yes, and of the majority who did not vote at all—with the aim of achieving a new and improved agreement, an agreement that all of Colombia could stand behind.

Not even four days had passed after the surprising plebiscite when the Norwegian Committee announced an equally surprising award of the Nobel Peace Prize.

I must confess to you that this news came as if it were a gift from heaven. At a time when our ship felt adrift, the Nobel Prize was the tailwind that helped us to reach our destination: the port of peace!

Thank you; thank you very much for this vote of confidence and faith in the future of my country.

Today, distinguished members of the Norwegian Nobel Committee, I come to tell you—and, through you, the international community—that we achieved our goal. We reached our port!

Today, we have a new agreement for ending the armed conflict with the Farc, which incorporates the majority of the proposals we received.

This new agreement was signed two weeks ago, and it was endorsed last week by our Congress, by an overwhelming majority, so that it can be incorporated into our laws. The long-awaited process of implementation has begun, with the invaluable support of the United Nations.

With this new agreement, the oldest and last armed conflict in the Western Hemisphere has ended.

This agreement—as set forth by Alfred Nobel in his will—marks the beginning of the dismantling of an army—this time, an irregular army—and its conversion into a legal political movement.

With this agreement, we can say that the American continent—from Alaska to Patagonia—is a land in peace.

And we can now ask the bold question: If war can come to an end in one hemisphere, why not one day in both hemispheres? Perhaps more than ever before, we can now dare to imagine a world without war.

The impossible is becoming possible.

Alfred Nobel, the great visionary whose legacy gathers us here today on the 120th anniversary of his death, once wrote that war is "the horror of horrors, the greatest of all crimes."

War must never be considered, under any circumstance, an end in itself. It is merely a means, but a means that we must always strive to avert.

I have served as a leader in times of war—to defend the freedom and the rights of the Colombian people—and I have served as a leader in times of making peace.

Allow me to tell you, from my own experience, that it is much harder to make peace than to wage war.

When it is absolutely necessary, we must be prepared to fight, and it was my duty—as defense minister and as president—to fight illegal armed groups in my country. When the roads to peace were closed, I fought these groups with effectiveness and determination. But it is foolish to believe that the end of any conflict must be the elimination of the enemy.

A final victory through force, when nonviolent alternatives exist, is none other than the defeat of the human spirit.

Seeking victory through force alone, pursuing the utter destruction of the enemy, waging war to the last breath, means failing to recognize your opponent as a human being like yourself, someone with whom you can hold a dialogue.

Dialogue . . . based on respect for the dignity of all. That was our recourse in Colombia. And that is why I have the honor to be here today, sharing what we have learned through our hard-won experience.

Our first and most vital step was to cease thinking of the guerrillas as our bitter enemies, and to see them instead simply as adversaries.

General Álvaro Valencia Tovar—a former commander of the Colombian army, a historian and humanist—taught me this distinction. He said that the word *enemy* gives a sense of a passionate struggle and a connotation of hate, unfit for military honor.

Humanizing war does not just mean limiting its cruelty but also recognizing your opponent as an equal, as a human being.

Historians estimate that up to 187 million people died during the twentieth century alone because of war. One hundred and eighty-seven million! Each one of them a precious human life, loved by their families and dear ones. Tragically, the death toll keeps climbing in this new century.

It is time to remember the haunting question sung by my fellow Nobel laureate Bob Dylan that touched so many youthful hearts in the sixties, including mine: "How many deaths will it take 'till he knows / That too many people have died? / The answer, my friend, is blowin' in the wind."

When people asked me whether I aspired to win the Nobel Peace Prize, I always answered that, for me, the actual prize was peace in Colombia. Because that is the real prize: peace for my country!

And that peace does not belong to a president or a government but to all the Colombian people, because we must build it together.

That is why I receive this prize on behalf of nearly fifty million Colombians—my fellow countrymen and women—who finally see the end of more than a half-century nightmare that has only brought pain, misery, and backwardness to our country.

And I receive this prize—above all—on behalf of the victims, the more than 8 million victims and displaced people whose lives have been devastated by the armed conflict, and the more than 220,000 women, men and children who, to our shame, have been killed in this war.

I am told by scholars that the Colombian peace process is the first in the world that has placed the victims and their rights at the center of the solution.

This negotiation has been conducted with a heavy emphasis on human rights. And that is something that makes us feel truly proud.

Victims want justice, but most of all they want to know the truth, and they—in a spirit of generosity—desire that no new victims should suffer as they did.

Professor Ronald Heifetz, founder of the Center for Public Leadership at the Kennedy School of Government at Harvard University, from which I graduated, once gave me a wise piece of advice: "Whenever you feel discouraged, tired, pessimistic, talk with the victims. They will give you the push and strength to keep you going."

And it has been just this way. Whenever I had the chance, I listened to the victims of this war and heard their heartbreaking stories. Some of them are here with us today, reminding us why it is so important to build a stable and lasting peace.

I would like to ask the victims here present—on behalf of the victims of the armed conflict in Colombia—to stand up and receive the homage they deserve.

Leyner Palacios is one of them. On May 2, 2002, a homemade mortar launched by the Farc, in the middle of a combat with the paramilitaries, landed on the church in his town, Bojayá, where its inhabitants had sought refuge. Nearly eighty women, men, and children—most of the victims were children!—died. In a matter of seconds, Leyner lost thirty-two relatives, including his parents and three younger brothers. The Farc has asked for forgiveness for this atrocity, and Leyner, who is now a community leader, has forgiven them.

That is the great paradox I have found: while many who have not suffered the conflict in the flesh are reluctant to accept peace, the victims are the ones who are most willing to forgive, to reconcile, and to face the future with a heart free of hate.

This peace prize belongs as well to those men and women who, with enormous patience and endurance, negotiated during all these years in Havana. They have reached an agreement that can be offered today as a model for the resolution of armed conflicts that have yet to be resolved around the world.

And here I am referring not only to the government negotiators but also to the Farc negotiators—my adversaries—who have demonstrated a great will for peace. I want to praise their willingness to embrace peace, to reach peace, because without it, the process would have failed.

In the same spirit, I dedicate this prize to the heroes of the Colombian armed forces, who have never ceased to protect the Colombian people, and who truly understood that the actual victory of any soldier or any police officer is peace itself.

And I wish to include a special acknowledgment—with all the gratitude in my heart—for my family: for my wife and my children, whose support and love throughout this task helped lessen the burden.

Finally, I also share this prize with the international community who, with generosity and unanimous enthusiasm, backed this peace process from the very beginning.

Let me also take this opportunity to convey my very special thanks to the people of Norway for your peaceful character and your extraordinary spirit of solidarity. It was because of these virtues that you were entrusted by Alfred Nobel to promote peace in the world. I must say you have done your job with great effectiveness for my country.

Norway and Cuba, in their role as guarantors; Chile and Venezuela, as witnesses; the United States and the European Union, with their special envoys; all the countries in Latin America and the Caribbean; even China and Russia . . . they all have reasons to take pride in this achievement.

The Kroc Institute for International Peace Studies at the University of Notre Dame in the United States has concluded, based on careful studies of the thirty-four agreements signed in the world to end armed conflicts in the past three decades, that this peace agreement in Colombia is the most complete and comprehensive ever reached.

As such, the Colombian peace agreement is a ray of hope in a world troubled by so many conflicts and so much intolerance. It proves that what at first seems impossible, through perseverance may become possible, even in Syria or Yemen or South Sudan.

The key, in the words of the English poet Tennyson, is "to strive, to seek, to find, and not to yield."

A few lessons can be learned from Colombia's peace process and I would like to share them with the world:

You must properly prepare yourself and seek advice, studying the failures of peace attempts in your own country and learning from other peace processes, their successes, and their problems.

The agenda for the negotiation should be focused and specific, aimed at solving the issues directly related to the armed conflict, rather than attempting to address all the problems faced by the nation.

Negotiations should be carried out with discretion and confidentiality in order to prevent them from turning into a media circus.

Sometimes it is necessary to both fight and talk at the same time if you want to arrive at peace—a lesson I took from another Nobel laureate, Yitzhak Rabin.

You must also be willing to make difficult, bold, and oftentimes unpopular decisions in order to reach your final goal.

In my case, this meant reaching out to the governments of neighboring countries with whom I had and continue to have deep ideological differences.

Regional support is indispensable in the political resolution of any asymmetric war. Fortunately, today all the countries in the region are allies in the search for peace, the noblest purpose any society can have.

We also achieved a very important objective: agreement on a model of transitional justice that enables us to secure maximum justice without sacrificing peace.

I have no doubt this model will be one of the greatest legacies of the Colombian peace process.

Ladies and gentlemen,

There is one less war in the world, and it is the war in Colombia!

This is, precisely, what we are celebrating today in Oslo, the same city that hosted the launch of the public phase of the negotiations with the Farc in October 2012.

And I must say that I feel honored and humbled to join the line of the brave and inspiring men and women who, ever since 1901, have received this most prestigious of prizes.

The peace process in Colombia—I say this with deep gratitude—is a fortunate synthesis of all what we have learned from them.

Peace efforts in the Middle East, in Central America, in South Africa, in Northern Ireland, whose architects have all received this award, showed us the way to move forward in a process specially designed for Colombia.

We also took up the legacy of Nobel laureates Jody Williams and the International Campaign to Ban Landmines. After Afghanistan, Colombia holds the shameful record of having the most mines and the most victims of mines in the world. We are resolutely committed to have our territory free of mines by 2021.

We have received the support of other Nobel laureates such as the European Union and President Barack Obama, who have also committed their countries to support the critical process of the implementation phase in Colombia.

And I feel that I must take this opportunity to reiterate the call I have been making to the world since the Summit of the Americas in Cartagena in 2012, which led to a special session of the General Assembly of the United Nations in April this year.

I am referring to the urgent need to rethink the world War on Drugs, a war where Colombia has been the country that has paid the highest cost in deaths and sacrifices.

We have moral authority to state that, after decades of fighting against drug trafficking, the world has still been unable to control this scourge that fuels violence and corruption throughout our global community.

The peace agreement with the Farc includes their commitment to cut all ties with the drug business, and to actively contribute to fighting it. But drug trafficking is a global problem that demands a global solution resulting from an undeniable reality: The War on Drugs has not been won, and is not being won.

It makes no sense to imprison a peasant who grows marijuana, when nowadays, for example, its cultivation and use are legal in eight states of the United States.

The manner in which this war against drugs is being waged is equally or perhaps even more harmful than all the wars the world is fighting today, combined. It is time to change our strategy.

In Colombia, we have also been inspired by the initiatives of Malala, the youngest Nobel laureate, because we know that only by developing minds, through education, can we transform reality.

We are the result of our thoughts; the thoughts that create our words; the words that shape our actions.

That is why we must change from within. We must replace the culture of violence with a culture of peace and coexistence; we must change the culture of exclusion into a culture of inclusion and tolerance.

And in that vein of coexistence, we have also learned from former US vice-president Al Gore and the Intergovernmental Panel on Climate Change and their determination to preserve the planet.

It is quite comforting to be able to say that the end of the conflict in Colombia, the most biodiverse country per square kilometer in the world, will yield high environmental dividends. By replacing illicit crops with legal ones, deforestation spurred by coca leaf growing will certainly diminish. And millions of barrels of oil will no longer be spilled in our rivers and seas because of attacks against our oil infrastructure.

We can say, in summary, that the Colombian peace process that you are recognizing today in Oslo is the synthesis and result of many positive efforts made throughout history and all over the world, efforts that have been valued and distinguished by this Nobel Committee.

Dear friends,

In a world where citizens are making the most crucial decisions—for themselves and for their nations—out of fear and despair, we must make the certainty of hope possible.

In a world where wars and conflicts are fueled by hatred and prejudice, we must find the path of forgiveness and reconciliation.

In a world where borders are increasingly closed to immigrants, where minorities are attacked and people deemed different are excluded, we must be able to coexist with diversity and appreciate the way it can enrich our societies.

We are human beings, after all. For those of us who are believers, we are all God's children. We are part of this magnificent adventure of being alive and populating this planet.

At our core, there are no inherent differences: not the color of our skin, nor our religious beliefs, nor our political ideologies, nor our sexual preferences. All these are simply facets of humanity's diversity.

Let's awaken the creative capacity for goodness, for building peace, that live within each soul.

In the end, we are one people and one race; of every color, of every belief, of every preference.

The name of this one people is the world. The name of this one race is humanity.

If we truly understand this, if we make it part of our individual and collective awareness, then we will cut the very root of conflicts and wars.

In 1982—thirty-four years ago—the efforts to find peace through dialogue began in Colombia.

That same year, in Stockholm, Gabriel García Márquez, who was my ally in the pursuit of peace, received the Nobel Prize in Literature, and spoke about "a new and sweeping utopia of life . . . where the races condemned to one hundred years of solitude will have, at last and forever, a second opportunity on earth."

Today, Colombia—my beloved country—is living that second opportunity; and I thank you, members of the Norwegian Nobel Committee, because, on this occasion, you have not only awarded a prize to peace: you helped make it possible!

The sun of peace finally shines in the heavens of Colombia.

May its light shine upon the whole world!

Index